Two-Party Politics in the One-Party South

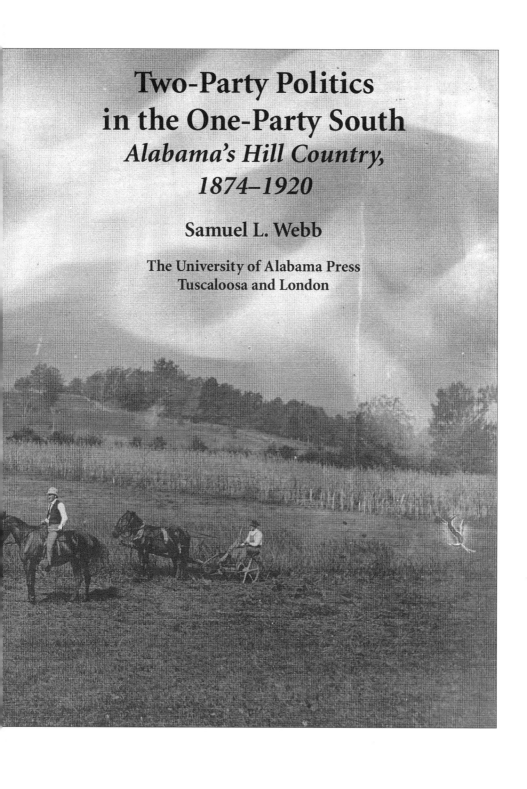

Two-Party Politics
in the One-Party South
Alabama's Hill Country,
1874–1920

Samuel L. Webb

The University of Alabama Press
Tuscaloosa and London

Copyright © 1997
The University of Alabama Press
Tuscaloosa, Alabama 35487-0380
All rights reserved
Manufactured in the United States of America
The paper on which this book is printed meets the minimum requirements of
American National Standard for Information Science-Permanence of Paper for
Printed Library Materials, ANSI Z39.48-1984.

Library of Congress Cataloging-in-Publication Data

Webb, Samuel L., 1946–
    Two-party politics in the one-party South : Alabama's hill
country, 1874–1920 / Samuel L. Webb.
        p.   cm.
    Includes bibliographical references (p.   ) and index
    ISBN 0-8173-0895-4 (alk. paper)
        1. Alabama—Politics and government—1865-1950.   2. Political
culture—Alabama—History—19th century.   3. Political culture—
Alabama—History—20th century.   4. Political parties—Alabama—
History—19th century.   5. Political parties—Alabama—
History—20th century.   I. Title.
F326.W43   1997
306.2′09761—dc21   97-20596

British Library Cataloguing-in-Publication Data available

Frontispiece: Shelby County, ca. 1900 (courtesy of the Alabama Department of
Archives and History, Montgomery, Alabama)

To the memory of my mother, Ruby Jones Webb, whose honesty, sincerity, sense of humor, and courage in the face of adversity impressed all who knew her. She played her music, and people listened.

Contents

Acknowledgments

All of the people mentioned below have been helpful to me, and if these acknowledgments sound a bit sentimental, I hope that the reader will forgive.

My fascination with the history of American politics began even before I entered elementary school, and no dinner table conversation in my parents' home neglected the subject. My father, Samuel L. Webb, Sr., was a local politician who taught me about the drama and significance of elections at the county level and about the important connections local politicians establish with state and national leaders. When I was seven he took me with him while he campaigned, and it was an experience I will never forget. Some of the most exciting nights of my life were spent with my father at the Sumter County courthouse waiting for election returns.

My maternal grandfather, Robert Sanders Jones, cast his first vote for William Jennings Bryan in 1908 and his last for George McGovern in 1972. He was living history, and he brought the past alive for me. His colorful storytelling ability and rhetorical flair grew from the great oral tradition that so many southerners of his generation shared. I never spent a dull moment with him. His house was strewn with magazines, newspapers, and good books, and no day passed that I did not find him propped on the side of his bed immersed in some dog-eared volume. I was very lucky that he lived next door while I was growing up, and the true origins of this book were the always wonderful times I spent with him.

Many teachers have helped me, and although some of them are now deceased, I must acknowledge their exceptional ability. My history teacher at Sumter County High School, Miss Vermelle Jones, inspired me and hundreds of other students. In the 1960s a group of dedicated English teachers gathered at Livingston University, including Robert Gilbert, Lynn Smith, Nathaniel Reed, Beverly Smith, and John Craiger. They were tough, thorough, and unrelenting in their battles against my ignorance, but they were also generous and decent gentlemen. At the University of Alabama at Birmingham, Ed Harrell, Tennant S. McWilliams, Virginia Hamilton, Dan Bjork, and Harriet Amos Doss all helped and encouraged me. Ed, Tennant, and Harriet (now my colleague) did their best to make me quit writing like a lawyer. My dream of getting a doctorate in history and of becoming a university professor would not have been possible without the help and support of Tennant S. McWilliams, who is now my dean. He has had a larger impact on my career than any other historian.

My decision to pursue a doctorate at the University of Arkansas proved to be a lucky one. The history faculty there went above and beyond the call of duty to help me. I am particularly grateful to Willard Gatewood for his thorough and speedy direction of my dissertation and for his continued friendship and advice since. While I was at Fayetteville and later, Michael O'Brien has been a great teacher, ally, friend, and advisor. I will never be able to repay Michael and his wonderful wife, Patricia, for their hospitality and patience with an aging, overly opinionated graduate student. David Sloan was a great teacher and good friend, and words are insufficient to express my deep appreciation to Professor David Edwards for his efforts to assure my material and emotional survival. Ed Harrell taught me both at UAB and at Arkansas, and more than once has been my benefactor. Others who were at Arkansas during my time there and who deserve many thanks from me are Elliot West, James Briscoe, Thomas Kennedy, and Randall Woods.

I owe a special thanks to all of my UAB colleagues for putting up with me, but especially to my friends, advisors, and department chairmen James F. Tent and James L. Penick. Margaret Armbrester has listened to my endless discussions of this book and offered sage advice. Debra Givens, who heads our department staff, has been more important to my career than even she knows.

There are a large group of historians whose work in southern political history has particularly influenced my own, but none more so than J. Mills Thornton, C. Vann Woodward, William Warren Rogers, Michael Hyman, Michael Perman, Robert C. McMath, Jr., Bruce Palmer, Worth Robert Miller, Allen Going, Wayne Flynt, and Paul M. Pruitt. I have shamelessly stolen from them all. I am also grateful to Robert David Ward and Mills Thornton for their thorough reading of my manuscript and for all of the suggestions they made about how it might be improved. Bill Rogers, Harvey M. Jackson, Henry "Mel" McKiven, Elaine Witt, and Amy Shields all read and criticized portions of my manuscript as well, and I appreciate their efforts.

I also had the help of many local historians, whose work too often goes unappreciated by academics, and of the descendants of some of the leading politicians discussed herein. George Longshore, grandson of A. P.

Longshore, encouraged this project, kept in touch with me, and furnished me with a wonderful picture of his grandfather. Morgan Reynolds, grandson of Lewis Reynolds, also searched out photographs of his grandfather. Larry Joe Smith of Jacksonville State University, an expert on the history of Marshall County, turned over his entire collection of photos for my use and worked tirelessly to find others for me. Smith and the Guntersville Historical Society have done a marvelous job of collecting photos of Marshall County. Karl C. Harrison and Frank "Butch" Ellis of Columbiana also sought photos for my use and took time to discuss the history of Shelby County with me. Mr. Harrison, who once boarded in the Longshore home, shared with me his personal memories of Judge Longshore. Morris Moatts of Clanton, a more recent Republican politician from Chilton County, also found photos for me through the Clanton Chamber of Commerce.

The employees at the southern history division of the Birmingham Public Library, the special collections department at the Harwell G. Davis Library at Samford University, the special collections section at the Gorgas Library of the University of Alabama, the library at Washington and Lee University, and the Department of Archives and History in Montgomery have been unfailingly helpful and courteous. There is no better state archivist than Ed Bridges, and I hope that the state legislature and the governor appreciate him as much as the state's historians do.

The management, board, and editors of the University of Alabama Press have been wonderful to me, and I appreciate their willingness to take a chance on this first book of mine.

There are, of course, people who are so special to me that thanks are inadequate. My brother Robert Ben Webb has been a source of strength for me through every difficult time in my life. My good friend Dr. Phillip Norris of the University of South Alabama has been my confidant for more than a decade and has learned more about these Hill Country politicians than he ever wanted to know. My children, Amy and Susan, do not always know exactly what I am up to, and I can only assure them that research, solitary thinking, writing, and editing are time-consuming processes. They and my stepson, Alexander, have been going through very difficult stages of their adolescent lives while I was trying to produce this manuscript, and I have not always been as understanding as I should have been. My wife, Ann, is also a historian and an academic of extraordinary ability and has given great support to all of my efforts. I am truly a lucky man to have her by my side.

Alabama counties

Two-Party Politics in
the One-Party South

Introduction

Among the plain white people of our state the plutocratic ideas . . . are not
indigenous. . . . It is not to the interest of the Black Belt to goad the plain
white people of the white counties on to desperation by disfranchising
them. If the plutocratic tendencies of our times continue in our Southland
the time is not far distant when the plain white people in their desperate
attempts to free themselves will bring desolation and ruin among us.[1]

Thomas Atkins Street, 1901

The politics of Alabama since Reconstruction, like that of other states in
that mythical election precinct called the "Deep South," has featured a
one-party system, a preoccupation with racial matters that often stifled
the ability of government to deal with pressing problems, and the triumph of archconservative public policies. Yet, Alabama's politics has
been far more complex, and the state's white people have been far less
unified, than these general characteristics suggest.

In 1949, political scientist V. O. Key wrote that no state that elected U.S.
senators such as Hugo Black in the 1920s, Lister Hill in the 1930s, and John
Sparkman in the 1940s could be stereotyped as a typical reactionary
southern state. Until the *Brown v. Board of Education* decision in 1954,
Alabama politics was rarely a simple morality play in which race played
the pivotal role. Most whites were not conservative except on race, and
they were certainly not unified. Fierce struggles over social and economic
issues more often pitted whites against one another than against blacks.
Populists, progressives, New Dealers, and liberal labor leaders were key
players in state politics. In 1946, Washington, D.C., columnist Stewart
Alsop described Alabama as the South's "liberal oasis." A more recent
observer, struck by the contrast between the state's liberal political heritage and the reactionary racist climate that surfaced after *Brown*, writes
that Alabama has proved to be "inscrutable, precisely as Russia was to
Winston Churchill—a riddle wrapped in a mystery inside an enigma."[2]

From Reconstruction to the 1950s, reactionary politicians were so har-
ried by reformers that they were forced to rely on extralegal and undemocratic methods to get power, and they often failed. Reformers dedicated
to raising the living standards and educational levels of Alabama's masses

won statewide office despite opposition from entrenched and unscrupulous economic interests. Until the post-1954 integration controversy successful racial demagogues were rare in Alabama politics, with the exception of the loquacious "Cotton Tom" Heflin, and even Heflin was known in the 1920s as a progressive supporter of organized labor and small farmers.[3]

Extreme conservatives did write the constitution of 1901 that disfranchised blacks and poor whites, legalized segregation, apportioned the legislature in a way that enabled reactionaries to control it for seventy years, and restricted the ability of the legislature to raise sufficient revenue for important public services. These stumbling blocks to the amelioration of ignorance, poverty, and racism were not erected by those bugaboos of southern history, the "Rednecks," but by gentlemen who ran plantations, cotton gins, and urban corporations. In spite of the success of this right-wing upper crust element, Alabama politics remained multifarious, intricate, and divided along regional lines.[4]

An intrastate geographic division played a major role in Alabama politics from the 1820s to the mid-twentieth century, but this split originated in socioeconomic differences rather than mere geography. South Alabama's Black Belt was blessed with rich soil, flat land, a staple crop, and transportation outlets to economic market places. North Alabama's Hill Country was rocky, hilly, subject to soil erosion, and more isolated from market centers. These factors led to disparities between the two regions in economic development, value of farm land, economic and social class of the farm population, and the percentage of black population. These differences generated ideological disagreements between the two regions that were "hardy and persistent."[5]

V. O. Key argues that a "progressive-conservative cleavage" grew out of this persistent sectionalism. Unity and conservatism existed in the Black Belt, but in north Alabama's Hill Country and the southeastern Wiregrass politics exhibited "a wholesome contempt for authority and a spirit of rebellion" born in antebellum times. Urban labor contributed to the election of Populists, progressives, and New Dealers, but rural north Alabama's Hill Country (also described herein as the "Upcountry") was the "seat" of political insurgence, and politics there retained a "strident radical agrarian tone" right into the 1950s.[6]

Most authorities recognize Hill Country dissidence, but they treat most significant pre-1960 political conflicts in Alabama as factional fights within the Democratic party family. Such a view is accurate when applied to statewide politics. No non-Democrat was elected to statewide office between 1872 and 1980, yet two-party politics was common in hill counties from 1868 to the 1920s. Because the rest of the state was so thoroughly Democratic, and statewide officials were all Democrats, Upcountry dissent against the ruling party is rarely analyzed. Except for the Populists, the written political history of Alabama since Reconstruction is almost exclusively a tale of Democrats. Unsupported assertions are often made about the origins and ideology of Alabama's post-1900 Hill Country Republicans, or they are completely ignored.[7]

Republicans elected to office at the county level are viewed as exotic exceptions to Democratic rule. Republican politics is considered insignificant because it was extraneous to the truly important statewide election process, which was the Democratic primary. The only serious effort by any historian to deal with early-twentieth-century Alabama Republicans characterizes them as motivated only by a desire to control federal patronage or loyalty to so-called lily-white or black-and-tan racial factions. Dewey Grantham's contention that the Republican party "declined to insignificant proportions" in the Deep South after 1900 and became a "skeleton party wracked by factionalism, perpetuated only by a desire of its leaders for federal offices and their quadrennial role in the national conventions" represents conventional wisdom.[8]

It is customary to argue that the Deep South GOP, after making critical gains among whites during Reconstruction, was driven into total remission by the mid-1870s because of its identification with blacks. Only in mountainous subregions of the upper South, in eastern Tennessee, southwestern Virginia, and western North Carolina did Republicans retain strength among whites after federal troops were removed in 1877. Upper South whites who had opposed secession and the Confederacy joined the party of the Union after the war, and their relatives remained loyal to it long after the turn of the twentieth century, but by 1900, writes Grantham, Deep South Republicans had been "discredited."[9]

The only Alabama county with post-Reconstruction Republican sympathies to receive attention from writers is Winston, located in the northwest Hill Country. "The story of mountain Republicanism" in counties "strung along the Appalachian highlands," writes V. O. Key, "is in essence the story of Winston County." It was filled with opponents of secession disgusted that their old party, the party of Jefferson and Jackson, had led them into war. "The highland yeomanry did not want to fight a rich man's war; the Democratic party was, or at least became, the planter's party and the war party." Because it had the fewest slaveowners of any Alabama county, Winston eagerly supported the party that had preserved the Union and freed the slaves.[10]

Historians neglect north Alabama counties such as Walker, DeKalb, and Randolph, where vibrant post–Civil War Republican sentiment also sprouted among white voters who had opposed the Confederacy. Between 1868 and 1880 these counties often backed Republicans in presidential elections and elected Republican state legislators. Other hill counties contained sizeable pockets of white Unionist-Republicans, but most Hill Country whites supported the Confederacy and opposed Radical Reconstruction. The GOP declined in north Alabama in the 1880s because Unionism, or war-engendered anger with the Confederacy, was not so widespread or enduring that it could sustain a two-party system against charges that Republicans were the party of Radical Reconstruction, blacks, and big business.[11]

This evidence of Republican decline is in accord with orthodox views about what happened to the Deep South GOP after the 1870s, but a sharp rise in GOP sentiment in north Alabama between 1896 and 1920 confounds the accepted notion that disfranchisement "dealt a final blow to whatever lingering hopes the Republican party had in the South." After disfranchisement, a larger percentage of Alabama's Hill Country whites were voting Republican than at any previous time, and few of them had anti-Confederate roots. In counties such as Shelby, Chilton, Marshall, and St. Clair, vibrant competition developed between Republicans and Democrats for the first time since the Civil War.[12]

In the 1920 presidential election, Republicans were neither extraneous nor insignificant. Thirty-two percent of Alabama's votes (nearly all white), a majority in nine hill counties, 49 percent in two more, and more than 40 percent in six others, went to the GOP. These seventeen hill counties cast 35 percent of the total vote in the state and held more than a half-million people, which exceeded the population of several American states. The fact that this large area existed within the boundaries of a "one-party state" does not render two-party politics in the section unimportant or grant historians a license to ignore it. It can be credibly argued that the two parties were more closely competitive in the hills than in some "one-party" New England and midwestern Republican states.[13]

Upcountry GOP voters were not just "presidential Republicans." They voted a straight ticket in 1920. GOP candidates for the U.S. Senate and three congressional seats won nearly the same percentage as presidential candidate Warren G. Harding. Republican Senate candidate Lewis H. Reynolds received majorities in eight counties won by Harding, and he took 51 percent of the vote in Walker County, where Harding fell below a majority. Reynolds exceeded 40 percent of the vote in eight other north Alabama counties, and GOP candidates for Congress in the Hill Country also exceeded 40 percent of the 1920 vote. Charles Kennamer, the Seventh District Republican candidate, lost by only 739 votes out of nearly 46,000 ballots cast. He would have won if Winston County had not been removed from the district by the 1916 Democratic legislature and replaced by Blount County. William B. Bankhead, scion of Alabama's most illustrious political family and the incumbent Tenth District Democratic congressman, got only 53 percent of the vote. Three of the seven counties in his district gave majorities to his GOP opponent.[14]

Hill Country Republicanism peaked in 1920, but it "fell to insignificant proportions" only after the "Hoover Depression" arrived. The sudden outpouring of Republican votes in a one-party state has not been fully explained. The 1920 election was the first after World War I and the first in which Alabama women voted. Democrats led the country into war in 1917, and newly enfranchised women may have lashed out at Woodrow Wilson's party in some states, but anti-war sentiment was not a factor in Alabama's Republican vote. John Burnett, the Seventh District's Democratic congressman at the time of the America's entry into the conflict, was one of the few Democrats to oppose the war. In the Seventh, where Republicans were stronger than in any other district, the GOP was the pro-war party. Republican congressional candidate Oliver D. Street questioned Burnett's patriotism, and Burnett's death in 1919 effectively neutralized the war issue. Hill counties supported Harding and other Republicans for reasons unrelated to the war.[15]

The GOP revival cannot be assigned to a recrudescence of Unionist Republicanism. Winston County was not a prototype for the rest of the Hill Country. Most white voters in Chilton and Shelby Counties, for instance, showed little interest in joining the Republican party during Reconstruction. No GOP candidate won these two counties from 1874 through 1892 despite a 19 percent black population in Chilton and a 29 percent black population in Shelby, yet Republicans won the two counties in seven of the nine presidential elections from 1896 through 1928. County governments in Shelby and Chilton (county commissions, probate judges, sheriffs, tax assessors, for example) fell to Republicans. This movement to the GOP after 1900 was stronger in Chilton and Shelby than in most hill counties, but it was substantial throughout the Upcountry.[16]

In some counties with a Unionist-Republican heritage, the post-1900 period also brought a GOP resurgence that was unrelated to anti-Confederate sentiment. DeKalb County's 95 percent white population returned majorities for Ulysses Grant in the 1868 and 1872 presidential elections, and it elected a Republican legislator in 1876. Democrats rebounded by winning more than 60 percent of the vote and the legislative seat in all elections from 1876 through 1892. After this twenty-year Republican decline, William McKinley suddenly won a plurality in DeKalb in 1896, and the county GOP vote stayed above 40 percent in every presidential election from 1900 to 1928. In 1920, Warren G. Harding won a majority in DeKalb, as did the GOP gubernatorial nominee in 1922. A burgeoning Republican party won control of the county government, and when Democrats finally won back the county offices during the Great Depression, the Alabama National Guard had to be summoned to dislodge the recalcitrant Republican officials from the courthouse.[17]

From 1900 through 1920, Republican nominees for Congress in the Hill Country's Seventh Congressional District won more than 40 percent of the vote eleven times in twelve elections. In 1910, Republican nominee Milford Howard took 48.6 percent of the district vote, and he did not poll less than 40 percent in any county. Charles Kennamer received 49 percent both in a 1919 special election and in the 1920 general election. Still, this Republican surge cannot be explained entirely by the ideology of Upcountry voters or by their attitudes toward national or state political organizations.[18]

Disputes about efficiency and integrity in county government, struggles for jobs at the courthouse, efforts to get public contracts, or personal jealousies played their usual roles in Upcountry politics, but it was unnecessary to become a Republican to fight over these local issues. Such conflicts could easily have been played out within the Democratic party, which abandoned tightly controlled nominating conventions in 1901 and thereafter selected its nominees in state and county primaries open to all whites. Local disputes differed from county to county, and they cannot explain a sudden surge of Republican votes among whites in a dozen different counties during the same period (1896–1920) in a state where Republicans were accused of racial treason. Thousands of Hill Country voters refused to participate in Democratic primaries and voted for Republicans because they made a conscious decision to reject the Democratic party. Some catalyst other than local factors led to that decision.

The rise of Upcountry Republicans between 1896 and 1920 can more clearly be understood as the third in a series of rebellions against the ruling elite of the Democratic party, which began as soon as Reconstruction ended. Each movement was propelled by distinct historical forces that set it apart from the others, but overlapping and interrelated motivations also existed. Most anti-Democratic voters were former Democrats, and few had ever been Republicans before 1900. Some of the same people participated in each protest movement, and their presence in the early-twentieth-century GOP flowed naturally from their support of the previous movements. Although their initial break with the Democrats occurred because of disagreements at the state and local levels, the actions of Gilded Age national Democrats on a variety of issues affected the evolution of the post-1900 Hill Country Republican party.

County political races were more hotly contested in the Hill Country than national or state contests, and county-level politics dominates this study. In the 1880s and 1890s, most Alabamians were farmers or engaged in farm-related activities. They rarely traveled to urban areas, and, if they went to town at all, they usually went to the county seat where they reluctantly paid their taxes, registered mortgages or liens, dealt with the sheriff, recorded wills or land deeds, demanded that roads be built, argued about the policies of burgeoning county schools, or registered to vote. Trips to the courthouse were major events, and the county impinged on the lives of farm families more than any other unit of government. Meetings between fiercely independent farmers and county officials made major impressions on both. A farmer's immediate "community" usually consisted of his family, nearby relatives, or farmer-neighbors, but the county was his larger community, and county politicians were his most direct connection to the state and national governments. As the table at the conclusion of this chapter suggests, the subjects of this study are counties that demonstrated substantial Republican sentiment in the post-1896 period.

Historians concentrate their attention on statewide political figures, on governors or U.S. senators, but the leaders of the Hill Country political revolts were second-tier officeholders (state legislators, probate judges, federal district attorneys, and the like), and it is probably because they labored at this lower echelon that their story has languished. It is a story filled with drama, competing ideologies, intrigue, violence, and moral

Table 1 Percentage Republican Presidential Vote in Alabama Hill Country

County	1880/1884/1888	1900/1904/1908	1912
Blount	19	41	49.9
Cherokee	17	38	50.7
Chilton	23	52	57.6
Clay	15	40	47.4
Cleburne	18	43	48.2
Cullman	30	44	56.6
DeKalb	29	43	44.2
Etowah	30	40	42.8
Fayette	27	45	48.6
Franklin	26	48	48.7
Marshall	10	39	52.1
Shelby	39	46	54.0
St. Clair	35	41	52.4
Walker	42	46	40.7
Winston	54	57	69.7

Source: Data from Louis Loveman, comp., "The Presidential Vote in Alabama," n.p., 1983.

Note: Percentages for 1880/1884/1888 and 1900/1904/1908 are averages. The 1912 percentage combines votes for the Progressive party, a Republican splinter group, with those votes for the regular Republican. The total 1912 non-Democratic vote was actually higher because Socialist Eugene Debs received 2.8 percent in Cherokee, 3.2 percent in Chilton, 3.6 percent in Walker, 4.1 percent in St. Clair and Franklin, and 4.9 percent in Etowah.

courage, but it does not juxtapose good against evil. Anti-Democratic politicians had no corner on virtue and were imbued with that quintessential American trait of "grasping the main chance." Their ambition sometimes led them into demagoguery, lying, vote buying, and other ethical lapses. Despite these faults, which were even more characteristic of Alabama's Democrats, Upcountry dissenters stood for what one historian has called the "humane preference," or the idea that human beings should not be subordinate to "money and system." This view did not suddenly come to them during the agrarian revolt of the 1890s, nor did it arrive with Farmers' Alliance lecturers. It was much older than that.[19]

Hill Country dissidents did share the racist attitudes of most white Alabamians (and of most white Americans) of all political persuasions, but the very fact of their opposition to the Democrats pitted them against the self-proclaimed "party of white supremacy." Hill Country anti-Democrats did not seek to exclude blacks from the political process and opposed all of the disfranchisement measures imposed on the state by white Democrats in 1901. These facts do not absolve them of racism, but they do demonstrate that race was rarely the dominant force in their political decision making.

The motives of Hill Country anti-Democrats can be found in the warning issued by Thomas Atkins Street of Marshall County that was cited earlier in this chapter. He feared moneyed elites whose "plutocratic ideas" were not "indigenous" to his area, and he resented the power of Black Belt planter-landlords who wanted to disfranchise Upcountry whites. The economic, regional, and class attitudes exhibited in Street's polemic motivated all three Hill Country rebellions, yet it was unlikely that such beliefs would lead Upcountry voters into a Republican party with a reputation for supporting blacks, monopolists, and northeastern bankers. One Hill Country man described the GOP as the party of "money managers and Negroes."[20]

The Republican surge cannot be understood without an analysis of the political culture from which it evolved, the historical events that helped produce it, and the colorful figures who led it. If the reputation of Republicans was as bad in most of the South in 1900 as the evidence suggests, we must understand what kind of Republicans hill people intended to become, how they intended to fit into that party, what they hoped to gain by opposing the Democratic party, and the degree of their success. This quest for understanding requires a thorough examination of local politics in several hill counties and an evaluation of the impact of state and national politics on county political leaders and voters. The first and last chapters focus on the presidential campaign of 1912 in Alabama, which involved most of the primary actors in this story and provides a stage on which to introduce them. That campaign also reveals much about the actors' ideas and character, and it places in sharp relief the historiographical questions examined here.

The rise and decline of Alabama Populism plays a central role in this story, and although I do not offer a comprehensive history of that movement, the evidence presented challenges past interpretations of it. Most analyses of Populism center on its economic origins. The primary focus here is on ideology, voters, candidates, elections, and political parties at the county level. Even though economic problems were the proximate cause of Populism, an obsessive focus on reactions by farmers to economic events of the late 1880s and early 1890s or a preoccupation with the Farmers' Alliance as the progenitor of agrarian reform can lead historians to ignore ways in which Populists were products of an older political culture that shaped their approach to public issues. Alabama Populism cannot be fully explained unless the political revolt that helped to create it and the one that came after it are also understood. Historians have not fully explored what happened to Populists after 1900, even though the rapid decline of support for the third-party movement after 1896 has raised questions about the seriousness of the Populists' commitment to ideals they expressed in their radical rhetoric. "Clearly the Populists were reformers," writes one commentator, "but to understand them better we need to know more precisely how their movement related" to post-1900 progressivism.[21]

1   The Old Guard and the Populists

> Roosevelt . . . had a special genius for phrasing and for galvanizing the
> progressive temper, and progressivism, for all its internal contradictions
> and doctrinal vagaries, gave a twentieth century thrust and cadence to the
> tradition of American reform. It translated Jacksonian precepts into a lan-
> guage relevant to an industrial nation.[1]
>
> John Morton Blum

The presidential election of 1912 featured major candidates from three
parties and was one of the most exciting in American history. The Progressive, or "Bull Moose," party nominated former President Theodore
Roosevelt after Republicans denied him their nomination. This new
party, formed in part by Republicans opposed to the conservatism and
patronage policies of President William Howard Taft, gained momentum
from the exposure of shady tactics used by Taft's agents to deny Roosevelt
the nomination. Some Taft delegates to the national GOP convention in
Chicago presented dubious credentials, and their right to be seated was
challenged by Roosevelt. Taft's supporters governed the GOP national
committee and the convention, and they "displayed blatant highhanded-
ness in awarding nearly every contested seat" to their man. One of the
most heated delegate quarrels concerned Alabama's delegation.[2]

When Republicans from Alabama's Ninth Congressional District met
in March 1912 in Birmingham, a majority chose delegates to the June national convention pledged to Roosevelt, but a pro-Taft group left the
meeting, chose their own slate, and claimed to be the legitimate Ninth
District delegation. Roosevelt supporters offered compelling evidence to
both the GOP national committee and the convention, evidence that
demonstrated that Taft was not the choice of most Ninth District Republicans, yet Taft's group was officially seated. Roosevelt, who said that Taft's
men acted with "scandalous disregard of every principle of elementary
honesty and decency," was especially mad about the decision on the Alabama delegation.[3]

After Taft's first-ballot renomination, Roosevelt's delegates decamped
to a nearby hall and formed their new party. Among those who escorted

Roosevelt to the platform of the rump convention was Birmingham attorney Oscar R. Hundley, one of the Ninth District Roosevelt delegates rejected by the Republicans. Insurgents shouted encouragement to their charismatic leader, who said he would be their candidate even if only one state supported him.[4]

A struggle to save the GOP from irreparable division shifted back to the state level when Taft's supporters went home to urge local party members not to jump ship, but they failed to stop the formation of state Progressive parties. The disagreement in the Ninth District further divided Alabama's Republicans, and pro-Roosevelt dissidents created Alabama's Progressive party at a Birmingham convention on July 24, 1912. They selected delegates to the new party's national convention, which met two weeks later.[5]

The Progressive party national convention resembled a giant evangelical revival. Delegates sang "Onward Christian Soldiers" and the "Battle Hymn of the Republic." Speakers regaled the crowd with the rhetoric of uplift. A leading Socialist charged those who wrote the party's platform with stealing "half the working program of the Socialist party." Roosevelt told delegates that their righteous cause would triumph even if he lost. "We stand," he said, "at Armageddon, and we battle for the Lord."[6]

Despite the high moral tone, those with sinister motives mingled with the pure of heart beneath the new political tent. Republican political hacks concerned about losing patronage under Taft, and steel industry executives thankful to Roosevelt for looking the other way when the United States Steel monopoly was formed during his presidency, shared convention seats with social workers, left-wing intellectuals, and reform politicians such as Governor Hiram Johnson of California, who became Roosevelt's running mate. An "outward unity" masked splits between urban progressives from the East, whose reform ideas did not include breaking up big business, and western or southern men who feared monopolies and supported trust busting.[7]

Roosevelt was not as committed to radical reforms as he wanted to appear. His largest campaign contributions came from wealthy businessmen whose ideology sharply conflicted with left-leaning reformers, but if he was not sincere, sophisticated progressives such as Learned Hand, Felix Frankfurter, and William Allen White, all of whom flocked to Roosevelt's standard, were badly fooled. "You could see," Frankfurter said of Roosevelt, "that he just sort of jumped out and was going to lead the armies of regeneration. All this about 'We stand at Armageddon,' wasn't just flap-doodle. That's the way he felt."[8]

The fact that Roosevelt had the heart of an aristocrat meant little to people who believed he spoke for them against selfish special interests. He had popularized reform by suing monopolies, attacking "malefactors of great wealth," calling for railroad regulation, and sympathizing with workers in labor disputes. He argued that the rights of labor were prior to those of capital, supported workers' compensation, and denounced child labor. Such attitudes broke with the pro-business views of past presidents of both parties. Taft was anti-labor; supported the use of the federal antitrust law to enjoin labor union activities; backed the dictatorial reign of the reactionary leader of the U.S. House of Representatives, "Uncle Joe" Cannon; refused to join progressive Republicans in an effort to protect American consumers from high tariffs; and backed away from Roosevelt's controversial forest conservation policies. Taft's administration actually sued more monopolies under the antitrust law than had Roosevelt's, but progressives viewed Teddy as a symbol of reform and Taft as an inept tool of reactionary "Old Guard" Republicans.[9]

Alabama's GOP leaders faced the same difficult decision as Republicans from other states. They could remain loyal to Taft and their party, despite its fatal split, and maintain good standing with the party hierarchy or risk losing their influence in the party by supporting Roosevelt's crusade, which had little chance of success. Despite the common dilemma, the various state parties did not mirror one another. Each one had grown out of a distinctive history, developed its own peculiarities, and contained unique personalities. State and local factors did have an impact on the nominees Republicans finally chose. The history of southern Republican parties is too often ignored because they operated in states dominated by Democrats, yet an understanding of why Alabama's Republican activists chose Roosevelt or Taft and the special role Upcountry leaders played in that choice can be gained only by examining the party's varied internal forces.

When the presidential campaign got under way in September of 1912, Prelate Demeck Barker could have been labeled the most successful Republican politician in Alabama's history despite never having won a single office in an election. He had come to Alabama from Connecticut at age twenty-two in 1857, established southern credentials by serving in the Confederate army, and was thereafter known to associates as "the Major."

The Old Guard and the Populists 13

He was trained as a lawyer, but after the war he worked in various areas of the cotton business in Montgomery and Mobile and briefly sojourned as an executive with a petroleum refining company in New York City.[10]

An active Alabama Republican since the early 1870s, Barker was a delegate to eight GOP national conventions between 1876 and 1912, served several terms on the state Republican executive committee, was appointed state collector of internal revenue by Republican presidents from Grant to Harrison, became Mobile's postmaster under President McKinley, and retained that job under both Roosevelt and Taft. He was a sensitive man, jealous of his status, and quick to anger. By the fall of 1912 he was both furious and bewildered. The acute strategic sense that had led to his control of the state Republican party since the spring of 1911 had deserted him, and real danger existed that Alabama Republicans, by a wide margin, would bolt their party and choose Roosevelt. Barker was a member of the Republican national committee, governing body of the party, and Taft's man in Alabama. Only Democrats could win statewide elections in Alabama, but if Roosevelt won a majority of Alabama's non-Democratic voters, Barker would be embarrassed.[11]

The major worked assiduously to insure that when the election was over he would remain Alabama's premier Republican. Such zestful politicking by a younger man would have been understandable, but at age seventy-seven, Barker's career should have been winding down. He had been granted rewarding positions by his party for more than forty years, yet he was especially driven in 1912. Past honors had not blunted his personal ambition, which shone through in letters he wrote to party operatives, but he was also motivated to protect his longtime GOP political friends and benefactors and to justify their long stewardship of Alabama's Republican party.[12]

Barker was the quintessential representative of men who had been active in the state Republican hierarchy since Reconstruction. Until just after the turn of the new century they had controlled the party, doled out patronage plums handed down from national GOP administrations, and divided party offices among themselves. Like Barker, few of them had ever run for office. They were motivated by a desire for federal office and their traditional roles in GOP national conventions. They had long since jettisoned any hope of making their party a serious challenger to Democrats in statewide elections, which no Republican had won since 1872. They were, said one observer, "pie counter" Republicans, or men whose sole reason for political activism was their desire for "political pie."[13]

Prelate D. Barker, ca. 1912 (courtesy of the Alabama Department of Archives and History, Montgomery, Alabama)

The history of the "Old Guard," as they were often referred to, was exemplified in the careers of Charles Waldron Buckley and Joseph W. Dimmick of Montgomery, Morris D. Wickersham of Mobile, and Julian H. Bingham of Talladega. Buckley, Wickersham, and Dimmick were all natives of northern states, had served in the Union army, and moved to Alabama after the Civil War. Bingham was a native Alabamian, but he was the son of a Reconstruction Radical Republican. Each man made a career out of gaining federal offices, including such positions as Mont-

The Old Guard and the Populists 15

gomery's postmaster, state collector of internal revenue, and chief clerk of the United States district court. They were never without a "place" while Republicans controlled the executive branch of the national government.[14]

The Old Guard lost their power in 1904 when a new group of men, loyal to Theodore Roosevelt, won the state party offices and seized control of federal patronage. Some of the old leaders died, and Barker was one of the few who remained in office under Roosevelt, but he was determined to oust the upstarts and put control of the party back into the hands of safe conservative men with strong ties to old party leaders. Barker achieved his goal by the summer of 1911, but only after several years of intense intraparty warfare.

The accession of Roosevelt to the presidency in 1901 marked the beginning of the Old Guard's problems. Roosevelt was not ideologically palatable to the dominant conservative hierarchy of his party, but his popularity with voters insulated him from a serious challenge for the GOP nomination in 1904. Doubts about his commitment to traditional Republican beliefs ranked second among Alabama's Old Guard to their concerns about Roosevelt's refusal to accommodate their patronage demands. In 1903 the president began to funnel patronage through a rising new group of Alabama Republicans, many of whom were very young. Sometimes he even appointed Democrats to significant offices.[15]

Roosevelt also demanded that blacks be included in party meetings and that they receive minor government posts. His appointment of a black woman as postmistress of a small Mississippi town in 1902 created a furor in the South. Some of Alabama's Old Guard had supported Negro rights during Reconstruction, but by the 1880s they had been assimilated into southern society. Supporting racial equality brought them diminishing returns, and most of them believed in white supremacy as ardently as the Democrats.[16]

The Old Guard had sometimes split into "lily-white" and "black-and-tan" factions, depending on how solicitous of black rights national Republican administrations were at any particular time and according to which faction best served their interests. Some longtime Republicans had been members of both racial factions, as necessity demanded; their allegiance was not to racial justice or racial oppression, but to officeholding. The national GOP had become tepid in its support of black rights after Reconstruction, but in the first few years of his administration, Roosevelt seemed more committed to racial inclusion.[17]

Roosevelt was influenced by the "Wizard of Tuskegee," Booker T. Washington, the country's most powerful black man, whose presence in Alabama was a constant source of irritation for older Republicans. The president brazenly consulted the black educator about patronage disputes and embarrassed state Republicans when he had dinner with Washington at the White House. Washington might have been acceptable to the Old Guard if he had shown proper deference to them, but he endorsed a new set of party leaders.[18]

Booker Washington's closest associate among Alabama's white Republicans, and Barker's archenemy, was Joseph Oswalt Thompson of Tuskegee. Thompson, with Washington's help, seized control of federal patronage coming to Alabama in 1903 and became chairman of the state GOP in 1904. Thompson, a younger brother of Black Belt Democratic congressman Charles W. Thompson, was the only Republican in his family. He declared his allegiance to the GOP while still a teenager, held low-level federal jobs during the Harrison and McKinley administrations, and won notoriety when he became the recipient of a moonshiner's bullet while trying to enforce federal revenue laws against illegal liquor. He was only thirty-three when he became party chairman.[19]

Thompson's opportunity came when conservative Republicans, anxious about Roosevelt's independent ways, backed Senator Marcus Alonzo Hanna of Ohio, who strongly supported big business, for the 1904 Republican presidential nomination. Hanna, a brilliant tactician who managed William McKinley's two successful presidential campaigns, had been chairman of the national Republican party. He knew grassroots Republicans in all regions but had no chance for the nomination because the party was not going to dump a popular incumbent. When Hanna died in early 1904, the anti-Roosevelt Republicans became a movement without a leader. Factions generated by this brief challenge to the president "persisted in several states" and divided Alabama's old guard. Unlike some of his political cohorts, who ruined their credibility with the Roosevelt administration, Barker astutely avoided the ill-fated Hanna boomlet.[20]

Thompson's subsequent exercise of power galled the Old Guard because his closest friends and some men he supported for federal offices had been Republicans for only a brief time. His chief advisor was Birmingham attorney Oscar R. Hundley, a shrewd political operator who had served several terms in both the state house of representatives and the state senate as a Democrat from Madison County in the 1880s and 1890s. Hundley abruptly switched to the Republican party in 1896 when he ran unsuccessfully as the GOP nominee for Congress from the Eighth District on a fusion ticket with the Populist party. He moved to Birmingham in 1901 after his marriage to Francis "Bossie" O'Brien, daughter of Democratic politician Frank O'Brien of Birmingham and a leader in the women's suffrage movement. Hundley directed the forces that elected Thompson chairman at the 1904 state GOP convention, and the new chairman relied on the ex-Democrat to outmaneuver the Old Guard during the remainder of the Roosevelt administration. Thompson's loyalty to the dexterous Hundley widened rifts among Republicans.[21]

In 1907, Thompson persuaded Roosevelt to name Hundley to a federal district judgeship, an appealing office that carried a lifetime appointment. Republicans with a longer span of service to the party sought the job. Stung by Hundley's methods and the ruthless manner in which Thompson exiled opponents, the Old Guard fought to keep the ex-Democrat from being confirmed. They received help from southern Democrats anxious to punish Hundley for switching parties. This strange alliance held up a vote on Hundley's confirmation for the remainder of Roosevelt's term. Under the law, Hundley became the "interim" judge while awaiting formal confirmation, but after Taft took office in 1909 the appointment was withdrawn, and Thompson's loyal lieutenant was forced to step down from the bench.[22]

This humiliating defeat marked the beginning of the end for J. O. Thompson as party chairman. The widely publicized patronage tilt showed how little influence he had with Taft. In an effort to save Thompson, Booker T. Washington arranged a meeting with President Taft that included Prelate Barker and other state GOP leaders, but the president would not override his Alabama supporters. Barker and his agents forced Thompson to step down as state chairman in 1911. His replacement was Walker County's Pope Long, and Barker was named Republican national committeeman. Taft's agents systematically removed Roosevelt's men from party offices. They understood that Roosevelt might run again in 1912, and they had to make sure that the party hierarchy in each state was loyal to the president. No serious internal dissent materialized before Roosevelt formally announced his candidacy in February 1912. Roosevelt later complained that Taft kept the party hierarchy loyal to himself by using "every species of dishonest pressure through patronage."[23]

These patronage victories for Barker's party faction in 1911 proved to be pyrrhic because in excising Roosevelt's men the Old Guard misjudged rank-and-file Alabama Republican voters. Barker must have understood that there was a progressive wing of the party represented by Roosevelt and that some Alabama Republicans were reformers, but he underestimated the role that reform ideology would play in splitting Alabama's Republican voters. He mistakenly viewed all of his enemies as varied groups of patronage seekers. This was probably a correct assessment of J. O. Thompson, but an influx of Hill Country whites into the GOP after 1900 altered the ideological nature and aims of the party rank and file, even as the character of the party hierarchy hardly changed. Hill Country Republicans were more interested in winning elections in their home counties than in federal patronage, and they also exhibited an interest in public policy issues. Barker believed that by the judicious use of federal patronage he could hold the loyalty of these new Republicans, but they were more independent than he thought, and they had grievances.

The north Alabama Hill Country was the seat of opposition to secession, and nearly three thousand men from the area served in the Union army. Unionist sentiment, particularly strong in northwest Alabama counties such as Lawrence, Winston, Walker, and Fayette, led many old Unionists into the party that preserved the Union. A majority of white Republican voters in postwar Alabama were concentrated in hill counties just south of the Tennessee River, yet most major federal offices in the state went to whites from south Alabama, where most Republican voters were black. Thus, from the Civil War to the end of the century the Alabama GOP hierarchy was dominated by white men such as Prelate Barker, from Mobile or the Black Belt, whereas a majority of white Republican voters came from the hills.[24]

This strange dichotomy, in which white leaders of the party came from one end of the state and most of the white GOP voters resided in the other, became even more pronounced after 1901 when a state constitutional convention disfranchised black voters. In 1902, 58 percent of the votes cast for the Republican gubernatorial candidate came from fourteen hill counties. The concentration of GOP offices in southern Alabama could be justified when blacks voted in large numbers, but after 1901 north Alabama Republicans could credibly argue that it was unjust to give them such a small voice in party affairs. Prelate Barker was cognizant of these facts when he supported Walker County's Pope Long for party chairman in 1911. Long's father, Benjamin McFarland Long, had been a pre–Civil War Unionist and a Republican party leader until his death in

1903. However, it soon became apparent to Barker that Pope Long and the descendants of the old Unionists might not represent a majority of post-1900 Hill Country Republicans.[25]

The largest group of new Republican voters were ex-Populists. Support for the GOP expanded in the hills only after the collapse of the Populist party, which had the loyalty of most Hill Country voters in the nineties. Older Republicans were frightened when these ex-Populists demanded a voice in party affairs. The Old Guard had been aware of this problem since the summer of 1902 when a former Populist with no direct connection to them or to Republicans with Unionist roots unwittingly provided the pretext for J. O. Thompson and Oscar Hundley to begin their drive to control the state party.

Joseph Columbus Manning of Clay County, in northeastern Alabama, had called for a meeting of Republicans in Montgomery in August 1902 to reorganize the state Republican party. Manning had been a Republican only since 1896, but before that he had gained recognition as the "Evangel" of Alabama Populism. At the age of twenty-two he had helped to organize the state Populist party, and at twenty-four he was elected to the legislature as a Populist, but when the national People's party fused with the Democrats in 1896, he became a Republican. His statewide reputation helped to generate surprising momentum for the 1902 Republican meeting.[26]

Manning was an idealist who cared nothing for the diplomatic subtleties or hypocrisies inherent in the art of American politics. For him winning elections or gaining temporary private advantage was secondary to the struggle against evil. He preferred defeat over compromise and would give up power rather than bend his knee to bad men. He believed Alabama's Democratic party was a desiccated institution that stood for white supremacy, elitist rule, and rigged elections. As a Populist, Manning championed yeomen farmers of the Hill Country, advocated the inclusion of blacks in party affairs, and opposed efforts to disfranchise anyone. He was an admirable man, but also a self-righteous and naive one, and more pragmatic men waited to use him.[27]

On August 14, 1902, Alabama Republicans, including many of the Old Guard, gathered at the Montgomery Opera House where they expected Manning and his followers to appear. The atmosphere was tense because Manning had made his reputation attacking the hierarchy of both major parties. In 1899 he drove one powerful Republican leader out of federal office with charges of corruption. No one knew what the "Evangel" might do or say. The Old Guard was already angry about public statements Manning made when he called for the meeting. He had begun by harmlessly declaring himself a "friend of President Roosevelt" and saying that the state GOP should move toward the "high ideals and hopes" of the president, but then he called for the ouster of the "office holding" element, whom he tactlessly described as political "debauchers" and "prostitutes." [28]

When Manning found out who was waiting for him, he refused to go to the Opera House, and a rumor surfaced that he might be in physical danger if he appeared there. Instead, he met in another hotel with a small group of men, who were either new to Republican ranks or very young. Their goals were less cosmic than Manning's. They too hoped to overthrow the Old Guard, but they were primarily interested in exercising the patronage power themselves. Manning performed their spadework by calling the meeting and publicly assailing the Old Guard. Manning and his temporary conspirators created the Alabama League of Republican Clubs, affiliated with a national Republican League, and selected a set of officers who agreed to work for a revitalized Republican party in Alabama. One of the vice-presidents of this new group was Joseph Oswalt Thompson. Another young man in his thirties, Charles Scott of Montgomery, became secretary, and William F. Aldrich of Shelby County became treasurer. [29]

Aldrich was an oddity in this circle. He was fifty-four years old and well connected in national Republican circles and had been elected to Congress three times in the 1890s. He was a wealthy coal mine owner and brother of Truman H. Aldrich, chief executive officer of the Tennessee Coal and Iron Company, Alabama's largest corporation. Thus, Aldrich was linked to wealthy Birmingham businessmen who were active Republicans. Among them were Erskine Ramsey, also of Tennessee Coal and Iron, and Joseph H. Woodward, head of another leading iron company. The fact that Aldrich, a representative of big business Republicans, was huddled in a room with Joseph Manning, the former leader of a political party best known for damning monopolies and the "money power," seemed incongruous, but it was not that unusual. [30]

In the 1890s Populists and Republicans had cooperated against Democrats, particularly in the north Alabama Hill Country, where pockets of Republicans with Unionist roots still existed. Many rank-and-file Unionist-Republicans were small farmers who sympathized with the radical agrarian Populist movement. In north Alabama, the two parties fused their tickets in many counties, and this merging led to victories at the county and district levels. Despite the common background of Populist and Republican farmers, cooperation with Republicans meant that Populists had to accept some GOP candidates whose public policy positions differed from their own.[31]

When William F. Aldrich first won the Republican nomination for Congress from the Fourth Congressional District in 1894, Populists extracted a promise from him that he would support the free coinage of silver. The national GOP leadership supported the gold standard, and Aldrich reneged on his promise, but Populists continued to back him and other conservative Republicans in return for GOP support for Populist candidates. Many black Republicans still voted in the 1890s, and fusion with Republicans was a key to gaining black support for Populists. Some Populists were not comfortable with fusion, and men such as Aldrich no doubt also felt peculiar about being on the ticket with a party that backed radical schemes such as public ownership of the nation's railroads; nevertheless, fusion paid dividends in the fight against the Democrats and created lasting bonds between many Republicans and Populists.[32]

Another factor bound Aldrich and Manning on that particular day in 1902. They were relatively new in Republican politics. Aldrich was a successful businessman who had entered politics only in the nineties. Born and reared in New York and educated as a mining engineer, he came to Alabama to buy coal lands in the 1870s. He did not serve on Republican committees or attend GOP national conventions before the nineties. Thus, the factor that set the upstarts apart from the Old Guard was not age, but recent entry into GOP politics. Few of Manning's collaborators were ex-Populists, but like Aldrich either they had been closely associated with Populists or their entry into active GOP politics coincided with the Populist upheaval. They needed to pry the Old Guard loose from positions that blocked their advancement.[33]

The day after the meeting in Manning's hotel room, a public gathering of his friends was held at Montgomery's Arlington Hotel, where the voluble ex-Populist called on the Republican party to become more concerned about voters and elections and less anxious about federal patronage. He named Republicans from the Hill Country who had faced voters and won elections, and he asked that they become the new party leaders. The Old Guard, said Manning, had done nothing in twenty-five years to make the GOP a credible organization or one concerned with winning elections. A few days after the Montgomery meeting, as if to confirm his reputation as an agitator, Manning described the party's leaders as "old carpetbaggers," "big pumpkins off from home," and "office-holding thugs." One old Republican declared that Joe Manning had "gone crazy." While Manning offended older Republicans with his vituperative rhetoric, J. O. Thompson went to work building Republican clubs loyal to President Roosevelt and himself. Manning had served his purpose as Thompson's stalking horse. After a few short months, Thompson abandoned the "Evangel." The idealist Joe Manning would always be the consummate outsider.[34]

Despite the personal attacks on the Old Guard, Manning's speech had made public the grievances of the Hill Country. The power center of the GOP needed to shift from southern Alabama to its new political base in the Hill Country, where white Republican voters actually lived. Disfranchisement made it impossible for Republicans to win the Black Belt, but William McKinley had won pluralities or majorities in ten hill counties in the 1900 presidential election. Possibilities for a competitive Republican party in north Alabama were obvious, particularly where Populists had been strong, but such a party could be built only if the Old Guard, few of whom could claim any credit for this new Republican surge, would open up the party to new men and new ideas.[35]

An influx of new voters into the party should have been welcomed, but the Old Guard feared new competition for patronage. As long as Populists were in their own party, merely cooperating with Republicans, there was no threat, but when they demanded a voice inside the GOP, friction was unavoidable. Populist doctrines were at odds with the GOP's capitalist orientation. It would be difficult to assimilate these radicals into the party of McKinley, but a party headed by Theodore Roosevelt might be different.

The public attacks of Manning, astute political maneuvering by J. O. Thompson and Oscar Hundley, and the ill will caused by the Hanna-for-president movement caused the collapse of the Old Guard and opened the way for Populists to enter the party of Roosevelt. When Thompson became chairman he removed the old Republicans who supported Hanna and put new party leaders, including ex-Populists, into federal offices. Gilbert B. Deans, a former Hill Country state legislator and former chairman of the state Populist party, became cashier of the customs service at the Port of Mobile in 1902 and then U.S. marshal for the southern district of Alabama in 1908. Warren S. Reese, an ex-Populist from Montgomery, was U.S. district attorney for the middle district, and Oliver Day Street, once a Marshall County Populist, became U.S. district attorney for the northern district in 1908. These appointments and Thompson's relationship with Oscar Hundley irritated older Republicans, including many who were loyal to Roosevelt.[36]

A longtime Republican from Cullman County who was a candidate for a postmaster's job wrote Oliver Street in 1911 to express dismay at competition from ex-Populists. He had attended Republican national conventions, he said, before some of his enemies were "out of swaddling clothes" and before "another political party preaching sixteen to one or other strange doctrines" threatened to "change our whole economics . . . and disturb our present prosperous relations." Joe Manning demonstrated that ex-Populists with radical ideas could be dangerous, and Barker was wary of them. Manning's unalloyed idealism and outspoken ways made him relatively ineffective, yet ex-Populist leaders who became Republicans were astute politicians even more dangerous than Manning. Barker thought that he could deal with these men, who were, like him, seekers of power, even some who had benefitted from Thompson's leadership. In 1911 Barker sought support for his political schemes from ex-Populists in the Hill Country, not because he trusted them, but because they could no longer be ignored. He turned for help to Marshall County's Oliver Day Street.[37]

Street's father, Thomas Atkins Street, was an early organizer of the third-party movement of the nineties. Oliver, also known as "O. D.," was the Populist candidate for Congress from the Seventh Congressional District in 1898 and the Republican nominee in 1902. He had supported the Thompson-Hundley faction in 1904 and owed his appointment as United States district attorney to them, but after Taft took office in 1909 Street held office at the sufferance of the president. If he showed signs of disloyalty to Taft or to the president's agents in Alabama, he might be fired or forced to resign. Before the end of 1909 Street privately began to help Barker's operatives clean the Roosevelt group out of office, and as a result he was one of the few Roosevelt appointees to stay in office until the end of Taft's administration. J. O. Thompson became aware of Street's duplicity in 1911, and while he was still chairman he withdrew his support for Street's reappointment as U.S. district attorney. Street then became a Taft delegate to the 1912 national convention and acted as counsel for the Alabama Taft delegates challenged by the Roosevelt campaign.[38]

Street was well-known in the Seventh Congressional District, which included Cherokee, Cullman, DeKalb, Etowah, Franklin, Marshall, St. Clair, and Winston Counties. District voters elected a Populist congressman in 1894 and 1896 and voted for statewide Populist candidates in the nineties. The Seventh presented the acid test of Barker's strategy for holding the new Upcountry GOP voters in line by the ruthless withdrawal or dispersal of patronage. By the fall of 1912, Barker had cause for concern because he had lost the support of leading ex-Populists from other hill counties.[39]

Lewis H. Reynolds of Chilton County and Adolphus P. Longshore of Shelby County particularly irritated "the Major." Chilton and Shelby Counties were not in the Seventh District, contained few Republicans of Unionist descent, and became Republican only after the demise of Populism. Closely contested two-party systems existed in each county. Reynolds and Longshore dominated their local Republican parties, but Barker hoped that his judicious use of the patronage power could create significant opposition to them within their own counties. He was frustrated in this effort because both men had powerful political bases among the ranks of former Populist voters in their counties who owed nothing to the state Republican hierarchy. Reynolds and Longshore, like their old ally Joe Manning, believed in grassroots democracy and feared machinations by elite groups at the state level, but unlike Manning they were subtle practitioners of the art of gaining and exercising power.[40]

The ideological concerns of Reynolds and Longshore became apparent when they caused what one Birmingham newspaper described as a "red-hot debate" at the state Republican convention in March 1912. The two ex-Populists spoke against an Old Guard resolution that declared that the state GOP opposed the "initiative" and "referendum," which were symbols of progressive efforts to take policy decisions away from political bosses and return them to the people. The initiative allowed citizens to put proposed laws on the ballot without going through the legislature, and referenda put certain legislative measures before voters for approval. Both were supported by Progressive leaders such as Robert La Follette of Wisconsin, Hiram Johnson of California, and Theodore Roosevelt.[41]

The Old Guard resolution was easily passed by the Barker-controlled convention, but it created an unnecessary battle at the state convention. Barker thought that Reynolds and Longshore would challenge him for control of the party at the state convention. When they did not, Barker's supporters offered the resolution, perhaps in an effort to bring the reformers out into the open, isolate them, and destroy their influence in the state party. Reynolds and Longshore freely entered the debate because they had a clearer perception than Barker of the minds of Hill Country voters, of how such a debate over the nature of democracy would be viewed by those voters, and of the lack of support in their counties for a Republican party controlled by a conservative elite.[42]

Days after the Republican national convention, Oliver Street wrote Reynolds to request that the Chilton County leader not bolt the Republican party. Street's letter came too late. Even before the Bull Moose movement, Reynolds's two brothers were supporting Roosevelt against Taft for the presidential nomination. Reynolds and A. P. Longshore joined the Progressives. If Shelby and Chilton went to Roosevelt, it was even more important for Barker to win the Seventh District. Although the Seventh had only 16 percent of the state's population, it had provided 30 percent of the total state Republican vote in the 1908 presidential election.[43]

Barker used all of his influence to stem the flow of Alabama Republicans to Roosevelt. During the last week in July, Joseph O. Thompson was ordered to resign as internal revenue collector, and he dramatized the event by refusing to leave his office. He was forcibly removed by federal marshals. Postal officials who refused to commit to Taft were fired, and many other federal officials were replaced by Taft loyalists. An old Republican commented that Barker was in control and "getting the offices for his men." If Upcountry Republicans had been concerned only about maintaining ties to men who controlled Republican patronage Barker might have held their loyalty, but Taft's election chances were fading, and Upcountry voters who did not hold federal positions could cast their ballots without fear of future reprisal. Barker's actions backfired, and his hopes of holding Seventh District Republicans for Taft began to fade by the end of the summer.[44]

It was up to Oliver Street to hold the new Seventh District Republicans in line. No one knew the district better. In addition to his excellent relationships with ex-Populists, Street was aided by Marshall County's Charles Brents Kennamer, the son of an ex-Union soldier who had close ties to Unionist-Republican families throughout north Alabama. Kennamer was Street's assistant U.S. attorney. The two men had been leaders in the Republican party since 1902. Street was the Seventh District GOP candidate for Congress that year and then managed the campaigns of Seventh District Republican congressional candidates in 1906 and 1910. In the latter year, the GOP candidate garnered nearly 49 percent of the vote. This alliance between the ex-Populist and a scion of the old Unionists was formidable.[45]

Surprisingly, Barker found that Street and Kennamer could not hold

O. D. Street, ca. 1912 (courtesy of Larry Smith)

Seventh District Republicans for Taft. "What is the trouble in the Seventh District?" the major angrily wrote to Republican chairman Pope Long in September. "There seems to be something the matter." Street had lost control of Republicans in the district, complained Barker. "How is it that all that crowd of Street's friends who were with him at his district convention are now leading the fight of our opposition?" Later, an exasperated Barker presented Long with a list of eleven men who had been active Republicans in various hill counties. "Will these men support Taft or Bull Moose? Kindly let me know which, if any of them, can be relied upon to oppose the Roosevelt crowd." Barker also informed Long that he was specifically encouraging opposition to Lewis Reynolds in Chilton County because he believed the old Populist was "the agitator behind the scenes, pulling the strings." Indeed, Reynolds had formally resigned from the state Republican executive committee and joined Shelby County's A. P. Longshore in helping to organize the Alabama Progressive party.[46]

The Alabama general election was a debacle for the Old Guard. Street and Kennamer, both from Marshall County, could not even keep Republicans in their home county from leaving Taft. Even though Democrat Woodrow Wilson won 70 percent of Alabama's presidential vote, he failed to get a majority in the Seventh District, where Roosevelt won nearly three-quarters of the non-Democratic vote. The total district vote was up nearly 20 percent over that cast in 1908, as opposed to a 10 percent increase statewide, and two-thirds of the Seventh District increase went to the Progressive party. The large voting turnout had been caused by Roosevelt.[47]

In Chilton and Shelby Counties, homes of ex-Populists Lewis Reynolds and A. P. Longshore, Roosevelt's Progressives led all parties, winning a plurality in Shelby and an outright majority in Chilton. In Clay County, where Joseph Manning had helped to form the first official Populist party organization in the state, the Progressive party won 45 percent of the vote, barely missing a plurality over Wilson, with Taft running a poor third. Thus, the insurgent Progressives won their largest totals in areas where Populists had been strongest, but the Populist experience was not the sole explanation for the 1912 response of the Hill Country.[48] Voters in southeastern Alabama's Wiregrass (Coffee, Conecuh, Covington, Crenshaw, Dale, Geneva, and Henry Counties), another area dominated by small white farmers, had been as committed to Populism as the hills, yet few Republicans lived there after 1900. Democrats easily reacquired the dominance they had exercised in the Wiregrass before Populism. A small Republican presence persisted in Geneva County, but no GOP candidates won local offices there after 1900, though Republicans won just over 40 percent of the Geneva vote in the 1900 and 1920 presidential elections. More than 70 percent of the Wiregrass's votes went to Woodrow Wilson in 1912, and although most of those who voted for someone other than Wilson did choose Roosevelt, their scant numbers confirmed that the anti-Democratic animus that still existed in the hills had already faded in the Wiregrass.[49]

Despite a common experience with Populism, the Hill Country political tradition differed markedly from that in the Wiregrass. Unionism had left pockets of Republican families in the Hill Country, and widespread and successful independent movements had also been prominent there just after Reconstruction. Contrarily, Wiregrass voters had been loyal

Democrats from the Civil War to the early 1890s. They had no pre-Populist tradition of anti-Democratic dissent. Ex-Populists in the Wiregrass who refused to go back to the Democratic party after 1896, unlike their counterparts in the hills, had no Republicans of Unionist heritage or longtime independents to form alliances with and had little hope of victory against the rejuvenated Democrats. Also, a large increase occurred in the black population of the Wiregrass between 1890 and 1900, while in most hill counties the black population either remained stable or declined during the decade. The increasing black presence in the Wiregrass was accompanied by growing loyalty to the party of white supremacy. Therefore, Republican activity in the Wiregrass was doomed to failure after 1900.[50]

Prelate Barker was confused about what happened in the Hill Country in 1912 because he did not appreciate the traditional factors that motivated voters there. The independent political mentality of Hill Country voters predated Populism and was reinforced by it, but as the 1912 election demonstrated, this mentality survived Populism. Sharp disagreements exist among historians about the nature of this Hill Country political mind.

In a "devastating" critique of Alabama's Populists, the historian Sheldon Hackney shifts the blame for their demise from the Democratic party hierarchy who stole elections from them in the nineties to their "mentality." Certain social-psychological factors so shaped their mentality, argues Hackney, that Populists were incapable of forming substantive political ideas or sustaining a successful, long-term political movement. Their ideas were irrelevant in a rapidly modernizing world, and their view of the future was unrealistic. They held fast to fading agrarian values, were disoriented by anxieties over their status in society, and were never "revolutionaries or reformers." After 1896 they became disillusioned and sour, gave up on politics, or turned reactionary. These facts proved their insincerity and a lack of continuity between their movement and the more realistic post-1900 progressivism.[51]

Hackney reached these conclusions after an unsuccessful search for ex-Populists among the ranks of progressive Democrats. Solid evidence of reform continuity could have been found among Hill Country Republicans who were once Populists. The behavior of ex-Populists in 1912 supports the view of a Populist mind more reform oriented, rational, sincere, and less cynical than the one Hackney describes. The Hill Country's Populist mentality was spawned by a complex interplay of substantive ideas, myths, experience, and fears that were part of the area's political culture. Anti-Democratic movements there were products of the Up-country political tradition, but each county functioned as a separate political entity and reflected its own distinct variation of the larger tradition. The choices that Oliver Street, A. P. Longshore, and Lewis Reynolds made in 1912 resulted from their individual experiences and needs and from the history of the counties that were their political bases.

2 James Lawrence Sheffield and the Roots of Hill Country Independence

Farmers in these up-country counties . . . might more profitably be understood as a distinct social class. . . . Unlike the [small] farmers of the plantation belt, they controlled the local political process and shaped a regional culture of their own.[1]

Eugene Genovese

The dilemma faced by Oliver Street in 1912 was not unfamiliar to him. Choosing between political parties was a problem his family had faced since Reconstruction, when he was a small boy living on a farm near the Tennessee River in northern Marshall County. In 1874, the year of the political upheaval that "redeemed" Alabama from Republican rule, Oliver's father, Thomas Atkins Street, led the Marshall County Democratic ticket as the candidate for probate judge, but older family members presented different role models. They insinuated that the Democratic party did not deserve their loyalty. James Lawrence Sheffield, stepfather of Thomas Atkins Street, argued that Democrats were dominated by elites who violated basic concepts of fairness to control party nominations. He broke with the Democratic party in 1874 and ran for Congress from the Fifth District as an independent against the "regular" Democratic nominee. The Fifth included the hill counties of Marshall, Etowah, St. Clair, Cherokee, and DeKalb, in addition to the Tennessee Valley counties of Madison, Morgan, and Jackson.[2]

Any sign of disloyalty to Democrats by whites was viewed as heresy during the Reconstruction era, but Sheffield's apostasy was extraordinary. State Democratic leaders had taken unusual measures in 1874 to insure white unity in the effort to defeat the hated Radical Republicans, identified as Negroes, carpetbaggers, and scalawags. Republicans had won the governorship in 1868, and though Democrats took it back in 1870, they lost it again in 1872. Small margins separated the parties in the previous two elections, and although Democrats won control of the Alabama House of Representatives, they were unable to win the state senate. This furious competition made white unity imperative, but it had not yet been achieved.[3]

The Union Loyal League, the Republican party's organizing arm, gained support in the hills immediately after the war (1865–1868), but GOP racial and economic policies so alienated the small farmers that Democrats swept the Upcountry in 1870. Two years later the Republicans capitalized on the unpopularity of incumbent state Democratic officials and won back some hill counties. Republicans were a minority among Upcountry whites, but gains among this group of voters were crucial to the 1872 GOP victory. Democrats had to hold these white counties in 1874 because black voters, who were loyal Republicans, constituted half of the state's electorate. The possibility that Sheffield might take white voters out of the Democratic party threatened not only Fifth District Democrats but also statewide Democratic candidates involved in close races.[4]

Restoring Democratic rule meant a return of white supremacy, and thus loyalty to Democrats was equated with loyalty to the white race, whereas disloyalty meant racial treason. Democratic newspapers warned that any break with the party, however slight, could lead to a Republican victory. An Upcountry Democratic editor who focused his anger on Sheffield wrote that the "principle was settled some time back by the Democratic press that there were to be no Democratic independent candidates in this election." If Sheffield persisted, he was "now and forever located in the ranks of the radical party." Independent candidates were "enemies to the cause of good government and social order . . . occupying a position false to themselves, to their country and to their God."[5]

State and county Democrats had created a convention nomination system calculated to control dissidents. Only regular nominees of authorized Democratic conventions could receive the party's blessing. Conventions were governed by rules that allowed elite groups to assure that only "safe" candidates would be chosen. Those dissatisfied with the nominees had little choice but to vote Democratic, or they would be censured by their communities as traitors to the party of white supremacy. County conventions were "mass meetings" called by members of the local Democratic executive committee who had few compunctions about setting the date and time of the meeting when their friends were available and their enemies indisposed. It was inconvenient for backcountry farmers to go to town, whereas town men, particularly lawyers and merchants, were nearly always in attendance. Nominations rarely represented the sentiments of most white Democrats.[6]

An influential Democratic editor, incensed by the arrogance of party elites, wrote that in each county "a few spirits work the wires and make up the conventions." People were asked to vote for candidates nominated by "intrigue and combination." Because most whites believed that they had to vote for Democratic nominees in the general election, the system "bound them hand and foot."[7]

Black Belt planters had a preeminent interest in efforts to control the party and insure white unity. Their control over black laborers had become problematic after slavery. Blacks had no land or means of employment and generally remained in plantation areas, yet they demanded a measure of distance from their ex-masters. A new agricultural system, including sharecropping and farm tenancy, replaced slavery. It was imperative for planters to control state laws on landlord-tenant relations, agricultural liens, mortgages, banking, interest rates, contracts, and even petty theft. Such laws formed the basis of economic relationships in the postwar period, and Black Belters had to be sure that safe Democrats were elected to statewide offices and the legislature. Furthermore, blacks and their allies held local offices in some Black Belt counties. This situation meant that law enforcement, control of the county treasury, the building of bridges and roads, and the collection of local taxes were in unsafe hands. Only total control of nominations and elections could dislodge these black-and-tan coalitions.[8]

Black Belters were so concerned about these matters that they claimed a personal interest in the politics of individual hill counties. If a few hill counties bolted from the party or picked unsafe Democratic nominees, white unity would be destroyed. Lowland planters formed alliances with Upcountry railroad men, merchants, mine owners, lawyers, and others with elite economic interests. As railroads cut into north Alabama's coal and iron ore country, the influence of this rising group of commercial interests increased. Birmingham, a new city located in the Hill Country, drew hundreds of new entrepreneurs. This coalition of planters and Upcountry commercial interests became the party hierarchy. These elite groups sometimes disagreed, but they negotiated arrangements that brought them together against politicians who touted the interests of small farmers, miners, and blacks. The party hierarchy was frightened by the alliance of lowland blacks and upland whites that helped Republicans win the 1872 gubernatorial election.[9]

James L. Sheffield's political past did not reassure leading north Alabama Democrats. If he had been an avowed Republican they could have denounced him as a radical allied with Negroes, and if he had been unknown the Democrats might have ignored him. Sheffield was, instead, a north Alabama native, a well-known politician whose public career as a Democrat spanned thirty years, a hero of the Confederacy, and an avowed opponent of Radical Reconstruction. He was closely identified with the political ethos and historical experience of Upcountry people.[10]

Sheffield, the son of a poor carriage maker who came to Alabama from Virginia, was born in Huntsville in 1819, the year Alabama became a state. In 1837, at age eighteen, he moved to Marshall County and clerked in a store near the Tennessee River, north Alabama's vital commercial highway. A small portion of Marshall County lay near the river, but the largest part rose steadily into hills and high mountains as one moved south away from the water. When Sheffield arrived, northeastern Alabama's Hill Country was being wrested from the Cherokee Indians. Marshall and neighboring Jackson, DeKalb, and Cherokee Counties did not finish removing the Native Americans until 1839. The Indians refused to go without a fight. White settlers, aided by the army, imprisoned the Cherokee in stockades and expelled them from the area. Thus, whites who moved into the northeastern hills in the early 1840s resided in frontier communities removed from even the amenities of rude small towns like Huntsville. They were often isolated from society by the mountain coves in which they lived.[11]

In 1840, the twenty-one-year-old Sheffield attended the state Democratic convention. Democrats swept north Alabama and Marshall County in the ensuing race against the Whigs. The Democratic party dominated the Upcountry in the 1840s, but Alabama had a closely contested two-party system. The political base of the Whigs lay in south Alabama's Black Belt plantation region. Hill Country farmers labeled Whigs the "broadcloth" or "royal" party because of the prominence of planters and wealthy businessmen among them. Economic and social differences between Whigs and Democrats within the Black Belt were not great because many large planters were Democrats, but substantial differences existed between rank-and-file Upcountry Democrats and plantation Whigs.[12]

Most Hill Country voters were staunch Jacksonian Democrats. Their "Jacksonianism" referred in part to Andrew Jackson but more broadly to an ideology that became fixed in the Hill Country mind even before Jackson's presidency. This way of thinking penetrated all regions of prewar

Alabama, was even popular among some Whigs, persisted beyond the Civil War, and was especially compelling to Hill Country yeoman, for whom it was orthodoxy. The yeomen constituted a majority of Hill Country people, and their attraction to Jacksonian ideas can be explained, in part, by their life-style and their mistrust of lowland planters.[13]

Yeomen usually owned farms of less than one hundred acres, grew their own food, and, unlike large planters, worked the fields with their families. Because Hill Country terrain was not conducive to the creation of large cotton plantations, few yeomen became slaveowners, and those who did usually held less than ten bondsmen. The yeomen's primary goal was economic self-sufficiency. They practiced a safety-first style of agriculture that led them to concentrate on food crops or livestock first and plant cash crops such as cotton only after they were sure that their families were fed. They had little cash money, and if they engaged in trade, it was usually by bartering one item for another. Despite this "pre-modern" economy, these people were not poor by their standards.[14]

Neighboring yeomen helped one another rather than engage in economic competition. They grazed livestock on the property of neighbors under a doctrine that made unenclosed land an "open range." This practice gave small landowners a larger area on which their animals could forage. If a neighboring landowner objected, he had to erect a fence to keep the animals out. The cooperative atmosphere of Upcountry life produced few fences. Relatives also settled near one another, and the ties to kin and neighbors gave the culture a more "communal" and "egalitarian" quality than plantation culture.[15]

Some yeomen aspired to become large planters and to create enough surplus to improve their lives materially, but most feared being controlled by unpredictable market forces or by the credit system that followed the market. Indebtedness created obligations that made men dependent on others. Yeomen equated dependency with the actual slavery of blacks they sometimes encountered. In the hills, freedom meant autonomy or the "absence of external forces manipulating one's life." Only independent landowners not ensnared in the credit system were free. Landowning made freedom possible, and yeomen were grateful to politicians who made more land available to them, even if it meant displacing the Indians.[16]

The Jacksonian ethos, so strong among yeomen, held that yeomen farmers were in a perpetual battle with elites who sought special privileges from government unavailable to average people. Often operating secretly, these elites threatened the independence of yeomen. They tempted politicians to raise taxes on the whole people to benefit wealthy private interests. Jacksonians believed that the chief victims of such funding schemes would be small farmers, mechanics, and laborers. The greatest threat to liberty came from the "money power" or stock jobbers, northeastern capitalists, state-chartered banks, and corporations.[17]

Jacksonians instinctively opposed internal improvements programs advocated by these market forces to stimulate the economy. Public money spent on roads, bridges, canals, and other public works came from everyone's pockets and benefitted only those engaged in the marketplace. Thus, internal improvement projects violated the principle of equality, or equal treatment for all white citizens, and threatened to enthrone a financial aristocracy. The issue of government aid to private economic forces sharply distinguished Jacksonian Democrats from their opponents. Whigs believed that internal improvements led to economic growth and thus to a greater range of personal choices for individuals trying to reach their full potential. Jacksonians took antigovernment positions, not because they were doctrinaire laissez-faire advocates, but because they did not accept Whig contentions that government support would lift all boats. Experience taught them that only elites benefitted from government aid.[18]

The phrase "equal rights for all, and special privileges for none" was the central tenet of Jacksonian thought. Protection against elite privilege lay in the ballot box. Jacksonians "campaigned for the abolition of all property qualifications for voting and officeholding." Public officials were subjected to frequent elections and were turned out of office with regularity by Jacksonians. In the eyes of these feisty voters, incumbency was a disadvantage. Jacksonian Democrats hoped that a broader electorate would use government to restrict the power of corporations, which were given artificial privileges by the government, advantages not held by individuals. "Class hatred and fear of corporate wealth was a continuing theme" in antebellum politics. Jacksonians believed that the Democratic party was a "trade union" of the electorate, which functioned as a counterweight against the privileged. This version of democracy flourished in the hills, whereas Whigs were more often found in areas closely connected to the market economy, such as the Black Belt, the cities, and the Mobile–Gulf Coast area.[19]

In the 1840s and early 1850s, a struggle developed over congressional redistricting that pitted Hill Country Democrats against Black Belt Whigs. Slaves outnumbered whites in the Black Belt, and planters there wanted slaves counted as part of the population for purposes of representation. The last vote on this issue occurred in 1854 when the white basis was sustained on a strict party line–sectional vote with north Alabama Democrats against the Whigs. This redistricting battle confirmed Jacksonian fears that a haughty planter elite, who already held the best land and most of the state's money, also wanted to control the political system. Upcountry Democrats were successful in creating a revenue system that hardly touched yeoman farmers, but taxed planters, banks, and corporations. Those who held slaves, carriages, and luxury items paid the highest taxes.[20]

Some Black Belt planter-Democrats, despite the class warfare rhetoric of Jacksonian politicians, were also motivated by the Jacksonian ethos, which was not confined to class or region. Planters, like yeomen, often lashed out at corporate power and the influence of impersonal bankers, but the need to market, transport, and finance the production of large amounts of cotton gave planter representatives a more favorable view of laws that aided railroads, banks, and steamboat companies. Andrew Jackson's battles against this kind of internal improvements legislation, his campaign against the recharter of the Bank of the United States, and his image as the champion of the farmers, mechanics, and laborers against sinister special interests won the hearts of North Alabama's yeomen. He was also an advocate of Indian removal, and after his battles with the Creeks and Seminoles, he became the symbol of that process. His policies led to the opening of thousands of acres of land to small white farmers in the Upcountry and increased their opportunity to become the independent landowners they idealized.[21]

Colorful Hill Country leaders practiced a unique Jacksonian political style in which they rhetorically pitted the masses against the privileged. The antebellum Fifth Congressional District, which included Blount, DeKalb, St. Clair, Jackson, and Madison Counties, as well as Marshall, was represented in Congress from 1849 to the Civil War by the redoubtable Williamson R. W. Cobb, an inveterate Jacksonian stylist. He pushed for a homestead act that would open up more public land at cheap prices for small farmers of his district. On the campaign trail, he played a banjo and sang a song that stated that "Uncle Sam is rich enough to give us all a farm." Cobb was so entertaining, said an opponent, that he had an unshakable "power over the masses," and he was always supported by those "who can't or don't read." He was often attacked for his lack of education, but this deficiency proved to be an advantage because common folk identified with him.[22]

The political career of James Lawrence Sheffield was carved out of this Jacksonian political culture, and its tenets were bequeathed to his children. As late as 1892, his stepson Thomas Atkins Street still defined himself as a "Jacksonian Democrat." In 1844 Sheffield married Mary Ann Street, daughter of a leading planter, widow of Presbyterian minister Oliver Day Street, and mother of two small children, including Thomas Atkins. Sheffield was elected sheriff of Marshall County in 1844, but after one term he briefly left politics for farming. Several Sheffield children were born, but the 1850 census shows that the former sheriff and his family were still residing with his father-in-law.[23]

During the 1850s, a cotton boom hit north Alabama, and some yeomen farmers entered the marketplace, became planters, and bought slaves. They followed a path described by W. J. Cash in *The Mind of the South* and moved from the "coon hunting population of the southern backcountry" to the "Big House." The 1860 census listed Sheffield as the owner of more than twenty slaves and five hundred acres of land. Only fifteen Marshall County men owned as many acres, and only twenty-one had as many slaves. Sheffield used most of his land for food production, but he also produced a substantial amount of cotton for sale.[24]

Despite the cotton boom, 80 percent of Marshall County farmers owned less than one hundred acres, and few owned slaves. Even Sheffield was land and slave poor when compared with Black Belt planters to his south and others in the Tennessee Valley. In Greene County, for instance, sixty-seven plantations contained more than one thousand acres, and 113 men held more than fifty slaves. Most Black Belt counties had a similar plantation demography. Only two plantations exceeded one thousand acres in Marshall County, and only four Marshall planters held over fifty slaves, although the county's white population was larger than most Black Belt counties.[25]

Despite economic, social, and cultural divisions between the regions, liberty-loving Upcountry yeomen supported the continuation and expansion of black slavery. Jacksonian Democracy's "ultimate paradox" lay in its support for both grassroots democracy and black slavery. Yeomen received few direct benefits from the slave system, but they favored white supremacy and feared that the collapse of slavery would introduce threatening market forces. Without slavery, economic elites would use their land, labor, and money as the market demanded, and this situation would inevitably lead to mills, factories, banks, a new class of white wage workers, and a complex system of rules and laws governing market relations.

James L. Sheffield, 1886 (courtesy of the Alabama Department of Archives and
History, Montgomery, Alabama)

Upcountry self-sufficiency would be eroded by forces of economic development. The absence of slavery, the decline of white supremacy, and the
introduction of northern-style capitalism could put yeomen into a state
of economic dependency alongside blacks.[26]

Yeomen support for slavery did not indicate their acceptance or emu-
lation of planter values or the hegemony of planters over yeomen, but the
opposite. The existence of slavery protected yeomen from being drawn
into the vortex of market capitalism and also from being entrapped in the
world of planters and slaves. Thus, slavery protected the liberty of yeo-

men to remain aloof from economic systems they feared. An examination of what happened to Upcountry yeomen after the Civil War, says one writer, confirms their rational analysis of what the end of slavery would bring.[27]

James L. Sheffield did join the cotton boom and gain economic prominence as a planter, but in Upcountry politics his planter status meant little. Deferential politics was anathema in the hills, and Sheffield needed the support of the feisty yeomen who were his neighbors. He demonstrated his ability to compete in the rough-and-tumble of Hill Country politics in 1855 and 1857, when he was twice elected to the state house of representatives. In 1861, Marshall County's small-farm electorate chose Sheffield as a delegate to the state convention called to consider the matter of secession.[28]

Most north Alabamians backed southern-rights Democrat John Breckenridge for president in 1860, but Marshall County gave a majority to the Unionist Democrat Stephen A. Douglas. Sheffield opposed secession and was a Unionist delegate. Most Upcountry and Tennessee Valley counties sent "cooperationist" delegates to the convention who did not oppose secession under all circumstances, but believed that Alabama should not secede until it learned the position of such upper South states as Virginia, North Carolina, and Tennessee. Most delegates from other areas were "immediatists" who agreed with the so-called fire-eaters that the South should secede without delay. A few Upcountry delegates were such avowed Unionists that they would agree to secede only as a last resort, and Sheffield was among them. He went beyond cooperationist rhetoric and argued to the convention that disunion was unwise. Even after delegates voted sixty-one to thirty-nine for secession, Sheffield would not capitulate. He signed a petition that called for a statewide vote on secession and refused to sign the ordinance of secession until ordered to do so by a mass meeting in Marshall County.[29]

After secession, Sheffield and most Hill Country whites gave their loyalty to the Confederacy, but a large group of Unionists in north Alabama would not capitulate. Despite connections between their independence and slavery, many yeomen would not fight for a cause that primarily benefitted big planters. Approximately three thousand whites from Alabama's hill counties joined the Union army, and thousands became "Tories" who refused to fight for either side. No other Alabama region was so bitterly divided, and as the war droned on, disillusionment with the Confederacy grew in the area.[30]

Upcountry Alabama was part of the war's "strategic crossroads," invaded by northern armies who laid waste to land, crops, livestock, and other personal property. Confederate armies also took provisions from the populace. Many hill men who went to war and survived came home to find their crops destroyed, their homes burned, and their personal property stolen. Desperate farm women in Randolph County attacked a Confederate supply depot in search of food. By the time of the Confederate surrender, many Upcountry families who initially supported the war had changed their minds. Women and children, some left behind by husbands and fathers killed in the war, roamed the roads in despair, near starvation, like the refugee freedmen in the plantation belt. In April 1864 James L. Sheffield begged Governor Thomas Hill Watts of Alabama to do something about starving people. "I find hundreds of them entirely destitute of everything upon which to live," wrote Sheffield, "not even bread."[31]

Sheffield was a prominent officer in Robert E. Lee's Army of Northern Virginia. He raised his own Confederate troops in the hills, was elected colonel, and spent nearly $60,000 outfitting and provisioning his men. The Confederate government promised to repay him, but it never did. He received a formal commission as a colonel in May 1862 and was wounded at the battle of Cedar Mountain that year, but he later commanded brigades at Second Manassas, Antietam, Gettysburg, and Chickamauga. At Gettysburg, Sheffield fought beside his troops on Little Round Top. After receiving a serious wound at Chickamauga in May 1864, he resigned his commission. His stepson, Thomas Atkins Street, also joined the Confederate army, was captured by Union troops, and spent the last two years of the war in northern prison camps.[32]

After the war, Sheffield made eloquent speeches about the "lost cause." As a state senator in the 1880s he led efforts to construct a Confederate memorial on Alabama's capital grounds. No two men could have been more closely identified with the South's "distinctive myths" than Sheffield and Street, yet postwar politics eventually led them into several phases of dissent against the party of white supremacy. By the 1890s they were even seeking alliances in anti-Democratic campaigns with a Marshall County family who had remained loyal to the Union throughout the war and had also supported Radical Reconstruction.[33]

The Kennamer family, who came from a mountainous section of Marshall County called "Kennamer's Cove," were led by a native Alabamian who helped his neighbors escape Confederate conscription agents, led others to join the Union army, spied and scouted for the Union himself, and was finally forced to escape behind Union lines. In the immediate postwar period, Sheffield and Street could not have felt kindly toward the "traitor" Seaborn A. Kennamer or his clan. Even after the war feeling ran high in the divided Hill Country. In the fall of 1865 a Marshall County grand jury indicted some citizens who had been identified with the Union army. The men were arrested but were ultimately released. Loyal Unionists denounced these actions and called on President Johnson for protection.[34]

Sheffield and his stepson returned home to find their plantation in ruins and their financial condition desperate. Young T. A. Street married, began a family, built a thriving farm, and became a large landowner and also the leader of the county Democratic party. Sheffield never recovered economically, and one newspaper described him in 1872 as "broken down in fortune and with poverty staring him in the face." He took in "boarders" who paid rent to live in his home. In the late 1880s he took clerking jobs for a private railroad company in Montgomery and in the office of the state superintendent of education. Despite economic reverses, Sheffield remained active in politics. He was elected to the first postwar session of the Alabama legislature, which met in 1865–66. Like other high-ranking Confederate officers, Sheffield was disfranchised by the Republican Congress of 1867. He was replaced in the legislature by Seaborn Kennamer, the Radical Republican and former Union spy.[35]

Kennamer joined the Union Loyal League, the organizing arm of the southern Republican party, and chaired the first meeting of the Marshall County Republican party on March 2, 1867. Among those who also joined Marshall County's postwar Republicans and became a Kennamer ally was Arthur C. Beard, another role model for Oliver Street. Like Sheffield, Beard had been an antebellum plantation owner and a slaveholder, but he also had been Unionist delegate to the secession convention. Beard and Seaborn Kennamer had also been among the few Marshall County antebellum Whigs, but, unlike Kennamer, Beard served in the Confederate army. A war-related injury brought him home from the army in 1862. In 1865, Beard's daughter Julia Ann married Thomas Atkins Street, and their son Oliver Day Street II was born in 1866.[36]

Young Oliver must have found political conversations at the Sunday dinner table confusing. He was surrounded by a diverse group of politicians: his father was a rising figure in the local Democratic party; his step-grandfather was an insurgent anti-Democratic dissenter; and his maternal grandfather had dared to become a Reconstruction Republican. In most of Alabama it would surely have been an unlikely collection of dinner companions, but not in the Hill Country. Thus, Oliver Street's political heritage was not confined to the Democratic party, and the only common theme he could glean from his disparate elders was that of independence.

A few Unionist-Republicans of the Kennamer-Beard stripe lived in Marshall County, and although they were more numerous in other hill counties, they never constituted a majority of Hill Country voters. Most hill men, including Sheffield and T. A. Street, had been Confederates after they were Unionists, were Democrats in the late 1860s and early 1870s, and opposed Radical Reconstruction. Most post-Reconstruction anti-Democratic movements came from this group, and although they sometimes won cooperation from Unionist-Republicans, the latter achieved long-term dominance only in Winston County. Nevertheless, the Republican presence was important in most hill counties. If 10 to 20 percent of the voters in any county were white Republicans, they were the balance of power in close races between independents and regular Democrats.[37]

Kennamer's election to the legislature resulted from the disfranchisement of men such as Sheffield and a white boycott of the state election. Only under these peculiar circumstances of 1867–68 did Republicans show substantial strength among Marshall County whites before the 1890s. In the 1868 presidential election, Ulysses Grant received 41 percent of the county vote, but the GOP percentage in Marshall declined to 33 percent in 1872 and 13.5 percent in 1876.[38]

Sheffield denounced Republicans, the Fourteenth and Fifteenth Amendments, and Radical Reconstruction, but his citizenship rights were restored, and he reentered politics. In 1872 he sought the Fifth District Democratic nomination for Congress. At the district nominating convention Sheffield won a plurality of the delegates, but even after fifty separate ballots were taken, he had failed to receive a majority. He withdrew in favor of John H. Caldwell, a Calhoun County attorney who was eventually nominated and elected.[39]

Sheffield came to the 1874 district convention with a majority of elected delegates in his camp, but he was denied the nomination again. According to an account written by Sheffield, Madison County Democrats elected twelve delegates pledged to Sheffield, but two Sheffield men from Madison failed to appear at the convention, and a delegate supporting incumbent congressman Caldwell was seated by a credentials committee controlled by Caldwell. This Madison County delegate was allowed to cast a proxy ballot for the other missing delegate. When Sheffield's forces lost by a vote of twenty-seven to twenty-four on a procedural call, it became apparent that the shift of the two Madison County votes had cost Sheffield his majority. Joined by a few delegates pledged to him, Sheffield angrily left the convention and prepared five hundred copies of a "circular letter" or pamphlet to Fifth District voters, which charged that the rules that were supposed to govern the convention were changed during the meeting to deprive him of the nomination.[40]

Sending the circular was necessary, said Sheffield, because "public journals" would not fairly present his contentions. He called on Caldwell to step aside and agree to another convention. If Caldwell refused, threatened Sheffield, the only "course consistent" with his "own honor" and that of his friends was "to settle it before the people." There had been independent candidates for lesser offices since 1868, but this was the most significant challenge to party convention rule at the congressional or state level since the Alabama Democratic party was reorganized in 1868.[41]

A Marshall County delegate who refused to bolt the district Democratic convention, despite his initial support for Sheffield, was Guntersville attorney Rufus K. Boyd, who had been elected to the legislature in 1870 and 1872. Boyd became the Democratic nominee for secretary of state of Alabama in 1874 and supported his party's ticket in the general election campaign. His party loyalty did not erase the fact that he probably posed a greater danger to the Democrats than Sheffield. Boyd was prominent in a faction of Democrats whose public criticism of their party's policies exposed intraparty ideological divisions and encouraged anti-Democratic dissent. Behind the formal unity presented by party leaders, factions who agreed to put aside conflicting views until the Republicans were obliterated eyed each other suspiciously. Issues that divided prewar Alabamians had resurfaced inside the party.[42]

The Civil War was not an unbridgeable chasm that separated older Democrats from their prewar beliefs. War and Reconstruction changed the context of politics, and the party lines of the old antebellum two-party system were confused and broken, but many postwar Democrats had grown up, reached maturity, formed their political views, and had their first political experiences before the war. "History did not begin for them in 1867." Rufus Boyd thought the party should stand loyal to its oldest principles, to the small farmers who were its political base, and against those willing to compromise with new groups in the party who threatened to change its ideology and character.[43]

In 1874 the Alabama Democratic party was held together by the patina of race. Most Hill Country yeomen returned to the party of their fathers after the war, but former Whigs who found Republican racial policies unpalatable also became Democrats. A forced marriage occurred between these old foes. Other potential factions included ex-secessionists, Unionists, hill men, Black Belters, mine owners, mine workers, landlords, merchants, tenants, big planters, and small farmers. Every identifiable group in Alabama except blacks and a few Unionists who could not stomach membership in a party with ex-secessionists joined this strained coalition. They had little in common except a desire for white supremacy.[44]

Whigs who became postwar Democrats exercised great power, and the party changed its name to the Democratic and Conservative party to assure Whigs that they were welcome. The first postbellum Democratic chairman was former Whig James H. Clanton. Several Whigs served on the state Democratic executive committee. Between 1870 and 1874, Democrats advocating Whiggish economic policies came under attack from the wing of the party that held Jacksonian attitudes. Civil War governor and Confederate attorney general Thomas Hill Watts, a prewar Whig, noted the tendency of postwar politicians to hold to "antebellum principles and traditions."[45]

The issue that created the greatest threat to postwar Democratic unity was state aid to railroads. During the 1830s and 1840s, differences of opinion on internal improvements formed a clear line of demarcation between Democrats and Whigs. Yet, in the 1850s when the cotton boom swept through north Alabama, some young Hill Country Democrats who believed railroads would bring riches to their region by connecting them with cotton markets and industrial cities backed state aid. Despite this effort to push Democrats closer to the Whigs, yeomen Democrats in the Upcountry opposed these new policies and drove advocates of state aid for economic development out of office. Governor John A. Winston, an obstinate and controversial opponent of internal improvements, vetoed a raft of railroad aid bills in the mid-1850s. His messages to the legislature were classic examples of Jacksonian rhetoric, as Winston claimed he was resisting the power of elite privilege on behalf of the people. His largest majorities in the 1855 gubernatorial election came from the hill counties.[46]

The railroad aid issue, albeit in a new context, recurred during Reconstruction, only a few years after Winston's widely publicized veto battles with legislators. The intrusion of secession and war did not prevent Alabamians of the late 1860s and early 1870s from remembering that they were revisiting an issue that had recently divided them. Many of the same people involved in the earlier struggle, including Winston, played a role in the later one. Three of Alabama's first four postwar governors had been either pro- or anti-Winston legislators in the 1850s, and each one was involved in the postbellum controversy.[47]

During Winston's second term as governor (1855–56), James L. Sheffield had supported efforts to fund the Tennessee and Coosa Railroad in northeast Alabama with state loans. The railroad would have passed through Marshall County. Sheffield briefly aligned himself with state aid Democrats. In 1857, Upcountry legislators who had opposed Winston's staunch Jacksonian policies were either turned out of office or left politics voluntarily. This outcome sent state aid advocates a strong message that Sheffield, the only state aid Democrat to survive the 1857 election in the Hill Country, did not forget. At the secession convention he joined other Democrats in putting into the 1861 state constitution a provision that barred the state from giving subsidies or lending credit to corporations. This issue revived old disagreements, party lines reappeared, and leading Whig delegates unsuccessfully opposed the amendment.[48]

Alabama's first two postwar governors, Lewis H. Parsons (1865) and Robert M. Patton (1865–68), were both ex-Whigs. Patton had been an outspoken opponent of John A. Winston and joined Parsons in supporting state funding of antebellum railroad schemes. They were allied with two wealthy prewar businessmen, Daniel Pratt and James W. Sloss, who pioneered Alabama's coal and iron industry. After the war, Patton and Parsons combined public service with efforts to get aid from Washington for their pet industries, in addition to tax breaks and land subsidies for their favorite railroads. Their Whiggish economic ideas permeated both postwar political parties. Parsons initially became a Democrat, but when Republicans demonstrated political strength in the late sixties he joined them. Patton remained a loyal Democratic-Conservative.[49]

New railroad entrepreneurs with an eye on the state's huge coal and iron ore deposits entered Alabama during Reconstruction. The state was peculiarly susceptible to domination by outsiders. The whole South suffered from a lack of capital after the war, but Alabama's coal and iron ore were important to the health of northern and European industrial economies. The state's valuable minerals lay primarily in the Hill Country, and aggressive outside capital poured in. Development efforts in Walker, Shelby, and Jefferson Counties pointed toward absentee control. The railroad men needed political influence to receive tax breaks, loans, and subsidies and to guide the making of all laws that affected their interests. Hill Country people were in danger of losing not only their raw materials but also control over their political system to either Black Belters or capitalists from afar.[50]

Railroad corporations lobbied for state funds to finance roads into the mineral belt. Those who got there first could buy up land and mineral rights. Local businessmen angled for alliances with outside investors and welcomed their involvement. A political battle erupted that implicated both political parties in financial deals that nearly bankrupted the state. Legislators in both parties were suspected of taking bribes from railroad men. The issues of which railroads would get subsidies, who would pay for them, and who would benefit had not changed since the 1850s. Republicans backed the Alabama and Chattanooga Railroad, whose capital came largely from the northeast, whereas most Democrats backed the South and North, a rail line begun by wealthy Alabama planter families.[51]

A postwar Democratic legislature, operating before Republican ascendancy, promised to underwrite bonds up to $12,000 per mile of railroad built by any company. The Radical Republican legislature that followed raised the ante to $16,000, underwrote an additional $2,000,000 in bonds for the Alabama and Chattanooga, and authorized smaller amounts for other railroads, including the South and North. While the state was passing this legislation, Alabama's city and county governments also approved railroad aid schemes that drove them deeply into debt. Neither political party was more to blame for these financial blunders than the other, but the statewide aid bills gave the Republican governor wide discretion in deciding when to endorse bonds, and he endorsed far more than were authorized by law. In 1871, the Republican-backed Alabama and Chattanooga Railroad defaulted on the interest payments due on the state-endorsed bonds and left the state with a huge bonded debt.[52]

Democratic governor Robert B. Lindsay, brother-in-law of former governor Winston, seized control of the A & C in 1871. Then, to the consternation of critics in his own party who wanted to repudiate the bonds, Lindsay agreed to pay those bonds that were validly endorsed or bought by "innocent purchasers." Some Democrats assailed the governor because his records could not confirm either the validity or innocent purchase of the bonds. Investigating committees exposed such extensive bribery and other corrupt actions by railroad men that even some ex-Whigs who favored internal improvements advocated repudiation of the debt, but the strongest support for refusing to pay off the bonds came from Upcountry

Democrats. Sixteen of thirty-three legislators who unsuccessfully voted for repudiation in 1871 came from the hill counties.[53]

James L. Sheffield was out of office and played no role in the railroad aid fight of the seventies, but Marshall County legislator Rufus K. Boyd helped lead the repudiation forces. Boyd and his friend Robert McKee, editor of the *Selma Southern Argus,* encouraged Democrats to reassert older party principles. McKee was a staunch Democrat and an opponent of Radical Republicans, but his editorial attacks on Lindsay's bond policies were so scornful that Democrats accused him of trying to split their party and aid the Republicans. Some historians label Boyd and McKee "Bourbons," which incorrectly implies that they were allied with an upper-class elite.[54]

Rufus Boyd grew up in Missouri, and his colorful past included filibustering expeditions to Nicaragua in the 1850s, service in the Confederate army, and a reported stint with the notorious Confederate guerillas, Quantrill's Raiders. He came to Alabama after the war. McKee was born in Kentucky and grew up there, the son of a poor blacksmith. He worked as a store clerk in his early twenties, became a journalist, edited the prosecession *Louisville Daily Courier* in 1860–61, and was indicted for treason by Kentucky Unionists. He came to Alabama during the Civil War. Boyd and McKee were not upper-class gentlemen, and their intentions were not to protect a "Bourbon" elite—quite the contrary. Their dissident Democratic faction was anticorporation, antirailroad, and antielitist. Their Jacksonian rhetoric linked them ideologically to the antebellum Democratic party. The prewar Democratic party that shaped their attitudes favored slavery and white supremacy, but it also opposed the concentration of governmental power in elite hands and distrusted large-scale capitalism.[55]

Although most Alabama Democrats refused to join McKee and Boyd in criticizing Lindsay, the two found support in the hills. The *Shelby Guide* warned Democrats in 1870 not to divide over issues that had once split the Whigs and the Democrats, but editor Willis Roberts also attacked Lindsay's attempt to pay the bonds and asked Democrats not to adopt the "fashions of the times." Shelby County legislator Burwell Boykin Lewis, nephew of one of Alabama's leading antebellum Whigs, George Shortridge, allied with Boyd in favor of repudiation. Lewis had an interest in a Shelby iron company, but he condemned government aid to business. The Shelby County Democratic executive committee adopted a resolution assailing Lindsay's actions and calling for a new Democratic gubernatorial nominee.[56]

Black Belt planters and urban commercial interests were anxious to placate this anticorporate faction that accused Lindsay and his supporters of selling out to a "railroad ring," but McKee's editorial criticism of railroad aid became so obsessive and unrelenting that he infuriated some Democrats. He blamed both parties for the funding scandal despite the negligence of the Republican governor who had endorsed the bonds. Other Democratic editors tried to silence McKee, and his debate with them became a leading sideshow in state politics. His editorials were reprinted throughout the state.[57]

"Under the pretext of development," thundered McKee, men sought to "tax and plunder" the state. Aid schemes, passed in the name of "progress," created a tendency toward "confiscation" from the masses "for the use of a few." Soon such schemes would include not only railroads but also "steamships, manufactures . . . agricultural enterprises, and . . . commercial ventures." Those responsible for this state of affairs, wrote McKee, were "a host of strangers," gathered around the people's representatives, "wearing sharp-toed shoes, short coats, side whiskers, stove-pipe hats, and eye-glasses." They were "pertinacious, brazen, shameless, impudent, with pockets full of money and heads full of schemes of plunder," and they enticed officials with "wine and cigars . . . feasts and revels . . . carriages and boxes at the theatre." If the Democratic party could not protect people "against the corrupt and grasping men and corporations combined against them," it was "impotent for good and should be buried out of sight forever." McKee, like the Jacksonians, believed the Democratic party was supposed to be a trade union of the people that protected them against sinister interests.[58]

McKee's rhetoric was reminiscent of John A. Winston and antebellum congressman W. R. W. Cobb. Winston was Governor Lindsay's brother-in-law, but he encouraged McKee and argued that Lindsay would not stand up to wealthy interests. Lindsay decided not to run in 1872, but when several hill counties voted Republican in the 1872 election, the Democrats realized that their initiation of the railroad aid program and Lindsay's apparent acquiescence in the fraud connected with it had damaged the party. The election results convinced party leaders that they would have to resort to open racial appeals to win in 1874 and that they would also have to reject railroad aid, placate Hill Country whites, and keep Whigs off the state ticket.[59]

A series of events added piquancy to this strategy. In 1873, Radical Republican state legislators introduced a bill that would have led to the racial integration of the public schools, which raised the anxiety level of whites and Democratic election chances in 1874, but the economy was also a major factor in the election. A nationwide depression that began in late 1873 was widely blamed on the Grant administration's financial policies, and Democrats all over the nation suddenly smelled victory.[60]

A sharp economic decline among southern farmers began even before the depression. Cotton prices fell, and Robert McKee implored Democrats to "offer some inducement to the hard-handed yeomanry of the land, hold out to them some reasonable promise of advantage." Cutting government programs would lead to lower taxes, which would give some relief to farmers. McKee wanted a complete moratorium on tax collection. Large amounts of farm land, he noted, were being sold for the nonpayment of taxes, and collecting taxes under those circumstances amounted to "confiscation."[61]

Calls for government retrenchment and low taxes were signally effective against Alabama's Republicans because they had raised taxes on small landowners. During the Republican administration of state government (1868–1870), land taxes were raised to finance new public schools and pay for the increased services that were needed when freedmen became citizens. Upcountry farmers felt the pinch of the tax collector for the first time. Antebellum Democrats had gouged big planters and kept taxes on yeomen to a minimum. Postwar Democrats complained that the irresponsibility of the Republican governor in endorsing so many railroad bonds had led to an increase in taxes. The Republican land taxes, the depression, and the school integration bill drove Upcountry yeomen who had voted Republican back into Democratic arms.[62]

Democrats nominated north Alabamian George Smith Houston for governor in the hope that he could keep Upcountry Democrats from bolting, but geography was only one aspect of his selection. Shelby County editor Willis Roberts happily described Houston as an "old Union Jackson Democrat." Houston was a Unionist who gave tacit support to the Confederacy yet played no role in the war or the Confederate government. He had been an antebellum congressman and a supporter of Jacksonian president James K. Polk. During Polk's administration, he opposed internal improvements legislation, but after the Civil War he formed a law partnership with the ex-Whig and railroad aid promoter Luke Pryor. Houston became a director of the powerful Louisville and Nashville Railroad. Thus, Jacksonian Democrats, ex-Whigs, Unionists, secessionists, bondholders, and repudiationists all had reason to believe Houston was their man.[63]

Many former Whigs were offended by the corruption and fraud surrounding railroad aid, yet Whig influence was reduced in the state Democratic convention. Delegates put only one former Whig on their ticket as the nominee for lieutenant governor, a position they later abolished in 1875. One Democrat wrote to a prominent ex-Whig of his fear that the party's actions might cost it the support of former Whigs. Historians who argue that "Bourbons" captured the Democratic party in 1874 should note that on economic issues the party actually capitulated to the Boyd-McKee faction and to their Jacksonian philosophy. Democrats promised tax and spending cuts, abolition of unnecessary state offices, a convention to replace the 1868 constitution written by Radical Republicans, and removal of the constitutional provision that allowed state aid to corporations. The most fervent supporters of this strategy were not "Bourbons," but Hill Country farmers. Rufus Boyd even won a place on the Democratic ticket as nominee for secretary of state.[64]

The "tide" was changing, and Democrats might win, Boyd wrote to McKee, "upon the basis of Democratic principles as understood in the olden time modified somewhat by the changed condition of the country." Orators returned to "the party's roots and essentials," and newspapers reintroduced into "discourse" the "traditional principles and basic tenets of the Democrats." One Hill Country editor waxed especially Jacksonian. He cited McKee's enormous influence, called for a constitutional provision ending state involvement in internal improvements, backed repudiation of the railroad bonds, endorsed the repeal of all "class" or "personal" legislation, and asked for the repeal of all tax exemptions for special groups. When a Mobile editor stubbornly broke ranks and called for state subsidies to steamship companies, McKee replied that Alabamians threatened with the loss of their homes by men who had deluded them with development schemes would consent to pay for "no more state aid projects."[65]

Some Democrats who denounced railroad aid supported an end to programs that they and their party initiated. Many Black Belt planters had backed aid in the late 1860s, but in 1874 a strange coalition of "agrarian" interests, lowland planters, and Upcountry yeomen held Republicans exclusively responsible for the state's financial problems. A leading planter spokesman was the prominent lawyer, former Confederate general, and future U.S. senator John Tyler Morgan. He had been legal counsel for the Alabama and Chattanooga Railroad during its fight for railroad funding, yet in 1874 he traveled the state assailing Republicans for mishandling the A & C bonds. Rufus Boyd and Robert McKee were dubious about the sincerity of George Smith Houston, who supported efforts to end any more state aid but not the repudiation of the bonds. Boyd wanted a clear declaration from Houston on repudiation. "The nomination of any man," wrote Boyd, "merely because it is hoped he is popular with the Tory element in North Alabama and will be able to carry them, is quite too conciliatory to suit my taste."[66]

Houston won every county in north Alabama except Winston, but received only 53 percent of the statewide vote because Republicans won such huge majorities in most Black Belt counties. Republicans also elected two black congressmen and thirty-three state legislators from the Black Belt. Historians assign racist rhetoric, violence, fraud, and the intimidation of black voters in the Black Belt as deciding factors in the Democratic victory, and they downplay the impact of economic issues in the white counties. Analysts should not dismiss the return of Democrats to their Jacksonian roots as a major reason for their party's success. An interpretation that emphasizes economic or other nonracial ideological motives by Upcountry whites need not reject the impact of racist rhetoric on all whites or ignore the venal tactics used against black voters in the Black Belt. All were significant.[67]

Despite efforts to maintain Democratic unity, thousands of Fifth Congressional District voters who cast ballots for George Houston also voted for James L. Sheffield. Houston received 16,177 votes, or 70 percent of the Fifth District vote, whereas John H. Caldwell, the Democratic congressional nominee, received only 13,011 votes, or 59 percent. In no other Alabama congressional district did so many people divide their vote. Houston's percentage differed by less than a point from Democratic congressional nominees in other districts. Blacks, the most avid anti-Democrats, constituted only 25 percent of the Fifth District population, yet Sheffield polled 41 percent of the district vote. Republicans did not field a candidate for Congress in the Fifth District, and blacks who voted for other GOP candidates probably also voted for Sheffield.[68]

In all districts except the Fifth, the anti-Democratic nominee was a Republican, but because Sheffield did not seek or receive the GOP nomination many whites who could not vote for a Republican were willing to vote for him. His vote total in the Fifth District far exceeded that of the

Republican candidate for governor. In St. Clair County, for instance, Sheffield received 755 votes, or 41.2 percent of the total, to only 621, or 36.7 percent of total vote, for the GOP gubernatorial nominee. All of the 1874 Republican congressional nominees got fewer votes than the GOP nominees had received in 1872, but Sheffield got 2,676 more votes than the Fifth District Republican candidate had polled two years earlier, an increase of 43 percent for the anti-Democratic candidate.[69]

The fact that so many white voters in the election to redeem Alabama ignored Democratic party instructions and voted for Sheffield is more impressive when one considers the hurdles they had to cross to do so. Because the state did not furnish ballots, each party had to print its own, which listed only its nominees, and voters who wanted to vote a straight party ticket merely deposited the party ballot in the ballot box. Republicans had no Fifth District candidate, and Sheffield's name may have been on their ballot. The difficulty involved voters who wanted to vote for all Democrats except Caldwell. These renegades, perhaps two thousand of them, had to scratch out the name of their regular party nominee and write in that of Sheffield.[70]

In the 1880s, many candidates broke with their old party and won elections, but Sheffield led the first serious challenge to the power structure from within the party, took severe criticism for his efforts, won notable support from whites, and encouraged others who resented the party lash. His circular had stressed elite control, which worsened after Redemption when elite groups tightened control over nominations and fixed election laws to make it more difficult for an opposition to develop. Such tactics were not well received in the hills, and charges of "ring rule" became common there. The ballot had given yeomen real power in the antebellum democracy, and procedures that decreased that power led to disillusionment. Like most anti-Democrats who followed him, Sheffield accepted the support of Republicans, but not their nomination. What eventually led so many Upcountry voters into the Republican party was a series of events between 1875 and 1900 that highlighted elite control of government.

Party bolts seemed remote in 1875 with the white men's government in office and whites apparently unified in support of a new constitution. Black Belt planters found their strongest allies in support of the new constitution among Upcountry farmers. An "agrarian" coalition pledged to put constitutional limits on the ability of the state to spend, raise land taxes, or grant subsidies and credit to corporations. This unusual union of Upcountry and lowcountry agrarians supplanted the older alliance of planter-landlords and elite commercial interests, but only temporarily, for the older alliance had a continuing interest in controlling labor and preventing joint action by blacks and Upcountry farmers.[71]

In 1875, hill counties gave a larger portion of their vote for a constitutional convention and for ratifying the constitution than any other Alabama regions. The constitution is often described as a "Bourbon" document, but that label is misleading. All over the South, says one writer, those most committed to abandoning the Whiggish policies of postwar southern governments were not planters, but those who lived in the Upcountry and operated on the margins of the farm economy. The new constitution cut tax rates and directly benefitted small farmers suffering from the depression. The new constitutional provision that banned state aid, loans, and bonds for private corporations was less Bourbon than "agrarian" or "Jacksonian." Even before the constitution took effect, elite economic groups influenced a shift in the ideological direction of state government. Instead of placating the Upcountry or anticorporate wing of the party, as occurred in the 1874 election campaign and in the new constitution, legislators passed laws heralding the return of elite economic elements to power. The new laws, which grew from efforts by planters to control black labor, adversely affected white Upcountry farmers already damaged by the national depression.[72]

The Houston administration had pledged to reduce taxes, but it played devious games with tax exemptions. Black Belt legislators successfully changed a law that allowed a person to exempt $500 worth of personal property from taxation by raising the total amount that could be exempted to $1,000, which ostensibly kept faith with the campaign pledge of lowering taxes. Unlike the old law, only certain items could be exempted. The items listed were plentiful on big plantations but not on small farms. The law reflected planter efforts to force blacks to pay taxes, but small farmers of both races were hurt because the amount they could actually claim declined. Robert McKee assailed the inequality inherent in the law, and a north Alabama editor who later became a leading Greenbacker argued that passage of the act betrayed the trust of Upcountry farmers who had supported Houston for governor. Efforts by Upcountry legislators to increase exemptions for small farmers were unsuccessful.[73]

Planter Democrats who worried about the security of their property and their control over commercial agriculture also persuaded legislators to increase the punishment for petty theft, and they banned small farmers from selling produce after dark. Planter legislators also tried to repeal the controversial crop-lien law. It had passed in 1866 at the behest of planters trying to create a credit system for former slaves who wanted their own farms, but lacked money or land with which to start them. The law allowed freedmen to pledge all or part of a future crop in exchange for supplies, cash, or rent, but it also permitted supply merchants who erected stores in the countryside to take liens on future crops as collateral for goods they sold on credit. Planters did not foresee the proliferation of supply merchants and failed to get legislators to specify who had priority when both a planter and a merchant had a lien on the same crop. Crop-liens were the only source of credit for some Hill Country farmers. Upcountry legislators successfully stopped repeal of the law, but Black Belters amended it so that landlords had priority over merchants.[74]

These legislative struggles highlighted growing animosity between Upcountry and lowland representatives similar to antebellum times, but the Houston administration's effort to compromise on the amount of the railroad debt came under the most severe criticism. Some delegates to the 1875 constitutional convention had moved to repudiate the debt in the new constitution, but Houston's agents convinced them to wait until legislators could approve a settlement worked out by a gubernatorial commission. When the settlement was announced in December 1875, Robert McKee angrily denounced it as too generous to bondholders, despite commission recommendations that large portions of the debt be repudiated. Some north Alabama newspapers joined McKee's denunciations of the settlement, and even those who disagreed with him printed some of his editorials.[75]

McKee insinuated, as he had in 1871 and 1872, that privileged elites worked secretly to steal from the people. The "yeomanry of Alabama, the tax-paying democratic masses," had no power in the legislature, he wrote, and they should take it back from the selfish men who had seized it. The *Montgomery Advertiser,* voice of the Democratic party hierarchy, accused McKee of dividing the party and exchanged rhetorical fire with the Selma editor for several weeks. McKee and other editors also charged that a caucus of Democratic legislators actually decided who would be the Democratic nominees for statewide office well in advance of the state Democratic conventions. By the summer of 1876, feeling "became so intense that many feared for the essential unity of their party." Charges circulated that McKee and his supporters had begun a third-party movement. Frank Baltzell, editor of the *Troy Enquirer* and a future Populist leader, argued that McKee's criticism was the primary force driving people out of the Democratic party.[76]

One man who did become a leading independent in the 1880s showed the influence McKee had on him. Former Tennessee Valley legislator Charles Raisler, who had voted with Rufus Boyd in 1871 for debt repudiation, thanked McKee for his editorials. The people in his region, wrote Raisler, thought it wrong to pay for "rotten R. R. rings," and Democrats seemed as willing as Republicans to tax the common people for the benefit of privileged groups.[77]

At about the same time as the controversy over railroad bonds heated up, a similar issue in Congress exposed more ideological fissures among postwar Alabama Democrats. Pennsylvania railroad tycoon Tom Scott asked Congress to fund his transcontinental railroad, the Texas and Pacific, which would run through parts of the South, connect the region to northern markets, and integrate it into the national economy. Most southern Democrats supported this Whiggish proposal, and people began to wonder, writes one historian, whether postwar Democrats traced their lineage to Henry Clay instead of Andrew Jackson. Strong editorial support for funding the railroad came from influential Democratic newspapers such as the *Mobile Daily Register* and the *Tuscumbia North Alabamian,* both of which called on former Whigs for help. One reader reminded the Tuscumbia paper that opposition to internal improvements formed one of the "cardinal principles" of the antebellum Democratic party. Could it be, asked this longtime Democrat, that the "element" that infused his party on the dissolution of the Whig party had taken control? "Spirits of Calhoun and Jackson," he exclaimed, "protect us!"[78]

Former Shelby County legislator Burwell B. Lewis, an ally of Boyd and McKee on the bond debt, was elected to Congress in 1874, and he was a principal opponent of the Texas and Pacific. The bill violated his party's principles, said Lewis, and put it on the side of the corporations. Heavily influenced by McKee, who assailed Scott's "gigantic plunder schemes," Lewis and Alabama's House delegation stood almost alone among southern representatives as opponents of the subsidy, though it did not pass. McKee and Lewis were not simply reiterating traditional southern state rights doctrine, for they were opposed to aid to corporations by state and county governments as well. Like old Jacksonians, they believed that such programs taxed the masses to build up the fortunes of a few.[79]

Criticism by the McKee faction may have hurt the Democrats in some parts of the state, but independents who nominated a statewide ticket in 1876 picked an unknown candidate for governor, offered no program, and publicly allied with the state Republican party. This ticket, which had no mission except to defeat Democrats, got few Upcountry votes. Black Belt Democrats asserted such control over voting in their region that the Republicans were virtually wiped out there. The number of Republicans in the legislature's lower house fell from thirty-five in 1874 to eighteen in 1876, and Republicans won only four of thirty-three senate seats.[80]

State Democratic officials were given even more control over voting when the legislature separated the dates for holding state and federal elections. Between 1875 and 1902, state elections were held in August and federal in November, which allowed state officials to avoid federal control of voting in state and local elections. Other voting provisions passed the legislature in 1879 that made state and local election officials virtual arms of the Democratic party led to the defeat of black officials. Although blacks still voted in large numbers in presidential and congressional elections, white Democrats mysteriously won congressional seats in majority black districts.[81]

Control over black voters in the Black Belt raised a new controversy over the apportionment of delegates to the state Democratic convention that added to Upcountry fears about lowland power. Despite a declining white population in the Black Belt, it claimed an inordinate share of delegates because apportionment was based on the total Democratic vote in a county. Upcountry whites knew that Black Belt officials boosted the number of delegates from their area by fraudulently putting the Republican ballots of black voters in the Democratic column. North Alabama whites protested this charade, but Black Belters refused to give up power in the conventions.[82]

The Black Belt elite also aligned with elite industrial interests in north Alabama counties that exploited the Upcountry's resources, entered its politics, and tried to control the Democratic party at the state and county levels. Criticism of state policies by editors such as Robert McKee signaled to the Upcountry that the Democratic party of old had vanished. Class and sectional conflict between rank-and-file Democrats, glossed over during the drive to defeat the Republicans, was rekindled. Instead of redemption, some Hill Country Democrats who had supported Houston and the 1875 constitution spoke of betrayal. The actions of James L. Sheffield in the last quarter of the nineteenth century were symbolic of the

Upcountry's reaction. He continued to assail the "Bourbon" hierarchy of the Democratic party, but he moved in and out of that party as events dictated. Like most Hill Country men, he wanted to be a Democrat and would not become a Republican, but the direction of his old party led him into new crusades against the elite elements that had seized it.

3 The Growth of Dissent: Anti-Democrats, 1876–1887

The present, so called, Democratic party is as different as day is from night from the grand old party Andrew Jackson led . . . against the moneyed aristocracy of his day. . . . Then, it was the people's party and in full sympathy and accord with the son's [sic] of toil. It consulted the wishes and interests of the masses. . . . There is nothing Democratic [about] the so-called Democratic party of Alabama.[1]

A. H. Brittin, *Huntsville Advocate,* 1879

Each Alabama election from 1876 through 1886 brought new evidence that hill counties did not defer to party elites and felt little loyalty to the postwar Democratic party. A tradition of party disloyalty formed in the Upcountry by 1886, despite legal and institutional constraints that discouraged dissent. This infidelity to the Democrats might have faded if the economic independence of Upcountry people had been assured. Politics was influenced by a declining farm economy that led to an economic-cultural revolution in the Upcountry, as once proud yeomen began to fall from self-sufficiency to dependency. Economic anguish revived and reinforced older ideas, myths, and impressions and gave birth to new ones that increased the tendency toward political revolt.

Efforts to revive farms decimated during the war, demands by creditors that debtors produce a cash crop, a brief postwar surge in cotton prices, and penetration of the Upcountry by railroads led Hill Country farmers into the marketplace. Cotton became the cash crop, but after a brief boom in the late 1860s, prices fell throughout the 1870s and 1880s. Yeomen were drawn into the credit system they feared, and the dream of a republic of independent farmers grew remote. Little capital existed in the South because the war wiped out southern investments. Merchants or bankers in the region who had money to loan generally borrowed it from northeastern creditors. A Civil War Republican Congress passed legislation that required huge amounts of start-up capital to charter a national bank. Thus, the nation's gold, the bank notes used as circulating medium, and interest rates were controlled by banks in New York, Boston, Philadelphia, and Baltimore.[2]

By 1875, the credit crisis and the crop-lien system competed with race and railroad bond debts for the attention of Alabama voters. Struggling farmers had little to use as collateral except land or crops. Declining prices led them to sell part of their land for badly needed money or to mortgage it to supply merchants, who often foreclosed. Between 1880 and 1900, Hill Country farms grew smaller, and many former landowners became tenant farmers or sharecroppers. White farmers were acutely aware that their plight increasingly resembled that of ex-slaves.[3]

Greenback dollars issued during the war were retired from circulation by the Grant administration in an effort to resume the gold standard. "Resumption" meant that creditors who had loaned cheap money would be paid back in more valuable dollars, and men who held government bonds bought with cheap paper currency would be repaid in specie. Currency contraction led to a rise in interest rates that was cruel in the South. Southern and western congressmen tried, but failed, to repeal resumption. Agitation mounted to increase the money supply by moving to a bimetallic standard that included gold and silver, but northeastern dominance of the nation's money supply was perpetuated into the twentieth century. This outside control of the money, rather than the amount in circulation, may have been the major problem for southern farmers.[4]

As the cash-nexus economy pulled more and more of them into its orbit, north Alabama's small farmers had to mortgage their crops to supply merchants in exchange for the things they needed. The crop-lien system was the only means of credit available to the farmers, but instead of buying them time so that they could make enough money to get out of debt, it became a burden. The price of cotton was rarely high enough to allow farmers to pay furnishing merchants, and they simply had to pledge more of their crop, mortgage their land, or sell the land outright.[5]

Even before the Greenback party entered Alabama and agitated for an inflated currency, influential Alabamians backed radical changes in the money system. The faction of Alabama Democrats most fervently opposed to public funding of railroads led the fight for an inflated currency. Some state newspapers edited by Democrats attacked the party's northeastern wing for its refusal to back the repeal of resumption and called for a new political system in which the South and West aligned against easterners in both major parties. E. G. Walker, a Shelby County independent in the 1880s, argued in a Columbiana newspaper in September 1875 that too much of the nation's money was held by northeastern national banks. He attacked the gold standard, called for greenbacks, and argued that the "money power" had created a dual society, with "enormous ill-gotten wealth on one hand, and squalid poverty on the other."[6]

Greenbackers found converts in many north Alabama counties, but especially in the Tennessee Valley. White farmers in the valley entered the cotton market at an earlier period than farmers in the Hill Country, and the economic misery that caught up to the Hill Country after 1880 had already come to the valley in the 1870s. Most black farmers became tenants or sharecroppers in the postwar period, but in Jackson and Morgan Counties, 83 and 71 percent white, respectively, nearly 50 percent of all farmers were either paying rent for their land or sharecropping by 1880. Dissidents in the valley tended to be Greenbackers in the early 1880s, whereas those in the Hill Country preferred to be called independents. At this time, there was a different emphasis in the two areas. In the early eighties, Hill Country anti-Democrats were more interested in political than economic reform. By the mid-eighties, the importance of the economic component grew in the hills as falling cotton prices, rising tenancy rates, and a reduction in farm sizes increased anxieties there.[7]

In 1878, the Greenback-Labor party held statewide meetings, established a state executive committee, and nominated candidates for district and legislative offices. Greenback theorists believed that only a "fiat" currency (paper money issued by the government) backed solely by the strength of the economy and uncontrolled by eastern banks could liberate people from the "money power." Population growth and the expansion of consumer goods meant that the supply of money to buy goods had to expand. When it did not, farm prices dropped. Farmers who increased production to make money only drove prices lower. Greenbackers also supported a bimetallic currency, but they did not believe silver was a panacea because it tied the nation to another form of "specie." Only a flexible paper currency unlimited by the shifting values of precious metals and uncontrolled by national banks could break the "money power."[8]

Greenbackers ran statewide tickets, and despite policy differences with Republicans they won cooperation from the GOP, but most anti-Democratic animus grew out of local disputes that differed from county to county. Between 1876 and the rise of the Alabama Farmers' Alliance in 1887, the Upcountry had given birth to a variety of anti-Democratic movements. Mounting agricultural distress and control of Democratic nominations by elite groups were staples of Hill Country discontent, but mone-

The Growth of Dissent 61

tary issues, the power of railroads, convict leasing, state debts, unfair tax rates or exemptions, the influence of impersonal or absentee groups over economic resources and local politics, efforts to end open range farming, new election laws passed to control dissidents, and an abiding animosity toward the Black Belt all fueled the growing animosity by small farmers toward the Democratic party.

Anti-Democratic movements were so diverse that they advocated conflicting policies, drew from all social and economic classes, and differed from county to county, but they commonly argued that the Democratic party was run by elite groups who sought special privileges instead of equitable government for all citizens. Most Upcountry people feared that divisions among Democrats might return "black Republican" rule to Montgomery, but local conflicts were exacerbated by the policies of Democrats who controlled state government. Party bolting increased sharply after 1876.

Robert McKee added to the mistrust of the party when he asked the 1878 state Democratic convention to endorse currency reforms and it refused. McKee wanted support for either greenbacks or a bimetallic currency, and when party leaders would not accede, he assailed them. A north Alabama Greenback editor noted McKee's continued criticism of the party and plaintively asked how the Selma editor could remain a Democrat. It was a question increasing numbers of Upcountry whites asked of themselves. An analysis of exactly why they did so requires a close examination of politics in individual counties. Events in Chilton, Marshall, Shelby, and Walker Counties are instructive, but the most successful anti-Democratic leader in north Alabama in the 1880s came from the Tennessee Valley.[9]

From 1878 to 1882, William Manning Lowe led anti-Democratic forces in a new congressional district that included counties from James L. Sheffield's old district. Lowe exposed corrupt control of elections by Democrats, popularized Greenback reform, and, unlike Sheffield, got elected. Born in 1842, the son of a prominent Tennessee Valley planter-Whig, Lowe served as a Confederate officer and practiced law in Huntsville after the war. Between 1865 and 1870 he was prosecuting attorney of Madison County, chairman of the county Democratic executive committee, and a legislator. Madison was a typical Tennessee Valley county. Despite some high mountains in its eastern section, it had an agricultural basin near the Tennessee River that had spawned large antebellum cotton planters, slavery, and a black majority that persisted after emancipation. More small white farmers lived in Madison than in Black Belt counties, but it was not Hill Country.[10]

Lowe had been a loyal Democrat, an opponent of Republican Reconstruction, a supporter of Governor Lindsay's bond policies, and a delegate to the constitutional convention of 1875. Only anger, ambition, or a sudden conversion account for his switch to a movement whose foot soldiers were white Republicans, Negroes, and poor white farmers. Whatever his motives, Lowe led the state's only true biracial post-Reconstruction political movement, and he might have broken the back of north Alabama's Democratic party well before Populism had death not taken him at the age of forty. In 1876, Lowe sought the Democratic nomination for Congress from the Eighth District, which was created by the legislature in 1875. The Eighth contained the Tennessee Valley counties of Colbert, Jackson, Lauderdale, Limestone, Lawrence, Madison, Morgan, and the hill county of Franklin. Events at the Eighth District convention in 1876 resembled the previous meetings that denied nominations to Sheffield. Lowe controlled a plurality of delegates, but after more than one hundred ballots another candidate was nominated. Lowe charged that unfair practices led to his defeat.[11]

In April 1878, writing in Huntsville newspapers, Lowe assailed the convention system and charged that Alabama politics was controlled by the state Democratic legislative caucus. Letters to newspapers from fellow Democrats and editorials by Greenback editor A. H. Brittin of the *Huntsville Advocate* endorsed Lowe's position. Lowe had shown no previous interest in Greenback issues, but he endorsed such Greenback demands as the repeal of resumption, abolition of the national banking system, taxation of government bonds and securities, the unlimited coinage of silver, and the issuance of all money by the government instead of banks.[12]

Lowe became the Greenback nominee for Congress, and a bitter campaign followed. Democrats accused him of being supported by Radical Republicans and blacks, but he could also play demagogue. He charged that his opponent, incumbent congressman W. W. Garth of Huntsville, was a "bond-holding aristocrat" and the candidate of a political machine dedicated to class interests. Even on election night, the victorious Lowe attacked wealthy interests. "Whosoever casteth out bondholding devils in the name of liberty," he said, "we hail him as friend and brother. We lock shield and shoulder with him now, and in 1880 we will march forward with him to victory in the great and final contest between the money power and the people." Antebellum Whiggery was Lowe's heritage, but he had mastered the lineaments of Jacksonian rhetoric.[13]

Lowe received 10,373 votes, or 55.6 percent of the total, and the incumbent Democrat took 8,279 votes, or 44.4 percent. Historians point out that the Greenbacker received significant support from black voters, and his overwhelming victory in majority black Madison County supports this assertion, but his victory in 90 percent white Franklin County demonstrates heavy white support. Independents angry about appointments made in Franklin by Governor Houston had won local elections there in 1876, and this local dispute may have contributed to the growing skepticism of Democratic rule.[14]

In the Hill Country's Seventh Congressional District (Marshall, Shelby, St. Clair, Blount, Cherokee, Etowah, DeKalb, Calhoun, and Talladega Counties), incumbent Democratic congressman William H. Forney easily won renomination, and district Democrats adopted a platform that endorsed radical currency reform. Among those on the platform committee was Marshall County's Rufus K. Boyd, Alabama's secretary of state and Robert McKee's old ally. Unlike the state Democratic convention, the Seventh District convention adopted resolutions that condemned resumption, extolled both silver and greenbacks, called for an end to "national bank currency," and condemned bondholders who benefitted from resumption. After giving their support to these inflationary nostrums, the convention then rejected a resolution that endorsed federal funding of the Texas and Pacific Railroad.[15]

In 1880, when Lowe sought reelection as a Greenbacker, Eighth District Democrats were determined to defeat him. They nominated the former Confederate general and war hero Joseph H. "Fighting Joe" Wheeler of Lawrence County and tried to control voting. Evidence of election fraud by Democratic election officials was abundant, but even with vote counters acting on his behalf, Wheeler led Lowe by only forty-three votes out of more than twenty-five thousand votes cast. Lowe contested the election in Congress, where he contended that he was defeated through election fraud carried out by Democratic party officials. The Republican-controlled lower house accepted this account of the election, unseated Wheeler, and declared Lowe reelected.[16] Greenbackers also nominated a ticket for statewide offices in 1880, but it received less than a quarter of the total state vote and won few votes from whites outside the Tennessee Valley.

Rufus K. Boyd (courtesy of Larry Smith)

One reason for the party's poor showing was that Democrats such as Forney adopted a Greenback position on finance.[17]

In 1882, Congressman Lowe's friend James L. Sheffield went to the Greenback-labor convention and won the party's nomination for governor. Sheffield's supporters, asked to define their candidate, responded that he was a "forty-year Jackson Democrat." It was not odd for a product of the "hard money" Jacksonian democracy to lead a Greenback movement. Greenbackers, like Jacksonians, wanted to stop a moneyed group from controlling the government, and during the postbellum period powerful eastern bankers were the ones who supported hard-money policies. Sheffield endorsed the Greenback platform, although his anger at the Democratic party hierarchy, said one editor, may have had more to do with his candidacy than his devotion to currency reform. Democratic newspapers gleefully reported that Sheffield accepted an endorsement of the Greenback ticket by the state Republican executive committee.[18]

Sheffield polled 32 percent of the statewide vote, the largest percentage received by a non-Democratic candidate for governor between 1874 and 1892. In north Alabama the Greenback candidate won majorities in Lawrence, Madison, Walker, and Winston Counties, and he exceeded 45 percent of the vote in Colbert, Coosa, Cullman, Limestone, Jackson, Jefferson, Morgan, and Talladega. Five of these counties had black populations of more than 40 percent, and black Republicans probably voted for Sheffield, but he won more votes from Upcountry whites than the third party received in 1880. The Greenback ticket won some lowland black majority counties, but Black Belt ballots were counted by white Democrats, and most counties in that region returned Democratic majorities. If blacks had voted freely in the Black Belt, Sheffield might have won. In Choctaw County, for instance, where prominent white leaders were Greenbackers (the same men later made the county the only Black Belt bastion of Populism), blacks probably voted freely, and Sheffield took 55 percent of the county's vote.[19]

In Marshall County, which had not given less than 67 percent of its vote to national and state Democratic candidates in the 1870s, Sheffield received 44 percent of the vote. He won several precincts that had shown no previous anti-Democratic tendencies, but most of them continued to oppose Democrats in the 1890s and after 1900. Thus, their disaffection with their old party preceded the Farmers' Alliance and continued after Populism faded. Despite his August loss, Sheffield demonstrated his commitment to the Greenbackers by stumping for William Manning Lowe in the fall campaign, in which he attacked "Bourbon" Democrats and the state's election system. Lowe died only a few days before the election, and Sheffield was a pallbearer at the Huntsville funeral. Even without Lowe, a stand-in Greenback candidate won 48 percent of the Eighth District vote. James L. Sheffield was also chosen as a presidential elector on the state Greenback ticket in 1884.[20]

Other anti-Democratic leaders in the Upcountry probably never met Lowe and blazed separate paths to political independence. While Sheffield and Lowe built third-party movements in the northernmost hill counties, Riley Monroe Honeycutt of Chilton County, Benjamin McFarland Long and John B. Shields of Walker County, and Thomas Harrison of Shelby

County demonstrated their dismay with the postbellum Democratic party.

Honeycutt, born in 1845 in the community that later sent him into politics and "educated between the plow handles," was a Confederate private, then a small farmer and a Primitive Baptist preacher. No anti-Democratic leader was more like the voters of his county. Chilton County, in the geographic center of the state, bordered hill and Black Belt counties, but it was demographically a hill county. Eighty-one percent of its population was white, and most whites lived on farms of less than two hundred acres. In 1880, Honeycutt owned and farmed eighty acres near the town of Jemison. He grew cotton on five acres in the year before the 1880 census and sold only one bale. Chilton County's only industries were the lumber companies that had taken huge chunks of the county's forests by the late 1880s. Some residents ran sawmills, yet some complained that local people got few benefits from the lumber because it was finished by manufacturers outside the county.[21]

Honeycutt did not seek public office until 1880, but his leadership of Chilton's independents so badly wounded the local Democratic party that it did not recover until the 1930s. It was ironic that Honeycutt, who refused nominations from parties, became the catalyst for a county political system in which the only way to gain office was through a political party. The party that dominated Chilton County after 1892 evolved out of the independent movements Honeycutt had led. Republicans and Greenbackers were scarce in Chilton in the eighties, and neither fielded local candidates during the decade. The county voted heavily Democratic in state and national elections in 1876 and 1878, and so the only competition took place in races for local offices. Voters objected to limits placed on this competition by the Democratic convention nomination system or by any organized party because they believed that such institutions allowed elites to limit true democracy.[22]

When an independent candidate running against a convention nominee was elected to the legislature in 1876, Democratic party officials got the message. In 1877, when a newspaper in the county seat of Clanton called for a Democratic convention to select nominees for an odd-year election, the county Democratic executive committee wisely refused to do so. Soon, the antiorganization bias of the county led the committee itself to disband, and candidates for county offices in 1878, 1880, and 1882 ran in a pell-mell general election in which no candidate was a party nominee. Riley Honeycutt, elected tax collector in 1880, believed all parties were tools of "rings" and denounced efforts to revive conventions. In 1884, the partisan Democrat who edited the *Clanton Chilton View* noted that no "regular Democratic organization" had existed for "several years," and he called for Democrats to create a formal organization or executive committee to exclude dissidents from the elections process. A local resident replied that although he always supported the party of the "white man" in state and national elections, he would not support nominating conventions that created "courthouse rings."[23]

Despite objections, a new Democratic executive committee was formed in 1884. It was dominated by Clanton merchants and lawyers, many of whom later joined the Merchants Association of Chilton County in 1885 to "protect themselves" from organizations of workers and farmers in the county. Thus, the split between the new executive committee and Honeycutt's independents reflected economic divisions. Chilton, like other counties in the Hill Country, was experiencing a decline in its farm economy. Not only had farmers begun to organize clubs, but the Knights of Labor had organized the county's lumber workers. Despite efforts by the economic elite to elect organized Democrats nominated in a convention run by the executive committee, Honeycutt was reelected tax collector against the Democratic nominee in 1884, and an independent candidate for county treasurer also defeated a regular Democrat. Honeycutt took 57 percent of the vote, won seven of the county's ten precincts, and ran especially well in the county's most rural and isolated areas. His defeat in the county seat of Clanton was a clear indication that he was the candidate of farmers against commercial and professional groups who lived in Clanton.[24]

The recently organized county Democratic committee, in an effort to meet objections to convention nominations, decided to hold a nominating primary in 1886 but limited voting to those who had cast a straight Democratic ticket in 1884. This limitation was an affront to voters who had cast an independent ballot. Details of how Democrats would enforce such a rule and who would identify impure voters went undisclosed. A "disaffected element claiming to represent the farmer's clubs" decided to run candidates against the Democratic primary nominees, and Riley M. Honeycutt was their candidate for probate judge, the county's most powerful office.[25]

The week after the election, the *Chilton View* reported that Honeycutt and his independents won each county office and elected their candidate to the legislature. The editor of Clanton's Democratic newspaper admit-

ted defeat and wrote that his party lost because its policy of stopping independents from voting in the primary was "unpopular." Only a few days
after this concession, Democratic election officials threw out the votes of
three precincts where, they charged, returns were improperly reported.
Two of the precincts had returned majorities for the independent slate,
and their removal allowed Democrats to claim victory.[26]

This suspicious and dramatic change in the election results was contested by independents, but such contests were heard before Democratic
officials, and the effort was futile. The Democrats had been too clever,
however, and the succeeding outcry was their undoing. They did not win
another Chilton County office until 1910, and the anger of Chilton's voters spilled over into state and national elections, in which Democrats had
previously won majorities in excess of 70 percent. Forty-five percent of
local voters cast their ballots for an independent congressional candidate
in November 1886. Voters demonstrated their independence at the local
level, and although a majority were unwilling to bolt the national and
state party, a consensus for doing that was building. In other counties, a
willingness to vote for Republicans was growing.[27]

Walker County's Benjamin M. Long was never a Democrat, before or
after the Civil War. Like James L. Sheffield, Long grew up on the old south-
west frontier and led a life of near epic dimensions. In 1827, he was the
first white child born among the Indian population of Carroll County in
western Georgia. His family rose to prominence and was active in Georgia
politics well into the twentieth century. Long fought in the Mexican war
(1846–48) under Robert E. Lee of Virginia and then came to Alabama's
Upcountry to investigate coal lands. In the fifties he pioneered the coal
business, founded the Walker County town of Cordova, and built a man-
sion there. He then became an active Whig and later a Know-Nothing.
Like Sheffield, Long was a Unionist who put aside his objections to secession, raised his own Hill Country troops, and fought for the Confederacy.
He also joined Sheffield in the 1865 postwar legislature.[28]

Long's choice of political parties before and after the war separated
him from Sheffield. The ex-Whig became a Republican in a county that
was only 15 percent black, but unlike most hill counties, Walker had sufficient white anti-Confederate sentiment to sustain a competitive postwar Republican party. When those who could swear they had remained
loyal to the Union became eligible for postwar federal pensions, Walker
had more applicants than any other Alabama county, and it gave 51 percent of its votes to Republican presidential candidate Ulysses Grant. Al-

though most of the county's residents were small farmers, many of whom had been Unionists, a group of coal miners was growing. In post–Civil War America workers favored a high tariff to protect their jobs from foreign competition and to keep their wages high. Therefore, black and white workers had good reasons to support Long's high-tariff Republicans.[29]

Long returned to Georgia in the early 1870s and was the only Republican elected to that state's legislature from Carroll County until the late twentieth century. In the mid-seventies he came back to Walker County to stay and dominated the local Republican party. His party fused with independents and Greenbackers, and the fusionist groups dominated county politics in the 1880s. Long was active in politics through the nineties, fathered a huge family, and saw his progeny become active political leaders in both parties. For a brief time in 1894, when he won the GOP nomination for Congress, Long faced the embarrassing prospect of opposing his son, who sought but did not receive the Democratic nomination.[30]

Coal miners as well as north Alabama farmers were also attracted to the Greenback-Labor party. An important figure on the state committee of that party in 1878 was Walker County's John B. Shields, whose career was inseparable from Long's. Shields was the son of a prominent antebellum Tennessee industrialist and a native of east Tennessee's fiercely Unionist Sevier County. Shields was also a Unionist who served in the Confederate army. After the war he was briefly a merchant and railroad station agent, but in 1872 he went to Carroll County, Georgia, to manage a paper manufacturing plant. His arrival in Carroll County coincided with the brief return of Benjamin M. Long. Shields married Long's younger sister and later followed his brother-in-law back to Alabama. Despite their ties, Shields and Long had political differences. Long's conventional gold-standard Republicanism was the antithesis of greenbackism.[31]

Shields's inflationist views were not unusual for a businessman of this era. During Reconstruction many northern manufacturers argued that more money was necessary for consumers to buy their products. In the seventies and eighties, Shields sought GOP support, but he preferred the independent or Greenback label. Southern Republicans and Greenbackers agreed on most matters other than money. In 1884, for instance, one north Alabama Republican who said he was a "hard-money, national bank man" argued that the struggle for fair elections in Alabama gave Greenbackers and Republicans "a common grievance." Both parties denounced convict leasing and included planks in their party platforms stating their opposition to replacing free labor with prisoners. Ben Long was a mine owner who opposed the convict system.[32]

When the votes were first counted in the August 1878 Walker County election, it seemed that John B. Shields, the Greenback nominee for a seat in the legislature's lower house, had won a narrow majority and would be Walker's first non-Democratic legislator since the 1860s. Then, in a series of events similar to those that would be repeated in other hill counties in the 1880s and 1890s, Shields was denied his office. A new law had removed portions of three Walker County precincts and placed them in other counties. Democrats claimed that voters who cast ballots in those precincts no longer lived in Walker. Shields had won each contested precinct, and when those precincts' returns were thrown out, the Democrats declared victory. Shields contested the seating of his opponent, and a committee of the state house of representatives assigned to rule on the contest issued a majority report that, unsurprisingly, sided with the Democrat. Two renegade Democrats issued a minority report in support of Shields, and Etowah County representative John P. Ralls moved that the minority report be adopted by the house, but the full house voted to seat the Democrat. The decline of Walker County's Democratic party began with this controversy.[33]

The election of independents and Greenbackers in north Alabama frightened Democrats, who revised the state's election laws in the 1878–79 legislative session. Each candidate had been responsible for printing his own ballot, but many voters of both races were illiterate, and party emblems or symbols were often placed on the ballot to benefit uneducated voters who had difficulty reading the candidate's names. The new laws commanded that ballots be a "plain piece of white paper, without any figures, marks, rulings, characters or embellishments thereon." Strict limits were placed on the ballot's length and width, and the requirement of putting a number on the ballot that corresponded to the voter's number on the poll list was eliminated. These changes facilitated Democratic control of independent and black voters and made it more difficult to contest a fraudulent election. Black Belt representatives unanimously backed the voting law, whereas many Hill Country and Tennessee Valley lawmakers opposed it.[34]

Despite the new election law, Ben Long accepted the Republican nomination for Walker County's seat in the house of representatives in 1880, and he became the only Republican elected to the house. The Republican-Greenback-independent coalition that supported Long held together in

Walker County for the remainder of the eighties. The election dispute of 1878 must have been a powerful tonic for the anti-Democratic coalition, for they won elections in Walker County at the same time that the revenue collection policies of the national Republican administration badly damaged the GOP in northwest Alabama.[35]

In 1877, federal officials decided on a policy of strict enforcement of internal revenue laws against the sale of untaxed liquor, and this decision led to warfare in the hills. The making of "home-brew" was integral to Upcountry culture and was viewed as part of the "liberty" of the people. In 1877, federal agents engaged in a pitched battle with moonshiners in Winston County, previously the state's most loyal Republican county. In 1880, for the first time since the Civil War, Winston voted Democratic in a presidential election. It would not do so again until 1900. Liquor enforcement policies were also felt in Walker County, which adjoined Winston, and the 1880 GOP national ticket managed only 27 percent of the vote there. Ben Long criticized the "internal revenue" in his campaigns. The GOP rebounded in both Walker and Winston after 1880, but Long could not have been elected without strong support from Greenbackers and independents. Republicans were more numerous than their allies in Walker County, but no anti-Democratic group was large enough to win on its own. A fusion ticket was necessary.[36]

In 1884 and 1886, the anti-Democratic coalition elected most of Walker County's public officials. John B. Shields was elected and seated in the house of representatives in 1884, and two years later was elected probate judge of Walker County. The probate judge was the most powerful county official in Alabama. In addition to his civil and criminal judicial functions, he was also a voting member and chairman of the county commission (also known as board of revenue). The commission had taxing power, and its primary duty was building or repairing roads and bridges. It could also appropriate money for a variety of public functions, including portions of the salaries and expenses of county officials.[37]

In 1886, Ben Long won the Republican nomination for Congress from the Sixth District and ran against Democratic nominee John Hollis Bankhead, patriarch of a north Alabama family that played a major role in Alabama politics through World War II. Bankhead, the warden of Alabama's penitentiary system, was accused of helping close friends in the mining business by manipulating the convict-leasing system in their favor. A newspaper run by Birmingham labor unions denounced Bankhead and endorsed Long for Congress. Long, said the paper, "never drove convicts into our midst to encroach on the rights of honest men."[38] Long debated the issues in joint appearances with Bankhead. The Republican endorsed the Blair education bill, which proposed to spend excess federal tariff dollars to improve schools in states with high rates of illiteracy. Long assailed the federal government because it would not allow rural people to make and sell liquor. The protective tariff issue loomed largest in the campaign, and Long supported high tariffs to protect a variety of American products, including Alabama's new iron industry. Bankhead won 64 percent of the general election vote, but Long won his home county of Walker.[39]

Long and John B. Shields were businessmen who differed from most Upcountry anti-Democrats. They did not dislike corporations or harbor suspicions of wealth, were not involved in farming or interested in radical agrarian reform, and believed that progress could not occur in the South until southerners joined the dynamic capitalist economy touted by northern Republicans. Newspapers that supported these anti-Democrats argued that the Democratic party was dominated by big planters whose backward racial and economic attitudes retarded economic development and corrupted politics. Despite the similarities of Long and Shields with "New South" industrial-minded Democrats, their supporters resented the fact that the state was controlled by men who sweated convicts and controlled the lives of tenants and sharecroppers.

In 1887, the *Jasper Protectionist,* a Republican organ that supported Long and Shields, assailed Alabama's Democrats for the low expenditures on state schools. "Illiteracy is weakness," said the paper, and "education is strength." The South had allowed the race issue to hold it "in vassalage to an aristocracy," and Democrats had to offer something more substantial than "memories and prejudice." Ben Long summed up his political attitudes in the *Protectionist* in 1888, when he invited all to attend a Republican meeting of those who favored "national aid to education, the repeal of internal revenue laws, the protection of agriculture and all other industrial interests . . . fair elections and an honest count" and all those who opposed "the English Cobden Club Democracy."[40]

Walker County's vital Republican party bore no resemblance to Marshall County's, which was moribund after 1874. Independents made headway in Marshall, where the county's Democrats, like those in Chilton County, gave up conventions in the late seventies and allowed all candidates for county offices to run in the general election. Marshall County's Rufus Boyd informed Robert McKee in 1882 that independent political movements were strong and conventions unpopular in all the upper hill counties. In 1884, two years after James L. Sheffield won 44 percent of the county's vote as the Greenback-Labor candidate for governor, more than 40 percent of Marshall's votes went to independent state senate candidate James L. Crichter, who argued that the multicounty Democratic convention that picked the Democratic senatorial nominee was conducted unfairly. In 1886, Democrats in the senate nominating convention won the independents back when they selected Sheffield as their candidate. Although he was elected to the senate as a Democrat, Sheffield had not reconciled with the party hierarchy, and he soon left his old party again.[41]

The desire to control nominations and elections seemed strongest where leading Democrats had major economic interests to protect. The alternative to such control meant turning the government over to small farmers and workers. Nowhere was the political power of an economic elite clearer than in Shelby County, where small farmers reacted against a local plutocracy. The county's independent leaders and the nature of political revolts there altered from election to election, but underlying them all was the tension between a rising commercial-industrial society and an older agrarian one. Shelby had coal and iron ore mines, two iron works, and a large nonfarm work force, yet it remained primarily agricultural. Pockets of white Republicans, a 28 percent black population, angry white farmers, and miners of both races sometimes allied as anti-Democratic dissidents, but these coalitions were fluid and impermanent. No Alabama county's politics was more competitive or diverse between 1880 and 1900. Shelby's elections often involved three political parties and more often than not were decided by thin margins.[42]

A substantial spur to anti-Democratic anger in Shelby was a feeling by local people that they were losing control of their political system to outside economic forces uninterested in their welfare. Willis Roberts, editor of the *Shelby Guide* from 1870 to 1876, and Shelby County legislator Burwell B. Lewis, an ally of the McKee-Boyd Democratic faction, assailed sinister economic forces in both major parties. Roberts and Lewis left the county in the mid-seventies just as it was invaded by forces hoping to control Shelby's rich coal and iron ore resources. A Whiggish, "New South" business-oriented faction, connected to economic entities operating inside but based and capitalized outside the county, soon dominated local government. Leadership of the local Democratic and Republican parties in the late seventies and early eighties was in the hands of business interests engaged in extracting natural resources.[43]

The Shelby Iron Works, a small producer of pig iron before and during the Civil War, was revived with northern capital, and men from Connecticut and Massachusetts came to manage it. An iron company at Helena managed by attorney Rufus W. Cobb but controlled by the Louisville and Nashville Railroad began operations in the 1870s. William F. and Truman H. Aldrich, mining engineers and New York natives who came to Shelby County in 1874, bought coal lands and pioneered the coal industry.[44]

Shelby County's small-farm culture was isolated from urban areas, the marketplace, and industrialization until the 1870s when it had to accommodate change with frightening suddenness. The new city of Birmingham, founded in 1871 in Jefferson County, was only a few miles away. It contained only three thousand people in 1880, but by 1890 the population totaled twenty-six thousand. Towns that were spin-offs of the rising city also grew up, and Jefferson County's population went from 23,000 in 1880 to 140,000 by 1900. Shelby County also grew rapidly, but Birmingham was the rail and commercial center of north Alabama and dwarfed its neighbors. By 1890, Shelby's economy was connected with merchant-creditors, mine owners, bankers, and myriad other business groups in Birmingham. This "Magic City," a den of iniquity filled with liquor and prostitutes, was just minutes from Shelby's women and children by train. Jefferson County and Shelby County newspapers ran stories about crime and violence in the new urban center.[45]

Shelby County's population rose from 12,000 in 1870, to 17,000 in 1880, to more than 23,000 by 1900. The L & N railroad cut through the county in the seventies and connected it with all major cities in Alabama, as well as with Tennessee and Kentucky. Large numbers of new people, interlopers from other Alabama counties, northern states, and foreign countries, moved in among farm families that had been in the county for several generations. In a county where almost everyone had been a farmer a new class of industrial wage earner grew. The arrival of the convenient railroad also stimulated more farmers to grow cotton for sale at the market, and more farmers were drawn into the credit system in the eighties. By 1880, more than four hundred men in the county worked in the mines. This occupation, in which mine workers were dependent on their employers, violated the ideal of the independent farmer that undergirded Upcountry political culture.[46]

Anxieties created by the rise of the new industrial economy and rapid changes in community life spilled over into the political system. The Knights of Labor organized chapters in Shelby County, and, at Helena, miners joined an organization formed to protest the use of convict labor by Shelby's mine owners. Because most convicts were black, racial resentments were stimulated. The New England managers of the Shelby Iron Works also preferred cheap black wage labor over that of local whites. In the early 1880s, local industrialists in search of a sober work force also began to support a rising prohibition movement. Entrepreneurs, lawyers, and merchants who were longtime residents of Shelby County, but who represented what one historian labels as "trans-local" forces, began to share political power with outsiders who invested in the county. The interests of these new investors did not necessarily coincide with that of the great mass of local residents.[47]

By 1876, some citizens began to criticize the "stocking" of Democratic conventions by a local political elite and their new commercial-industrial friends, but a new Democratic editor, Needham A. Graham, had no objections to elite control. In 1876, John W. Pitts, a wealthy Harpersville planter who founded the *Shelby Sentinel* to compete with Willis Roberts's *Guide,* turned over control of his paper to Graham, a lawyer with influential business and family connections. Roberts left the county soon afterward. Graham, a Shelby County native of Whig ancestry who entered the Democratic party "in the dark days of Reconstruction," married the sister of probate judge James T. Leeper, a former Whig-Unionist who held the county's most powerful office from 1867 until his death in 1888. Leeper was connected to Alabama's rising industrial class through his marriage to the niece of a prominent iron entrepreneur. Graham, Leeper, and their cohorts dominated the county's Democratic party between 1878 and 1888.[48]

Graham's most powerful local Democratic friend was Rufus W. Cobb, a leader of the New South industrial wing of the Democratic party who was elected to the state senate in 1872 and 1876. In addition to a law practice, Cobb managed an iron company at Helena that was partly owned by the Louisville and Nashville Railroad. The L & N, controlled by northern and European capital, had invested in Alabama's mineral belt and Birmingham's iron industry. Railroaders were acutely interested in a pliable state government, and Rufus W. Cobb had led George Smith Houston's effort to stop the 1875 constitutional convention from repudiating the state's railroad debt. Cobb was elected governor of Alabama in 1878 and 1880.[49]

A revealing incident binding Needham Graham and Cobb occurred in 1878, when Cobb, a candidate for governor, was criticized by a north Alabama newspaper for sponsoring legislation to exempt iron companies from certain taxes. Graham devoted an entire editorial page to Cobb's defense. Cobb had acted from "Whig principles" in encouraging manufacturing in Alabama, said Graham, and he would be better off if he did it more often. Judge Leeper, Graham, and Rufus Cobb's other lawyer-merchant associates dominated Shelby County's Democratic conventions in the late 1870s and 1880s, but Graham was their public voice.[50]

Graham eventually invested in several industrial concerns and in a real estate development company called the Calera Land Company. He welcomed outside businessmen who came to Shelby County with their capital and technical skills. His connections extended to business leaders of all political faiths, including the recently arrived northerners, some of whom had been Union soldiers and were avowed Republicans. At least two of the investors in the Calera Land Company were Republicans with northern roots. Graham never viewed the interlopers as carpetbaggers, yet he despised Napoleon Bonaparte Mardis, a Shelby County native Alabamian and antebellum politician who had become a Republican during Reconstruction. Graham treated these diverse Republicans differently because Mardis spent more time boosting the political rights of blacks and forming alliances with them than in pushing industry and commerce. Blacks constituted 29 percent of Shelby County's population and had more political clout there than in most hill counties. Potential white and black coalitions threatened the Democratic establishment.[51]

Pockets of native white Unionist-Republicans, active since the war, lived in several precincts. Presidential election results in 1876 showed that 38 percent of Shelby's voters cast Republican ballots in a county only 28 percent black. Graham kept a wary eye on these Republicans, who had to be defeated or controlled. The continued unity of the vast majority of Shelby whites inside the Democratic party was vital, but Graham shrewdly made friends with the newest Republican interlopers. The editor was a loyal Democrat and chairman of the local Democratic executive committee, yet he openly championed the northern Republican businessmen.[52]

James D. Hardy, the most influential and active white Republican businessman in Shelby County in the 1880s, was often praised in Graham's *Sentinel*. Hardy was a New York transplant instrumental in the growth of Calera, a town born after the war. Located at the junction of two major railroads, including the L & N, Calera was also near large outcroppings of limestone. Hardy established a large limekiln near the town and expanded his business operations to include a lumber mill, a general merchandise store, and the iron business. When he joined other businessmen in advocating removal of the county seat from the older town of Columbiana to Calera, additional tensions between old and new residents of the county were created.[53]

From his perch at Columbiana's *Sentinel,* Needham Graham was a bridge between Republican J. D. Hardy and the county's Democratic leaders. The reasons for this circumstance were clear. Because Hardy's purposes in the county were similar to those of the Democratic hierarchy, he posed no threat to them and helped to make the local Republican party a safe institution. Hardy's conservative business instincts and his relationships with local blacks helped to keep the local GOP from becoming too "radical." Alabama Republicans were already divided into factions, one that supported black rights and another that was "lily-White." Both wanted patronage from national Republican administrations. Hardy was a member of the white faction, but he often counseled with black Republicans.[54]

Despite the hegemony of this commercial elite, in 1880 most of Shelby County's people lived on small farms, and the suspicions of the farmers toward the two political parties are not difficult to understand. The Republicans, aside from the small group of local white Unionists who joined the party right after the war, were northern-born businessmen or Negroes, whereas the Democrats were controlled by a clique of ex-Whigs and wealthy entrepreneurs whose economic attitudes were similar to the Republicans. No one seemed to represent the white farmers.

In 1877 and 1878, when some independents angry about the manner in which local Democratic conventions were held ran against local Democratic nominees, Graham warned against the return of Radical Republicanism. Despite his judicious associations with the newer Republicans and the political weakness of these independents, Graham insisted that even minor breaks with the Democratic party threatened stability and white supremacy. When several Shelby County men attended the state Greenback-Labor party convention in 1878, Graham charged that Greenbackers were "Communistic and Socialistic" and that one Greenbacker demanded "that Negroes shall be put upon the juries of this county." When Graham listed the names of Shelby men who attended the convention, he carefully italicized the names of three local blacks who were there.[55]

The editor was far more worried about ex-Democrats who broke with their party to create third-party coalitions than with loyal Republicans.

By itself, the GOP was a permanent minority, and Graham's friend J. D. Hardy would intervene to steer Republicans in the right direction. Only schisms that led disgruntled Democrats to create alliances with Republicans could defeat Graham's friends, and the effort to contain dissent and control the local Democratic party led to trouble in 1880. Like local Democratic parties all over the Hill Country, the institution was too small to contain the competing ambitions and differing ideological positions of so many diverse groups. Shelby Democrats were deeply divided.[56]

When ex-sheriff Thomas Harrison was denied the Democratic nomination for the state house of representatives in 1878 by the local convention, he left the party. Harrison was from a wealthy planter family, a Confederate veteran, and the first sheriff elected by Shelby's postwar Democrats. He attended the state Greenback-Labor convention in 1878 after his alienation from the Cobb-Leeper-Graham–controlled party. The political oscillations of the Harrison family between 1865 and the 1930s are an object lesson in the fluidity of Hill Country politics. They were Democrats, Greenbackers, independents, Populists, Republicans, Bull Moose Progressives, Republicans again, and New Deal Democrats.[57]

To stop further defections, the county Democratic committee adopted a rule in 1880 that no one could be nominated unless the person won two-thirds of the vote of the local party convention. For the first time in his career, James T. Leeper had difficulty winning the nomination for probate judge. Twelve ballots were taken before he obtained the necessary votes. Harrison did not ask Democrats for the legislative nomination in 1880, but he ran as an independent against Democratic nominee Henry Wilson, a Columbiana attorney and former law partner of Governor Cobb. Harrison and independent candidates for other county offices, all angry about Democratic nomination procedures, almost caused Judge Leeper's defeat.[58]

In the general election several independents, including Harrison, polled more than 42 percent of the vote. White independents joined blacks and white Republicans in voting for Republican Napoleon Mardis for probate judge. Despite several tries for public office, Mardis had never won significant white support before, but he ran impressively in 1880, losing by only eighteen out of twenty-seven hundred votes cast. The reaction against Leeper can only be explained as part of a general reaction against the small elite that controlled Shelby's politics, for no other policy issues were discussed. Mardis received a sizeable vote in predominately white precincts where voters had been Democrats in the past, but majority black and Unionist-Republican precincts did not support Harrison. Republicans simply refused to vote in races between independents and Democrats. Because independents such as Harrison were former Democrats who had opposed black rights during Reconstruction, blacks had no reason to trust them, and this failure to form a racial alliance hurt future anti-Democratic movements. Voters at Bear Creek, a predominately white precinct that was heavily Unionist before the Civil War and Republican afterward, also refused to vote for Harrison or his Democratic opponent.[59]

Democrats won the 1880 local elections, and Rufus Cobb won 70 percent of his home county's vote in his campaign for reelection as governor, but the election campaign and results presented clear evidence that the Democratic party was in trouble in Shelby County. The actions of Thomas Harrison, a prestigious Democrat from an old Shelby County family, lent credibility to the party bolters. A majority of voters in several white precincts had broken with the Democrats, and many had even voted for the scalawag Mardis. Soon, party bolting became a habit.[60]

In 1882 a new set of forces challenged Shelby's Democrats, but they were less dangerous than the previous group and polled fewer votes. In June 1881 Needham Graham noted the "temperance movement" in the county, wished it success, and suggested that it stay out of politics. One of the county's largest towns voted for prohibition within the town limits, and Republicans, including J. D. Hardy and Napoleon Mardis, began to tout prohibition. A prohibition ticket supported by J. D. Hardy ran against the Democrats in 1882, but independent voters were not enamored with prohibition. Events suggested that many people were also bitter toward Hardy and other outsiders who had bought up the county's resources and now sought political control. Hardy had been active not only in the effort to drive liquor out of the county but also in the push to move the county courthouse from Columbiana to Calera.[61]

The day after the election, Hardy found the following note attached to his front gate:

> We, Mr. J. D. Hardy, think you have done enough in this community against the good people who live here to notify you to pursue a different course to what you have, less an extreme penalty, we will not nor can tolerate your course, hope you will take warning—please do so for your sake.[62]

If this note had simply been the work of a single crank, Hardy might have ignored it, but he was worried enough to report the incident to Needham Graham and other Democratic editors. They printed the note and defended Hardy. Hardy was a "northern man," a "prohibitionist," and a "Republican," said one editorial, but he was an "energetic, enterprising, thrifty proprietor" who was "highly respected by the leading people of Shelby County." Such men, "who have come among us to develop the resources of our country, should be encouraged in every way, and be made to feel that they are appreciated and esteemed." These comments by Democratic editors in support of a Republican were unusual in a time when the southern press was so partisan, but Hardy's continued success in business and his presence in Republican councils was important to the hierarchy of Shelby's Democratic party. Democratic editors made it clear that Hardy was their kind of man.[63]

Dissatisfaction with Shelby's changing way of life and with the power of interlopers was obvious in 1884. Needham Graham moved his newspaper from the county seat at Columbiana to Hardy's Calera, described by Graham as a New South boomtown led by visionary capitalists. A correspondent to the *Sentinel* described only as "Q. R. X." sounded a discordant note in April 1884. Calera was not, he argued, the town Graham depicted. Since Hardy and the new economic forces had taken it over, real estate prices had gone up so fast that it had become impossible for average people to buy a lot or house. Another correspondent argued that the county should stop electing politicians who supported railroads and "corporations that manipulated the prices of farm produce" for the "plethoric purses of pampered monopolists." Shelby's politicians had to learn that the "tiller of the soil" was not an "insignificant factor" in public affairs. Shelby County needed officials more concerned about "home-felt wants and necessities."[64]

Dissatisfaction with the power of outside forces in Shelby, combined with anger at elite control of the local Democratic party, produced a successful political revolt in 1884. E. G. Walker, who led the revolt, had been active in local Democratic politics and had severely criticized the prohibitionist-Republican coalition of 1882, but he was a longtime advocate of greenback currency reform. He sought the Democratic nomination for state representative in 1884 and was defeated at the party's county convention. The convention also elected Needham Graham chairman of the local Democratic party, and he "appointed" an executive committee to run the party. Walker and his supporters argued that they were treated unfairly, held their own independent convention, and nominated a full ticket for county offices.[65]

The independent ticket denounced courthouse "rings," "third-term men," and convict leasing. They also endorsed the Blair education bill pending in Congress, which proposed to distribute excess federal revenue from the tariff to states with high rates of illiteracy, who would then use the money to improve their schools. Many of the independents had long been active in the local Democratic party, and no Republicans were prominent in their meetings. To show that they were the "real" Democratic party, they endorsed the Democratic national platforms of 1876 and 1880 and the reelection of the incumbent Democratic governor.[66]

Shelby's Republicans, white and black, were placed in a dilemma by the independents. Black Republicans had little reason to support white men who still claimed to be Democrats despite their formation of a new party. Neither Napoleon Mardis or J. D. Hardy had much in common with the new independents, but Republicans ran the risk of splitting the anti-Democratic vote if they offered their own ticket. If they refused to participate they would have no influence with the victors after the election. Because they could not publicly endorse Democrats, local Republicans, with J. D. Hardy in the lead, supported the independents. Hardy's decision to join the dissidents later paid dividends for the local establishment.[67]

Needham Graham rolled out standard Democratic accusations against the insurgents and in desperation resorted to some novel ones. He accused the independent candidate for the legislature, E. G. Walker, of being a "Radical Republican" and a tool of blacks. Then, Graham sought to deflect charges against his own elite group by charging that Walker was the candidate of "the rich." Because Walker was a well-known merchant, this charge had some plausibility, but Graham was not through. With time running out, he resorted to an accusation of dubious opprobrium in Shelby County. Walker, said Graham, was really an "Englishman"! None of these ploys had much effect. In the August general election, the independent ticket smashed the local Democratic organization.[68]

The independents won control of the county commission and elected E. G. Walker to the legislature. The two largest black precincts in Calera and Helena voted for the independents along with several previously Democratic white precincts. Each independent candidate took between 53 and 54 percent of the vote. This consistency proved that people were voting for the entire independent ticket. In November, 44 percent of Shelby County's vote went to Republican presidential candidate James G. Blaine. It was the largest vote for a GOP national ticket in Shelby County since the Civil War. Most Republican votes came from predominately black or Unionist-Republican precincts, but a sharp increase in support for the Republican ticket occurred in formerly Democratic precincts that were almost exclusively white. All but three of the county's seventeen precincts had now cast a majority of its vote for either an independent or a Republican in one of the various local, state, or national elections in 1880, 1882, or 1884.[69]

Most of Shelby's white voters, like the independents they elected, still considered themselves Democrats, but the state Democratic party frowned on actions that went outside the bounds of party regularity. Even if the party divisions grew from local disputes and were only temporary, those who operated outside of regular party channels were a threat to the power structure. Shelby voters found that political independence carried a heavy price.

E. G. Walker also claimed to be a Democrat, yet he found that legislators who had not won "regular" party nominations were banned from the Democratic party caucus and would not be treated seriously by other legislators unless their votes were badly needed on a closely contested bill. Needham Graham endorsed the exclusion of E. G. Walker from the Democratic caucus. Graham and his cohorts could not control Shelby County from within, but they could count on help from Democrats outside the county to punish locals who strayed. Even before the election a Selma newspaper pointed out that "Black Belt leaders" would "insist upon the ruling out of the Democratic caucus every representative who defeated a nominee." This willingness of the state Democratic hierarchy to step in and aid local party establishments became more apparent in the late eighties and early nineties.[70]

Walker joined Greenbackers John B. Shields of Walker County and James H. Branch of Lawrence County outside the caucus. He introduced controversial legislation on behalf of groups who had supported him, including a bill "to secure equal accommodations to persons of African descent on the railways" of Alabama and another to protect the "health and safety" of coal miners. Both were doomed to defeat, but their introduction demonstrated the sponsor's courage. When the issue of railroad regulation came up, Walker was less courageous. Hill Country Democrats were prominent in getting a bill passed during the 1881–82 legislative session that created a railroad commission, and in 1884 some legislators supported a bill to grant the commission power to enforce its rate decisions. Railroads began a propaganda campaign to defeat the new measure, and petitions against the bill flooded the legislature. Lawrence County Greenbacker James Branch called for an investigation of railroad lobbying. The campaign against the railroad bill was particularly strong in Shelby County, and one member whose vote may have been influenced by it was E. G. Walker.[71]

The campaign to influence Walker signified that the railroad bill's opponents believed that Walker's vote was in doubt. A petition opposing the bill signed by twenty-five businessmen, merchants, and lawyers appeared on Needham Graham's editorial page. Former governor Rufus Cobb, his law partner Henry Wilson, and Graham all signed, but Walker was probably most affected by the signature of J. D. Hardy, whose support had been crucial in marshaling Republican support for Walker. Much to the relief of the local elite, many of whom had transactions with railroad companies that either owned or invested in iron and coal companies, Walker voted against the bill, and it was defeated. John B. Shields of Walker County also opposed the measure, but no record exists that Shields came under the kind of pressure exerted on Walker. Shields, a manufacturer who did business with railroads, was not anticorporation despite his Greenback affiliation, but Greenbacker James H. Branch supported increased powers for the commission.[72]

No independent won in Shelby County in 1886, but several non-Democrats from north Alabama were elected to the legislature. The entire independent ticket won in St. Clair County. Independent and Republican house members came from St. Clair, Blount, Etowah, and Walker Counties, as well as Colbert and Lawrence Counties in the Tennessee Valley. Some newspaper accounts indicate that the number of independents elected was even greater. Accounts of southern politics that contend that anti-Democratic movements went into decline after 1882 and did not regain life until the Farmers' Alliance arrived do not apply to the Hill Country. The Alliance was not a presence until the spring and summer of 1887.[73]

Independents in the 1886–87 legislature had a major impact on public policy. In the lower house they supported two bills to give workers a lien on the property of their employers in the event that they were not properly paid. Such laws would have given white and black workers in industry or on farms an important legal tool. Black Belt and Gulf Coast Democrats united to defeat the bills. Upcountry independents backed efforts to exempt small farmers from certain taxes, opposed tax exemptions for landlords and merchant-creditors, and tried to kill the state convict-leasing program by voting to limit the use of convict laborers to the counties in which they were convicted. Most independents successfully supported a resolution endorsing the Blair federal aid to education bill.[74]

When a measure to exempt cotton from taxes "while it was in the hands of the producer" came up, the senate's only non-Democrat, Greenbacker James H. Branch of Lawrence County, amended the bill to exempt "one horse or mule" from taxation. The amendment lost, seventeen to fifteen. Hill Country senators, including James L. Sheffield of Marshall County, who had been elected as a Democrat, were solidly for it. The economic dimension that underlay the concerns of Upcountry legislators was obvious. The fact that even this meager effort at giving relief to small farmers was defeated was a clear demonstration of the power of the elite wing of the Democratic party.[75]

From 1876 through 1886, at least seventeen north Alabama counties sent independents, Greenbackers, or Republicans to the legislature. Some counties elected anti-Democrats to other local offices. By the time the Farmers' Alliance arrived, the Upcountry had already broken with local leaders of the Democratic party. It was no giant step for Hill Country voters to bolt the party, yet anti-Democrats from the various counties were not unified. Walker County's Republican-Greenback coalition, led by businessmen, was markedly different from Chilton County's "farm club" dissidents or the farmers who feared a loss of local control in Shelby.[76]

The Farmers' Alliance brought greater unity and tried to work from within the Democratic party as the only apparent avenue to statewide power, but when Alliancemen could not achieve reform as Democrats, they found willing party bolters among those who had split with the Democrats before. The Alliance embodied the multiple dynamics of Hill Country political discontent, including concerns about currency or credit, anger over Democratic nominating procedures, fear of the Black Belt, and a lack of room for the competing ambitions of politicians within the elite circles that dominated Democratic politics. The post-1890 anti-Democratic movements spawned by Alliance organizing had more credibility and lasted longer in the Upcountry than in other parts of the state because it was not unusual, unexpected, or socially demeaning to break with the Democratic party there. By the time the Alliance arrived party bolting was normal.

4 Alliancemen, Populists, and Republicans, 1888–1892

> The uneasy alliance calling itself the Democratic and Conservative party
> that emerged from Reconstruction proved a Trojan horse through which
> the old Jacksonians were . . . betrayed. At the end of the century, forced
> into increasing alienation by the social and economic attitudes now domi-
> nant in the party, those citizens who still remembered the antebellum
> tradition undertook one last crusade to recapture the state government—
> and the dream to which that government had once given form.[1]
>
> J. Mills Thornton

Historians credit the Farmers' Alliance with creating a movement culture
that galvanized southern farmers to fight a financial system they believed
was oppressing them. The Alliance tried to break the hold that a "system
of finance capitalism," concentrated in "Eastern commercial banks," had
on the agricultural economy of the South and West. There was no "conspiracy" in the East to control the hinterlands, but market forces dictated
that easterners would gain financial power because of the absence of capital in the South, and the self-interest of easterners dictated that they use
whatever political clout was necessary to protect their advantage. Alliance
leaders hoped to reform the nation's credit system and asked farmers to
join cooperative ventures that would free them from dependence on supply merchants and landlords financed by eastern bankers. Southern farmers who tried to maintain their independence by supporting the Alliance
clashed with political forces in and outside the region that sought to but-
tress the prevailing system. The battle that inevitably ensued in the South
was for control of the Democratic party.[2]

The Alliance began in Texas and won early successes there in the mid-
1880s. Texans sent lecturers across the South and West to form new chapters and train lecturers to appeal to farmers. Alliance meetings resembled
religious revivals, and members acted as if they were joining a Mani-
chaean fight against evil. Lecturers called on farmers to pool their resources and create their own mercantile stores, manufacture products

they needed, and start organizations that would loan them money at reasonable interest rates. In addition to criticizing eastern banks, lecturers aimed rhetorical fire at merchants who charged usurious interest rates, the pervasive crop-lien system, monopolistic corporations, and railroad warehouse and freight charges. Alliance leaders advocated strong antitrust laws, government ownership of railroads and telegraph lines, a revival of greenbacks, and a bimetallic currency.[3]

The subtreasury plan, the most radical aspect of the Alliance program, was unveiled at a national meeting in St. Louis in 1889. It called for the creation of federal crop warehouses in every county that yielded more than $500,000 worth of agricultural produce. Farmers would store such nonperishable crops as cotton, tobacco, rice, wheat, oats, and wool in these "subtreasuries" and then wait up to a year for the price to reach a higher level before selling. They would receive a subtreasury certificate of deposit, under which they could borrow up to 80 percent of the local market price of their product upon storage. The certificate was negotiable or saleable at the market price during the year. Farmers would pay a small fee for storage, grading, and insurance.[4]

Alliance programs inevitably produced political conflict because they threatened to circumvent men who benefitted from the loans, liens, or mortgages entered into by farmers of both races. Merchants and landlords held powerful positions in Alabama's Democratic party, and the Democrats had erected a legal system that served creditor interests. Cooperative farm clubs were no threat as long as creditors made the laws and controlled government. The Patrons of Husbandry, or the Grange, also advocated farmer cooperation, and it had been active in the state, but it was largely controlled by planter-landlords in the power structure. Democratic newspapers that initially praised the Alliance carefully warned it against political involvement, and although Alliance leaders initially disclaimed an interest in partisan politics, their presence created a feeling of uncertainty that disturbed entrenched elites.[5]

Any organization that won the loyalty of the masses and had the capacity to mobilize them threatened state party leaders and courthouse rings. Alliance leaders could control local Democratic organizations by sending farmers to county conventions or churning them out to vote in party primaries. Democratic leaders felt anxious because Alliance programs could not be adopted without political action, and the organization would eventually have to choose between candidates on the basis of their stances on these programs.

Marshall County Farmers' Alliance, 1892 (courtesy of Larry Smith)

The Alliance had to appeal to Congress to achieve most of its goals, but congressman were unlikely to fear groups that could not threaten their nomination or election, and so the organization had to gain power first at the grassroots level. The Alliance had to make a political effort at the state and local levels because Democratic party nominating procedures, general election processes, and the legal system that enforced the rules of commercial agriculture were in the hands of men opposed to Alliance aims. Alliance leaders who asked members to stay out of local and state politics were unrealistic, and Democratic leaders were justifiably suspicious of such antipolitical rhetoric.[6]

The Agricultural Wheel, a radical farm group, formed a chapter in Lawrence County in 1886 and found members in hill counties at the same time that the Knights of Labor, a national union of both skilled and unskilled workers, was creating chapters in Upcountry coal, iron, and lumber industries. In the spring of 1887, the Farmers' Alliance began its search for members in areas of Alabama most distressed by the declining farm economy. Hill Country and Wiregrass areas were ready for the Alliance. By 1888 the Knights, Wheel, and Farmers' Alliance had formed a coalition dominated by Alliancemen that called for the unity and cooperation of farmers and workers. Alabama was a banner state for the Alliance, and by the spring of 1889 it had garnered 125,000 state members.[7]

The Alliance was more than a spur to political activism. Local chapters became a vital part of the culture. Alliance activities included recreational gatherings, dinners on the ground, tent meetings, and other mass conclaves. It was no accident that many Alliance orators were Baptist ministers experienced at motivating large crowds. For people whose only outlet from the drudgery of farm life was the church, the Alliance added a welcome dimension. Farm women soon formed auxiliary chapters, held meetings of their own, and raised their voices on behalf of reform. Black farmers became members of the Colored Farmers' Alliance, which was affiliated with the parent organization. White and black Alliances generally met separately, but numerous instances of integrated meetings between these people at the bottom of the economic order was a hopeful sign of the possibilities of change.[8]

The arrival of the Farmers' Alliance in Chilton County in June 1887 followed closely on the heels of the dispute that deprived Riley M. Honeycutt and his independent ticket of their election. The political dynamics that initially led to the rise of the independents and the anger that grew out of the election debacle of 1886 stimulated interest in the Alliance. Honeycutt had been supported by pre-Alliance "farmer's clubs" formed in Chilton to support cooperative efforts. Connections between the independents of 1886 and the new farm organization became clear when Honeycutt was elected president of the Chilton County Alliance, a position he held through the 1892 elections. Voting precincts that backed independents supported Alliance candidates and then Populists.[9]

Labor union members also played a role in the Alliance. A Knights of Labor chapter, which included miners and lumber workers, fused with the Alliance. The two organizations held a joint barbecue and parade at Jemison on July 4, 1887. By 1888 the Chilton chapter of the Knights was Alabama's largest. This solidarity among varied economic movements demonstrated a class consciousness that disturbed the editor of Clanton's Democratic newspaper, the *Chilton View,* and he revealed his own class loyalties when he cast aspersions upon "the material" that constituted the Alliance.[10]

A white Republican leader tried to capitalize on the growing rift between Honeycutt's supporters and the "organized" Democratic party. H. A. Wilson, head of the tiny local GOP, invited "all Republicans, Knights of Labor, Farmers Alliance and Laborers" to a convention. Few accepted the invitation, but his call showed the efforts at party crossbreeding that characterized the GOP in the eighties and nineties. Wilson may have believed that dissension existed between labor and the Alliance that might lead one group to support Republicans. A split in reform ranks did occur when some Alliancemen attended a state Labor Union party convention, which endorsed radical notions such as the single-tax theories of Henry George. A petition signed by a large group of Alliance members denounced their brothers for attending the "Socialist" gathering, but some attendees answered that they had no apologies for supporting the "laboring element." This rift quickly healed, and Republicans won no immediate benefits from it.[11]

When local Democratic party leaders realized that the Alliance, unlike independents, was so well organized that its members could win Democratic nominations in county primaries, the Chilton County Democratic executive committee abandoned primaries in 1888 and returned to conventions. In response, Alliancemen and independents formed an "Independent Democratic party," held their own primary, and offered a slate of candidates against the regular party ticket. The local Democratic editor, at a loss to describe the new party, simply characterized it as "Alliance, labor or third-party or whatever."[12]

Independents won the Chilton County legislative seat and elected the sheriff, tax collector, and county treasurer. Seven precincts that had also backed Honeycutt's 1886 independents returned majorities for the new party's ticket. Honeycutt, who opposed party nominations throughout his career, did not seek reelection. The fact that candidates on the winning ticket were "nominated" may have led to his withdrawal. His attitude toward institutional control of politics was reminiscent of Jacksonians, but it soon became apparent that only "organized" political institutions that demanded group loyalty could win elections.[13]

The Democratic editor of the *Chilton View* admitted that the Alliance held a numerical advantage over its foes, but he argued that its members were "financially weak" and that he was not worried about losing their subscriptions because he was supported by the "better off element." Farmers should not support the Alliance, he wrote, because it was "taking in Negroes," and the coalition between the Alliance and labor was unnatural because laborers were consumers and farmers were producers. The Alliance put this strange coalition together by "unnecessarily" raising "class" issues.[14]

The birth of Shelby County's Alliance was even more acrimonious. A dispute marked by sharp rhetorical exchanges created the potential for violence after the first Alliance lecturer came to the county in July 1887.

In a letter to a Democratic newspaper written after the first chapter was formed at Harpersville, the prosperous planter J. L. Walthall contended that the lecturer was a "first-class fraud and imposter" and that those who joined the Alliance were motivated by "stupidity." The Alliance aimed to destroy the local merchant, who was "the miserable cuss that has been carrying us year after year." Only "hard work," said Walthall, not "cooperation," would save farmers. John W. Pitts, once a leader in the Graham-Leeper Democratic faction, angrily described Walthall as a "willful and malicious liar." Walthall challenged Pitts to a duel, though the two disputants never met on the field of honor.[15]

Pitts was an odd Allianceman. He was a native of Selma in the Black Belt, son of a Whig-planter, and a Confederate veteran who moved to Shelby County after the war and became a successful cotton planter. He founded the local Democratic party organ, the *Sentinel,* in 1875 and later sold it to Needham Graham. As editor, Pitts advocated abolition of the crop-lien system, which was then supported by small farmers. He was elected to the legislature in 1878, but he was surprisingly independent. He voted against an election law backed by the state Democratic committee that made it more difficult for the uneducated to vote for independents or third parties. Pitts's name soon disappeared from the rolls of the county Democratic committee, and he did not participate in politics again until the formation of the Alliance. The intensity of his dispute with Walthall demonstrated the vehemence of his anger with the party establishment he once supported.[16]

The Alliance spread rapidly in Shelby County, and in 1888 H. G. McCall bought the *Columbiana Sentinel* and temporarily converted it into an Alliance paper. McCall was accused by local Democrats of having been a Reconstruction Republican, and he confessed to this indiscretion, but he distanced himself from the GOP by claiming that his Republican period had been a "mistake." This rapid disavowal of the Republican party revealed the repugnance most Upcountry whites still felt about the Radicals of the "Tragic Era," despite the existence of Unionist-Republicans in the area.[17]

In addition to the newspaper, the Alliance set up a cooperative mercantile store run by members, designated a committee to help negotiate with merchants, and supported a "shoe [horseshoe] manufacturer." Democratic editors warned the Alliance not to enter politics, and some leaders of the farmers organization supported this nonpolitical stance, but Alliancemen in Shelby County proved to be even more political than their brothers in other counties in the state. Their initial goal was the takeover of the local Democratic party.[18]

Shelby County's most able Alliance advocate was the colorful orator Adolphus Parker Longshore, who was admitted to membership in the farm organization despite being a practicing attorney. He began his political career as a Democrat (1880–88), then became an "independent Democrat" (1888–92), a Populist (1892–1904), a self-described "Populist-Republican" (1904–10), a Republican (1910–12), a Bull Moose Progressive (1912–16), and finally a mere Republican once again (1916–22). Longshore served four terms in the legislature, three as probate judge and one as chairman of the county board of revenue. He was a delegate to several national political conventions between 1896 and 1920, chaired two state Populist party conventions, served on the executive committee of three separate political parties, ran unsuccessfully for Congress three times, and competed once for the U.S. Senate. No figure so clearly symbolized links between the Alliance, Populist, and progressive Republican politics of the post-1900 era.[19]

Longshore was born in Chambers County in 1854, the son of Levi Longshore, a farmer who migrated to Alabama from the South Carolina Piedmont around 1850 and later fought for the Confederacy. Unlike some who later aligned with Populists in Walker, Winston, Lawrence, DeKalb, or Randolph Counties, Longshore had no Unionist-Republican roots. After the war, Levi ran the Longshore House hotel at Dadeville in Tallapoosa County. A. P. Longshore was sent to Washington and Lee College for a year, but he dropped out for a "lack of funds," returned to central Alabama, and read law. He was admitted to the bar in 1878 and practiced briefly in Tallapoosa County, where he served as county solicitor (prosecuting attorney). The Longshore House at Dadeville burned in 1884, and the family suffered severe financial reverses. Levi opened a mercantile store in Columbiana, and his son followed him there in 1885. A. P. Longshore began his political career in Shelby County by attending the 1886 Shelby County Democratic convention, which then selected him as a delegate to the party judicial nominating convention.[20]

Soon after Longshore's arrival in Shelby County, his law firm won a $1,500 verdict against a railroad company associated with the Louisville and Nashville Railroad, which was represented by Rufus Cobb's former law partner, Henry Wilson. Longshore did not content himself with law practice, however; he opened a general mercantile store that specialized

A. P. Longshore, ca. 1912 (courtesy of George H. Longshore)

in a variety of seeds for local farmers, became partners in a real estate firm, and offered to loan money at "eight percent per annum" on "improved farm land." These activities were not sufficient to contain his energies or ambitions, and he soon turned to politics.[21]

Shelby voters who supported independents in 1884 had returned to the local Democratic party by 1886, but only temporarily and probably because they had little choice. Republican leader J. D. Hardy claimed that his support for the independents in 1884 was supposed to be reciprocated by their support of a Republican for probate judge in 1886. When independents claimed that no such deal had been struck, Hardy and the Republicans withdrew their support from the dissidents, and no independent slate was offered in 1886. Thus, the Democrats recaptured Shelby's legislative seat, and Judge Leeper won a fourth term, but Hardy hurt his own cause by breaking with the independents. He was the Republican nominee for Alabama's secretary of state in the August elections and the nominee for Congress in November. He lost Shelby County in both races.[22]

These events revealed the dilemma of independents who accepted support from Shelby Republicans and refused to return the favor. If they openly aligned with the GOP, they risked losing many of their supporters, yet they eventually had to reconsider their approach to the Republicans despite their distaste for them. Republicans were a small minority and could not win elections on their own, as Hardy's defeat demonstrated, but they were the potential balance of power in county politics. Contests between regular Democrats and party renegades were so closely contested in the eighties and nineties that Republican voters often decided the elections. Anti-Democrats had difficulty mobilizing a majority without Republican help.

The Alliance initially sought power through the Democratic party and supported candidates for delegates to the Shelby County Democratic convention, which met on May 4, 1888. The pro- and anti-Alliance factions were nearly equally divided, as voting in the convention eventually demonstrated, and neither one seemed to be in control. The delegates selected a chairman, John W. Pitts, who defeated former governor Cobb by a vote of sixty-two to sixty-one, but delegates from one precinct changed their vote, and Cobb became the convention's presiding officer.[23]

Delegates to the meeting were supposed to be selected from each precinct by direct election of Democratic voters, but voters suspected of past disloyalty to the party had been excluded from voting in some precincts. After some men were nominated for office at the convention, pro-Alliance delegates began to object to the manner in which delegates had been chosen, and the convention was hastily adjourned. An angry John W. Pitts charged that only those known to be pro-Alliance had been excluded from voting and that certain precinct delegations had been stacked by the "ring" against the Alliance-supported candidates. Democratic election officials appointed by the Graham-Leeper wing of the party replied that only "known Republicans" were excluded. Pitts accused former governor Rufus W. Cobb, who presided over the aborted convention, of unfairly thwarting the will of a majority of Democrats.[24]

Supporters of the old hierarchy correctly noted that the Alliance had tried to seize control of the convention. Alliance leaders argued that an open primary should be held to nominate candidates, but the county Democratic committee voted to hold another convention. When the county convention met again in early July, a month before the general election, so many farmers were elected delegates that the convention was totally governed by Alliance leaders. A. P. Longshore was elected chairman of the convention rules committee, and every motion that carried during the meeting was moved by either him or John W. Pitts. Needham Graham was ousted as party chairman, the old executive committee was abolished, a new Alliance-controlled committee was selected, and Alliance-endorsed candidates were nominated, including Longshore, for the state house of representatives. A new political "ring" had replaced the older one. Charges by Needham Graham that many Alliance leaders had not been loyal Democrats were valid. Longshore was joined on the Alliance ticket by three men who had been on the independent ticket of 1884. The new chairman of the local party, A. C. Keller, had also endorsed the independents.[25]

An angry Graham-Leeper faction held a separate convention presided over by Judge Leeper's son, nominated their own slate of candidates, and claimed to be the legitimate county Democratic party. They also argued that the old Democratic executive committee and chairman Graham could not be ousted because their terms had not expired. One of their leaders wrote to a local newspaper that the Alliance-controlled convention had "deviated" from the "original landmarks" of the party in "disregarding the power and the sole power" of the executive committee. The Alliance, he said, had allowed the "ignorant voting masses" to dominate the convention.

Despite their tradition of accusing independents of being mere stalking horses for Radical Republicans, the Graham-Leeper group quickly appealed to Republicans to join the fight against the Alliancemen. In 1884, Needham Graham had wrongly accused E. G. Walker and his ticket of being dominated by Republicans, but in 1888, Graham's pragmatic use of his friendships among Republicans such as J. D. Hardy nearly brought his faction success.[26]

J. L. Vandiver, a Unionist-Republican from Bear Creek, a white precinct that had been in the GOP column since the Civil War, cooperated with the Graham-Leeper faction and agreed to be their candidate against Longshore. Vandiver had been a Reconstruction scalawag, but he gained acceptance from Democrats during the controversial campaign to redeem the state in 1874, when he broke with the GOP over the race issue, supported the Democratic ticket, and called for a government of white men. He became a "lily-white" Republican, and the anti-Alliance group shrewdly used him in 1888 to draw white GOP support. The Alliance ticket won each office in the ensuing election, but its lack of support from Republicans ensured a narrow margin of victory. Alliance candidates won some support in majority black precincts, however, and Longshore defeated Vandiver by 138 out of 2,678 votes cast.[27]

Between 1888 and 1890, events further divided the wings of Shelby's Democratic party. Judge Leeper died in 1889, and John W. Pitts wanted to replace him, but Black Belt governor Thomas Seay appointed ex-governor Rufus W. Cobb to the unexpired term. This action further alienated Pitts, who only a few months earlier criticized Cobb's conduct as presiding officer of the county Democratic convention. Farmers' Alliance editor H. G. McCall charged that the appointment was "against the wishes of the Shelby Democracy."[28]

McCall, who went on to edit a statewide Alliance newspaper, pointed out the close connections between the Alliance movement and the 1884 independents. The people of Shelby, he wrote, proved that they did not belong to any man or group "six years ago" when, "aroused at last by the indignities and outrages perpetuated upon them by a lot of cormorants that had fed upon the county treasury for a quarter of a century," they "repudiated them at the polls." In McCall's mind the two movements were linked.[29]

Sheldon Hackney has charged that "agrarian" leaders were "primitive rebels" opposed to raising revenue for public services that led to modernization, yet Shelby's Alliance Democrats were criticized for initiating efforts to raise more revenue for public education. H. G. McCall endorsed a referendum to increase local taxes for the schools, and it passed by a wide margin. A. P. Longshore sponsored a bill in the 1888–89 legislative session that gave the Shelby County commission increased authority to raise and appropriate money for schools. The proposal was assailed in a Democratic newspaper by an Alliance enemy who feared the money would be used for Negro education. He was right, for Longshore's measure stipulated that at least one-third of the money had to go to Negro schools, even though the population of Shelby County was only 28 percent black.[30]

Pro-and anti-Alliance splits existed among Marshall County Democrats by 1890, but they evolved differently from those in Shelby. The route of the Sheffield-Street family to the Alliance was more circuitous than that of Honeycutt or Longshore. Neither James L. Sheffield nor Judge Thomas A. Street encountered much difficulty inside Marshall County's

Democratic party before 1890. Street was a local party leader, and Sheffield's disagreements with Democrats had been at the congressional and state levels. In 1886, a multicounty Democratic convention nominated Sheffield for the state senate. According to the *Guntersville Democrat*, which backed him in 1886, Sheffield had repented his political sins and reentered the Democratic fold. Sheffield and Street soon learned that they could not continue to disagree with the policies of state and national Democrats and remain safely inside their local party.[31]

Street was easily reelected probate judge in August 1886, but he began to sow seeds of dissension among Democrats when he engaged in a bitter dispute with Seventh District Democratic Congressman William H. Forney. Street accused Forney of protecting wealthy and powerful railroad men to the detriment of the Marshall County's small farmers. Tracts of land had been given to the Tennessee and Coosa Railroad Company by the federal government in the 1850s in return for the company's promise to build rails through Marshall and other north Alabama counties. The work was unfinished when the Civil War began, and the T & C ceased work on the road. New settlers who entered Marshall County from Georgia and Tennessee wanted to live on the company's land, but heirs and successors of the railroad property refused to relinquish control. Some of the new Marshall countians "squatted" on the railroad's land, though they had no legal title. The hope of Upcountry farmers for landed independence was still alive, and Street became their champion.[32]

Forney refused to introduce legislation requested by Street to force the company to give up title, and Street refused to back the congressman in his 1886 reelection bid. Forney easily won another term, but Marshall County gave a majority of its votes to Shelby County's J. D. Hardy, the Republican nominee. It was the first time since the 1860s that a Republican had won a majority in Marshall County, yet it represented no groundswell of support for Hardy and the Republicans. Democrats, in testimony to Street's influence, had simply refused to vote. The dispute with Forney continued through the 1890 election and combined with a separate and growing dispute in the state Democratic party to drive many Marshall County Democrats out of their old party.[33]

The dispute at the state level in 1890 concerned efforts by the Alliance to nominate one of their own, state commissioner of agriculture Reuben F. Kolb, for governor. Kolb had strong support in the Hill Country and Wiregrass areas. The Chilton County Democratic convention of 1890 was dominated by Alliancemen who instructed all six of their state convention delegates to vote for Kolb, and the Shelby County convention so instructed five of its six delegates. Opponents of Kolb walked out of both county conventions, formed their own separate executive committees, held rival conventions, and selected rival convention delegations.[34]

In a move that plagued Chilton delegates to the state Democratic convention, leaders of the Alliance-dominated Chilton County Democratic convention forced each potential candidate for local office to declare their stand on the subtreasury plan, though they nominated one candidate who said the plan would "bankrupt the government." The editor of the *Chilton View* admitted that the convention was "representative of the yeomanry of the county," but he questioned the way that Alliance leaders had run the meeting.[35]

Friction between pro- and anti-Alliance factions in Marshall County existed, but Judge Street did not become a Kolbite until after the state Democratic convention, and the local party did not divide over the 1890 gubernatorial race. Kolb won only two of Marshall County's seven state convention delegates. Also, because candidates for Marshall's county offices were not nominated in convention, no public forum was provided through which the party could formally split. Alliance candidates ran in the county's general election without Street's support and were defeated. It was not until the summer of 1890, after the state Democratic convention, that the Alliance won the allegiance of Marshall County's voters and Judge Street. Events at the state convention increased sympathy in the county for the Alliance.[36]

Reuben Kolb came to the state convention with a plurality and a chance for a first-ballot nomination, but the party hierarchy stopped him. A credentials committee run by anti-Alliance men ruled that Kolb delegations from Shelby, Chilton, and Lee Counties were improperly selected and ordered that they be divided evenly between pro- and anti-Kolb men. Convention chairman William H. Denson, a Gadsden attorney, refused to allow the Alliance delegates to vote as their conventions had instructed. On the thirty-fourth ballot, L & N Railroad attorney Thomas G. Jones of Montgomery received 269 votes to Kolb's 256. If the Shelby, Chilton, and Lee delegations voted as instructed, Kolb might have won. His supporters had little time to form a third party, and he asked them to stay in the party so that they might take control of it in 1892.[37]

James L. Sheffield attended the convention and wrote to Oliver Street that he remembered every election campaign in Alabama since 1840 but had "never witnessed anything to equal" the Kolb-Jones race, which was "the harshest and most exciting political contest ever decided on Alabama soil." Kolb was defeated, said Sheffield, by the "unjust rulings of the chairman." Party leaders resorted to "every strategy and device" to deprive Kolb of victory. Alliancemen shared these views, but they went along with Kolb's call for party loyalty. Wiregrass editor Frank Baltzell expressed their anger when he wrote that he would vote the Democratic ticket again, but those who ran the convention could not "wipe from their records the wrongs perpetrated in order to secure the victory they gained."[38]

As Democrats divided into pro- and anti-Alliance factions, the state Republican party hoped for a resurgence. In 1889, partly in response to the possibility of capturing more dissident white Democrats to their cause, some Republicans tried to create a white party. They divided into two separate factions, both of which claimed to be the real state Republican party. One group was lily-white, and the other continued to support black political rights. In 1890, the lily-whites nominated Benjamin M. Long of Walker County for governor. He received less than 25 percent of the statewide vote, and Jones won the Hill Country despite his fight with Kolb. Long's poor showing dashed Republican hopes that they could win large numbers of white voters. To defeat Democrats, Republicans had to cooperate with a party acceptable to a larger number of whites.[39]

Benjamin Long won 49 percent of Walker County's vote in 1890 despite statewide defeat. The Long-Shields coalition had dominated the county since 1880, and although the Farmers' Alliance won converts in Walker, the GOP remained the primary vehicle to defeat Democrats there. Later, in 1894, Long and his party fused with the third party created by local Alliancemen, just as they had with Greenbackers, but the relationship was difficult. Long's hard-money, protariff Republican views hardly suited him to Populism. In most hill counties, Republicans hoped for a small place in a temporary coalition, but in Walker County the Alliance hoped that local Republicans would allow them a small place at the GOP table. Long sympathized with those who wanted fair and free elections.[40]

Despite their support for the state Democratic ticket, voters in the Upcountry vented their anger at the Democratic convention in county elections. Kolb's defeat led to permanent divisions in Democratic ranks. In Shelby County the two Democratic party wings formed separate committees, and those who ran the state executive committee recognized the Graham-Leeper or anti-Alliance group as the legitimate county party.

State leaders could not allow Kolbites to have local control because delegates to state conventions and members of the legislature would be chosen at the county level.[41]

A. P. Longshore and John W. Pitts attempted to heal the party rift by proposing that the two groups fuse their committees and hold a joint convention, but after it won the imprimatur of the state committee, the anti-Alliance wing had no incentive to fuse with Alliancemen, who might overpower them. Because they were no longer "real" Democrats, the Alliance group described themselves as the "Independent Democratic party," selected a slate of candidates for county offices, and renominated Longshore for the legislature. This party split created the basis of a closely contested two-party political system in Shelby County that emerged in 1892 and remained in place until 1932. Alliance supporters and their progeny created the political base of Shelby County's opposition to the Democrats until the New Deal. Close general elections became the rule.[42]

In a move that was welcomed and perhaps encouraged by the Graham-Leeper wing, Republicans held a county convention in 1890 and nominated J. D. Hardy to oppose Longshore. Hardy's effort typified his actions throughout the eighties. Despite his stated opposition to the Democratic party, his views had always been more like those of the Democratic establishment than those of the independents, Greenbackers, or Alliance Democrats. Because a majority in the GOP meeting were black Republicans, the white Republican nominee for superintendent of education withdrew from the ticket, denounced Hardy, and said that when "the colored man participates in our meetings and says who is to run, it is too much for me." Such divisions in GOP ranks were important to the Alliance's success because the task of defeating a coalition between the old Democratic establishment and a united Republican party was formidable.[43]

When A. P. Longshore was accused by a Democratic newspaper of asking for votes from Republican "laboring men" as well as Democrats, he believed it necessary to distance himself from the GOP despite his need for Republican votes. In a letter to a local newspaper, Longshore denied that he sought Republican votes but admitted that he wanted the votes of all "laboring men" who "work earnestly for those great reform measures that are demanded by the men who produce the wealth of this country."[44]

Longshore's remarks about laboring men placed him within an ideological tradition that held that those who actually did the labor that "produced" crops or goods, not those who sat in bank or corporation boardrooms, created economic value for society. This producer ideology underlay Alliance demands and had deep roots in Upcountry Alabama. Its most militant advocates were antebellum Jacksonians, who believed that a "just republic" must first serve the needs of "hard-working plain people." Jacksonians had opposed government involvement in the economy because it seemed that government only helped the nonproducing, or investing, class. The postbellum growth of gigantic corporations, monopolies, and a market system that involved so many average people caused men who believed in Jacksonian producerism to revise their anti-government philosophy. Unlike their pre–Civil War predecessors, post-bellum producer advocates argued that government should be a balancing wheel to protect farmers and laborers from monopolies and eastern banks. Populists used the Jacksonian phrase "equal rights for all, and special privileges to none," but believed that unless government acted on their behalf, the grossly unequal distribution of wealth would get worse.[45]

Personal attacks on Longshore and the race issue were the basis of the Democratic campaign in Shelby. Longshore was the acknowledged leader of Shelby's Alliance and was so described in a poem in a Democratic party newspaper that accused him of being a "whiskey drinker," a "poker player," a "bully boy," and a man who did not care about the "color line." There was ample evidence that Longshore and the Alliancemen were generally racist despite the fact that the Alliance invited cooperation from black farmers, sat in open meetings with them, and asked for their votes. This integration was superficial, but it broke entirely with practices of the Democratic party. Longshore's prior effort to increase funding for Negro schools also gave credibility to the Democratic allegations.[46] Despite the racial charges, Longshore defeated both Hardy and his regular Democratic opponent in 1890, but the Alliance ticket won only a plurality. Longshore received 41 percent of the vote, the anti-Alliance Democrat 35 percent, and Hardy a surprising 24 percent. Months later a Democrat noted that the Alliance ticket was supported by "nearly all the independents who left the party six years ago," but the close results should have served as a warning to the Alliancemen that the Republicans could not be ignored.[47]

The state Democratic executive committee that anointed the anti-Alliance wing as Shelby County's official Democratic party also ruled that Chilton's state convention delegates and Democratic nominees were improperly chosen and forced Democrats there to hold another county convention. Both rival factions participated. Alliancemen controlled the new convention in Chilton and nominated all local party candidates. An anti-

Alliance editor wrote that the "Alliance has politics in her hands," that the new leaders of Chilton's Democratic party were "farmers," and that men "not members of that class" could not expect county political "plums" to come their way. Alliancemen easily won the August election.[48]

A growing Farmers' Alliance movement in Marshall County, events at the 1890 state Democratic convention, and a rift between Judge T. A. Street and town-based men may have forced Street into the Alliance. He had made no commitment to the Alliance economic nostrums, but his strongest support had always come from Marshall County's small farmers. He could ignore their attachment to the Alliance only at his peril. At an Alliance meeting in July 1890, Street's oldest son, Atkins, announced the family's support for the organization's candidates. Street's fight with Congressman Forney alienated old-line Democrats in the towns, and their anger with the judge led him to move toward a coalition with the popular Alliance. In the fall of 1890, the Streets joined a group associated with the Alliance and supported an "independent Democrat" against Forney in the general election. Forney won, but his opponent polled 36 percent of the vote. Sentiment grew to exclude those who opposed Forney from participation in Democratic party councils. A pro-Alliance newspaper felt compelled to assert that Alliancemen would "not be driven out of the Democratic party."[49]

Bitterness against Street among prominent Marshall County professional and business leaders may also have grown out of the tragic death of a well-known local physician, Dr. William "Buck" May. Southerners reared on the antebellum frontier sometimes resorted to violence to save their families from dishonor, and James L. Sheffield had been Marshall County's sheriff when such activity was sanctioned by society. On June 20, 1890, the seventy-one-year-old Sheffield was in Marshall County at the home of his married daughter, Lucy Taylor, Judge Street's half-sister. The *Guntersville Democrat* reported that Sheffield, employed in Montgomery as chief clerk in the office of a Marshall County man who was state superintendent of education, had been called home by a telegram on a "private matter" that "concerned the honor of his family." Dr. May, a former boarder in Sheffield's home, knew the family well. He came to Mrs. Taylor's house where Sheffield met him on the front steps, and they exchanged words. Sheffield reentered the house, emerged with a pistol, and shot May, who was evidently unarmed. The doctor died, and a few days after the November 1890 election Sheffield was tried for murder.[50]

The background of the principal figures in the trial was a fascinating study in the complexity of politics and the irony of history. Presiding Judge S. K. Rayburn had, back in 1861, been an unsuccessful secessionist candidate for delegate to the convention called to consider whether Alabama should leave the Union. He had lost that election to the ardent Unionist James L. Sheffield. William H. Denson of Gadsden, whose conduct as the presiding officer at the 1890 state Democratic convention led Sheffield to accuse him of making "unfair rulings" that deprived Reuben Kolb of the nomination, was the chief defense counsel. One of the prosecutors brought in to assist Marshall County solicitor John Lusk was the noted Birmingham trial lawyer Colonel E. T. Taliaferro, who happened to be a close friend and advisor to Reuben Kolb. Lusk, a longtime political opponent of the Streets, evidently brought in Taliaferro to appeal to Kolb supporters or Alliance members on the jury. Three other lawyers, including Sheffield's step-grandson Oliver Street, joined the defense team.[51]

No record of the trial is extant, but the event uncovered a bizarre scandal that embarrassed Sheffield and the Streets. One of Sheffield's daughters had been under the care of May. She charged that the doctor not only had engaged in sex with her while she was under the influence of a drug he administered to her but also had led her to become dependent on the drug and asked her to commit criminal acts against her neighbors while she was under its influence. Indeed, she was arrested for arson against one neighbor, but she was never put to trial for it. Newspapers reported the names of the lawyers in the murder case, a brief account of the facts, and the point that Sheffield was acquitted. Sheffield returned to Montgomery, suffered no retribution for his deed, and continued to campaign for Alliance candidates. In 1891 he made speeches on behalf of Warren S. Reese, the Alliance candidate for mayor of Montgomery. In his speeches, the old Jacksonian Democrat described politics as a struggle of the "strong against the weak" and of "money against labor."[52]

In March 1892, when Marshall County's Democrats held a mass meeting to select delegates to the state convention, the inevitable formal division in their ranks occurred. The Streets and their allies came to select Kolb delegates, and they outnumbered their opponents. As a pretext to get rid of Kolb supporters, anti-Kolb delegates argued that anyone who had opposed William H. Forney for Congress should be banned from the hall. Many Kolb supporters hailed from precincts that opposed Forney in 1890, and the motion led to a veritable melee. Pro-Kolb Democrats, whether they had opposed Forney or not, refused to leave, and the two factions held separate meetings on different sides of the hall. Judge Street stood on a table and presided over the pro-Kolb group.[53]

These events marked the birth of a new political party in Marshall County, though both factions still considered themselves Democrats. Once Reuben Kolb gave up his useless fight for the 1892 Democratic nomination, Judge Street's version of the Marshall County Democratic party could choose to remain inside a party run by the anti-Kolb state Democratic executive committee, become Republicans, or associate with either of two new statewide political parties. The first two alternatives had no appeal.[54]

The National People's Party, or Populist party, founded in 1891 in Cincinnati, Ohio, was organized in Alabama's Hill Country in the spring of 1892. The party platform was essentially the same as that of the Farmers' Alliance. It endorsed the subtreasury, supported strong government regulation of railroads and telegraph lines, called for the direct election of U.S. senators, and asked Congress to enact a federal income tax. The first county in Alabama to affiliate with the national party was Clay, where the leader of the movement was twenty-two-year-old Joseph Columbus Manning, the "Evangel" of Alabama Populism. In April 1892, groups in Shelby, Walker, Cleburne, Cullman, Etowah, Calhoun, and Jefferson Counties followed Manning and formed local branches of the new party.[55]

Reuben Kolb and his supporters decided against attending the Democratic convention. If Kolb had competed for the nomination on the convention floor, he would have been bound to support the eventual party nominee. A. P. Longshore advised Kolb that he would walk "into a trap" if he attended the convention, which was controlled by men who would not let him have the nomination. Kolb and his supporters met in a separate convention near the site of the Democratic meeting and founded the Jeffersonian Democratic party. Unlike Populists, the Jeffersonians refused an open break with the national Democratic party and futilely selected delegates to the national Democratic convention as rivals to those selected by the regular Democrats. In the preamble of their platform they reaffirmed their "devotion and allegiance to the principles of Democracy as enunciated by Jefferson, taught by Madison, and practiced by Jackson." Their aim was to "restore Democracy to its old landmarks, as the exponent of the rights of the people."[56]

The Jeffersonians called for the free coinage of silver, abolition of the national banking system, a graduated income tax, equitable taxation at the state level, an elected railroad commission, and an end to convict leasing, but they did not endorse the subtreasury plan or governmental ownership of railroads. They nominated Kolb for governor and picked nominees for other state offices. Some who attended the meeting, including Longshore, feared that the Jeffersonians had not broken clear of the Democratic party, and this more radical group became outright Populists.[57]

On June 2, 1892, A. P. Longshore published the first issue of the *Columbiana People's Advocate,* which became the Shelby County organ of the People's party. He wrote that the national banking system was a "hideous monster" and that nothing short of "political revolution" would "break the shackles and free the people" from the power of eastern banking. In an appeal to Hill Country voters, Longshore also wrote about the unfairness with which the Black Belt controlled Alabama's Democratic conventions. He argued that voters from white counties in north Alabama and the Wiregrass were grossly underrepresented at the conventions. Shelby, Chilton, Calhoun, and Cleburne Counties had a joint population of eighty-two thousand to Dallas County's forty-one thousand, yet Dallas had twenty-six delegates, and the four Upcountry counties had a combined total of only twenty-three. Staying inside the Democratic party, wrote Longshore, was futile for north Alabamians. Sectional bitterness, producerism, and fear of the political and economic power of eastern banking were the core of Longshore's ideology.[58]

On June 4, 1892, a mass outdoor meeting called by a Farmers' Alliance lecturer was held in Calera to organize Shelby County's Populist party. It was, said a witness, "the largest assemblage of Shelby County people ever brought together in Calera for political purposes." The meeting adopted resolutions that endorsed the national People's party platform; picked delegates to state, congressional, judicial, and senatorial conventions of the new party; set up a primary election to nominate local candidates; and selected an executive committee. Alliance leaders from both Shelby and Chilton opted to be Populists instead of Jeffersonians. They were committed to the entire program of the Populist party and later became "mid-roaders," or members of the most zealous and uncompromising wing of the party. Immediately after this convention, a Shelby County Democratic newspaper raised a charge used against every anti-Democratic movement. Populists, said the editor, were "Negro sympathizers." He was partially correct.[59]

In late June, the Alabama People's party held a convention in Birmingham, and Longshore was chosen to preside over the meeting. He opened the session by remarking that he was a lifelong Democrat, never a Republican, that he opposed the "McKinley tariff" passed by Republicans in 1891, and that he endorsed the free coinage of silver. The Populists wanted a clean break with the state and national Democratic party and resolved to hold their conventions and select an executive committee separate from the Jeffersonians. Instead of endorsing the Jeffersonian Reuben Kolb directly, the Populists asked voters to choose between the "perpetuation of bossism and machine rule, and a rule of the people."[60]

The precocious Joseph C. Manning, a moving force behind this statewide meeting and chairman of the committee that selected delegates to the national Populist convention, which met later that summer in Omaha, recommended that Alabama's People's party select a black delegate. A Birmingham delegate said that this action would brand the party as a gathering of "Negro lovers," but Manning prevailed, and a black delegate was chosen. Longshore praised this black Populist in a *People's Advocate* editorial.[61]

Among the delegates at the Birmingham convention was Lewis H. Reynolds, who eventually replaced Riley Honeycutt as Chilton County's most influential politician. The son of a farmer and Confederate veteran who came to Chilton County from the Black Belt in the 1870s, Reynolds grew up in relative poverty with little formal education, but at the age of twenty-eight he was the county's senior Alliance lecturer and had been one of the ill-fated Kolb delegates from Chilton at the 1890 Democratic convention. He had held various jobs, including that of bill collector for a rural merchant, which probably alerted him to the tragic situation of Chilton County's farmers. Later, Reynolds managed the Farmers' Alliance store at Jemison and was endorsed by the county Alliance for the 1892 Democratic nomination for state senator from Chilton, Shelby, and Elmore Counties. He withdrew from the race, joined the Populist party, and sought the Populist senate nomination instead. He lost his bid for the senate, but he remained a major figure in Alabama's Populist party.[62]

Reynolds's decision to leave the Democratic party was probably hastened by the interference of the state Democratic executive committee in Chilton County's election. The Alliance had dominated the selection of the local Democratic ticket in March 1892, but the state committee refused to recognize the candidates as official party nominees. Thereafter, the Alliance candidates were endorsed by the local Populist party, even though they were not "nominated" in a Populist convention or primary.

Riley Honeycutt was endorsed by the Populists as their candidate for probate judge.[63]

Before Reynolds left the Democratic party, his loyalty to the "Democracy" was challenged in the *Chilton View* by a critic who wrote that no man could be a true Democrat who supported the platform adopted by the Farmers' Alliance national convention in Ocala, Florida. The Ocala meeting demanded the subtreasury and government ownership of the railroads, said the critic, and these remedies violated the antigovernment precepts of Jefferson and Jackson, the founders of the Democratic party. Reynolds was asked to define how Alliancemen fit into the Jeffersonian-Jacksonian tradition, and he proved equal to the task.[64]

Reynolds did not retreat from his devotion to the antebellum Democracy. The Ocala platform, he replied, was in accord with the "true principles of Democracy." He would never support a program that conflicted with the Jacksonian principle of "equal rights to all." Reynolds went to the core of what linked him to the older Democratic party when he wrote that he stood with Jefferson and Jackson against the power that financial interests exercised in the government. He used quotes from each of the party founders to prove that "Alliance precepts" were "exactly in harmony" with the founders. "Banking institutions," said the Jefferson quote, were "more dangerous to our liberties than standing armies," and the quote from Jackson endorsed paper money controlled by the people but not "delegated to the individuals and corporations." The quotes were significant because they proved that Reynolds believed that the primary issue motivating him in politics was not voting reform, but the influence of financial interest groups in politics.[65]

The economic views emphasized by Reynolds tied him to an ideology older than his nation. Like "country opposition" writers of early-eighteenth-century England, Jeffersonian Republicans, and Jacksonians, the Alliancemen battled the influence of the "money power." Reynolds believed that government had to balance the economic scales and that both major parties endorsed policies that served eastern financial interests. National banks had "raised up a financial aristocracy," and the Democratic party could not return to first principles until it turned "Wall Street loose first." Reynolds did not suggest that eastern financiers were engaged in a conscious conspiracy. The actual concentration of economic power in the northeast in the late nineteenth century led him to a perfectly rational assumption that those who had that power would act to protect it. For nearly thirty years, Reynolds and A. P. Longshore, whose political careers ran a strikingly similar course, worked side by side in political battles and eventually led their Populist cohorts into the Republican party. They were committed to the Ocala demands and to the program of the national Populist party, and even after the nineties their reform impulse remained vital.[66]

Unlike Longshore and Reynolds, the Street wing of Marshall County's Democrats chose to join Reuben Kolb's Jeffersonian Democratic party. In the summer campaign of 1892, Judge T. A. Street supported Kolb's third-party ticket, but unlike Reynolds and Longshore, he did not entirely break with his old party. In the fall, with federal offices at stake in the November general election, Street supported Democratic nominee William H. Denson for Congress in the Seventh District and Democratic presidential nominee Grover Cleveland. Denson's defense of James L. Sheffield in the murder case may have influenced Street, but the Democratic nominee had spoken at Alliance meetings, praised the Alliance, and was an advocate of free silver. Thus, Street's support for Denson did not signify an innate conservatism. The Streets also supported reform measures to aid farmers and laborers, believed the Black Belt–dominated Democratic party was too elitist, and backed reforms to ensure fair elections, but they never supported radical programs such as the subtreasury or government ownership of the railroads. Their support for the anti-labor, pro-gold Grover Cleveland separated them from more radical third-party men.[67]

Judge Street was a member of the Jeffersonian state executive committee, but he would not participate in the meetings of Marshall County's small Populist party, which maintained a separate executive committee from the larger Jeffersonian group until 1896. The two dissident groups finally merged at the state and local levels in 1896. The leader of Marshall County's Farmers' Alliance since 1888 was W. M. Coleman, a Jeffersonian who also supported Denson and Cleveland, and Judge Street's late arrival into Alliance circles made the two men rivals. Populists and Jeffersonians cooperated in Marshall County in 1892 and held what they described as the "Alliance primary." Judge Street was nominated for probate judge, and W. M. Coleman was nominated for the state house of representatives. Marshall County Republicans followed the lead of the state GOP and endorsed the third-party candidates.[68]

The small Republican group was led by the old Union spy and Reconstruction legislator Seaborn A. Kennamer. A Marshall County Democratic editor charged that Judge Street posed "before our people as a Jacksonian Democrat," but he was openly aligned with Republicans. Street "finds himself applauded and cheered by a lot of men who lay out in the mountains and sneaked into federal camps with traitorous news of the movement of Confederate armies."[69]

James L. Sheffield's activities on behalf of the third party were more radical than Judge Street's. A Democratic newspaper charged Sheffield and other Alliancemen with creating secret organizations in Marshall County that were part of a more formal group called "Gideon's Band," which threatened Democrats with violence. A local Populist editor admitted the existence of the groups, but he argued that they were formed to protect Populists from the Democrats. Sheffield died only a few days before the August elections after a political career of more than half a century. His 1874 campaign for Congress, the first substantial effort to oppose the corrupt nomination processes of the Democrats, had paved the way for the successful campaign of his friend William Manning Lowe. Sheffield's willingness to lead the Greenback cause in 1882 increased anti-Democratic dissent and created support for currency reforms later pushed by Populists.[70]

Reuben Kolb lost the 1892 election despite unified support from the two reform parties and the endorsement of the Republican executive committee. Historians contend that Kolb's defeat resulted from stolen votes and ballot fraud in Black Belt counties. Outside the Black Belt Kolb led Jones by more than 16,000 votes, but Black Belt counties returned Democratic majorities so large that Jones overcame this deficit. In some Black Belt counties where whites constituted no more than 20 percent of the population, Jones received more than 80 percent of the vote. It was "demonstrable to the dullest understanding," Robert McKee wrote to a friend, that Kolb received a majority of the white vote. McKee, a loyal Democrat since the antebellum period, complained about the failure of Democratic party leaders to understand the economic difficulties facing farmers, and he admitted that he too had bolted his party and voted for Kolb.[71]

The *Birmingham Age-Herald* chastised Black Belters for having "no conception of conditions in North Alabama." The paper's editor admitted that Democrats acted unfairly and called on the Black Belt wing of the party to stop election fraud. White unity, he wrote, had been maintained for the benefit of the Black Belt, but a "feeling of resentment" had grown up in "North Alabama," where people were "impatient of the restraints of conventions and party organizations." Mass defections from the party would continue in the Hill Country unless clean elections were restored. "We lay this matter before our fellow Democrats in the Black Belt for their consideration. They dominate the Democratic party."[72]

Despite his defeat, Kolb lost only four counties in the Hill Country, and he also carried three Tennessee Valley counties. He won every precinct and more than 70 percent of the vote in Chilton County, where the entire Alliance ticket was elected. Kolb won 63 percent in Marshall County, where Judge Street and the Jeffersonian ticket were elected. Benjamin Long's Walker County Republicans supported Kolb who, along with some members of a joint Republican-Populist ticket, won in Walker. Kolb won in Shelby County, but the vote was close, and most local Populist candidates lost by a few votes. Democrats kept the influential probate judge's office. The Populist defeat in Shelby resulted from the efforts of Republican J. D. Hardy, who once again fielded a GOP ticket with himself as candidate for the legislature. He did not win, but he polled more than a quarter of the vote, and this division in non-Democratic ranks led to the defeat of the local Populists.[73]

A. P. Longshore did not seek reelection to the legislature, but in August he accepted the Fourth District Populist nomination for Congress. Like Shelby County's Populists in August's elections, Longshore was also caught between a Democratic nominee and Republican nominee George W. Craig, from the "black and tan" wing of the GOP. The district was composed of both hill and Black Belt counties. Craig was a white native of Selma in Dallas County, but he had been a Radical during Reconstruction, which assured that Longshore would lose votes among blacks. J. D. Hardy refused to support a black-and-tan Republican, and the *People's Advocate* accused Hardy of asking white Republicans to vote for the Democratic candidate.[74]

Craig had little impact outside Shelby County, but the votes he received there caused Longshore to lose Shelby to the Democratic nominee by 149 out of 3,655 votes cast. Longshore received 32 percent of the total district vote, and Craig received only 7 percent, but it was clear that voter fraud led to the Democratic victory. Dallas County, with a black population of more than 80 percent, had the largest number of voters of any county in the Fourth District. Craig, a Reconstruction Republican and supporter of black rights, should have won his home county, yet Dallas reported a whopping 85 percent of its vote for the nominee of the self-proclaimed party of white supremacy. This outcome was absurd, and the *People's Ad-*

vocate charged Democrats with stealing the election, but Longshore did not file a formal contest in Congress.[75]

Shelby County's Populists did not have the luxury of ignoring the Republicans, as their cohorts did in Chilton and Marshall Counties. No Republican ticket had been offered in Chilton County since Reconstruction, and although Judge Street accepted the support of the Republican Seaborn Kennamer in 1892, he could have won without it. However, Shelby County's Populists had to remove J. D. Hardy as the major power in the local GOP and grant Republicans a role in a governing coalition because the elections pointed unmistakably toward Populist fusion with Republicans as the only feasible strategy for defeating Democrats. In 1894 a fruitful relationship began between Shelby's Republicans and Populists that led to their joint control of the county for two decades and the end of Hardy's influence. Hardy had little in common with Alliance ideology, and his business interests impelled him toward coalitions with conservative Democrats. In 1892, he admitted that although he would like to see the Democrats lose state elections, he believed Jones would be a better governor than Kolb.[76]

The congressional election in the Hill Country's Seventh District between Democratic congressional nominee William Denson and Cullman County school superintendent W. M. Wood was much closer than the race Longshore lost. Wood, another Populist linked to the independent politics of the early 1880s, ran for the state legislature as an independent in 1882 and was a presidential elector for the Greenback party in 1884. In 1892 he received 46 percent of the Seventh District vote, won his home county of Cullman, took 60 percent in St. Clair County, and led in Winston. Wood received 48 percent of Marshall County's vote without the support of Judge Street or W. M. Coleman. The large vote for Wood in Marshall may have convinced Judge Street and Coleman that they could not continue to be national Democrats and local third-party men. By 1894 they were out of the Democratic party entirely.[77]

Reuben Kolb and leading Jeffersonians stumped the state in the fall campaign, accusing Democrats of election fraud in the state elections, but Kolb did not endorse Populist presidential candidate James B. Weaver until a week before November's election. Despite the belated endorsement, Weaver's 36.6 percent share of Alabama's vote was larger than he received in any other southern state. In the Hill Country he won a majority or plurality in Chilton, St. Clair, Winston, Fayette, and Randolph Counties, exceeded 45 percent of the vote in five other hill counties, and received more than 40 percent in two more. In the Wiregrass and Upcountry the voting turnout was far below that of August's elections. Weaver's strongest Alabama support came from counties with large Republican contingents. Republican chairman R. A. Moseley and the state GOP executive committee endorsed Weaver, who won Winston County, some Black Belt counties, and two Tennessee Valley counties where blacks exceeded 40 percent of the population. Republican support for Weaver left GOP presidential candidate Benjamin Harrison with only 4 percent of Alabama's vote.[78]

A lack of interest in Weaver's candidacy by Kolb voters may have been purely practical. Weaver had no chance of winning, and southern voters viewed the election from a different perspective than their counterparts in the West who had once been Republicans. A Weaver surge in the South could only help Harrison by taking southern electoral votes away from Grover Cleveland. For southern Populists, Harrison was no better than Cleveland. The state Republican committee's endorsement of Weaver signaled that a vote for the Populist was, in effect, a vote for Harrison. Some Populists publicly stated their fear of this Republican strategy in the South.[79]

A. P. Longshore, Lewis Reynolds, and Populist newspapers in their counties did support Weaver and denounce Cleveland before and after the election. In the *People's Advocate*, Longshore argued that Cleveland's victory gave a new lease on life to a national banking system that sucked money from the South and West into "the coffers of the Eastern Capitalist." When an economic depression hit the nation in late 1893 and Cleveland called for the demonetization of silver as a remedy, Longshore's prediction seemed confirmed. The president's actions led Lewis Reynolds to write in the *Clanton Banner* that he felt sorry for "some of our Cleveland free silver Democrats." Longshore and Reynolds were not tepid reformers or reluctant Populists, and they had no residual affection for the party of white supremacy, but some historians cannot accept the notion that nineteenth-century southerners of any kind had the capacity to break out of the mental or cultural boundaries prescribed by the Redeemers, Bourbons, or "old captains" who ran southern Democratic politics. Even if southern Populists did make such a break, these commentators believe that a reactionary mentality or a subconscious conservatism lurked just beneath the mental surface of all southerners and that it hampered the reform efforts of the Alliance and Populist movements.[80]

Norman Pollack, citing W. J. Cash's *The Mind of the South* as authority, contends that southern Populists were encased in the same "cultural straight jacket" that held all southern whites. Their strong "language of defiance" against the Democratic party was either a form of "bravado" that hid an innate conservatism or a way of rhetorically "discharging emotion" that grew from a "regional gift for hyperbole" and a "luxuriant dispersion of mental activity" typical of southern whites. Southerners were ingrained with "habits of deference" toward the old captains of the Democratic party, says Pollack, and southern Populists were so distracted by the herculean effort it took just to get people to bolt their old party that they gave insufficient support to radical economic reforms. Pollack admits his "apparent severity" with southern Populists and concedes that they were among the most committed advocates of their party's platform, but he contends that such strong commitments were expressed in blustery, emotional, and insincere behavior. Northwestern Populists were, of course, more sincere and less limited by cultural boundaries.[81]

Pollack's contention that southern Populists were overly emotional and unable to break free of a deferential past is wholly Cashian in origin, assumes a monolithic southern mind, puts Upcountry and lowcountry folk in the same cultural straightjacket, ignores diverse political cultures within southern states, and fails to note that many southerners inherited an ideology as democratic, independent, rebellious, and egalitarian as any in the nation. Pollack's contentions are at odds with recent scholarship, break with his own generally favorable impression of American Populists, and contain a stereotypical description of southern whites not unlike the characterization of southern blacks contained in W. J. Cash's work. Alabama's Upcountry Populists, the region from which they came, and the independent tradition that produced them bore little resemblance to the southern Populist mind or regional political culture described by Pollack.[82]

5 Who Were the Populists, and What Did They Believe?

> Populism developed among people who were deeply rooted in the social
> and economic networks of rural communities, not, as some would have it,
> among isolated and disoriented individuals. . . . The movement . . . did not
> spread among people so ensnared by habits of deference and enthralled by
> the pageantry of politics that they could not imagine freeing themselves.
> . . . Rather, it began among people who possessed as part of their birth-
> right, cultures of protest-patterns of thought and action growing out of
> their own history on the land.[1]
>
> Robert McMath

Historians disagree about what kind of people the Populists were, their
economic and social background, the ideology that motivated them, and
their degree of commitment to reforms pushed by the Farmers' Alliance
and the national People's party.[2] The most significant attempt to define
the character of Alabama's Populists and determine their motivations
comes from Sheldon Hackney in his *Populism to Progressivism in Alabama.* Populists were, he writes:

> only tenuously connected to society by economic function, . . . personal
> relationships, . . . stable community membership, . . . political partici-
> pation, or by psychological identification with the South's distinctive
> myths. Recruited heavily from among the downwardly mobile and
> geographically transient, they were vulnerable to feelings of powerless-
> ness. They were largely superfluous farmers or ineffectively organized
> workers . . . not linked to influential Alabamians by kinship or close as-
> sociation. They tended to come from isolated areas . . . experiencing ex-
> traordinary influxes of population . . . areas with increasingly large con-
> centrations of tenant farmers. . . . Their opportunities for the sort of
> psychological integration with the state's social system that developed
> from long-term personal interaction was limited. Populists also tended
> to come from the ranks and regions of Alabama life where the Old

South, the Lost Cause, and the New South were myths with very little resonance.[3]

The top men in Alabama's third parties were motivated by "restless aspiration," writes Hackney, "linked to experience with failure." Populist leaders "at a lower level were recruited from social strata below that of comparable Democratic leaders," and in the eyes of the "better element" of society they were "nobodies" who only entered politics in the late 1880s or early 1890s.[4]

Hackney's assertion that Populism was strong in Alabama counties that were experiencing growing tenancy rates and huge influxes of new people has been confirmed. In these counties the number of farms increased and their size decreased, and making a living from them grew more difficult. Counties suffering most from the downturn in the farm economy were a logical place to find people ripe for revolt.[5] However, Hackney portrays Populists as existing at the outermost rim of community and society, outside social acceptance and beyond consideration as serious people by rational and sober community leaders. Populists were failures and crackpots with foolish or irrational ideas, who dealt with deep status resentments and other private insecurities by attacking society's leaders.[6]

Contrary to Hackney's contentions, Upcountry Populist leaders who can be identified at the "lower level" were rooted in their communities, related to community leaders by blood and association, and committed to the preservation of their values and their society. The communities in which they lived were often stable and had few transients. Farm tenancy might be an index of Populist strength in some counties, but the economic crisis in the Hill Country was more complex than that. It cut across class lines and led small, middle, and big farmers alike into the protest movement. Far more Unionists and outright opponents of the Confederacy were found in the Upcountry than in other areas, but most Populist leaders there had been loyal to the "Lost Cause," and their service to it rivaled that of their Democratic opponents.

Hill Country Populists were steeped in the ideas, fears, myths, hopes, and dreams of the society in which they and their families had lived for many decades. They argued that it was elitist Democrats, not Populists, who departed from the widely accepted democratic and egalitarian ethos of their political culture. Far from providing the acid to dissolve their communities, Populists fought instead to preserve the older, more settled, less materialistic society that had nourished their ancestors. Some Populist politicians were probably failures operating on the periphery of society, but that was rarely the case in Chilton, Etowah, Marshall, St. Clair, or Shelby Counties. "Lower level" third-party leaders did not come from the "lower strata" of society, but from the same broad middle class that produced Democratic party leaders.

All Populist officials elected in Chilton County in 1892 were born during the antebellum period, and although Chilton had not been a county before the Civil War, seven of ten men elected on the Populist ticket lived all of their lives on land that became part of the county. Six served in the Confederate army. All had been engaged in the same occupation for many years, and most raised extensive families in the county. Seven were full- or part-time farmers, but the group included a postmaster, a public school teacher, and a gin owner, and one had been the county surveyor of Elmore County before holding the same job in Chilton. The school teacher, one of three Populist officials not a Chilton native, graduated from the University of Tennessee, lived briefly in South Carolina, and came to Chilton County in 1888. He might have been a transient, but he was certainly not on the fringes of his society. Nine of these men had not held public office before, but Probate Judge Riley Honeycutt had served two terms as county tax collector. One officeholder did admit that he had once been a Republican.[7]

In St. Clair County the profile was similar. Five of seven Jeffersonian-Populist officeholders elected in St. Clair in 1892 were lifelong county residents. State representative W. S. Forman, son of a former Democratic legislator, was in the real estate business and had been mayor of Springville. Probate Judge A. G. Watson, a former school teacher, had served "several terms" as the Democratic county tax collector. Three of the seven officials had been in the Confederate army, and Watson lost an arm in the war. J. W. Box, the Populist tax collector and member of the state Populist executive committee, was the brother of Leroy Box, a longtime Democratic circuit court judge.[8]

The lives and careers of other Jeffersonian-Populist officials in the Up-country confirm their importance and stability in their society. W. M. Coleman, president of Marshall County's Farmers' Alliance and a Jeffersonian legislator, was a lifelong resident of the county and grandson of James L. Crichter, who served Marshall County in the legislature in the 1860s. Coleman was also a Mason, an Odd Fellow, and a member of the Knights of Pythias. Judge Thomas Atkins Street, the stepson of antebellum politician James L. Sheffield, served in the Confederate army, became a large landowner during the postbellum period, and was three times elected probate judge as a Democrat before switching parties.[9]

Populist legislator Pinkney L. McCall was a school teacher in Etowah County for more than forty years and founder of a successful private academy. W. B. Beeson, another Etowah County Populist legislator, was born in 1829 and spent his entire life in either Etowah or nearby Blount County, except for his time in the Confederate army. He fathered eleven children and sent many of them to college. Even before Beeson became a Populist, one of his sons became a lawyer and mayor of Gadsden, another earned a Ph.D. in chemistry at Johns Hopkins in the nineties, one headed the Marengo County Female Academy, and a fourth was a student at the state college at Auburn. We do not know whether Beeson experienced "failure" as a farmer, but the success of his children does not suggest that their lives were shaped by a resentful or insecure mind.[10]

Doctors, dentists, and lawyers also participated in the third-party movement. Populist state senator James Alpheus Hurst of Etowah County, the son of a noted Upcountry politician, was born in Rockford in Coosa County in 1865 and graduated from the Medical College of Alabama at Mobile. He moved to Walnut Grove in Etowah County where he practiced medicine in the 1890s. Dr. Jonathan S. Hollis of Fayette County practiced medicine while serving as a Populist legislator, and Populist representative R. D. Evans of Clay County was both an ordained Methodist minister and a practicing dentist. Dr. Henry Wilson Harrison, son of Thomas Harrison, the successful planter and Reconstruction sheriff of Shelby County, was a lifelong resident of the county, a graduate of the Mobile medical college, and a practicing physician. Dr. Harrison was an avowed Populist. A. P. Longshore, A. T. Goodwyn, Oliver D. Street, and many others were lawyers.[11]

Several leading Populists were ministers. Riley M. Honeycutt pastored a Baptist church at Jemison. Samuel M. Adams, who was president of the state Farmers' Alliance and chairman of the state Populist party, led Baptist churches in both Bibb and Chilton Counties. Populist T. M. Barbour was born in Tuscaloosa County in 1830, served in both the Mexican war and the Confederate army, and became a Baptist minister in Tuscaloosa after the war.[12]

Roy S. Nolen of Coosa County, John W. Pitts of Shelby County, and John Harvey Wilson of Talladega County were sons of antebellum planter families. Nolen was born in Georgia in 1837 but lived in Coosa County after 1849 and served in the state house of representatives as a Democrat in the early eighties before his election as a Populist in 1892. Wilson, the son of a South Carolinian who came to Talladega County in 1836, still owned a portion of his family plantation in the late 1890s. He had also served in the Confederate army and was briefly a prisoner of war. After the war he became a farmer and saw mill operator, in addition to serving as a justice of the peace and superintendent of Talladega County schools before his election to the legislature as an Alliance Democrat during the 1888–89 session. Later, he was secretary and treasurer of the state Farmers' Alliance.[13]

The life and career of A. P. Longshore breaks with the notion that Populists were motivated by feelings of resentment that grew from "experience with failure." Longshore was no aristocrat, but he associated with young men who were the leadership class of southern society. In 1873 he matriculated at Washington and Lee College in Lexington, Virginia, a gathering place for the children of the southern upper class. Because of a lack of funds he only stayed one year, but records in the college archives show that he enrolled in courses in Latin, Greek, mathematics, and modern languages and that his grades were consistently in the top quarter of his class. Longshore learned he could compete with the leading sons of his region. For his time, Longshore was a well-educated young man and, if his grades were an indication, a self-assured and hard-working one. When he dropped out of school for lack of funds it signified no failure on his part and did not derail his spirit. He returned home, worked as a public school teacher, read law in the office of a distinguished attorney, and was admitted to the bar in 1878.[14]

Rank-and-file Populist voters came from isolated rural areas experiencing economic upheavals, as Hackney asserts. Thomas Atkins Street, Lewis Reynolds, and A. P. Longshore all expressed the view that small farmers, not wealthy or professional classes, were their voters. Precinct voting returns confirm their analysis. Their support came primarily from the most rural voters, and they usually lost the larger towns. Longshore and Reynolds assailed courthouse "rings" and professional men in the towns who opposed reform, yet census records of staunch Populist precincts raise additional questions about Hackney's thesis that rank-and-file Populists were transients from unstable communities. An analysis of residential persistence in these places sends contradictory messages, but it does not sustain Hackney's contentions.

The Chilton County town of Jemison, which produced Riley M.

Honeycutt and Lewis H. Reynolds, gave majorities to independents in the eighties, backed Populists in the nineties, supported Republicans from 1900 to 1912, and was not an unstable place. A majority of male heads of household living in the Jemison precinct in 1880 were still there in 1900. The same was true of Spring Creek in Shelby County, which gave more than 80 percent of its vote to Populist candidates in the 1894 and 1896 elections. These Populists were committed to their land, their farms, their families, and their neighbors. The Populist precinct of Friendship in Marshall County first became anti-Democratic after its residents voted for James L. Sheffield for governor on the Greenback ticket in 1882. It did not show a majority of residents persisting from 1880 to 1900. Also, large numbers of people from other states moved into the precinct in this period. It was an area in flux. Community instability, marginality, tenuousness, or transience may have influenced voters in Friendship to become Populists, but no evidence suggests that this precinct was a prototype for Populist communities.[15]

People in Upcountry counties reacted against the economic forces that they feared were abusing them, not by picking up and moving away or by rejecting the society in which they lived, but by joining the Farmers' Alliance. That act, in itself, was one of community. Alliancemen reached out to others in trouble to meet and act together. They assisted each other in "bearing the burdens and crosses of life." People shunned by society or who had no stake in the community and no interest in its preservation would not have unified with neighbors against common foes. The Alliance, like the Masonic Lodges that proliferated in the rural South, had rituals in which members referred to each other as "brother" or "sister." Parades and secret passwords marked the unity of the members.[16] Thus, Upcountry revolts were led by people who hoped to preserve the life-style and independence their families had always known.

In Black Belt counties, "lower strata" farmers may have been marginal or transient people who were beneath the large planters that dominated the political and economic life of that region, but Upcountry "community" or "society" differed greatly from the Black Belt. It was a small farmer society, more egalitarian and less deferential than the lowcountry. In the Upcountry it was those who failed to associate with the small farmers who were outside the dominant society. Politicians who did not consider the viewpoints of small farmers were in serious political trouble by the nineties. Small Upcountry farmers found strength in their joint commitment to common political and social values. When the postwar cash-nexus economy created economic-political elites, small farmers reacted against them. In Shelby County, revolts against the Democratic party in the eighties and nineties were at least partly stimulated by longtime residents who resented the subversion of settled forms of life by an elite group of capitalist interlopers who sought to change the economic, social, and political power structure of the community.[17]

Farm tenancy was not the primary cause of Populism in the Hill Country. In Chilton and Marshall Counties farm tenancy grew rapidly between 1880 and 1890, but in many counties with strong Populist movements, that was not the case. In St. Clair County, tenants increased from 371 to only 404 in the decade, and the percentage of tenants in Shelby County actually declined. From 1890 to 1900, farm tenancy expanded in all hill counties, but factors other than tenancy made the Farmers' Alliance powerful by 1890.[18]

Farm owners were as likely as tenants to be angry about their circumstances. They were losing their grip on their land and farms and often had to sell land or mortgage their property. Even large farmers such as John W. Pitts of Shelby County could see the possibility of disaster looming at the end of the eighties. The total number of farm owners in Shelby County hardly changed between 1880 and 1890, but those who owned farms of more than one hundred acres fell from 715 to 581. In St. Clair County farm owners cultivating farms of less than 100 acres rose from 501 to 675, and the average size of farms there fell from 147 to 132 acres. In Chilton County the number of farm owners with farms less than one hundred acres went from 466 to 634. Fayette County farms were larger than those in most hill counties, averaging 163 acres in 1890, but a decade earlier they had averaged 198 acres, and farms larger than 500 acres in Fayette fell from 102 to 69.[19]

A comparison of Populist counties to the one hill county that never gave a majority to a Populist gubernatorial candidate or state legislator is revealing. Marion County was staunchly Democratic even though it had once been home to many Unionist-Republicans. Tenancy rates remained almost constant there between 1880 and 1890, and farms averaged 166 acres in 1890, the largest in north Alabama. A majority of farms in Shelby, Chilton, and Marshall Counties were smaller than one hundred acres in 1890, but 63 percent of Marion's farms were larger than that. The economic misery was simply not as widespread in Marion County, but the farm economy was not the sole factor in political decision making.[20]

Chilton County farm family, ca. 1900 (courtesy of the Clanton Chamber of Commerce and Helen Carter Teel)

Voters were also influenced to join third parties by the arrogant way in which local Democratic leaders responded to the economic crisis and to political competition from Alliance leaders. When Alliancemen seized control of hill county Democratic parties from 1888 to 1892, elite Democrats reacted by attempting to manipulate election results, trying to get state Democratic authorities to interfere on their behalf, and using callow racial charges. "Permit me to remind you," wrote an ex-Populist to a Democratic friend, "that one of the chief elements of strength in the People's Party was its hostility to old party leaders."[21]

Deep sectional resentments combined with this dislike of party leaders. Upcountry Democratic leaders often cooperated with the Black Belt–dominated state party and held influence in the party because of their connections with lowcountry leaders. White supremacy was imperative for Black Belt whites, and they pushed the Upcountry toward white unity. The *Birmingham Age-Herald* pointed out in 1892 that this desire for white unity made it necessary to discriminate against dissident factions, which inevitably led to elite control and to growing disaffection in north Alabama. Black Belters dominated state Democratic conventions by apportioning delegates among counties on the basis of the number of Democratic votes in state elections, which gave the Black Belt an advantage because of its manipulation of black voters. Lowland control of the party led to efforts to eliminate conflict and dissent. Hill Country Democrats who believed that the party of their antebellum fathers had stood for the "people," or for small farmers, chafed under this apparent fraud by the lowland leaders.[22]

Alliance leaders such as Riley Honeycutt fought this hierarchy before the Alliance arrived. Fair nominations and elections had been important to these rebels since the late seventies, when Democrats made the first attempt to disfranchise dissenters. There was good reason to fear that the state Democratic party would do whatever it took to control ballots. Unfortunately, commentators claim that Populists who seemed more interested in election reform than in economic change were insufficiently radical. A "free ballot and a fair count" did not promise reform of the economic system, yet economic reforms could not be achieved without basic election reforms. A "free ballot," said Honeycutt, was more important to the long-term interests of his community than free silver.[23]

This preoccupation with voting processes leads historians to contend that Populists had no serious "ideology." Sheldon Hackney asserts that Populists had no beliefs "that would connect their sad economic plight" to "a train of causation leading back to the political process." They only had "conspiracy theories" and needed ideas to give "cohesion and direction to their unformed yearnings for change." Historians who do believe that Populists had serious or complex political ideas too often center their studies on the 1880s and 1890s and portray Populist ideology as simply a product of economic circumstances or Farmers' Alliance lectures. Support for Alliance measures did not create, but merely reflected, an ideology. The subtreasury or government ownership of railroads were remedies, and although support for remedies often grew from what Lawrence

Goodwyn describes as an "ethos," this ethos did not suddenly appear just in time to bolster the remedial proposals offered by Alliance lecturers. It formed a long time before the existence of the Alliance. We must look for a Populist mind that evolved over a period of several decades.[24]

Influential Jeffersonian-Populist leaders were born, reared, educated, and had their earliest memories of politics before the Civil War. Reuben Kolb, Philander Morgan, John W. Pitts, Roy Nolen, T. M. Barbour, W. B. Beeson, T. A. Street, Riley Honeycutt, and many others all reached manhood before the war. Nineteenth-century rural society handed down political ideas, party identification, and attitudes toward American political history from one generation to the next. Ineluctably, Longshore, Reynolds, and T. A. Street were influenced by those who grew to manhood between 1825 and 1850. In Street's case, James L. Sheffield was a guiding figure for half a century. Antebellum ideas about political economy played an integral role in postbellum Upcountry politics.[25]

One historian of northern politics demonstrates that an antebellum political socialization process kept postbellum politicians in states such as Indiana, Wisconsin, and Maryland loyal to beliefs and prejudices of their prewar youth. A recent study of Mississippi politics also confirms the persistence of antebellum ideas in the period after the war. The determination that Populists "had no ideology" before the advent of the Farmers' Alliance or had deferential or irrational ideas suffers from a failure to analyze attitudes prevalent in Upcountry political culture well before the 1880s and from a failure to connect these older attitudes to the actions of third-party men. If one believes, like W. J. Cash, that southerners had no minds or were culturally encased or so obsessed with race that nothing else mattered, then one may conveniently avoid an analysis of ideology and simply explain Upcountry political revolts as the product of mental pathology, social "anomie," bigotry, anger, fear, resentment, or "feelings of impotence."[26]

Upcountry Alabamians were the inheritors of a "historic ideology of opposition to privilege and power" familiar in the South since the age of Jackson. Sheldon Hackney contends that Populists advocated an antebellum-style "passive" or "referee" state. Populists did fear a powerful central government and the effect of government involvement in the economy, but they were less interested in keeping government small than in keeping governmental power out of the hands of the wrong people. Populists updated the ideology of their antebellum Democratic forbears when the rise of gigantic corporations and monopolies in the Gilded Age made the use of government necessary to protect "the people" from depredations committed against them by the new and impersonal economic forces.[27]

Vital connections existed, as some historians note, between Populists and the Jacksonian ideology that was "orthodoxy" in antebellum Alabama's Hill Country. If Jacksonian ideas faded in some places by the 1850s, they were revived in Alabama during that decade by an ideological battle over the funding of railroads. Jacksonian ideas reemerged in the 1870s when writers such as Robert McKee, a product of Kentucky's antebellum Democratic party, assailed attempts by Alabama and the national government to fund railroads as raids on the treasury by the financially privileged. Governor John A. Winston, who opposed the use of state money for railroads in the late 1850s, was referred to by the press organ of the Alabama Jeffersonian party in 1896 as "Alabama's Old Hickory." If "primal honor" or other antebellum "mentalities" were alive and well in postbellum Alabama, historians cannot overlook the survival of a Jacksonian ethos deeply embedded in Hill Country culture.[28]

Jacksonians and Populists feared the same enemies, made the same arguments about how society functioned, wanted the same ends, and used strikingly similar rhetoric. They were both pro-producer, biased toward values inherent in an agrarian culture, believed that banks should not control the currency, argued that labor created economic value, feared the power of impersonal financial institutions, and wanted political power in the hands of the widest number of white people. Efforts to limit democracy, they thought, came from forces whose economic privileges could best be protected by restricting the franchise. The Farmers' Alliance organized Upcountry farmers, gave them specific progovernment remedies, and made them bold, but it did not furnish them with a political consciousness or ideology. Alliance lecturers found fertile ground for their ideas in north Alabama because people there were already attuned to Alliance rhetoric and aims.[29]

On August 2, 1893, A. P. Longshore began to run a series of articles in the *People's Advocate* titled "The Old and the New," which compared the Democratic party of "fifty years ago and the so-called of today." The articles reprinted a lengthy speech made by Jacksonian political theorist Theophilus Fiske in 1848. Portions of the speech ran for three successive weeks in Longshore's paper, and it was, said the *Advocate*, "Full of Genuine Populist Ideas." Fiske assailed an aristocratic social system, the power of banks to issue money that put people into debt, the insidious influence of a credit system that made people dependent, the power that corporations had "wrested from the people," the granting of "exclusive privileges" to corporations, the amorality of the marketplace, and the monopoly of land by a favored few.[30]

Fiske advocated a government that not only fought monopolies but also limited the amount of land that one person could own, gave wealth to "those who toil," made the "right of suffrage independent of taxation," strictly construed the Constitution, created strict economy in government, selected its officials without the "intervention of caucuses, delegates, conferences, or conventions," and placed strict limits on the authority of creditors to collect debts. Not even Fiske believed in a mere "passive" or "referee state." He wanted government to protect producers from the parasitic forces of organized wealth, and that is what Populists intended to do.[31]

Populists supported new and expensive government programs for struggling farmers at the same time they adhered to Jacksonian ideas against using the tax money of the many for the benefit of the few. The same mentality that backed the subtreasury system opposed new internal improvements programs. The editor of the St. Clair County *Ashville Southern Alliance,* a committed supporter of the subtreasury and the entire Alliance program, was appalled that the federal government might build a canal through Nicaragua with money from the sale of government bonds. When Alabama's senator John Tyler Morgan proposed such a scheme, the St. Clair editor censured him. "We are not opposed to the canal being built, in fact we are in favor of it, but we are opposed to the government saddling a hundred million dollars of bonded debt on the people."[32]

The same A. P. Longshore who thundered that "the way to avoid railroad ownership of the government is to have government ownership of the railroads" ran an editorial by Robert McKee in the first edition of the *People's Advocate* that criticized a congressional rivers and harbors bill because it would take tax money from the many and use it for the benefit of the few. There was no inconsistency in Longshore's attitudes. Populists opposed programs that benefitted big corporations, Wall Street bondholders, and others at the economic apex of American society. They supported initiatives that benefitted those who needed help, or "the people," narrowly defined by Populists as the nation's producers or workers. Their ultimate fear was that those in control of the nation's money would get control of the government and use their power to perpetuate an economic system already fixed against the people. Like Jacksonians, Alabama's third-party men believed that monopolies flourished because of government favoritism and that corporate privilege grew from the ability of the wealthy to exercise political influence.[33]

Alabama Populists realized that their movement was not merely the result of Alliance organizing but also the outgrowth of two decades of dissent against a party that had abandoned its anti-monopolistic, anti-bank traditions. The post–Civil War Democratic party no longer represented the principles and people it was created to protect and had become the handmaiden of powerful moneyed interests, but Populists had kept the old faith. A Shelby County Populist sent an "exposition of principles" to the *People's Advocate* in which he argued that "those who still adhere to the old Democratic party" should study its principles, and they would find that they were in accord with those of the People's party.[34]

Southern Bourbons sold out the party to a financial elite after the Civil War, argued Populists, and Democrats had not been on the right track since. For "twenty-five years," said a *People's Advocate* editorial in July 1892, the Democratic party had "failed to make good on almost every promise it has made to the people, and its leaders have almost been a unit on the side of monopoly and against the laboring man." The party boasted that it was the "champion of the poor and oppressed," but for "the past twenty-five years its representatives in congress have been voting with great unanimity to rivet the chains of serfdom more tightly upon the toilers of the country." It was the mythical party of Jackson that party bolters hoped to restore in the "Populist moment." Even the more conservative third-party leaders were wedded to this notion. When he left the Democratic party, Judge Thomas A. Street described himself to a critical Democratic editor as a "Jacksonian Democrat," implying that his old party was no longer Jacksonian and that the men who were should leave it. The preamble to the Jeffersonian party platform called for the "restoration" of the Democratic party to the principles of its founders.[35]

Alabama Populists, like those in many other states, sounded "like religious enthusiasts" of the "restorationist traditions in American religion, who believed that by shunning the old churches they were restoring Christianity to its original purity." When Democrat Grover Cleveland defended the national banking system and the gold standard, Alabama's third-party leaders pilloried him with references from their Jacksonian view of American history. State Farmers' Alliance president Samuel Adams wrote that Cleveland Democrats were for all things "for which the Democratic party was organized to overthrow; the system that Jackson was elected to overturn." A St. Clair County man wrote that Cleveland was elected as a "Jackson Democrat," but had surrendered to the "very influence the crushing out of which sixty years ago made Jackson's name immortal." Another correspondent wrote that congressmen who professed "to be Democrats" but who perpetuated "bank currency" violated Jacksonian principles. Jackson ordered men who supported the issuing power of banks "to be kicked out of the party."[36]

In December 1893, in response to Cleveland's actions in restoring the gold standard, the Populist editor of the Chilton County *Clanton Banner* printed that portion of Andrew Jackson's farewell address that denounced the "moneyed power" and drew a distinction between the power of the wealthy and the lack of power among the "agricultural, mechanical and laboring classes" who were "the people." A. P. Longshore commonly used rhetoric similar to that of the antebellum Jacksonians when he stated that he was committed to the "farmers and mechanics" in politics and that the national banking system was a "hideous monster."[37]

What Populists believed about their history had an impact on their public stances. They referred to Thomas Jefferson as their hero and described themselves as Jeffersonians. This historical view of Jefferson was filtered through a "Jacksonian understanding" of American history, for Jacksonians thought Jefferson was democratic and egalitarian. Jacksonian Democrats and Populists characterized American history as a dual struggle of Jeffersonians against Hamiltonians, symbolic of the struggle of the privileged against the weak and corporations against agrarian masses.[38]

On July 2, 1896, the *Clanton Banner* printed a speech on its front page by Mississippi Populist Frank Burkitt, who stated that the Democratic party of his fathers was not as much the party of Jefferson as it was of Jackson. Burkitt, who understood that Jackson had moved the country away from the elite politics of gentlemen who dominated the early republic, contended that the Populist stance on the "financial question" was identical to that of Jefferson and Jackson but that Jackson had made the Democratic party a "people's party." Jackson's attacks on national banks were delivered "under precisely the same conditions and for precisely the same purposes that inspired honest, patriotic members of both the old parties to assemble at Omaha, Nebraska on Independence day, 1892." Burkitt claimed to be an heir of the Jacksonian tradition, but he endorsed government ownership of the railroads and saw no inconsistency.[39]

Like Jacksonians, Populists did not support equality for blacks in Alabama, but Populist editors did support the right of blacks to vote and opposed efforts to discriminate against them. Both A. P. Longshore and Joseph Manning supported the inclusion of a black delegate to the national Populist convention of 1892, and Longshore praised the black delegate in an editorial. At the 1894 Populist state convention, Manning called for the support of the political rights of all black citizens. In the early years of the twentieth century, Manning joined the famed "Niagara movement" that founded the proequality National Association for the Advancement of Colored People, but Longshore supported the decision of the 1894 Jeffersonian state convention to bar black Republican leader William Stevens from their meeting. Populists also adopted a plank in their 1894 platform that called for the creation of a separate homeland for blacks.[40]

In 1893 Longshore published editorials against the adoption of a state constitutional amendment that would have restricted funds going to Negro schools. The proposal tried to shift responsibility for funding schools from the state to the counties. The *People's Advocate* argued that the state should properly fund all public schools, particularly those in "poor districts" that did not have enough revenue at the local level. "We believe that the state should educate all the children of the state" and that discrimination against Negroes would simply lead to "other discriminations" until there was "no telling" where it "would end." The same Longshore who took this position on education assailed "Negro loafers" and used crude racial stereotypes to show his solidarity with whites.[41]

Longshore publicly appealed to black voters to cast their ballots for Populists because such votes were in the political and economic interests of all of the economic underclass, but rhetoric aimed at blacks by Populists seemed calculated to get their votes rather than to benefit their lives. Populist editors engaged in running battles with Democratic papers in which they accused each other of receiving the most support from blacks. Longshore's *People's Advocate,* for instance, asked for support from black voters, yet condemned Democrats for doing the same thing. This inconsistency grew out of the dual desire to both win elections and placate the racial fears of the white majority, but the overall stance of Populists on racial questions was more tolerant than that of the Democrats. Populists were racists, but that charge could have been made about every white-dominated political party in the United States in 1892.[42]

Anyone who left the Democratic party to vote for Populists or Jeffersonians said, in effect, that white unity was less important than other issues. Democrats who sympathized with Populist aims but would not bolt their old party were usually constrained by race. Editorial writer Robert McKee, who supported the Farmers' Alliance and voted for third-party candidate Reuben Kolb in 1892 and 1894 despite a personal distaste for Kolb, brought this crucial distinction into focus in his correspondence with Senator John Tyler Morgan. Morgan and McKee had similar economic views, but the senator was appalled by the revelation that McKee was a Kolbite. If men like McKee voted for Kolb, white men would be split into warring factions that would ultimately drive them into the "arms of the Negroes." This "fearful exigency," believed Morgan, was the prime reason for Democratic party loyalty. McKee disagreed.[43]

McKee was a white supremacist, but the economic component in politics and honest elections were as important to him as race. He had been an antebellum Jacksonian Democrat, and long before Populism he assailed Democrats who did not stand up for producers against railroad magnates, eastern bankers, and bondholders. His criticism of the party in the 1870s was so strident that he was accused of trying to split it, but he consistently argued that Democrats must not allow race solidarity to blind them to issues such as tax rates, government debts, mortgage debts, wages, working conditions, corporate privilege, and the problems of farmers. McKee berated a Black Belt Democratic congressman when Grover Cleveland endorsed the gold standard and the national banking system. "The newspapers and the big and little bosses of your own wing of the party," he wrote, "have gone off with Cleveland in opposition to the most important article of the old Democratic creed."[44]

McKee did not learn his priorities from the Alliance. They were part of an ideology he had adhered to for a long time. Third-party leaders were aware of their political kinship to him. In 1891, when he wrote pro-Alliance editorials for a north Alabama newspaper, McKee received praise from Thomas Atkins Street, who wrote that he saved McKee's editorials. A. P. Longshore reprinted and cited McKee's editorial views.[45] When Democratic congressman William Denson of the Hill Country's Seventh District faced another challenge from the Populists and wanted the nomination of both Democratic and Populist parties, he wrote to McKee, who lived on the district's southern edge. Denson knew his man and did not make race the basis of his appeal. The struggle in American history, he wrote, had always been between:

> monarchy and Democracy, imperialism and free institutions, privileged classes vs. the masses, money vs. the people, capital vs. labor . . . doctrines of Hamilton vs. the principles of Jefferson . . . high taxes, high cost of living and low rate of wages, all to oppress labor and to establish a moneyed aristocracy, against low taxes, low cost of living and high rate of wages, the doctrine of Jefferson.
>
> National banks, funding schemes and protection to create and foster trusts and combines, aggregate money in the hands of a few, and then oppression of the masses, this is Hamiltonianism.[46]

Denson did not, as Sheldon Hackney charges, state a conspiracy theory of history, but affirmed a Jacksonian view of the Jeffersonian tradition similar to the one advanced by Frank Burkitt. The "dualistic" political struggle Denson depicted had often been described by McKee and was not unlike the one later delineated by progressive historian Vernon Louis Parrington, who was a Populist. Four months after his letter to McKee, Denson also thought it necessary to inform Thomas Atkins Street that he was for "popular democracy as taught by Jefferson and Jackson."[47]

Unlike McKee, Longshore and Lewis Reynolds did support the reform remedies in the Populist platform, but that difference should not obscure the common ideological heritage they shared with the Jacksonian Democrat James L. Sheffield, the Jeffersonian party leader Thomas A. Street, and the dubious Kolbite Robert McKee. They all drew from a "language of social criticism that was steeped in the discourse of pre–Civil War America" yet "focused on the ills of an industrializing nation." Nevertheless, they were not "isolated" from the "mainstream of national reform ideas." Their ideological tradition led them to believe that capitalist greed, monopolies, the northeastern money power, and elite control of elections threatened the independence of small farmers and the egalitarian democracy of white men. If they disagreed on remedies, they all agreed that wealth producers had to unite against the forces of privilege and financial power.[48]

6 Triumph, Tragedy, and Disillusionment, 1893–1898

> For a great party with almost two million votes, we occupy a most humiliating attitude as we bow the knee before the Democratic throne. . . . I feel inclined to join some sort of movement to relieve ourselves of our present humiliating attitude. . . . We are all at sea.[1]
>
> Congressman Milford W. Howard (1896)

The years from 1893 to 1896 were a time of confusion in Alabama's party politics. Jeffersonian leaders could not decide whether they were genuine third-party men or just Democrats on temporary leave from their old party until it agreed to treat them fairly and return to first principles. Populists, stretched between the demands of practical politics and their commitments to national Populist party programs, nurtured coalitions with Republicans and Jeffersonians while publicly minimizing their devotion to the radical economic reforms proposed by their party.[2]

Some Alabama Democrats tried to lure third-party men back into their fold by sounding Populistic. They advocated free silver, assailed corporate power, called for fair elections, and damned President Cleveland as a tool of northeastern bankers. Silver was the rallying cry of Congressman William H. Denson and Senator John Tyler Morgan, both Democrats who faced reelection battles in 1894 and sought to expand their political base. A silver-based reform movement also threatened to seize the national Democratic party, and although free silver was the minimum demand of Populists, many Jeffersonians were drawn toward the silver Democrats. Efforts by Democrats to capture the reform mantle posed a genuine threat to Populists because the new Democratic rhetoric sounded increasingly like the moderate reform statements of such men as Reuben Kolb.[3]

Republicans learned that their party could not win statewide elections by itself. Their best hope for defeating Democrats lay in cooperation with third parties, but some GOP leaders thought cooperation insufficient. At state and county levels they demanded places on the reform tickets, which

led to conflict among third-party men, some of whom feared that asso-
ciating with Republicans would truncate Populism and hand the Democrats an effective issue. The GOP was identified with gold, high tariffs,
and Negroes, despite its lily-white wing, and Reconstruction was not a
dim memory. Third-party leaders such as Judge Street had actively opposed Radical Reconstruction in the 1870s, but President Cleveland's
commitment to gold, his use of the army to break the famed Chicago
Pullman strike in 1893, and the depression of 1893–94 made the Republican party attractive by contrast. In the 1970s, a woman who grew up in
Shelby County in the 1890s still recalled the horror of what she described
as the "Cleveland depression."[4]

Republicans cemented relationships with some third-party men by
calling for an end to election fraud, an issue that grew in significance
when Democrats in the legislature, fearing that the third-party might actually win in 1894, passed the Sayre election law. The Sayre law, initiated
by Black Belters and opposed by Populists, required voter registration by
a particular date, forced voters to bring registration certificates to the
polls, stipulated that the ballot could contain no party names or initials,
compelled printers to list candidates in alphabetical order, allowed printers to list offices in any order they desired, and specified that the governor
would appoint all voter registrars and poll officials. Populists and Republicans were not even guaranteed observers at the polls, and only officials
appointed by Democrats could assist illiterate voters.[5]

The new law made it possible for state and local elections to be totally
controlled by the Democratic party, and it assured that voter fraud could
not be discovered. The law aimed to disfranchise hill and Wiregrass whites
and allowed officials to manipulate Negro voters in counties where they
needed them and to disfranchise them in places where they did not. It
would not help to disfranchise Negroes, observed one Democratic editor,
unless the "corresponding ignorance of North Alabama" was also excised.
An Alliance editor warned that the votes of "mountaineer" whites were
threatened.[6]

Populists and Jeffersonians attacked the law. One of the most publicized arguments against it came in 1893 from the pen of Oliver Day Street
of Marshall County, then a twenty-five-year-old Guntersville attorney,
who wrote a legal brief that questioned the law's constitutionality. Some
newspapers that published excerpts from Street's argument confused the
young attorney with his father T. A. Street and referred to him as "Judge
Street." The law's validity was actually irrelevant because it would un-

doubtedly be upheld by Democratic judges, but it presented a major problem for third-party men who faced the 1894 elections.[7]

Populists and Jeffersonians divided on the strategy they should use in the 1894 statewide campaign. The Jeffersonian executive committee made a surprise offer to the state Democratic executive committee that called for a "white primary" in which all white voters would participate. Jeffersonian leaders believed that excluding blacks would stop the disfranchisement of Upcountry and Wiregrass whites, allow Kolb to win such a primary, and reunify the Democratic party. Rank-and-file Jeffersonians who supported the programs and success of the national Populist party were dubious about this gambit. St. Clair County editor W. S. Griffith, an Alliance lecturer affiliated with the Jeffersonians, refused to endorse the reunification of the Democratic party.[8]

After the state Democratic executive committee rejected the olive branch, the Jeffersonian committee offered yet another joint primary proposal, and it too was rejected. Populist leaders were horrified, and a Chilton County Populist editor pointed out that Jeffersonians were not part of a national political party like the Populists. Populist participation in a joint primary with Democrats would betray the national People's party. Some Populists considered rejecting Reuben Kolb and selecting their own candidate for governor. Kolb did not support the national Populist program and had made the Jeffersonian party his own personal instrument. When the Populist state convention met on February 8, 1894, in Birmingham, delegates threatened to walk out rather than cooperate with the Jeffersonians. Convention chairman A. P. Longshore and Clay County Populist Joseph Manning successfully urged the delegates to maintain their arrangement with Kolb's party. The Populist delegates then met jointly with the Jeffersonians, who had held their own convention nearby, and the two parties unanimously chose Kolb again as the gubernatorial nominee.[9]

This unity took place despite the fact that the Jeffersonians had adopted a controversial platform. In addition to supporting free silver, a graduated income tax, fair elections, and the abolition of the convict-leasing system, they supported "a tariff for revenue" to protect the jobs of those who worked in "mines, mills, and factories." Democratic newspapers that accused the Jeffersonians of selling out to Republicans knew that the tariff plank was included out of deference to lily-white Republican chairman R. A. Moseley, who once again got his executive committee to endorse Kolb and the reform ticket. A few days before the August election, Moseley spoke in Shelby County and endorsed both county and statewide Populist-Jeffersonian candidates.[10]

In 1888, 1890, and 1892, Shelby's Republicans had refused to support Alliance Democrats or Populists against the Graham-Leeper Democratic faction. Republicans who voted for Kolb in 1892 either refused to vote in local races or voted for their nominee, J. D. Hardy, for state representative, which allowed a Democrat to win the legislative seat and cost the Populists control of the probate judge's office and the county commission. In 1894 a different situation prevailed. Statewide cooperation between lily-white Republicans and third-party men carried over to local races. Even J. D. Hardy supported Kolb, and Republican voters backed all third-party candidates. Kolb received 58 percent of Shelby's vote, and the Populists won all contested county offices.[11]

A. P. Longshore did not seek reelection, and G. B. Deans, a Virginia native who came to Shelby County in the 1880s and who had been a member of the county Democratic executive committee, won the county's legislative seat as a Populist. Deans became a leader of the state Populist party and Longshore's rival for control of the party in Shelby County. Despite his absence on the ticket, Longshore campaigned for the Kolb ticket and toured the state in support of Populists and Jeffersonians for Congress. A Lamar County Democratic editor reported that in a speech in that county "Longshore delivered himself a tirade against national banks and the Democratic party for an hour." He blasted President Cleveland for his opulent life-style, particularly for his use of expensive carriages. The Lamar editor wrote that Longshore was "conceded to be the ablest man the Jeffersonians have."[12]

Strikes by organized labor in 1894 led to greater tension in Alabama politics. Seven thousand coal miners, led by the United Mine Workers, went on strike in the Birmingham area in April. Bombings and other violence occurred in Walker and Jefferson Counties. By July, the Chicago Pullman Palace Car strike spread to railroad workers in Birmingham. When Governor Jones sent troops to break the coal strike, Populists endorsed the workers' demands, assailed Jones's actions, and argued that Kolb would have backed the strikers. Mine workers endorsed Kolb, which probably helped in mine-rich Walker County where Reuben Kolb was victorious again.[13]

Marshall County had few miners, but politics there in 1894 was enlivened by Democratic criticism of the county commission, chaired by Judge Thomas A. Street. The commission's Jeffersonian majority, led by

Street, raised property taxes to fund local public services such as schools and roads. A Democratic newspaper and other local Democrats criticized the tax increase, but Street defended it, and his popularity was apparently unaffected. The *Montgomery Advertiser* wrote that a "majority" of the uneducated and illiterate Marshall County voters were "brought up under the Great Street's training" and believed him to be "almost a God." Street held the Jeffersonian-Populist-Republican coalition together in his county. The "question is not whether a particular party shall prevail," said Street, "but whether the individual liberties of the common people are preserved." People should join the Populists and Republicans, said Street, to return "a free ballot and a fair count" to state elections. Kolb received 60 percent of Marshall County's vote, and W. M. Coleman won a second term in the legislature.[14]

Chilton County gave nearly three-quarters of its vote to Kolb and the entire Populist ticket after a campaign that revolved around Democratic charges that the local Populist party had issued an "edict" that required its nominees to endorse publicly the Omaha platform. Local party chairman and Populist state legislator O. M. Mastin, who said he was the first member of the Alabama Farmers' Alliance and was a member of the Knights of Labor, contended that candidates in the Populist primary did not deserve nomination if they did not support the Omaha demands. Mastin, a candidate for reelection to the legislature, had no use for Jeffersonian moderation. Chilton County voters must have agreed.[15]

Populists and Jeffersonians won many county offices by larger percentages than they had managed in 1892, but because of Democratic landslides in Black Belt counties, Kolb's state ticket lost again. Even in the few majority black counties that Kolb won in 1892, the vote was completely reversed. The Sayre law also discouraged Upcountry whites from voting, and even in the hill counties where Kolb got a larger percentage of the vote than in 1892, his total vote fell. In Marshall County the total went from 2,157 votes to only 1,773; in Chilton County the total dropped from 1,785 to 1,242; and in Walker County Kolb received 428 fewer votes than in 1892. In Shelby County Republican cooperation held Kolb's vote steady, but only in St. Clair did he get a significant increase. The total number of statewide votes for both gubernatorial candidates fell from 242,000 to 192,000, and Kolb's total went from 115,522 in 1892 to 83,394 in 1894. Black Republican leader William Stevens, who was excluded from the Jeffersonian convention, endorsed Democratic candidate William C. Oates for governor. Stevens may have damaged the third party in majority black counties, but he was probably less important than the impact of the Sayre act, which worked its magic on voters of both races.[16]

Democracy had not been allowed to operate, and Populists had no method of redress. The law did not allow third parties to contest elections on a fair basis. Legislators refused to pass a contest law when Populists demanded that it be made retroactive to the 1892 election. Contested elections were controlled by Democratic officials who had no intention of allowing Kolb or other renegades to gain office. Frustration among third-party leaders boiled over as some urged the use of force to take over state government, and the fall congressional campaigns were particularly bitter.[17]

Populists had more support in the Seventh Congressional District than in any other, but tensions ran so high there at the end of 1894 that Oliver Street labeled it the "bloody Seventh." The law partner of Populist congressional nominee Milford W. Howard was beaten by a Democratic mob during the campaign. Howard, a self-righteous man with an immense ego and mercurial political views, was a Georgia native who came to Fort Payne in DeKalb County to practice law in 1881 and made money in a brief business boom that centered around the iron ore trade in the late 1880s. Howard was chairman of the DeKalb County Democratic executive committee from 1888 to 1894, a delegate to the Democratic national convention in 1892, and supported the state Democratic ticket that year. One historian argues that Howard lost money in the 1893–94 depression and blamed the Democrats, but for whatever reason, his conversion to Populism came suddenly, in August 1894, after DeKalb County's Populists sent him a telegram urging that he accept their nomination and oppose incumbent Democrat William H. Denson.[18]

Howard became a noted Populist propagandist and wrote two books, one of which was very controversial. In *If Christ Came to Congress*, published before the election, the fledgling author charged that drunks, wastrels, and crooks roamed the halls of Congress engaging in immoral and nefarious activities. His opponent said the book was obscene. Later, Howard published *The American Plutocracy*, which attacked the power of giant corporations and eastern banks.[19]

Democratic nominee William Denson also asked Populists for their nomination, but before the Populist district convention met, Howard accused Denson of accepting $500 dollars to speak for Kolb and then refusing to carry out his end of the bargain. At the Populist convention in late September Denson said that Howard was "a liar blacker than hell." Rhetorical exchanges between the two almost led to a fistfight during the meeting, and Howard said he had to avoid a pistol fight with his opponent afterward. Because he was already the Democratic nominee, Denson's name was not placed in nomination at the Populist convention. Judge Street had wanted the Populists to nominate Denson and initially endorsed him, but Street supported Howard after the Populist convention.[20]

Populism was so strong in the Seventh District that Denson tried to steer a middle course between his party and the Populists. He must have known he was in trouble when Kolb polled 62 percent of the district's vote in August. Denson criticized Grover Cleveland, said he would "tote his own skillet" without help from the Democratic party, endorsed free silver, and offered his own loan program for small farmers, but he would not endorse the subtreasury or other radical Populist demands. Howard emphasized economic issues, endorsed the Populist platform of 1892, and, despite his recent conversion to Populism, became one of the most uncompromising supporters of Populist demands. Denson's moderate free-silver appeal to members of both parties failed. Howard received two-thirds of the vote and won every county in the district. No other anti-Democratic candidate for Congress in Alabama fared as well. The Seventh had more white Republicans than other congressional districts, and Howard's victories in Winston and DeKalb were won with the help of Upcountry farmers of Unionist-Republican descent. Democrats were unable to take the district for granted again until the late 1920s.[21]

A Populist agreement to back several Republican congressional nominees in exchange for GOP help for Populist nominees in other districts drew some criticism on the grounds that Populists had little in common with national Republicans. William F. and Truman H. Aldrich, Republican nominees in the Fourth and Ninth Districts respectively, were wealthy businessmen with anti-labor reputations. The high-tariff, gold-standard advocate Benjamin M. Long was the Sixth District GOP nominee. Populists had trouble justifying their support for such men. William F. Aldrich endorsed a bimetallic currency, but a Shelby County Democratic editor denounced him as a "monopolist," a "high tariff protectionist," and a "national bank director." J. D. Hardy, the editor went on, had made "good Republicans" out of A. P. Longshore and his Populist friends.[22]

Events on election day in November in Shelby County involving John W. Pitts, the new chairman of the state Populist executive committee, exposed a political atmosphere thick with tension. Pitts lived in the Shelby County precinct of Harpersville, which had a large black population but returned Democratic majorities in the state elections of 1892 and 1894. In light of the fraud practiced by Black Belt Democrats and the disastrous application of the Sayre law in August, Pitts and his son John Singleton Pitts decided to take action. On election day, they led a group of Populists to Harpersville's polling place and demanded a Populist poll watcher. Because the Sayre law made no provision for such an onlooker, the Democrats refused the request. Populist frustration and Democratic obstinacy collided, shooting broke out, and newspapers disagreed about who was to blame, but members of both parties exchanged fire. A black man, described as a Democrat by a local newspaper, was killed in the crossfire, and the younger Pitts was wounded.[23]

Populists feared returning to the polling place after the shooting, and no votes were registered for their candidates at Harpersville. Populist chairman John W. Pitts and his son were indicted for murder and arraigned a few days after the election. They were represented at the arraignment by A. P. Longshore, but there are no accounts of a trial or records showing that the two men were ever tried. Given the pro-Populist political atmosphere, a conviction was unlikely. John W. and John S. Pitts continued to be active in Shelby County politics for many more years.[24]

Local Democrats were shocked when W. F. Aldrich got 1,772 votes to his Democratic opponent's 992. "Tis passing strange, indeed almost incredible," wrote a Democratic editor, "but nevertheless true that Shelby County, a white county, inhabited largely by white people, has gone Republican." If anyone had told a Populist a decade earlier "that he would ever vote the Republican ticket, he would have taken it as a gross insult." Chilton County's Populists, who were among the state's most radical devotees of the Omaha platform, also gave Aldrich a large majority. Such votes for Aldrich by members of the reform party did not signify an ideological conversion by Populists to the GOP, but rather their loyalty to the arrangement they had made with the Republicans. Nevertheless, it was the first time a Republican had received a majority of the vote in Shelby or Chilton, and it began a long and fruitful relationship between the two parties in both counties.[25]

Aldrich's majorities in Shelby and Chilton were not sufficient to overcome Democratic landslides in the district's Black Belt counties. Democrats again resorted to voter fraud. Republican Truman Aldrich and Jeffersonian A. T. Goodwyn were also denied election by Democratic arithmetic. All three candidates contested the results in the U.S. House of Representatives. An investigation by the Republican-dominated house led to the seating of all three. Thus, two Republicans and a Jeffersonian joined the Populist Milford Howard in Alabama's nine-member House delegation.[26]

Eight of thirty-three state senators and thirty-five of one hundred members in Alabama's house of representatives were Jeffersonians, Populists, or Republicans. All eight counties in the Seventh District sent anti-Democrats to Montgomery, as did Shelby, Chilton, Walker, Fayette, Cleburne, and Lawrence Counties. Sheldon Hackney asserts that a progressive, pro-silver wing of the Democratic party led by Jefferson County state representative Sam Will John was more concerned about reform than Populists during the 1894–95 state legislative session. Populists, writes Hackney, opposed reform efforts by Democrats. The evidence does not support a conclusion that Populists were antireform and contradicts the notion that a unified "progressive" wing of the Democratic party existed. Unfortunately, legislative journals do not reveal the true intentions of legislators because these records do not contain the members' speeches or expose their behind-the-scenes stratagems. Policy disagreements presented by Hackney as clear struggles of reform against reaction were far more murky than he contends.[27]

Populists failed to support the abolition of the draconian convict leasing system, writes Hackney, after Democrat Sam Will John introduced an amendment "aimed at doing just that." The amendment lost by a vote of thirty-four to thirty, with eleven Populists against and ten in favor. Yet, the house *Journal* discloses that the amendment was not clearly "aimed at" ending the system. John did not propose to abolish or even reform its most egregious features, but merely asked for a change in the convict governing board. Populists and Democrats were equally divided on the issue. On its face the amendment was innocuous, but John made his motivations clear. In a formal protest made later in the session and published in the house *Journal,* he attacked convict leasing as an evil and said he would like to see it abolished, but he also said he intended to increase revenue coming to the state from the system. Thus, his attempt to reorganize the convict board grew more from his concerns about the system's efficiency than from his opposition to it.[28]

In his protest, John assailed members of his own party, rather than Populists, for their failure to support his changes. When a final bill to maintain the system essentially as it was passed by a vote of fifty-one to twenty-seven, John could muster only seven other Democrats to oppose it, but they were joined by nineteen Populists. When John tried to place his protest in the *Journal*, some Democrats tried to stop him, but the Populists voted overwhelmingly for a successful motion to publish the remarks.[29]

Hackney criticizes Populists because most of them voted for a Democratic proposal to repeal a state law prohibiting employers from compelling women and also children under the age of fourteen from working more than eight hours per day. Democratic governor William G. Oates, says Hackney, "recommended" repeal "to lure outside capital into the state." The house backed him by a vote of fifty-three to seven. A majority of Populists voting supported the bill, but six of the seven men who voted against it, including G. B. Deans of Shelby and Joseph Manning of Clay, were Populists. The charge by Hackney that those who backed the measure were insufficiently reform minded says more about those he describes as "progressive" Democrats than about Populists. Sam Will John did not vote, and if opposition to the bill was a litmus test of progressivism, John's wing of the Democrats failed it and the six Populists who did oppose it confirmed that their party contained far more reformers than either "wing" of the Democrats.[30]

Hackney charges that a bill to centralize tax assessments was a progressive measure because it "could have been a demand for a change in the tax structure" that discriminated against owners of real property devoted to agriculture. Populists opposed it because it was undemocratic. It was, said Joe Manning, an attack on "local self-government" because it proposed to take taxing authority from locally elected tax assessors and give it to a three-member county board with only one elected member. O. M. Mastin of Chilton County was the only Populist to support it.[31]

When Populists failed to support a measure that would have raised the state tax rate from four to five and one-half mills, says Hackney, they demonstrated that they were "still wedded to the idea of minimum government." Actually, Manning and other Populist legislators denounced the tax increase as a burden on small farmers already hard hit by a growing economic depression. In his protest, Sam Will John criticized all legislators who failed to support the tax measures, which he believed would shift the tax burden from farmers to corporations. A part of the tax measure would have given the state better tools to determine the actual value of property, which might have raised taxes on wealthy corporations and Black Belters, but the bill offered little to third-party legislators because no assurance was given that taxes on farm land would go down.[32]

Another revealing dispute involved efforts by the Democratic administration to pass a measure guaranteeing payment of interest on new state bond issues in gold. Thirty-three Populists and fifteen Democrats joined to defeat the measure on a forty-eight to forty vote. Later, when some Populist opponents were absent, three Democrats switched sides, and the goldbugs won by a forty-two to forty-one margin. This demonstrated how little influence "silver" Democrats had. The administration needed the support of 80 percent of the Democrats to pass this measure, and it got them. Many urban Democrats joined Black Belters in support of the bill. Conflicts between an economic elite and a mythical "silver" Democratic bloc over monetary issues were not apparent.[33]

The voting records of legislators do not present nearly as much confusion for historians as do the 1896 elections, when Alabama's convoluted political party alignments became absurd. Only the fact that Alabama scheduled state elections in August and federal elections in November saved voters from being totally confounded by the new party entanglements. A sensible move came when Populists and Jeffersonians abandoned separate executive committees and became one party, but before the year was out Populists were trying methods of fusion with Republicans at the state and local levels while fusing with Democrats at the national level. These tangled alliances threatened the identity of the third party, for fusion might produce electoral victories, but it obscured the ideological reasons for the existence of the Populist party.[34]

Politicians from all parties fought for electoral advantage by aligning with whomever they believed would help their immediate cause. Coalitions differed from county to county. Populists such as Longshore tried to distance themselves from Republicans who were clear ideological opponents of Populism, but once alliances with Republicans were created, reciprocal obligations bound leaders of the two parties together. Ideological consistency was left behind in the scramble for power. Few political leaders were entirely satisfied with the varied coalitions that emerged, but once they were forged it was difficult to shed them.

When third-party men discussed strategy in late 1895, the question of what to do about Republicans weighed heavily on them. Former state Populist chairman Samuel M. Adams, who moved to Chilton County in 1895, denounced fusion with Republicans. Black Belt Republicans, he said, had voted for the Democratic candidate for governor in 1892 and 1894, and north Alabama Republicans were already full-fledged Populists. Therefore, there was no need for fusion. A. P. Longshore and Populist congressman Milford Howard also opposed fusion, but Populist leaders changed their minds about the efficacy of fusion during 1896 as political circumstances altered. Sheldon Hackney correctly notes that a Populist's stand on fusion with Republicans in 1896 revealed little about his ideology or commitment to reform.[35]

Adams was only partially correct in asserting that Upcountry Republicans had left their party for the Populists. Republican leaders of Unionist descent such as Napoleon B. Spears of St. Clair County and Walter Powell of Cullman County had become Populists, but Benjamin M. Long of Walker, Marshall County's Kennamers, and the Winston County GOP had not. Most Republicans cooperated with third parties in statewide elections, but their loyalty was to the GOP. They did not want to see their party swallowed by Populists.[36]

The GOP had loyally supported Populists for state and local office in 1894 and only received two Republican congressional seats for its labors. Some Republicans wanted to fuse formally with the Populists by splitting a state ticket between the two parties. This fusion proposal went beyond the mere "cooperation" that had previously marked the relationship. In April 1896, when Populists nominated Congressman A. T. Goodwyn for governor, new Republican chairman William A. Vaughn demanded that his party have places on the ticket with Goodwyn in exchange for an endorsement of other Populist candidates by the GOP state executive committee. The state Populist convention was controlled by fusionists, and the delegates mollified Vaughn by adding Republican candidates for attorney general and secretary of state to their slate. Longtime Republican Julian Bingham, who was active in the Farmers' Alliance, was nominated for state treasurer without the prompting of Vaughn. Some Populists were so angered by these moves that they denounced their party and left it, but most, including antifusionists A. P. Longshore and Milford Howard, remained loyal. Upcountry Populists from counties with large pockets of Unionist Republicans were unlikely to reject fusion because they needed GOP votes.[37]

The biggest problem for Populists in 1896 was the popularity within their ranks of Democratic candidates whose oratory sounded Populist themes. The shrewdest leader of the reform wing of the Democratic party was Joseph Forney Johnston. He had served in the Confederate army, then moved to the Black Belt and practiced law in Selma. He served as state Democratic party chairman in the late 1870s and was a typical Black Belt leader who disclosed no reform tendencies. In 1884 he moved to Birmingham, became a successful banker, and sought the Democratic nomination for governor in 1890. He received little delegate support and joined a coalition that denied the nomination to Reuben Kolb. In 1892 he personally wrote into the state Democratic platform a provision asking for the passage of election laws that would "secure the government of the state in the hands of the intelligent and the virtuous" white men.[38]

After his aristocratic vision was translated into reality through the Sayre law, Johnston ran for governor again, but the right wing of his party was already occupied by prominent candidates, so he conceived a new strategy aimed at forming a coalition of urban workers and small farmers and winning back the Populists. Johnston's speeches emphasized his support of fair elections and free silver. The sudden switch to a reform image was the first in a long series of actions by Johnston that led people to note his reputation as a "political trickster" who "could not be true to principle or friends." His "entire anatomy," said one observer, "seems to be built on lines that lead to ingratitude, treachery and deceit." Johnston's own private secretary Chappell Cory, searching for a way to sell the dexterous Johnston to Robert McKee, argued that his boss had "rubbed along on the practical roads of life" and was "not a saint whom the rascals can fool."[39]

Johnston lost the 1894 gubernatorial nomination to the reactionary goldbug William C. Oates, but when the national economic depression deepened and the Cleveland (gold) wing of the Democratic party was discredited, Johnston attacked the pro-gold state party hierarchy more stridently, and his strategy began take shape. He put together a meeting in Birmingham in the fall of 1895 of the pro-silver forces in the party, including Senator John Tyler Morgan, who supported Johnston for the gubernatorial nomination. In October 1895 Johnston bought the *Birmingham Age-Herald,* renamed it the *State-Herald,* and turned it into Alabama's largest free-silver paper. The pro-gold *Montgomery Advertiser,* organ of the Black Belt hierarchy since the Civil War, engaged in a war of words with Johnston's upstart paper. The mere fact that the *Advertiser* opposed Johnston probably attracted some Populists to his side.[40]

Johnston so successfully changed his image that he "blurred the lines between reactionary and reformer" and increased the likelihood "that some old Jeffersonians" would return to the Democrats. Leading Populists recognized the danger. G. B. Deans of Shelby County, the newly elected chairman of the state Populist party, reminded his party that Johnston was a chameleon who had collaborated in the nomination of a reactionary Black Belt governor in 1890 and 1892. Johnston's commitment to free silver was questionable, wrote Deans, because Democratic campaign chairman John B. Knox was himself an avowed goldbug.[41]

Johnston won the Democratic nomination for governor after a bitter battle with Congressman Richard H. Clarke of the First District, a gold advocate and representative of the planter elite. The state Democratic executive committee, controlled by Johnston and Senator John Tyler Morgan, had opened the Democratic nominating primaries to all white voters regardless of past party affiliation. Clarke's supporters charged that their candidate lost some primaries because Populists entered them to vote for Johnston.[42]

A free-silver takeover of the Democratic national convention presented a greater threat to Alabama's third-party cause than Johnston. The Populist national convention took place after the Democratic convention, and Populists would split the reform cause if they nominated a candidate to oppose a silver Democratic nominee. Such a nominee would also rob Populists of their charge that reactionary Clevelandites controlled the Democrats. The Democratic convention created a special problem for Alabama's Populists because it took place two weeks before the August state elections. If silver forces triumphed at the convention, the euphoria of their victory would be felt immediately in state and local elections. Alabama's Populist legions might be induced to return to the party of their fathers.[43]

Much to the chagrin of radical Alabama Populists such as A. P. Longshore and Wiregrass leader James M. Whitehead, the Democratic convention nominated silverite William Jennings Bryan after his famous "Cross of Gold" keynote speech. Longshore wrote that the "wrong people" had supported Bryan. Democrats "will adopt free silver," wrote Whitehead, and then "will be furnished just money enough by Wall Street to pay for drum beating and torch light processions and such, so as to keep as many free silver men out of the Populist party as possible." Although Bryan did not endorse the subtreasury or other Alliance-Populist programs, the Democrats contended that his nomination made Populism superfluous.[44]

Many Alabama Populists favored the nomination of Bryan by their national convention also, but Longshore, Manning, and Congressman Milford Howard vigorously opposed fusion with the Democrats. They never wavered, but Reuben Kolb and his supporters backed Bryan, and fusion gained ground among the delegates. As the time for nominations grew near and it became apparent that Bryan might be the Populist nominee,

Milford Howard argued that his nomination might destroy the party. In the South, he feared, men would simply return to the Democratic party. Howard and other midroaders persuaded the delegates to nominate Georgia's famed Populist Tom Watson for vice-president. The Democrats had nominated the conservative easterner Arthur Sewell to run with Bryan, and Howard argued that only by nominating Watson could the Populists retain a party identity separate from the Democrats.[45]

When Bryan won the Populist nomination, the antifusionists demanded to know whether he had actually accepted it. Fusionists would not disclose Bryan's intentions, and Alabama's delegation, led by Milford Howard, caused a near riot at the convention podium. The fusionist leaders would not tell the delegates the truth, that Bryan had actually refused the Populist nomination, because they were determined that he would carry their banner anyway. Bryan never recognized Watson as his running mate, and Populists left St. Louis with a hybrid ticket satisfactory to few delegates.[46]

Most Alabama Populists had little choice but to support Bryan, but others were so angry with their national party for giving up its autonomy that they became Republicans despite the ideological gulf separating them from the GOP presidential nominee, the goldbug William McKinley. Among the Republican converts was the idealist Joseph Manning, who found it intolerable to make common cause with men such as Joseph Johnston, who had collaborated in the Democratic party's election thefts. Manning's integrity was laudable, but his switch to McKinley was not without irony. The men Manning detested most, former Democratic governors Thomas G. Jones and William C. Oates, were so angry about Bryan's nomination that they broke with their national party and supported a "Gold Democrat" for president. Since the gold candidate had no chance of winning the presidency, their only possible reason for supporting him was to take enough votes from Bryan in Alabama to aid McKinley. Indeed, Jones and Oates sought money for their campaign from Republicans. Manning had unwittingly entered the camp of his old enemies.[47]

It was not yet clear to some Alabama Populists that their movement had been dealt a lethal blow by Bryan's nomination, but the identity of their party as the only instrument of reform was threatened. Their coalitions with Jeffersonians and Republicans required Populists to play down the radical features of their national program in favor of an emphasis on free silver and fair elections, which made their message seem indistinguishable from that of the Democrats. Many Populists saw the charismatic Bryan as an enduring symbol of agrarian reform and the return of the Democratic party to its Jacksonian roots. Bryan's anti-monopoly, anti-gold oratory certainly sounded Populistic. No man benefitted more from Bryan's nomination than Joseph Forney Johnston, the Democratic nominee for governor, who now claimed that both his national and state party had been captured by reformers.[48]

A Democratic editor from Jackson County invited the Streets of Marshall County to help lead the reform "wing of the Democracy." The pro-silver Democratic national platform, he wrote, was a "fair settlement and adjustment of the principles contended for by the Populites, omitting the ownership of railroads and telegraph lines," which his party could adopt later if it was "deemed wise." The Streets refused the offer, but their party had allowed itself to be pushed into a corner. It had consummated a political alliance with the state GOP for the August elections only a few weeks before the Democrats sharply differentiated their party's economic policies from that of the Republicans.[49]

A. P. Longshore found that many in his local party were again committed to supporting the McKinleyite Republican William F. Aldrich for Congress. Shelby's Populists, with Longshore's support, had already fused with local Republicans by dividing their county ticket with the GOP. Populists nominated Longshore for another term in the legislature. Luckily, his opponent was not a Bryan-Johnston reformer, but Needham Graham, the old Democratic editor and lawyer who had led the anti-Alliance wing of the local Democratic party.[50]

Longshore's differences with Graham on economic issues could not have been greater. The old Democrat was a Cleveland goldbug, whereas Longshore had become even more radical by 1896. He had opened two new Populist newspapers in 1895, one in Calhoun and the other in Cleburne County, both of which advocated radical Populist ideas. The post office, "owned and controlled by the government," was a success, wrote Longshore, and "so would the ownership of railroads and telegraphs be." In March 1895 he argued that "the money question" was the "only question" and that "the Omaha platform is our ticket." He even compared socialism to Christianity, but said that the socialist philosophy was too idealistic to succeed in America. Longshore's editorials in his Calhoun County paper stressed "anti-monopoly greenback issues" and downplayed free silver as an antidote. As late as July 1896 the Shelby Populist refused to say whether he would support Bryan and wrote that he would "defer" judgment on the matter to a later time.[51]

The fusion of the Shelby County and state Populists with the Republicans allowed Needham Graham to build his campaign around the theme of white supremacy. Third-party gubernatorial candidate A. T. Goodwyn, while a member of Congress, had given racial ammunition to Graham and the entire Democratic press. In deciding a contested congressional election out of South Carolina, Goodwyn voted with the Republican majority to seat the GOP Negro contestant over his Democratic opponent, a one-armed Confederate veteran. Goodwyn had little choice, for Republicans had voted to seat him in an earlier contest. A week before the state election, Needham Graham published a cartoon that depicted Goodwyn shaking hands with the triumphant black man while a one-armed Confederate in full military regalia stood downcast behind them.[52]

The race issue hurt Populists in the August elections. White voters most threatened by race were influenced by the racist Democratic message. Johnston won the Black Belt by margins similar to those received by the two previous Democratic candidates for governor, but he also won some majority white counties with high black populations that had previously voted for Kolb. Outside the majority black counties, the election was almost even, although Democrats gained some ground in the Hill Country.[53]

Joseph Johnston won the three counties, Walker, Winston, and DeKalb, with the largest percentage of white Republican voters in north Alabama. Despite fusion at the state level, local Republicans in these counties would not fuse their county tickets with Populists again. The GOP offered its own ticket in Winston and Walker. GOP candidates for state representative and sheriff defeated Democratic and Populist candidates in Winston County. In each race the Populist finished last, which disclosed the relative power of the three parties in the county. Johnston won Winston, not because Republicans voted for him, but because they refused to vote for either him or Goodwyn. In Walker County, Populists also ran last in the three-way races, but, just as in the 1880s, the divided vote of the two anti-Democratic parties allowed the Democrats to win local elections there.[54]

The refusal of the Walker and Winston County Republicans to fuse with the Populists had its consequences. Unlike Shelby and Chilton Counties, where Republicans and Populists grew closer after 1896, in Walker and Winston they divided. In Shelby, Chilton, Marshall, St. Clair, and other hill counties the Republicans got a boost when Populists entered their ranks after 1896, but in Walker and Winston no such boost occurred. Some Populists must have returned to the Democrats because the GOP went into decline in both counties for several elections. Bitterness toward the Populists among Republicans in Walker and Winston in 1896 grew, no doubt, from the fact that so many Populists supported the Democrat Bryan for president. Republicans were also tired of cooperating with Populists and getting little cooperation or tangible benefits in return. In the fall election, Seventh District Republicans decided not to support the Populist congressional nominee.[55]

Problems in the upper Hill Country did not affect fusion in Shelby County, and the race issue did not affect the outcome of the election there. All of Shelby's Populist-Republican candidates won landslide victories in the August elections, although it was noteworthy that each Populist candidate received between 60 and 63 percent of the vote, whereas Republicans only got 55 to 58 percent. Shelby's voters were still more Populist than Republican, and a few Populists still refused to vote for any Republican. Longshore, the most outspoken and committed midroad Populist in the county, got a higher percentage of the vote than any other candidate.[56]

Shelby County's Populists saved the most important local offices, such as sheriff, state representative, and a majority of the county commission, for themselves and backed Republican candidates for tax collector, superintendent of education, county coroner, and one member of the county commission. This brand of fusion, with the Populists as the directing and dominant group, remained in place as long as a separate Populist party existed in the county, but major gains for the GOP occurred despite its subservience to the Populists. A majority of Shelby County's Populist voters voted for some Republicans, worked with GOP officeholders in the courthouse, and grew accustomed to their presence there. The loyalty of the Shelby GOP to the Populists, which began in 1894 and continued through the 1890s, also led to obligations. Populists had to stand by their fusionist brothers.[57]

John W. Pitts, who had taken over editorial control of the *People's Advocate*, urged Populist-Republican fusion even if it meant supporting candidates opposed to Populist ideas and programs. Longshore disagreed. He could support Republicans for local offices and accept support from them at the county level because candidates for local offices did not have to discuss cutting edge national issues such as currency reform. Congressional offices were a different matter. Longshore, like other Populists, supported William F. Aldrich for Congress in 1894 because he endorsed a bi-metallic currency, but Aldrich openly supported the pro-gold Republican William McKinley for president in 1896.[58]

Longshore broke with Aldrich and became a political enemy of the Republican coal operator. In his *Anniston Alabama Leader* Longshore wrote that Populists endorsed Aldrich because the Republican told the Populist executive committee that he would support the Bryan-Watson electors "in the event his party nominated a gold standard man on a gold standard platform." Since then, Aldrich had declared for McKinley. Longshore could not support "a man who would vote for a gold standard man for president." A continuation of gold currency would "impoverish and ruin the laboring people." A Shelby County Democratic editor also commented on the absurdity of free-silver men supporting a gold-standard advocate and admitted that Longshore was "consistent in his position." Longshore's stand also led to an open break with his old ally John W. Pitts.[59]

The GOP had not offered any nominees in Chilton County since Reconstruction and had a small presence there, but Chilton's Populists did not object to fusion with the GOP at the state or congressional level. Without fusion, local Populist candidates received more than 70 percent of Chilton County's vote in the August 1896 elections. Lewis Reynolds, manager of the Alliance store at Jemison, was elected to the legislature. Frank Crichton, editor of the Populist *Clanton Banner*, endorsed William F. Aldrich for Congress, and Reynolds accepted a position on the fusion congressional campaign committee at the same time that both Crichton and Reynolds were also asking voters to support the midroad Bryan-Watson ticket. This ideological inconsistency caused little anxiety in Chilton County, but Bryan's candidacy worried the founding father of Chilton's anti-Democratic movements.[60]

In a letter to the *Banner*, Probate Judge Riley M. Honeycutt questioned the efficacy of free silver as a remedy for farm problems and criticized the national Democratic ticket. Honeycutt wrote that he had never been a "party man," but an "independent" who always "supported the man nearest in accord with my views on the important questions of the day, regardless of party affiliations." He would vote for Bryan-Watson, but he "did not have the utmost confidence in the sincerity of Mr. Bryan." Populists should support the "southern man," Tom Watson, for vice-president. Democratic vice-presidential nominee Sewell was from New England, which was the "center of all the corruption and iniquity in American politics," and Sewell was connected to "wealthy corporations." Honeycutt did not "think the free coinage of silver at 16 to 1" was "the relief of all these troubles which some people try to make us believe. In fact, I think that it has very little to do with it." The real problem lay in who controlled the money. Honeycutt then endorsed Aldrich for Congress, and the inconsistency between his statements and that endorsement seemed to escape him.[61]

If the ideology of Reynolds and Honeycutt seemed inconsistent with the views of Republican coal magnate and gold-standard advocate William F. Aldrich in 1896, the multifarious, convoluted nature of political jockeying was even more bizarre in Marshall County. The GOP there was tiny and since Reconstruction had offered no candidates. In 1890, when the state Democratic party split, local Republicans reorganized under the leadership of Seaborn Kennamer. In 1892 and 1894 they endorsed third-party candidates but had no slots on a fusion ticket. In 1896 Marshall County's GOP sought a fusion agreement with the third party. Charles Brents Kennamer, the son of Seaborn and a young attorney in his twenties, publicly chastised Judge Street's party for its patronizing attitude toward Republicans. He proposed that the local GOP nominate half the anti-Democratic ticket and Populists the other half. When the Populists rebuffed this offer, Republicans nominated their own ticket.[62]

Populists attempted to reconcile with the Republicans, but a local GOP leader reported that "fusion will not be possible in Marshall County this year." He was wrong, but the fusion that resulted was certainly of a peculiar character. When the hapless Marshall County Democrats, badly defeated in the past two elections, met in April and decided not to nominate a ticket, the Democratic chairman said that the county Republican nominees were "splendid men personally." The local party of white supremacy then entered a strange fusion arrangement with the party dominated by the scalawag Seaborn Kennamer and his progeny. Judge Street's Jeffersonian-Populist group had seemed unbeatable, but 1896 was a volatile year. In many upper hill counties it was difficult to know how many third-party voters had returned to the Democratic party of Bryan and Joseph Johnston or how many had simply decided, like Joe Manning, to become Republicans.[63] When formerly loyalist Democratic voters in Marshall County also decided to cast ballots for Republican candidates, Judge Street's party suffered a stunning defeat in the race for Marshall County's seat in the state house of representatives. Republican Thomas Kennamer, another son of Seaborn, defeated the Populist nominee by 25 out of 2,657 votes cast. Kennamer's largest majorities came in previously Democratic precincts, which remained loyal to the statewide Democratic ticket.[64]

Republican disaffection from Populists in several upper hill counties carried over into the Seventh District congressional race, in which Milford Howard sought reelection. The state Republican committee had not endorsed all Populist candidates for Congress. Only in the Fourth District had Populist and Republican committees agreed on a candidate, W. F. Aldrich. Republicans nominated James J. Curtis of Winston County to oppose Howard. Curtis, the son of a Unionist-Republican, had supported Populists in state elections, but his loyalty was to the GOP. The contest turned into a four-way race when a gold Democrat also entered the field.[65]

Congressional and presidential races were complicated by the fact that Reuben Kolb and some of his leading supporters abandoned the Populist party during the fall campaign. Kolb and his longtime ally Peyton Bowman endorsed Bryan-Sewell over Bryan-Watson and supported some Democrats for Congress, including Milford Howard's opponent. These actions could not be ignored, and the Populist state executive committee read the renegades out of the party. Kolb and Bowman, said the committee, had "basely betrayed" the Populist cause. Some Populists had always been suspicious of Kolb and were glad to see him leave. In a letter to a Chilton County newspaper Lewis Reynolds bid the two men a less than fond "farewell." Despite the evident delight of men such as Reynolds, the loss of Kolb and his endorsement of Bryan-Sewell damaged the Populist cause.[66]

Milford Howard had received two-thirds of the Seventh District vote in 1894, but in 1896 he got only 35.8 percent of the vote to 32.7 percent for the Democrat, 28.9 percent for Curtis, and 2.7 for the Gold Democrat. Howard won majorities only in Cherokee and St. Clair Counties and pluralities in Cullman and Marshall. The large vote for Curtis was surprising, and there was also a GOP surge in two hill counties in the presidential race. In Blount County, where Republican presidential candidates had won only 23.7 percent and 16.6 percent respectively in 1884 and 1888, McKinley got 51.2 percent. In DeKalb County the GOP had not received more than 40 percent in a presidential race since 1876, but McKinley got 46.6 percent. Blount and DeKalb had loyally backed Reuben Kolb in 1892 and 1894, but many former Populist voters in these counties, like Joe

Manning, would not vote for Bryan. Their movement into the Republican camp in the congressional and presidential elections was a harbinger of the future.[67]

The Bryan-Watson ticket ran poorly because most Upcountry voters simply chose the Democratic presidential ticket. The endorsement of Sewell by Reuben Kolb hurt the midroad ticket, and national Populist headquarters also gave voters mixed signals. National party chairman Marion Butler of North Carolina wavered between support for Watson and statements that the party would not insist on Watson for vice-president. In the Hill Country, Bryan-Watson led the regular Democratic ticket only in Chilton, Cherokee, St. Clair, and Fayette Counties. Populist leaders must have feared that many of their rank and file had followed Kolb back into the Democratic party or had become Republicans. Efforts by Howard and Longshore to maintain a distinct Populist identity had been ruined by fusion.[68]

Actions by Alabama Democrats after 1896 had a greater impact on the future direction of Populists than national politics. Governor Joseph Forney Johnston presented himself as a crypto-Populist, but this tepid reformer never clearly defined his path. By 1900 his party had divided into two relatively cohesive factions. He sought support from ex-Populists, but his faction included urban Democrats and business interests who were not agrarian minded. The other faction was led by the Black Belt but also included more conservative urban business interests. Only on the issue of voter disfranchisement did the differences between Johnston and his party's reactionary faction become clear to Populists. On issues other than disfranchisement Populists viewed Johnston's brand of reform with suspicion. Johnston and his urban Democrats wanted some kind of tax reform and railroad regulation, but it was unclear whether these "progressive" economic policies would benefit the great mass of Alabamians or simply aid a new kind of urban-commercial elite.[69]

Johnston sought a brand of economic modernization that required government to raise taxes and pass the kind of regulations that would ease the process of industrial and urban expansion. Ostensibly, this modernization process would move people out of the economic system that tethered them to crop-liens and farm mortgages, but it might also lead them to unhealthy coal mines, some of which were still worked by convict labor, or to textile mills where small children ran dangerous machines. Some of Johnston's most significant supporters, modernizers such as the

Anniston cotton mill boss B. B. Comer, were the most vocal opponents of child labor reform, did little to oppose convict leasing, and opposed labor unions. Their support for railroad regulation, an issue that obsessed them, grew more from their desire to increase the profits of their businesses than from compassion for the masses. Populists were skeptical about the people who would be put into power in the bureaus and agencies advocated by these "progressives" and about the loss of grassroots control in a government run by experts and regulators.[70]

A. P. Longshore's actions in the 1896–97 legislative session exhibited his concerns. Populists in the legislature nominated Longshore for speaker of the house of representatives and for the United States Senate. With only twenty Populists in the house and eleven in the state senate, he had little chance of getting either office, but he did play a major policy-making role. Longshore, with support from Chilton County's Lewis Reynolds and other Populists, got the house to amend the Sayre law so that registration and voting would be easier for uneducated, rural people. Reynolds also backed a measure that would have allowed women to practice law in Alabama, the first in a long series of actions by the Chilton County Populist in support of women's rights.[71]

Longshore has been criticized as antireform or unrealistic for opposing a bill offered by Governor Johnston that would have created an elected railroad commission. The Populist leader was less concerned about the creation of the commission than about who would serve on it. In Alabama, an elective railroad commission, like many regulatory agencies in the progressive era, might actually serve the interests of the business it was created to regulate. There was no assurance that the Louisville and Nashville Railroad, which played a key role in nominating and electing Thomas Goode Jones governor in 1890 and 1892, would exercise self-restraint in using its power in the Democratic party to nominate and elect its candidates to the commission. Populists had been counted out of other elections, and there was no reason to believe that things would change when railroad commissioners were elected.[72]

Far from opposing the commission, Longshore merely offered an amendment that stipulated that no single party should elect more than one of the three commission members. That act would have created a place for a Populist. When the legislature turned his proposal down, he opposed the commission and helped defeat it. Events proved that Longshore was more prescient than unrealistic. When Democrats finally got a railroad commission act through the 1903 legislature, two of the three commissioners were backed by the L & N railroad and consistently voted with railroads rather than consumers.[73]

Joseph Johnston usually sought support from Populists, but in 1898 he benefitted from a disillusioned Populist rank and file rocked by three successive statewide defeats, rampant election fraud, and frustration over their inability to challenge election authorities. Their lethargy helped Johnston win a second term as governor. Despite the salutary revision of the Sayre law, the total vote in the gubernatorial election fell 27 percent below that of 1896, and the Populist candidate for governor, G. B. Deans of Shelby County, received only 31 percent of the vote. Deans polled 39,000 fewer votes than A. T. Goodwyn had received two years earlier, but a lack of interest was not confined to the Populists. Johnston also received 18,000 less votes than in 1896. The Populist decline was caused, in part, by the failure of the third party to fuse with Republicans, who did not offer a state ticket but had little incentive to back Populists in state elections. In some counties with large Republican contingents the failure of fusion at the state level had an impact on the vote in county elections.[74]

Populists would not be able to mount another serious challenge to the Democrats in statewide elections, but their party retained vitality and power in some hill counties. Longshore, Reynolds, and Oliver Street all sought elective office in 1898 and won impressive support in their home counties, which, along with St. Clair, Cherokee, and Coosa, were the only Upcountry counties to give majorities to Populist nominees for governor in all four elections in the 1890s. Populism was strongest in these counties, where Populists won local offices in 1898 and beyond despite the overall decline of their movement, but even in these counties Populists eventually had to face the problem of how to maintain power at the local level when they no longer had a credible statewide or national party with which to align. Even if the primary interest of Upcountry Populists was in local, rather than in state or national issues, their isolation from the only political parties with state or national influence would inevitably dissolve their influence at the local level.

7 What Happened to the Upcountry Populists? 1898–1904

I told you about the number of drinks you should take before speaking.
. . . Two good drinks for a Republican speech and three good drinks for a
Populist speech, taken twenty minutes apart . . . will produce results on
election day.[1]

Napoleon B. Spears (1902)

Upcountry Populists watched the decline of their party with trepidation, and they did not relish becoming members of either of the two major parties. William Jennings Bryan and Joseph Johnston had great appeal, but if Populists returned to the state Democratic party they would have to contend with the same reactionary group that had rejected Farmers' Alliance candidates in 1890. Populism's most bitter enemies still held high offices in the state and local Democratic parties. Joining the Republicans seemed remote. In 1898, national GOP leaders stood at opposite poles from Populists on economic issues. The state Republican hierarchy had been ambivalent about fusion with Populists, and it was infested by political relics whose goals had less to do with public policy than with getting federal jobs. A. P. Longshore, Lewis Reynolds, and Oliver Street chose to nurse the hope that their party would revive, but temptations to leave it grew as circumstances changed the texture of politics. A close analysis of the responses of these three Populists leaders and their supporters to the events of the period between 1898 and 1904 leads to a better understanding of the motives, intentions, and ideology of Upcountry Populists.

In early 1898 A. P. Longshore was assailed by the *Columbiana People's Advocate,* which he founded and which had been the organ of the Shelby County Populist party since 1892. Longshore had turned over editorial control to John W. Pitts, but their disagreement over Longshore's failure to support Republican W. F. Aldrich for Congress led to an ugly public fight. When Pitts claimed to be the legal owner of the paper's presses, litigation ensued. For several months they published two versions of the paper, but Longshore won sole control in the summer of 1898. He hired a new Populist editor, J. Frank Norris, and in the political battles of two more decades, Norris's editorial views reflected those of Longshore.[2]

The Longshore-Pitts controversy divided Shelby's Populist party. In 1898 Longshore ran for probate judge, an office that would give him more power over Shelby County affairs. State senator G. B. Deans, with Pitts's support, opposed Longshore in a Populist primary. Deans and Pitts had both been chairman of the state Populist party, but their prestige was no match for that of Longshore. In the face of charges by Pitts that he was a corrupt "mercenary" and treasonous to his party, Longshore won 56 percent of the primary vote, then graciously supported Deans for governor and led another Populist-Republican fusion slate that demolished Shelby's Democrats in the August elections. Longshore's victory gave the probate judge's office to Populists for the first time, and fusionists occupied every county office.[3]

In a celebratory editorial, Frank Norris noted that the fusionist victors were direct descendants of the victorious independent movement of 1884. He wrote:

> Fourteen years ago . . . independents broke the ranks of the Democrats. The plans were gotten up by the best people in the county. We met at Moore's corner and got up the plan and the ticket. The Democrats gave it the name of Mulberry Corner and the mulberry is still living, and has answered all purposes, but now the Democrats are routed and hereafter we can hold our caucuses in the courthouse with our people. We know that it is hard for the Democrats to give up their strong hold, but to the victors belong the spoils. Now let us cherish the old mulberry like the people did the charteroak at Hartford.[4]

Norris had focused on a variety of issues during the campaign. A week before the election, he condemned "gold bugs," "mortgages on the land of the poor," "vote stealers," "educational qualifications for voting," "disfranchisement," and "stock law advocates." The reference to stock laws raised an issue of increasing concern to Hill Country farmers, who had always grazed their livestock under an open range system that allowed animals to forage on the unfenced land of their neighbors. Small landowners could thus get sustenance for their livestock that the animals could not obtain if confined to their owners land.[5]

In the 1880s a push began to force farmers to fence in their animals and pay for damages their stock might cause neighboring property owners. Independent movements in the Tennessee Valley in the early eighties were stimulated, in part, by the effort to end the open range, but the issue did not become significant in the many Upcountry counties until the late 1890s. Stock law advocates were often large landowners who sold their produce to smaller farmers. The farmers increasingly bought such staples as butter and milk from the large landowners or merchants. In 1885, a Shelby County farmer observed that a motivation behind the stock laws was to increase the opportunities for "the rich man to sell his yellow butter" to his less fortunate neighbors.[6]

Black Belt legislators easily won passage of stock laws that applied to their counties. Because most small farmers in that region were black, the laws created little white opposition. The Hill Country escaped such legislation until the late nineties, but as large farmers there got interested in the commercial prospects of their produce their desire for stock laws increased. Between 1898 and 1901 the issue became an emotional one in the Hill Country. Shelby County and Chilton County Populists defended the open range.[7]

Frank Norris also assailed new efforts to disfranchise voters, which became a leading issue in state politics. In the fall of 1898, a Shelby County Democratic editor endorsed disfranchisement of the "uneducated." This editorial reflected a growing movement among Democrats to enact laws that would restrict voting by blacks and poor whites. With Governor Johnston's support, Democratic legislators enacted a law in December 1898 that called for a constitutional convention on voting.[8]

One legislator who voted against the convention and opposed stock laws was Lewis H. Reynolds, who had become the dominant figure in Chilton County politics. When Reynolds drew opposition in his race for reelection in 1898, one Populist argued that stock laws were the leading issue in the campaign. If Chilton County voters did not want a Democratic representative "hired to serve a few landlords," he wrote, then they should vote for Reynolds and "protect" their "summer woods pasture."[9]

Reynolds and Chilton County's Populists had backed candidates supported by the Farmers' Alliance in 1892, but none of these candidates had been formally nominated by the Populist party. The decision of Populists to hold a county party primary in 1898 alienated Probate Judge Riley Honeycutt, who refused to enter it. His stand was consistent with the position he took as an independent in the eighties. He admitted that he had voted for all Populist nominees since 1892, but he regarded "conventions and primary elections" as "party machines in which political schemers may by their manipulations unfairly defeat the will of the people." He

Lewis H. Reynolds, 1903 (courtesy of the Alabama Department of Archives and History, Montgomery, Alabama)

would run only in the general election, where the "whole white people" participated. This stand created a dilemma for local Populists, who had come to power under Honeycutt's tutelage, but they could not concede the election to a man who refused to participate in their party's processes.[10]

Former state Farmers' Alliance president Samuel M. Adams, a Baptist minister and one of Alabama's most widely known Populist leaders, won the Populist primary nomination for probate judge. He had served Bibb County as a Populist legislator and moved to Chilton County in 1895. No man did more to stimulate Populism than Adams, and none did more to forge opposition to organized Democrats in Chilton County than Honeycutt. Democrats saw a chance to drive a wedge between Honeycutt and Populist leaders and wisely declined to nominate any candidates, but some Democrats sought office as independents. Populists angrily accused Honeycutt of trying to ruin the movement he had pioneered. Reynolds won reelection handily, but the race for probate judge was closer. Honeycutt, running as an independent, won support from loyal Democratic precincts. Populists, demonstrating that they were more committed to their movement than to personalities, backed Adams, who won a plurality. By 1902 Reynolds and Adams were political enemies, and Reynolds had joined Oliver Street in the Republican party, a scenario that seemed improbable at the end of 1898.[11]

The Streets had followed a more ambiguous course to Populism than Reynolds, Adams, or Longshore, and Oliver Street's road to the GOP between 1898 and 1902 was also circuitous. The Streets were loyal to the Populist party through 1898 and referred to themselves as Populists after 1900, but when reform-minded Democrats sought their help, they gave it. Like many Upcountry Populists they began a period of oscillation between the three parties. In 1898 Thomas Atkins Street decided not to seek reelection as probate judge, an office he had held since 1874, but the entire Marshall County Populist ticket won without him. The coalition of Republicans and Democrats that had cooperated in the county in 1896 had broken up. Republicans received less than a quarter of the vote and finished behind not only Populist and but also Democratic candidates. Despite the strength of Populism, after the Seventh District congressional campaign of 1898 it seemed that Oliver Street would return to the Democrats.[12]

The year 1898 marked the rise of Oliver as the leading politician in his family and a major figure in the Hill Country. As early as August 1897, T. W. Powell of Cullman County, a Populist with a Unionist-Republican heritage, organized "Street clubs" in the Seventh District. Milford Howard, a committed and radical Populist, had been an embarrassment. He was accused of drunk and disorderly conduct on the floor of the Congress, a charge he denied, but his personality and politics were unsteady. He shocked Populists by voting for the Republican-sponsored Dingley tariff, which raised rates on imports. Grassroots Populists criticized him, opposition to his renomination grew, and Street was poised to contest his candidacy.[13]

On August 10, 1898, a week before the Seventh District Populist nominating convention was held in Marshall County, Howard told a DeKalb County newspaper that he would not be a candidate. He could have been nominated had he asked, but he said that he withdrew because he needed to come home and make money. Howard expressed fears that he could not win another three-way race like the one in 1896. Street was nominated, and Howard remained his ally in many campaigns that followed.[14]

Street faced major obstacles. Some Populists had voted for Republicans, some had become Democrats again, some had grown disillusioned with politics, and factions had sprouted in local Populist parties. Republican J. J. Curtis's 28 percent of the 1896 congressional election vote and William McKinley's victory in DeKalb County disclosed a revival of the Seventh District GOP. Street did not know whether the voters who had supported Republicans in 1896 were protesting against Populist fusion with Bryan, or whether they had actually become Republicans. The question was important because the GOP had already nominated a candidate, and the chances of fusion looked dim.[15]

GOP leaders resented the fact that, after they helped Populists in the 1896 state elections, most third-party men backed a Democrat for president in that year's fall elections. Since the "national fight" of 1896, T. W. Powell wrote Street, "Republicans have had as much antipathy for us as for the Democrats." State GOP leaders refused to fuse with Seventh District Populists and rebuffed all efforts by Populists to secure the withdrawal of GOP congressional nominee Frank Lathrop, a wealthy St. Clair County lumber man. Republican leaders argued that they helped Howard win in 1894, and Populists should reciprocate. The three-way race Howard anticipated materialized and made it unlikely that a Populist would win.[16]

T. W. Powell did not believe the 1896 Republican vote in the Seventh District represented loyalty to the GOP. Forty percent of the vote Curtis had received, he said, would go to Street and his Democratic opponent, John Burnett. Still, many Street supporters believed that it was imperative to get Lathrop to withdraw. If he did so, one man wrote, Street would get three-quarters of the GOP vote. Dealing with Republicans on this issue was difficult because the GOP hierarchy was split between two patronage factions, one led by former chairman R. A. Moseley and the other by newly elected chairman William Vaughn. If Street got help from one faction, he risked losing the other. Seventh District Populists claimed that Vaughn agreed to support Street if Populists would support GOP nominees in other districts, but the chairman denied making such a deal. Powell found that rank-and-file Republicans would not back Street. Populists had to "go it alone," he said, because Republicans did not appreciate the help they had received from Populists in other districts. Some Populists were relieved by this turn of events. One wrote Street that he was "sick" of fusion with a party that had "no affinity whatsoever" with Populists.[17]

Republican support for Lathrop meant that Populists had the daunting task of getting a larger turnout of their voters than August's election had generated. One Populist advised Street that the "plebeians" were "tired of so much politics when they are getting nothing out of it." A St. Clair County Populist wrote that the August elections had "depressed and discouraged" his local party members, and a Franklin County Populist editor wrote that subscriptions to his paper were so low he would have to stop printing it. Street tried to stir crowds with emotional attacks. He charged that his Democratic opponent, Cherokee County attorney John Burnett, was a "gold bug" raised in a wealthy family. Street focused attention on railroad corporations by raising an issue that obsessed his family. Land in northeast Alabama given to railroads by the government had not been used to build rail lines. Street argued that it should be given to farm families for homesteads, but Burnett would not address that problem, said Street, because he was an "attorney for the railroads."[18]

T. W. Powell's search for a way to motivate voters led him to ask Georgia's famed Populist Tom Watson to campaign in the district. "No other man in the Union," wrote Powell, "could accomplish so much" by speaking for Street. Powell also proposed that a "referendum" be held on election day to allow Populists to express their attitudes about recent actions of the national People's party. Remnants of the party had already met and selected candidates for the 1900 presidential election, two years ahead of time. Both candidates were northerners, and southerners, who had few delegates at the meeting, were furious. A referendum on whether to accept or reject the nominees might bring out Populist voters.[19]

The efforts of Street and Powell proved unavailing, as a low voter turnout and the lack of fusion aided the Democrats. Burnett won a plurality with 44 percent to 32 percent for Street and 23 percent for Lathrop. The total vote fell by 10 percent from that of 1896, and Street polled eleven hundred fewer votes than Howard received that year. The Populist nominee got a majority only in Marshall County. Some Etowah and Cherokee County Populists charged that Negro voters were paid by Democrats, but the Populists did not have entirely clean hands. Oliver Street had offered to pay $100 to a Republican who said that he could deliver the votes of one faction of Etowah County Republicans to the Populists. Street, an ostensibly pious Methodist layman, did not allow ethical scruples to interfere with his ambitions.[20]

Populists were bewildered by the events of 1898, which dealt a death blow to their national and state parties. In a dispiriting letter to Oliver Street, Cherokee County editor I. L. Brock, once a member of the state Populist executive committee, argued that the Populist party was a "goner" and could not "be resuscitated." Brock considered the options. "Politically I am at sea," he wrote. "I am a Populist. Believe that we are right. But what are we to do to accomplish the results sought?" Oliver Street was unhappy with the Republicans because Lathrop's candidacy caused his defeat, and in September 1899, when Brock suggested that they realign with the Democrats, he initially agreed. A few months later they began to correspond with reform Democrats, including Governor Johnston, who was seeking John Tyler Morgan's senate seat.[21]

Morgan, a free-silver Democrat, had helped to elect Johnston governor, but obligations to the senator did not thwart the governor's ambitions. Johnston prepared for his campaign against Morgan by engaging in a series of devious actions that made him an outspoken opponent of disfranchisement, which he had previously supported. In 1898 he had given his approval to a legislative act that set up a referendum on whether to hold a constitutional convention on voting restrictions, yet when he needed Populist support in the senate race he castigated disfranchisement, attacked "machine" politics, and in February 1899 persuaded the legislature to repeal the convention act he had signed into law only three months earlier. It was an extraordinary performance.[22]

Repeal of the convention measure was a relief to Upcountry Populists, who believed voting restrictions would disfranchise poor white farmers as well as blacks. When newspapers and politicians despised by Populists attacked him for his reversal, Johnston gained support, although many people noticed that he had been on both sides of the issue. Judge T. A. Street offered to help Johnston, and in January 1900 the governor slyly appointed Oliver Street as a trustee of the Seventh District agricultural school. Democrat Jesse Stallings, a three-term Wiregrass congressman, pro-silver Bryanite, and an opponent of disfranchisement, ran for governor with the support of many ex-Populists, including the Streets.[23]

In the spring of 1899, Lewis Reynolds offered a resolution, passed by Chilton County's Populist executive committee, that commended Johnston's new stand on disfranchisement. In the summer Frank Crichton, editor of the Populist *Clanton Banner*, asked Populists to support reform Democrats and proposed dismantling the Populist executive committees. In November 1899 Judge Samuel Adams advocated that Populists vote for Johnston in the 1900 Democratic primaries but did not suggest that they abandon their local party organizations. Reynolds did not support Johnston but said he would be bound by the action of the 1900 state Populist convention. Populist activity on behalf of Johnston was almost entirely stimulated by the governor's conversion on disfranchisement, but it forced the state Populist party to act.[24]

On November 24, 1899, the Populist state executive committee met in Birmingham to debate whether Populists should enter the 1900 Democratic primaries to aid reform Democrats. Committee members rejected a resolution that urged this course but endorsed one by St. Clair County legislator Napoleon Spears to keep the Populist state committee intact and permit Populists to make their own decisions about voting in the primaries. This action was significant because Populists had been discouraged from participating in Democratic nomination fights. Opposition to Spears's resolution came from Shelby County, where *People's Advocate* editor Frank Norris condemned Populist participation in the Democratic primary.[25]

The state Democratic executive committee, controlled by Morgan, hurt Johnston's effort to get Populists into the primary. It scheduled the county primaries all on one day, which benefitted Morgan, and in November 1899 it resolved to limit the power of non-Democrats in the legislature by a method that confirmed Upcountry fears about elite control of the state. Non-Democratic legislators, said the committee, must get approval from the Democrats they had defeated to get local bills (bills that applied only to the legislator's home county) passed. The resolution was an effort to stifle political independence in the Upcountry. A concerned Lewis Reynolds, who sought the 1900 Populist nomination for state senator from Chilton, Shelby, and Elmore Counties, denounced the committee's action. Reynolds's disenchantment with the Democrats grew, but actions by the Streets led people to believe that they had become Democrats again. "Like you," wrote I. L. Brock to Oliver Street in March, "I thought that the proper thing to do was to ally ourselves with the free-silver wing of the Democratic party."[26]

The Democratic primary results gave pause to many Upcountry Populists who dallied with reform Democrats. Johnston's strongest support came from hill counties, but John Tyler Morgan won sixty-one of sixty-six counties, and William T. Samford, a Black Belt planter, easily defeated Jesse Stallings for the gubernatorial nomination. The primary, writes Morgan's biographer, "helped perpetuate and extend aspects of a sterile, conservative political environment well into the twentieth century." This evidence of the futility of attempting a reform takeover of the Democratic party caused many Populists to pull back from the Democrats. Frank Crichton of the *Clanton Banner* decided to support Populists for local offices in Chilton County's general election, and Oliver Street was soon trying to elect a Populist to Congress in the Seventh District. However, events within the Populist party at the national and state levels in 1900 made it difficult to continue the third-party effort, no matter how committed Populists might be.[27]

Remnants of the antifusionist wing of the People's party held a national convention in 1900, with Lewis Reynolds and Milford Howard as delegates. Northern Populists insisted on the ticket selected two years earlier, that of Wharton Barker of Pennsylvania for president and Ignatius Donnelly of Minnesota for vice-president. Barker was an unknown, and neither candidate appealed to the South. Howard was suggested as an alternative to Barker, but delegates would not alter the ticket, and northerners threatened to bolt if their candidates were removed. "From any standpoint," writes John W. Hicks, "the ticket was ridiculous." Georgia Populist Tom Watson refused to participate in the national campaign, and some Populists actually held a separate fusionist convention. These events dealt the final blow to Populism as a national movement.[28]

The efficacy of offering a statewide Populist ticket in 1900 was also questioned. With so little support left in the Wiregrass and no chance of fusion with Republicans, statewide success for the Populists was impossible. Yet, a state Populist convention met in the spring and nominated a ticket. Chilton County's Samuel Adams, who had backed Johnston in the Democratic primaries, was nominated for governor, and Lewis Reynolds was named chairman of the state campaign committee. Shortly after the convention adjourned, Adams refused the nomination and endorsed the Democratic nominee. Another Chilton County Populist turned down the nomination for state treasurer. Both men seemed resigned to Democratic hegemony.[29]

Because of these defections, Populists tried to hold another convention, but they could not assemble enough delegates to make new nominations. In desperation, the Populist state executive committee arbitrarily picked a ticket, which included Perry County physician Grattan Crowe as candidate for governor. Crowe had little support, and Chilton County editor Frank Crichton questioned both the wisdom of the nominations and the committee's authority to make them. Crowe received only 11 percent of the vote in the August elections, and won only Shelby, Chilton, and St. Clair Counties. Populists were no longer a serious threat in state politics, and although they had not decided on their future direction, they had to be impressed with the vote received by Republican gubernatorial candidate John A. Steele, who led Crowe in most Upcountry counties. Steele won just under 30 percent of the Seventh District vote. Defectors from Populism were voting for both major parties.[30]

The confusion of Upcountry Populists became evident when W. F. Aldrich declined to run for Congress again. The Populist and Republican executive committees of the Fourth District could not agree on a "fusion" nominee for Congress and adjourned without nominating one. The Populist committee finally endorsed Democratic nominee Sidney Bowie of Talladega County, part of the Bryanite wing of his party, who ran unopposed. Populist editor Frank Norris, at his party's request, endorsed Bowie but urged his readers not to desert the Populist party in its hour of maximum danger, and he endorsed Populist electors running on the Wharton Barker ticket against Democratic nominee William Jennings Bryan. He "would prefer a Populist for congress," wrote Norris, but Bowie was "in thorough accord with the Populists as to the leading demands of the party." Norris cited not only Bowie's support for free silver but also his endorsement of "municipal ownership of public utilities and the telegraph," a favorite issue of Norris that reflected the views of reformers in the nation's largest cities.[31]

These endorsements left Norris and A. P. Longshore in a quandary because the *People's Advocate* endorsed no Republicans. The Populists were obligated to Shelby County's Republicans, who had fused with Populists in four consecutive state and local elections, and in August 1900 the fused parties had won all contested county offices again. Neither party could win without the other. A week before November's election, Norris conspicuously printed on his editorial page the names of Alabama's Republican presidential electors. Because the editor had already endorsed the Populist national ticket, he could not endorse the Republican electors, but he had to show solidarity with the GOP. The newspaper had now given aid to three separate political parties and reflected the confused mentality of the Populist rank and file. Norris's progressive mentality made Bowie acceptable, his loyalty to the Populist party made the endorsement of the Wharton Barker ticket essential, and his debt to Republicans made his tepid sanction of their electors necessary. All three dynamics continued to influence Norris and Longshore for another decade.[32]

Lewis Reynolds was influenced by other factors. He was already angry about the Democrat's effort to limit the power of non-Democratic legislators when he became embroiled in another dispute with Democrats that had an impact on the direction of Chilton County Populists. Reynolds had been the Populist nominee for the state senate from Chilton, Shelby, and Elmore Counties, and his Democratic opponent was Shelby County lawyer W. P. Oliver. In the August elections Reynolds led in both Chilton and Shelby, but Oliver's margin of victory in Elmore County, which was 47 percent black, was so large that the Democrat won. Reynolds charged that white Democrats stuffed ballot boxes with the votes of blacks, and he formally contested the election with the state senate. The senate did not act on the matter until after the November election, but the dispute was widely publicized before the election and may have influenced voters.[33]

Oliver Street agreed to serve on the 1900 campaign committee of the Seventh District's Populist nominee for Congress, Napoleon Bonaparte Spears of St. Clair County. In 1898 Street had not enticed Republicans away from Frank Lathrop, but Spears was a former Republican, and his ties to the GOP seemed to unite the two parties. He even persuaded Lathrop to be his campaign manager. The two anti-Democratic parties fused their campaign committees. Thus, only a few months after supporting reform Democrats, Oliver Street took a seat on a fusion committee headed by the Republican who had cost him a seat in Congress in 1898![34]

Napoleon Spears was born and reared in the east Tennessee mountain county of Bledsoe. Several Tennessee mountain counties furnished more Union than Confederate soldiers, and Spears's father had been a Union general. Napoleon attended Emory and Henry College after the war, read law, was admitted to the Tennessee bar, practiced in Bledsoe County, and was elected to Tennessee's house of representatives as a Republican in 1874. In the early 1880s, he moved to St. Clair County and practiced law in Pell City. Spears became active in his county's Republican party, but St. Clair was the state's most loyal Populist county, and in 1896 Spears became an outright Populist. He was elected to the legislature as a Populist in 1898, reelected on the Populist ticket in August 1900, and won the Populist nomination for Congress in September.[35]

Many people doubted Spears's commitment to Populism. A Franklin County Democratic editor described Spears's speeches as "Republican smeared over with a thin coat of 'Populist sugar' hoping to catch the unwary Populist voter." Spears endorsed the Omaha platform of the national People's party, wrote the editor, but he had made a "Republican speech" in Franklin County in which he endorsed high tariffs. In a letter to Oliver Street only three weeks before the fall election, St. Clair County Populist Noah B. Hood charged that Spears had backed Lathrop in 1898. Hood could not "take Spears" and was disturbed by reports that Spears was trying to lead St. Clair's Populists into the GOP. Like Samuel Adams, I. L. Brock, and many other Populists, Hood was unwilling to join the Republicans.[36]

The race issue was injected into the campaign when a letter Spears wrote to the "Colored Citizens of St. Clair County" was printed in Democratic newspapers. The letter was patronizing (Spears encouraged blacks to stay sober on election day and not sell their votes), but he did ask for their help and pledged to stand by them on issues such as disfranchisement. Spears was sincere and later spoke out against racial discrimination, but his campaign manager, Frank Lathrop, had typical white views. Lathrop informed a GOP leader that it would "take two hundred dollars to control the negro vote at Gadsden on election day. . . . We want those two hundred and fifty negro votes that I lost in Gadsden beat two years ago."[37]

The outcome of 1900's November election shocked Alabama's Democrats. With Bryan as their candidate for president again and Populism dying, they looked for a great triumph. Black Republicans still "voted" in many counties, but by 1900 the Black Belt counties were so dominated by white election officials that a unified anti-Democratic vote by blacks was unlikely. If Democratic insecurity had faded, as an 1899 legislative vote not to call a constitutional convention act revealed, the 1900 election revived it, created new anxieties, and led to the realization that disfranchisement was necessary to insure Democratic dominance.

Incumbent Seventh District Democratic congressman John Burnett received only 51.6 percent of the vote. Bryan fell below 50 percent of the vote in fifteen north Alabama counties and lost to McKinley in twelve of them, ten of which were in the Hill Country. Shelby and Chilton Counties, neither of which had ever returned a majority for a Republican presidential candidate, gave more than 60 percent of their votes to McKinley. Even in Wiregrass counties, most of which returned large majorities for Bryan, McKinley got impressive support. Wiregrass whites were drifting back toward the Democratic party, as the 1898 and 1900 state elections verified, but McKinley defeated Bryan in two Wiregrass counties. McKinley received only 35 percent of the statewide vote, but tight control of voters in Black Belt counties kept the state Democratic. In some counties where blacks constituted more than 75 percent of the population, the Democratic party received more than 90 percent of the votes.[38]

Burnett was the first Democratic congressional candidate to receive a majority of the Seventh District vote since 1892, but he won by only 626 out of 20,000 votes cast. Spears led in two of the eight counties in the district and came within fifty votes of winning another. Burnett was lucky. Local political disagreements led to a sweep of Winston County by the national Democratic ticket for the first time since 1880 and to Burnett's victory there. The Winston County vote may account for Burnett's reelection, but he could not depend on Winston to remain in the Democratic column.[39]

The editor of the Democratic *Anniston Hot Blast* was incensed by the large vote for Republicans in the predominately white Hill Country. A week after the election he raised the possibility that Upcountry whites might actually align with lowcountry blacks and seize control of the state. Election returns from "white counties," said the editor, "point very clearly to a future coalition between many of the white populists and negro republicans." These white Populists must "retrace their steps and get upon the sunlit hills of white supremacy." Populists once had "the tolerance if not the sympathy of very many democrats who did not cooperate with them," but "making Kolb governor and putting the bottom rail on top" were "two different things." A man who wants to "make a white nigger of himself," the editor went on, would bring on himself the "contempt" of "right thinking people."[40]

Former Populist Frank Crichton of the *Clanton Banner,* who had endorsed Bryan and Bowie, was mystified by McKinley's large vote in Chilton County. Crichton first argued that the higher price of cotton had led people in his county to vote Republican, but he did not believe that his old Populist allies had become "believers" in "Republican doctrine." They had probably voted for McKinley as a "compromise with themselves at the present moment" because they had "not determined their future course of action." *People's Advocate* editor Frank Norris explained that the national Democratic party was still too evenly split between the Cleveland and Bryan wings for Populists to go back to it. Only when the Cleveland wing "was gone" would Populists "be ready to unite with the representatives of the pure democracy."[41]

Bryan did seem to be losing support in his party, and when he did not gain ground on the GOP in 1900, southern Bourbons crowed that his nomination had been a mistake. By early 1901 conservatives were taking their party back from the coalition of small southern and western farmers who had nourished Bryanism. "Conservatives and reactionaries" who had little influence in the party between 1896 and 1900 "now burst into print" to demand a return to the southern planter–northeastern business coalition that elected Cleveland.[42]

McKinley's support in white counties helped inspire a new drive for disfranchisement. In December 1900 state legislators authorized a new referendum to take place on April 1901 on the question of whether to hold a constitutional convention. The goal of convention supporters was to enact voting requirements that would protect Democrats. Black Belters had kept power by managing black voters, but if thousands of white Hill Country farmers would not conform even after the Populist movement expired, the threat of an alliance of lower-class blacks and whites still existed. The Democratic hierarchy sought safety so that, as one leading Democrat later put it, politics could remain in the hands of "the supremacy of virtue and intelligence in this state." Frank Norris called on voters to oppose a convention that would be "composed of delegates, one-third of whom would be agents and attorneys of the corporations." The "common people" could bid "farewell to their liberties" if such a convention succeeded. Chilton County's Populist executive committee denounced the convention, and rank-and-file Populists expressed fears that whites would be disfranchised.[43]

The Street family was offended by the call for a convention. When Edgar Gardner Murphy of Montgomery, the well-known Episcopal minister and opponent of child labor, endorsed an educational qualification for voting in a March 1901 pamphlet, Thomas Atkins Street bitterly rebuked him. Street accused Murphy of writing in the language of a Black Belt "oligarch" and a "deceiver," and he warned Murphy that if efforts to eliminate upland voters went forward, "the plain white people in their desperate attempts to free themselves" would "bring desolation and ruin among us." Murphy's "plutocratic ideas," noted Street, were not "indigenous" to the Hill Country. Genteel reformers such as Murphy often opposed mass democracy and believed that society must be guided by enlightened elites such as themselves, a stand that sharply differentiated their brand of progressivism from the more democratic reform ideology of the Populists.[44]

Oliver Street, who had attacked the Sayre law in a legal brief that brought him statewide attention in 1893, argued later in his life that disfranchisement "overshadowed" all other issues. "The strangle hold of the Black Belt on the white sections of the state was locked in 1901," said Street, "and the key thrown away." Democrats were losing the support of Hill Country Populists such as Street, who had seemed willing to reenter the Democratic party.[45]

Black Belt election officials recorded such huge percentages of black voters in favor of a convention called, in part, to disfranchise blacks that the measure passed. Most hill counties, the entire Seventh Congressional District, more than 75 percent of Marshall and Chilton County voters, and 60 percent in Shelby County opposed the convention. Upcountry voters also chose convention delegates who, like Lewis Reynolds of Chilton County, opposed disfranchisement. Only seven delegates were Populists, but Republicans Napoleon Spears of St. Clair County and J. B. Sloan of Blount County had been Populists, and Republican delegate W. H. Bartlett of Marshall County was supported by Populists from his county.[46]

Democrats also created another issue that drove Upcountry Populists away from the Democratic party. The resolution of the Democratic executive committee that called for reduced influence by non-Democratic legislators led to the 1900–1901 legislature actually imposing laws on Shelby and Chilton Counties. Democratic legislators passed a stock law that applied solely to Chilton County even though Chilton's Populist state representative L. B. Pounds objected to it. *Clanton Banner* editor Frank Crichton noted that few measures could generate more emotion. If you wanted a successful mass meeting in Chilton County, he wrote, just mention a stock law and "that'll fetch 'em." The stock-law controversy "revived the old spirit of antagonism" between Populists and Democrats. A letter to Crichton from a self-described Chilton County "cracker" denounced the "wicked" advocates of the stock law who had "drawn out the sword" against small farmers. Later, at the constitutional convention, Lewis Reynolds sought the passage of a bill that required all stock laws to be approved by the voters.[47]

The Democratic legislature ushered through a similar stock law for Shelby County. Angry farmers filed their objections to the law in a lawsuit heard by Judge A. P. Longshore. Despite his lack of authority in the matter, Longshore declared the law invalid and unenforceable. When the state senate also rejected Lewis Reynolds's contest of W. P. Oliver's election to the senate because they claimed Oliver was not properly "served" with contest papers, the Hill Country was ripe for revolt. Reynolds said that he was "counted out by a Democratic board" and that a "Democratic legislature endorsed the steal." Disfranchisement had the greatest impact, but efforts to limit the power of non-Democratic legislators, the passage of stock laws, the refusal to hear the contest filed by Lewis Reynolds, and the defeat of Democratic reformers in the 1900 primaries all alienated Upcountry voters. The constitutional convention and the process of ratifying the constitution made it almost impossible for Street, Reynolds, or Longshore to become Democrats.[48]

Lewis Reynolds demonstrated his commitment to reform and to grass-roots democracy at the 1901 constitutional convention. He voted against every effort to restrict voting, but the convention's Democratic majority severely restricted the right to vote. Reynolds supported the right of property-owning women to vote and opposed a proposal to take the suffrage from strikers. He voted for a strong antitrust provision, introduced a consumer measure to make bank stockholders individually liable to customers in case of bank failures, and backed a child labor provision designed to prevent employers from hiring boys under the age of twelve and girls under the age of fourteen. The latter provision would have stopped the payment of children's wages to their parents, a practice that had made it difficult to end child labor. Reynolds opposed a measure that would have prevented the state from lending "its credit" or funding internal improvements. A Black Belt delegate said that supporters of this measure feared the internal improvement schemes Populists had "mothered in the Ocala platform."[49]

Despite Reynolds's record in these areas, Sheldon Hackney charges that he and other "agrarian" delegates opposed "Progressive" forces in the convention because they voted to limit the taxing and debt limit authority of cities. However, when a measure to lower the tax rate that could be levied by the state for public schools came before the convention, Reynolds spoke against it. Supporters of the lower state rate contended that taxes for education should be raised by individual counties and not by the state. Reynolds, acutely aware of the low value of Upcountry land and the consequent lack of revenue available in hill counties, believed the state should take the lead in funding education. The problem before the convention, he said, was "what to do with the ignorant white man" in Alabama. "I represent the hill billies," asserted Reynolds, who argued that education increased property values and helped poor white children.[50]

When a delegate sought to give large landowners more authority than other citizens to decide when to increase property taxes, Reynolds angrily attacked the proposal. A special privilege for wealthy landowners, he said, was a "remarkable proposition and something new in the history of our country." When war came, big property owners would not do the fighting and dying because they were "the biggest cowards who ever lived in the country. Wealth is always cowardly, and the poor people are those who fight the battles." As a legislator, he had opposed special taxes on one group or special privileges for anyone, said Reynolds, "because the statute books should bear equally on all classes alike." There was class resentment in Reynolds's speech, but he also displayed the Jacksonian idea of a government that treats everyone equally.[51]

The constitutional convention of 1901, more than any other event in Alabama's history, pointed out the cooperation between the Black Belt and elite industrial interests. John B. Knox, "perhaps Alabama's richest railroad lawyer," was chairman of the convention and of its rules committee, which appointed all other committees. Knox named Black Belt representative Thomas W. Coleman of Greene County chairman of the committee on suffrage and elections, and the two men were the convention's most influential figures. Winston County delegate N. H. Freeman understood that Black Belters would ratify the constitution with the votes of the very people it was written to disfranchise, so he offered an amendment to limit the ratification process to whites only. "I respectfully submit that it is enough to disfranchise the Negro," said Freeman, "without making him an involuntary party to his own disfranchisement. We should not call upon him in the Black Belt to be the victim of a ballot he never cast." In addition to the suffrage provisions, Black Belters apportioned the legislature so that they could control it, and the lowland region resisted reapportionment until the late 1960s.[52]

Frank Norris wrote that he would "fight the ratification of the new constitution to the best of our ability from start to finish." The "sole object" of the convention, he wrote, was to "perpetuate the Democrat party in power." The Shelby County Populist executive committee asked voters to oppose ratification. In a debate with convention chairman John B. Knox at the courthouse in Columbiana during the ratification campaign, A. P. Longshore said the constitution would cost the "poor laboring boy" his right to vote. Lewis Reynolds described the constitution as the work of the Black Belt and said he had also tried to have the referendum restricted to white voters only, but was ruled out of order. The "uneducated," he said, would be hurt by ratification.[53]

In a final act of hypocrisy, Black Belt election officials recorded the votes of blacks in favor of a constitution that created a property qualification, a literacy test, and a poll tax for voters. The total vote for ratification was 108,613, or 57 percent, versus 81,734, or 43 percent against, but in six counties where blacks exceeded three-quarters of the population (Dallas, Greene, Hale, Perry, Sumter, and Wilcox), more than 95 percent of the vote was recorded in favor. In two other counties with similar racial populations (Macon and Marengo), more than 85 percent of the votes were counted for ratification. If all majority black counties had been excluded, the constitution would have been defeated.[54]

"The new constitution has been ratified," wrote Frank Norris, "but it was not done by the white counties." The Hill Country overwhelmingly opposed ratification. Marshall County's voters cast the largest percentage against ratification, 84.7 percent, of any county in the state. Chilton and St. Clair County's voters both recorded 81 percent, and Shelby's voters 79 percent, against the constitution. This result was an extraordinary demonstration of white sentiment against suffrage restrictions. A credible argument can be made that most Alabama white voters opposed the 1901 constitution. It was no accident that areas where Populists were strongest returned the largest percentages against ratification. At the nearly all-white precinct of Dunnavant in Shelby County, where Populists won overwhelmingly in the 1896, 1898, and 1900 elections, all fifty-three ballots cast were recorded against ratification.[55]

"The Democratic party," boasted the *Montgomery Advertiser,* "through its most patriotic spirits, called the convention, framed the new instrument, [and] adopted it at the polls." Hill Country Populists were well aware of the truth in that statement, and no one was more disconcerted by it than Lewis Reynolds. When Chilton County's Populists met in convention at Clanton in December 1901 to discuss their party's fate, Reynolds brought his accumulated anger. He proposed, and the delegates adopted, a resolution that denounced the new constitution as a "disgrace" and appealed to Congress to restore "a republican form of government in our state . . . and by so doing prevent revolution which will surely come unless this crowd of monarchs is dethroned." Reynolds then asked the delegates to join the Republican party because the Populist party no longer existed. The request marked the beginning of a long debate between Reynolds and Judge Samuel Adams, who spoke against the notion that Populists should become Republicans.[56]

Clanton Banner editor Frank Crichton, a former ally of Reynolds, expressed dismay at his old friend and asked that the Democratic party take Populists back on a "free and open basis." Another critic argued in a letter to the *Banner* that joining the Republicans would divide white men, who should "stand as a unit." After these attacks, Reynolds equivocated. In another public letter addressed to local Populists, he both denied that he intended "to land the Populists in the Republican party" and reiterated his belief that joining the GOP was the best course of action. He had not intended "to scare anybody to death" and would do what the "majority" of Populists wanted, except "go into the Democratic party." For Reynolds, the only options for Populists were to maintain their local party or to become Republicans formally.[57]

The state Democratic executive committee and the legislature adopted a statewide Democratic primary for whites, formally restricted to Democrats only, but in practice the Populists could participate. Because the primary would be held in August, beginning in 1902, both state and federal general elections were thereafter held in November. Joseph Johnston, an advocate of the primary, sought a third term as governor in 1902. He appealed to Populists by labeling his opponents "the machine" and charging that the 1901 constitution was adopted by fraud practiced in the Black Belt. Because Johnston's opponent in the August Democratic primary was the Black Belt conservative William Dorsey Jelks, the ex-governor's appeal to Upcountry reformers attracted the Streets into his camp once again.[58]

Johnston's candidacy also stirred the growing debate in Chilton County between Lewis Reynolds and Samuel Adams. The Populist executive committee of Chilton County met again in July 1902 to settle the question of what to do about their party's future. Reynolds argued again that they should become Republicans while Adams opposed Reynolds's suggestion and expressed his support for Johnston. Reynolds replied that although he supported Johnston's views, he could not vote in the Democratic primary. The Populist committee decided to lay the issue before the party's voters in an extraordinary party election. The question that Chilton County's Populists had to decide were: "1. Shall the party maintain its organization? 2. Shall the Populists join the Republican party?"[59]

In a letter to the *Clanton Banner,* Reynolds sought to take the sting out of the idea of becoming an avowed Republican. "Now, we are not to join the Republican party, but we are to call the same party we belong to now the Republican party." Frank Crichton found this notion absurd and described it as a call for a "sham republicanism." Reynolds continued his pragmatic campaign by arguing that the absence of Populist state and national organizations made it imperative for local Populists to join a party with a voice in state and national affairs. After joining with Republicans, he said, "We will be the same . . . [party] that we are now." Reynolds was accused of telling Chilton's voters that even if they agreed to go into the GOP, they would not be real Republicans. A critic who watched this controversy unfold described Reynolds as a "very remarkable person . . . a circus performer in the political arena . . . an adroit slack wire walker." When he was with the Republicans, "he was a Republican," and when he was with Populists he was "still a Populist." Chilton County's Populists narrowly rejected the proposal to join the Republican party when they voted 168 to 149 to remain Populists.[60]

The adroit Reynolds was not dismayed. He resolved his dilemma by claiming to be a Populist in local matters and a Republican in state and national politics. He received the Populist nomination for the lower house of the legislature at approximately the same time that the Fourth Congressional District Republicans chose him to serve on the state GOP executive committee. One old Populist declared that he was "disgusted" with Reynolds and that the GOP was the party of "money managers and negroes." Frank Crichton wrote that Reynolds should end his fiction of being a Populist. Another of Reynolds's former allies wrote that his friend had joined the party of monopolies, tariffs, and the gold standard. "You wire in and wire out," wrote Samuel Adams in a published letter addressed to Reynolds, "but no man can tell whether the spoke that made the track is going in or coming back."[61]

Even though Chilton County Populists such as Adams and former circuit clerk E. B. Deason had returned to the Democratic party, and it was not certain what party the rank and file would eventually choose, the Republican stance of Reynolds did not hurt him with the great mass of his old supporters. He accepted the Populist nomination for another legislative term, and won 55 percent of the general election vote. A majority of those who voted for him also cast ballots for the GOP candidate for governor and the Fourth District Republican congressional nominee, each of whom won the county. Still, it was not apparent whether Chilton's Populists had become Republicans or voted for the GOP because no statewide Populist ticket was available. Apparently, they intended to continue voting against Democrats in national, state, and even local elections, but as the special party election held earlier had shown, a large faction of Populists were not yet prepared to denominate themselves as Republicans.[62]

Election returns also disclosed that many Upcountry voters had been disfranchised. Only sixteen hundred ballots were cast in Chilton County in 1902, whereas in 1900 twenty-one hundred people had voted in state and local elections. A similar change occurred throughout the Hill Country. In Shelby County, 3,313 voters cast ballots in 1900's gubernatorial election, but by January 1903 only 3,206 people were registered to vote in the county, and only 1,919 voted in the 1902 gubernatorial race. Shelby, with a 28 percent black population, lost far more voters than Chilton County, where blacks made up only 19 percent of the population, but thousands of whites were disfranchised. In the 90 percent white Seventh Congressional District, for instance, the number of people voting in the 1902 race for Congress fell by more than three thousand from the 1900 election. All of these voting declines took place at the same time that the population in nearly all north Alabama counties was growing rapidly. The Black Belt had achieved most of its aims through disfranchisement.[63]

A week after the election, Lewis Reynolds charged that every "merchant, lawyer, doctor and professional man" had opposed him. Frank Crichton described this statement as an unwarranted appeal to "class interests," and another critic charged Reynolds with "seeking to build himself up politically on the prejudice of a certain class of our people" against another. It was clear that Reynolds hoped to take the county's small farmers into the Republican party with him and that the kind of Republicans he admired were not those that represented big business or elite financial interests. Despite this initial failure to make Populists into Republicans, events in 1902 continued to alienate Hill Country Populists from the Democrats.[64]

Joseph F. Johnston was defeated in the Democratic primary by the Black Belt Bourbon William Dorsey Jelks in a landslide conservative victory. The new constitution affected Johnston's vote-getting ability. Many former Populists in the Hill Country and Wiregrass were disfranchised. Johnston wrote Judge Street that the constitution succeeded in keeping "more than half the men who would like to have participated" from the polls. This severe blow to hopes for a progressive takeover of the Democratic party left little doubt among Populist leaders about the direction of the Democratic party.[65]

Three days after the Democratic primary, Oliver Street received a letter from Etowah County Republican W. H. Standifer, who argued that it was Street's "duty" to accept the 1902 Seventh District GOP nomination for Congress "and then afterwards of the Populists if necessary." The men "that are to be lined up in this fight," wrote Standifer, "are those who at one time affiliated with the Populist party, and you are the man to do that." Winston County Republican J. J. Curtis favored "nominating a Republican with Populist tendencies or a Populist with Republican tendencies." Napoleon Spears contended that there was a "strong disposition" by Republicans to nominate Street if they could be assured that he would support the national Republican administration and was "at heart a republican." Republicans would allow Street to receive the Populist nomination "first" if he desired. Spears warned that four thousand white voters in the Seventh District were disfranchised by the poll tax and that "three thousand of this number are Republicans and Populists; one thousand Democrats."[66]

Despite warnings from Johnston and Spears about the effects of disfranchisement, the close race run by Spears against Burnett in 1900 made the Seventh District race attractive to Street. If he could only unite Populists and Republicans he had a chance, yet a St. Clair County Populist who opposed fusion wrote Street that there was "nothing in common" between the two parties. Cherokee County's I. L. Brock wrote that he had become a Democrat, supported the new constitution, and backed Burnett for reelection. "I know full well and so do you," wrote Brock, "that the populist party, as an organization is a thing of the past. . . . So it is now up to those who once followed the flag of that party to decide whether they will unite with the Democrats or republicans or be mugwumps." Brock asked whether Street would run as a "Populist or republican" and warned that if he ran as a Republican he would "necessarily have to make some kind of compromise" with the GOP "that it seems to me might be humiliating to you."[67]

Street accepted the nomination of both parties, which did not signal that he was a Republican, but it was a break with fusion as Populists had practiced it in most hill counties. Populists had accepted "cooperation" from Republicans and allowed the GOP places on fusion tickets only after Populists secured the nominations for the most important offices. This method was also used in creating statewide tickets, but Populists had accepted Republican "nominations" only in counties such as Winston and Walker, where there were more Republicans than Populists. Street's dual nomination was a large step toward Republican affiliation. State GOP chairman William Vaughn, who had refused to support Populists in previous Seventh District campaigns, offered to campaign for Street.[68]

After it became common knowledge that Oliver had accepted the GOP nomination, Judge Thomas A. Street received a remarkable letter from Democrat Joseph Johnston, who wrote that if he lived in the Seventh District he "certainly would be greatly tempted to vote for Street. . . . He is infinitely a better man than Burnett and would serve the people better." Johnston offered to send one hundred copies of a Birmingham newspaper that supported progressive causes to be "distributed" in the Seventh. He

What Happened to the Populists? 177

believed this reform paper would help Street's cause. One Republican found evidence that "Johnson [sic] Democrats are openly opposing ticket of machine." Thus, in at least one congressional district the "progressive" Democrats and old Populists did work together.[69]

What Street needed was campaign funds, but he did not receive any help from the national Republican party. He requested aid from the national GOP chairman, who wrote back that it would give party leaders "great pleasure to aid you materially in your campaign" but that money was short and that it was too late to help Street. In other Seventh District campaigns between 1902 and 1920, parsimonious behavior by the national GOP contributed to Republican defeats. GOP leaders were loathe to spend money in this southern congressional district despite the voting strength of Upcountry Republicans.[70]

Despite Street's acceptance of the GOP nomination, Populist leaders campaigned for him. Wiregrass Populist Frank Baltzell and Milford Howard traveled through the district with Street, and Dr. Grattan Crowe, Populist candidate for governor in 1900, sent four thousand circulars into the Seventh District asking Populists to vote Republican. Upcountry Republicans campaigned just as actively. J. J. Curtis was "exhausted" by the campaign. Napoleon Spears humorously explained the hybrid nature of the fusion campaign to a Republican friend. One should have "two good drinks for a Republican speech and three good drinks for a Populist speech, taken twenty minutes apart before speaking," wrote Spears. This prescription, he advised, when "adhered to strictly will produce results on election day that will be talked about by the people around their firesides to their children for many years to come."[71]

Victory was possible only if Populists and Republicans could be unified, and they could not. Populist S. J. Petree warned Street that in Franklin County some Populists not only had returned to the Democratic party but also were on the local Democratic ticket. Even this small percentage of ex-Populists in Democratic ranks damaged Street, and he lost. He won ten of fifteen Marshall County precincts that had given majorities to Populist gubernatorial candidate A. T. Goodwyn in 1896 and received 53 percent of the county's total vote, but in most Upcountry counties the Populists were not united. Seventh District anti-Democrats had lost another round in their longtime war for Upcountry political independence, but they had come close to victory. Burnett received 9,298 votes, or 52.8 percent, to Street's 8,044 votes, or 45.7 percent of the total. An independent candidate received 213 votes. Disfranchisement and a lack of money led to Street's defeat. His supporters were upset about the lack of support from the national Republican party, and a few days after the election, he wrote President Roosevelt to complain about his treatment by the GOP national campaign committee.[72]

Oliver Street's younger brother, E. C. Street, an attorney living in Texas, wrote a consoling letter that gave some insight into the Streets' view of political parties: "Several of my friends asked me if that was my brother who was a republican back in Ala.[sic] and my reply was always that you were a populite with the support of republicans. I had rather have a populite brother than a republican, and I would rather have either than to have one who would associate with the Democratic ring in Ala." Judge Thomas A. Street never became a Republican, and Oliver Street's private correspondence showed his preference for Populism, but he joined Lewis Reynolds in the GOP.[73]

Reynolds's pro-labor stance in the 1903 legislative session demonstrated that the Republican party he hoped to join was not the party of Old Guard conservatives or big business. He opposed an antiboycott bill offered by the conservative Jelks administration in an effort to stifle Alabama's growing labor movement. Reynolds backed restrictions on child labor and offered a bill to make peonage a crime. He emphasized his opposition to the Democrats when he wrote a Chilton County newspaper that disfranchisement had led to control of the state by "corporations."[74]

A rising progressive wing of the Republican party was far more congenial to Reynolds's brand of politics, but even before the legislature adjourned he began a strategic retreat from his association with the Republicans. The *Montgomery Journal* reported that Reynolds had denounced new rules of the national Republican party that favored black participation in party affairs and that he would leave the GOP if it did not remain a white institution. This statement was unusual from a man who rarely mentioned race in political speeches. The national GOP had moved from a lily-white stance long before Reynolds first became a Republican, and he later became an active supporter of precisely those men in the state GOP hierarchy who benefitted from the new rules. Events in 1904 explained his sudden reversal of positions on political parties. The national Republican rules simply provided a pretext for Reynolds to take a temporary leave from the GOP.[75]

Like A. P. Longshore, Reynolds sought the office of probate judge, which would give him more power than he could exercise in a 105-member state legislative body. If he ran as the Populist party nominee with

Republican cooperation, as he had in 1902, he stood an excellent chance of winning. If he accepted the GOP nomination, he risked losing Populist voters who had already stated that they did not want to be Republicans. In January 1904, in a move to bolster his standing with Populists, Reynolds hosted a large dinner party to celebrate the tenth anniversary of his involvement in the Farmers' Alliance store. Forty-six people, including the old Alliance leader Riley M. Honeycutt, attended. In February a Republican newspaper in Birmingham reported with surprise that Reynolds had resigned from the state GOP executive committee.[76]

Reynolds followed these astute political maneuvers by calling for a mass meeting of the Chilton County Populist party to "find out what a majority of our people want to do." He would "abide by a majority of our voters or their wish." At the March 1904 meeting Reynolds acted as chairman and asked those who wished to go into the Democratic party to stand. No one stood, but Reynolds did not ask how many wanted to become Republicans. Instead, he read a telegram from state Republican activist Joseph Oswalt Thompson, a Roosevelt supporter engaged in an internal GOP fight against a party faction that had supported Marcus Alonzo Hanna for the 1904 presidential nomination. Thompson, whom Roosevelt had named as head of a new committee to decide who would receive patronage from the national administration, asked Chilton County's Populists to "stand pat" in their party and not vote for Democrats. If they did as he asked, said Thompson, Chilton County's Republicans would back the Populist ticket. Chilton County's Republican party had been moribund before Populism arrived, but it had grown since 1896, and Thompson's promise of support from local Republicans was important to the Populists.[77]

A deal between Thompson and Reynolds, who were first cousins, was also obvious. The *Birmingham Times* reported that Reynolds was being supported for probate judge by a Republican newspaper run by the pro-Roosevelt or Thompson faction of the state Republican party. Shortly after these events, Reynolds announced that he would seek the Populist nomination for probate judge. With Republican cooperation sewed up, winning the election against the Democrats would be easier. It was also clear that Reynolds had engaged in a charade earlier in the year when he temporarily left the GOP. After he secured the Populist nomination and was elected probate judge, he publicly reentered the Republican party.[78]

A. P. Longshore was reelected probate judge in 1904, but unlike Reynolds he did not claim to be a Republican. Unlike Oliver Street, he never considered becoming a Democrat or helping Joseph Johnston either. He insisted that he was a Populist and accepted the nomination of the local Populist party for another term as probate judge. Yet, Longshore and Populist editor Frank Norris were inseparably tied to a coalition with Shelby County's Republicans that benefitted local Populists. When a newly formed but weak national Populist party organized and nominated Tom Watson for president in 1904, Norris endorsed Watson, but the local coalition with Republicans prevented Longshore and Norris from criticizing Populists who wanted to vote for Roosevelt.[79]

Party affiliation problems did not stop the *People's Advocate* from backing reforms after 1900. Norris applauded most progressive causes, including the national "good roads" movement, higher taxes for the modernization of Shelby County's roads, more revenue for education, and the trend toward municipal ownership of such local utilities as water and electricity. The *People's Advocate* was not anti-industrial, but Norris did call for people to "throw off" the power of private "railroads and corporations," and he was pro-labor. He endorsed building a modern cotton seed mill to furnish employment for Columbiana citizens, assailed a new antiboycott law, endorsed the eight-hour day, and called for recognition of unions for bargaining purposes. Norris wrote that Populists could not return to the party of "Cleveland and the gold standard" until it returned to the "principles of Jefferson and Jackson."[80]

In the absence of a national political party with real influence to attract them, Norris and Longshore searched for a national cause with which to link their local movement. In 1902 Norris endorsed the formation of the Allied People's party in Louisville, Kentucky, a conglomeration of socialists, the public ownership party, prohibitionists, and fusion and nonfusion Populists. The party platform supported government ownership of public utilities, the initiative and referendum, and an end to what it described as the "whiskey ring." Longshore and Norris also supported and joined a national cotton farmers organization that advocated policies similar to the Populists. These organizations had a dim future, but the interest of the Shelby County Populist leaders in them was a clear signal that the reform impulse that motivated Populists in the nineties was still vital. Norris's most eloquent editorials concerned disfranchisement. Even "the poorest boy in Shelby County, whether he can read or write or not, had just as much right to vote as the best educated man in the county." The right to participate in government was "inherent and inalienable," and whenever that right was limited to the "educated and rich" the "liberties of the people" were in danger.[81]

When it became apparent that the national Democratic party was going to nominate Judge Alton B. Parker, a conservative member of its Cleveland pro-gold wing, for president in 1904, Populists in both Chilton and Shelby Counties denounced the Democrats. Chilton County's Populist executive committee condemned Parker, and Norris reminded people that a vote for Parker was a vote for Cleveland, who caused the 1893–94 depression. Despite his endorsement of Watson, Norris defended local Republicans against a charge in a local Democratic newspaper that a vote for Roosevelt was a vote for "social equality" of the races. This defense of Roosevelt voters was followed by public criticism of Norris and Longshore by longtime Populist leader J. P. Pearson, who claimed that he was the only Populist still sincerely backing Watson for president.[82]

A local issue intruded when the county commission, led by chairman Longshore, attempted to enforce a tax on the property of railroads that ran through the county. Longshore started to seize railroad property when the roads failed to pay. Local Democratic newspapers, run by conservative editors who supported Alton Parker and attacked Bryanite Democrats, condemned the tax as illegal and went to court to have it declared void. Longshore defended the tax and said the common taxpayers should not have to bear the burden of raising county revenue. This issue allowed Frank Norris to turn the campaign into a struggle between corporations and the people. Because both Longshore's opponent and the chairman of the county Democratic executive committee had been part of the party hierarchy that took the local Democratic party away from the Alliance Democrats back in 1892, it was like old times. Norris and Longshore characterized the campaign as a "fight between the common yeomanry of the county and the money power and manipulators."[83]

The victory margin for both Longshore and Lewis Reynolds in their respective races for probate judge was narrow, but Longshore's victory surprised the Democrats, who had won several county offices in 1902. Indeed, so many white farmers and black Republicans were disfranchised that Democrats must have expected to take control in Shelby, but Longshore's campaign rejuvenated the county's anti-Democratic movement. The apathy that accompanied disfranchisement in many counties evaporated in Shelby County; 2,450 voters cast ballots, a nearly 30 percent increase as compared with 1900. A particularly large increase occurred in the old Populist precincts, and Longshore won by sixty votes.[84]

Alton Parker won only a plurality in Shelby and Chilton Counties and received a narrow 51 percent majority in Marshall County. He did not receive more than 57 percent of the vote in any Seventh District county, and he fell below a majority in three of them. Parker's pluralities in some counties grew from a divided opposition vote. Populist Tom Watson, who had no chance of winning the presidency, received a quarter of Shelby's vote, 21 percent in St. Clair, 15 percent in Chilton, and 11 percent in Marshall. Even with disfranchisement, a unified vote for Roosevelt would have defeated Parker in six hill counties, but some Populists were not yet prepared to say they were Republicans, even if they adamantly refused to be Democrats. Yet, a plurality of voters in precincts that had been in the Populist column in the nineties did vote for Roosevelt.[85]

A week after the election, with no further advantage to gain, Longshore issued a defiant statement that revealed much about his radical ideology, the class consciousness of Populism, and the direction the movement would take. A Democratic editor referred to it as Longshore's "manifesto," but it was titled "The People Shall Rule and Not the Bosses." The campaign, he wrote, had been one of "the plain working people against organized greed and predatory wealth," and his most loyal supporters had been the "farmers, miners, and laboring people." "I regret to say," he added, "that with few exceptions, the lawyers, doctors, and merchants championed the Democratic cause." At one precinct, he charged, merchants had closed their stores "to do more effectual against a ticket composed almost exclusively of farmers." Longshore endorsed the "principles" of the Populist party and wrote:

> We have the most glorious country ever fashioned by the Almighty, rich in natural resources, and yet the wealth of this country is being concentrated in the hands of a few. All over this land from sea to sea, the legions of honest toilers go forth in the morning to conquer the forces of nature and produce the vast wealth of this country. Does it stay in the homes of working men who toil for it? It does not. All the vast wealth of the mines and all the industries of the land, less the amount that is necessary to feed and clothe the laborer, goes into the hands of men who never did an honest day's work in their lives. This is all wrong, those who produce the wealth should have their just share

of it, and the platform of the Populist party is the only one that demands such a distribution of the wealth of this country. Let us all stand true to the principles of our party and work for the enactment of them into law.[86]

Some criticized Longshore's class-conscious accusations against the county's professional men, and he apologized to lawyers and doctors who voted for him, but he insisted that most did not. When a Democrat charged that Longshore had become a Republican, he responded that there was not "a word of truth" to the charge because he was "continually jumping on the Republican party" during the campaign. At age fifty, Longshore still thought of himself as a Populist, but the term "Populist-Republican" was increasingly used to describe his supporters. Only a Republican party that was Populist in orientation would suit him.[87]

A new two-party system did not mature in the hill counties until more Upcountry Populists joined Reynolds and Street in making the transition to the GOP, and Reynolds had initially been unable to convince his followers that they should become formal members of the Republican party. Leaders of Chilton County's Democratic executive committee summed up the dilemma of their county in a statement that applied to Shelby and several other hill counties. People did not recognize Chilton as Republican, they said, "because they know that she is not Republican. She is not recognized as Populist, because there are no other Populists to recognize her. She is not recognized as Democratic, because she has not been Democratic."[88]

8 From Populists to Progressive Republicans, 1904–1912

The *Advocate* has, since the first issue of this paper, stood by the principles of the People's party. . . . President Roosevelt has endorsed more of these principles than any president since Andrew Jackson.[1]

Frank Norris, 1908

The charge that a retrograde mentality led Alabama's ex-Populists into the Republican party has no basis in fact, and the contention that no continuity existed between Populists and progressive reform in Alabama cannot be sustained in light of the activities of many ex-Populists in the years between 1904 and 1912. The events of the 1912 election campaign alone are enough to demonstrate substantial continuity. Populists tended to become Republicans, in part, because of their attraction to the GOP progressive wing and to Theodore Roosevelt as a leader. They also had strong personal attachments to neighboring Republicans of Unionist family backgrounds and obligations to Upcountry Republicans who had sided with them in local elections, but Hill Country Populists could not have been more different from the leaders of the state Republican party in 1900.

Most white Republican voters in Alabama in the late nineteenth century were small farmers from the Hill Country or Tennessee Valley, yet the state GOP gave most of its important party offices and political plums to south Alabamians, particularly from Mobile and Montgomery. These lowcountry leaders had been active in the party during Reconstruction and still held important federal patronage jobs in the nineties. By 1890, Republicans associated with rising business and professional classes in Birmingham had moved up in the party, and Birmingham attorney William Vaughn became chairman of the state GOP executive committee in 1896. The Birmingham businessmen and the older Republican officials had little in common with north Alabama's small farmer Republicans, particularly those who had been Populists.[2]

The state's GOP leaders were passionate about few things except getting federal government jobs, but they were generally committed to pro-business, high-tariff, "sound money" planks in their 1896 and 1900 national party platforms. They were also racists, but they swung back and forth between lily-white and black-and-tan wings of their party as the situation demanded. Questions of economic policy and race were subordinated to the unceasing quest for patronage. A Franklin County editor warned Populists not to be cornered by Republican leaders interested only in the "political pie counter."[3]

Populists had little use for the old denizens of the state GOP hierarchy, yet Upcountry Populists admired their Republican neighbors, who were of Unionist descent. Unionist-Republicans usually cooperated or fused with Populists as a way to defeat Democrats, but some did so for more than pragmatic reasons, and many actually joined the third party. Republican farmers were drawn to the pro-yeomen, anti-monopoly, anti-creditor core of Populism. Like Populists, they believed in grassroots democracy and "resented the control of government by and for the benefit of the people who lived in the big houses in the lowlands." In 1895, a Winston County Populist leader contended that state legislator D. B. Ford of Winston, despite being a Republican, fairly represented the Populists in Montgomery. A Cherokee County Populist editor wrote that rural Republicans were "about as good Populists as we need in our business."[4]

When Populists began to enter the GOP after 1900 the long-existing ideological division between rank-and-file Upcountry Republican voters and the state Republican hierarchy widened, and an ideological split among national Republican leaders sharpened the internal party conflict in Alabama. In 1896, the primary differences between the rivals for the GOP presidential nomination, William McKinley and House Speaker Thomas B. Reed, were on foreign policy. Both favored high tariffs, gold currency, and big business, and both feared the growing power of labor unions. Yet, after 1900, the party began to divide over issues concerning labor, business regulation, problems caused by industrialization and urbanization, tariff revision, and control of the party by a conservative elite. The GOP split into progressive and "Old Guard" conservative wings. Theodore Roosevelt, Robert La Follette, Hiram Johnson, George W. Norris, and other Republican reformers tried to force the party to adopt a new reform identity.[5]

Between 1900 and 1916, as the party oscillated between ideologies, grassroots Republicans had to consider public policies as significant factors in making their decision about who to nominate for national office.

Before, when the party was more ideologically homogeneous, the rank and file chose nominees based primarily on which candidate would favor them or their friends with patronage. The new ideological dimension in national GOP politics became acute in Alabama by 1910, after ex-Populists became an integral part of the Republican party.[6]

As a reform movement, progressivism was more inclusive than Populism, which had been confined to agrarian interests in the southern and western states. Many progressives, like Roosevelt, hailed from eastern cities and were interested in a broader array of reforms than the Populists. Post-1900 reform was a hodgepodge; some progressives viewed solving the problems of labor and human welfare as most important, whereas others believed that reforms in the electoral process or changes in the management of government would suffice. Some supported a myriad of reforms. Older problems such as child labor, monopolies, prison reform, the fairness of the tax system, and proposals that Populists had pushed, such as the direct election of U.S. senators and a progressive income tax, remained high on progressive agendas. No single formula existed, but portions of progressivism particularly appealed to Alabama's ex-Populists.[7]

Upcountry Populists were naturally drawn to the anti-party nature of progressives, who sought support for direct primaries and such devices as the initiative, referendum, and recall, all of which were part of an effort to take government decision making out of the hands of party bosses. Alabama Populists, infuriated by the manipulation of state Democratic nominating conventions, the crude theft of elections by Democratic officials, the manipulation of black voters by Black Belt Democrats, and the passage of laws by Democrats that took the franchise from common people, were acutely sensitive to remedies that might empower grassroots voters. Frank Norris of Shelby County admired a variety of men who were members of several parties. Sometimes, in the same editorials, Norris praised William Jennings Bryan, William Randolph Hearst, Thomas E. Watson, Robert La Follette, and Theodore Roosevelt. These men had gained their power not from party leaders but from their appeal to the masses.[8]

No politician was more representative of this anti-party trend than Theodore Roosevelt. He became immensely popular with Upcountry Populists despite his northeastern origins, upper-class background, and efforts to include Negroes in his party's affairs. From Grant to McKinley, presidents had either been party tools or "safe" men comfortable with conservative party bosses. Grover Cleveland was personally independent, but his economic views made him the darling of his party's wealthy eastern elite. Roosevelt's power came from outside his party's elite, with rank-and-file voters. He took big business money for his campaigns, but Republican money managers and bosses had to support him in 1904 because he could go over their heads directly to the people.[9]

Roosevelt's antitrust lawsuits against the companies of J. P. Morgan and John D. Rockefeller, the help he gave striking miners in the great coal strike of 1902, and his support for laws that stopped railroads from granting rebates to favored customers such as Rockefeller were signs that the country finally had a president who understood Jacksonian-Populist ideology. Roosevelt believed that elite business interests wanted to dominate the government and that societal ills were exacerbated by government favoritism toward the financially privileged. No prior president, Republican or Democrat, had ever openly supported the rights of labor over those of business. The historic ideology of opposition to privileged economic power groups that infused Greenbackers, independents, and Populists, drew ex-Populists to Roosevelt's progressivism.[10]

In 1904, when Roosevelt ran for president as both the head of the Republican party and the national symbol of progressive reform, the national Democrats decided that they had been wrong to support William Jennings Bryan, capitulated to their northeastern business-banking wing, and nominated the goldbug Alton B. Parker of New York for president. This ill-conceived Democratic effort to run to the ideological right of Roosevelt coincided with the effort of Populists to find a new political home. Famed Kansas Populist Mary Elizabeth Lease described Roosevelt as a "man of destiny, an instrument in God's hands," and another midwestern Populist leader said that the president's speeches sounded like a "preamble to the Populist platform." Georgia's Tom Watson, a hero to southern Populists and a third-party candidate in 1904, assailed Parker, but not Roosevelt. Alabama's Upcountry press reported Watson's statement that he had "no words of abuse" for Roosevelt, believed the president was an "honest and conscientious man," and could understand how people "could work for the Republican party and vote its ticket with enthusiastic zeal."[11]

On January 19, 1905, the *Columbiana People's Advocate* published an article from the conservative *Springfield (Mass.) Republican,* whose editor argued that "Populism has secured a foothold even in the White House" and that some of the "crazy schemes advocated by Populists" had "become orthodox in the seats of the mighty who once denounced them." Between 1904 and 1906, Lewis Reynolds and Frank Norris publicly praised Roosevelt for his anti-monopoly campaign. In 1906 the Shelby County Republican executive committee, already infused with Populists, praised the president for his attacks on "unlawful combinations of capital and for applying the law fairly and equally to all regardless of wealth." The take-over of Alabama's Republican party by Roosevelt men, led by state GOP chairman Joseph Oswalt Thompson, made the GOP more attractive to the Populists.[12]

In October 1905, when President Roosevelt came to Alabama, Lewis Reynolds arranged with pro-Roosevelt state GOP chairman J. O. Thompson for the president to stop his train in Chilton County at Clanton before it went on to Montgomery. Roosevelt stayed long enough to shake hands with a few people and shout greetings to the crowd. The first man on the platform to grasp his hand was Judge Lewis Reynolds, whom Thompson introduced to Roosevelt. A Democratic party newspaper gave Reynolds sole credit for causing this exciting event, which began Reynolds's long association with the progressive Republicans. The Chilton County leader moved into public alliance with Thompson's ruling faction of the state GOP, but he did not do so because he sought federal patronage or wanted to hand out "political pie." His consistent loyalty to Roosevelt after 1905, even following the party schism of 1912 and Roosevelt's defeat in that election, reflected the progressive intentions of a variety of Populist leaders after their party died.[13]

When Oliver Street and I. L. Brock, who both eventually revealed that they were far more conservative and less ideological than either Reynolds or Longshore, considered leaving the Populist party and becoming Democrats, they gave no public support to either the pro-business or Black Belt conservative wing of the ruling party. Between 1898 and 1902 they had backed ostensible reformers such as Joseph Johnston and Jesse Stallings. Adams endorsed Johnston in the Democratic primaries, and although Lewis Reynolds never aligned with Johnston, he demonstrated that he was pro-labor, anti-monopoly, and pro-Roosevelt. As late as 1908, A. P. Longshore and Frank Norris adamantly claimed they were still Populists, but they endorsed Roosevelt's policies and praised his "excellent record." Norris called on the reform elements of both parties to combine against the reactionary forces in each.[14]

Oliver Street had not abandoned his emotional commitment to Populism despite his association with the Republican party. In November 1905 he informed Georgia Populist Tom Watson of the death of Oliver's father, Thomas Atkins Street. Judge Street had run for probate judge as an independent Populist in 1904 and lost by only a few votes to his Democratic opponent. He died a month later. "You may rest assured," Oliver wrote, that Judge Street was "still a Populist" at his death. "The very last year of his life he spent fighting a desperate fight for the cause of Populism" and on his "deathbed" thanked God for permitting him to lead this last battle "at the head of the Populist column, as Populist principles were with him a passion, a deep-seated conviction, a part of his very nature." Street added prayers for the success of Watson's new magazine "and for the ultimate triumph of our principles, in which alone lies the safety of our Republican government."[15]

Democrats were aware of the Populist mold in which the new Upcountry Republicans were cast. When a Chilton County Democratic editor invited his readers to explain why the county had voted for Republicans for local offices in 1906, one correspondent wrote that the "division and bitterness of feeling engendered in our county, by the Farmers' Alliance movement coupled with the heated Kolb campaigns for the governorship" had been "kept alive by the political leaders of the opposition party to the Democrats."[16]

Democrats understood the continuing commitment to reform by the ex-Populists. In 1907, when the Chilton County Populist executive committee voted formally to join the GOP, a Shelby County Democratic newspaper noted that Reynolds had finally achieved his goal and ran headlines that said: "Old Time Populists Merge with Republicans." Democratic editor Frank Crichton pointed out that the merger was a "personal tribute" to Reynolds, who not only "held the opposition to the democracy together in Chilton" but was "in thorough sympathy with the reform policies" of the progressive wing of the Democratic party.[17]

Many Populists who became Republicans were worried about losing their former political allies to the Socialists. When the Socialist party of Eugene Debs began to organize in Alabama, the group solicited the membership of Oliver Street because he represented what they described as the "reform" forces in the state. Street did not accept, but in 1904 a Chilton County Democrat correctly noted that the Populist-Republican ticket in that county included a "Socialist." Former Populist state representative L. B. Pounds of Chilton County had announced in August 1903 that he would become a "missionary" for Socialism. Populism had been destroyed by the "cunning craft of capitalism," said Pounds, but Socialism had "rekindled" the "old fire." Democrats trying to defeat the new Republicans in local elections sometimes pinned their hopes on the possibility that Socialists would draw votes from the Populists.[18]

The most radical of the old Populists continued to be Shelby County's Longshore-Norris group. As labor-management problems became violent in Shelby between 1908 and 1910, and as miners went on strike there, Norris and Longshore supported the unions. During a 1908 strike Frank Norris supported the drive of the miners for recognition of their union by the coal companies, and he reported the "miners side" of the story in the *People's Advocate*. In 1909 Norris said he had learned from "reliable authority" that "the miners of the state will all pay up their poll tax and register at the proper time and be ready to strike next year for liberty and freedom and give the Democratic party a death blow."[19]

Some of Norris's most virulent criticism was of Democratic governor Braxton Bragg Comer, a protégé of Joseph Forney Johnston and leader of the "progressive" wing of Alabama's Democratic party. Norris had praised the reform rhetoric of Comer during the 1906 campaign. A millionaire textile producer, Comer was elected in 1906 on a reform platform that included support for railroad regulation and prohibition. His time in office between 1907 and 1910 was primarily spent supporting those causes, but his progressivism was combined with some reactionary attitudes toward the lower classes. This former Black Belt plantation owner and "cotton mill boss" had been the most public opponent of child labor reform, and he tried to suppress Alabama's labor movement. In 1908, when Comer called out the national guard to break a coal strike in the Birmingham area, Norris wrote that it was "all right with Comer and his democrats for the coal operators to form a union, but it is a violation of the law for coal miners to form a union or meet in a crowd to discuss their own interests." Comer, said Norris, should be "hurled from office" for his anti-labor activities.[20]

In 1909, a Democratic editor accused A. P. Longshore of interfering with the deliberations of a grand jury to keep it from indicting miners accused of committing violent acts against a coal company. In 1910, as the county court judge who heard misdemeanor cases, Longshore was called on to preside over the trial of nine black coal miners accused of setting off dynamite at a mine. Longshore found the miners, all members of the United Mine Workers, "not guilty," but the Democratic prosecutor appealed this decision to the circuit court. "After thoroughly investigating the cases," wrote Frank Norris, the prosecutor "found that no evidence whatever could be produced" against the miners by the state, and they "were allowed to go free after being confined in jail about eighteen months on charges they were absolutely not guilty of."[21]

Norris had expressed doubts about Theodore Roosevelt in 1904, primarily because the president was a Republican. Norris praised the president's trust-busting, but he believed it would not last because of Republican connections to Wall Street. During his second term, as Roosevelt moved further to the political left and alienated much of the Old Guard, Norris and the People's Advocate were drawn to him. As Norris wrote in 1906:

> Populist principles are forging to the front and being upheld by more men than ever before. President Roosevelt, Senator La Follette, Thomas Lawson [anti–big business journalist], W. J. Bryan, and W. R. Hearst, nick-named Populist by their Wall Street despisers, are the greatest men of their parties, and it is their Populist tendencies alone that have made them more highly esteemed than their ordinary fellow partisans.[22]

Portions of the Populist platform had been endorsed by "a large number of the most prominent men in the two old parties," Norris went on, but the Republicans "understand that Roosevelt is the only man in the Republican party who can defeat the Democrats."[23]

In 1908, even after it became clear that Bryan would be the Democratic nominee for president, Norris claimed that Thomas E. Watson was still the "ablest exponent" of "Populist principles," but Roosevelt had "advocated and endorsed more of these principles than any president since Andrew Jackson." Despite Norris's pro-Roosevelt pronouncements, he and Longshore found it difficult to abandon the remaining remnant of their party to become Republicans. Norris endorsed Tom Watson for president again in 1908, and Longshore was one of Alabama's Populist presidential electors, even though it was clear that Watson's campaign was more of a gesture than a serious effort.[24]

Progressive attitudes by Populists were also displayed at the local level between 1904 and 1910. Longshore's county administration not only enforced a tax against railroads and defended the rights of labor but also raised county taxes for a variety of services, including modernizing Shelby County's roads and building a new courthouse to service a growing county population. In 1905 the *People's Advocate* endorsed new taxes for local schools, and a special school tax was enacted by a three-to-one majority of the county's voters. A conservative Democratic editor used the tax issue against Populist-Republicans in 1906. "The tax rate has more than doubled," he argued, since the Democrats were in power. "There is now an enormous debt upon the county that will not be paid in twenty years, if, in fact, it is ever paid."[25]

Shelby County's Democrats grew frustrated after Populist-Republican fusion tickets won county offices in 1906 and again in 1908. In 1909 an angry Democratic editor analyzed the dilemma of his local party when he wrote that for "half a generation" Shelby County had "been in the grip of the Longshore forces," which were "made up of two elements—independent citizens who have always been democrats, but were dissatisfied with democratic leadership and record in the county; and of an element whose opposition dates back to the Civil War." The latter group had "nursed their grudge" against the Democratic party for causing the war. The two elements were "in hostile array against the Democratic party of Shelby County," and their success was "decidedly significant."[26]

Exasperated local Democrats copied the methods of their predecessors and persuaded the Democratic state legislature to pass two laws designed to break the power of Longshore and his supporters. One stripped Longshore of a portion of his power as judge. Another, designed to divide the ruling Shelby County fusion coalition, commanded political parties that selected their candidates in separate meetings to put separate tickets on the ballot. Instead of ending the Populist-Republican alliance, however, the law backfired on the Democrats. It forced ex-Populists who had thus far refused to become Republicans to make that commitment finally.[27]

On February 19, 1910, the Populist and Republican executive committees of the county agreed to hold a unified primary to select their nominees, and the two parties' governing committees formally combined their operations in the spring under the aegis of the Republican party. Longshore and Norris continued to say that they were Populists, or at least "Populist-Republicans," but the joint primary and committee meant that only one party existed. Efforts by Democrats to break up the coalition had actually unified the anti-Democratic forces for the 1910 election.[28]

The prohibition of alcoholic beverages divided both the Democratic and the Republican parties into pro- and anti-liquor factions by 1910, and it also divided ex-Populists. In 1907, the legislature banned the manufacture and sale of liquor in Alabama, but prohibition forces wanted the ban put into the state constitution so that the legislature could not change its mind by a mere majority vote. Prohibition was a "progressive" issue that appealed to the reform impulse to purify society, but the issue of freedom to control one's private life without state interference also raised its head in the Hill Country. Oliver Street and Lewis Reynolds were avowed prohibitionists who supported the "bone-dry" statute and the constitutional amendment banning liquor, but Milford Howard opposed both. Longshore also opposed the amendment. It was one of the few times that he and Reynolds disagreed on a public issue.[29]

Prohibition did not affect Longshore's career, but it had an impact on Reynolds, who stumped his county in 1909 for the constitutional amendment on prohibition. Chilton County voted overwhelmingly against the amendment, and in 1910 the Democrats used the issue against Reynolds in his campaign for reelection. He lost by sixty-seven votes to Democrat E. B. Deason, also an ex-Populist. One of Reynolds's leading supporters assigned his defeat to hard feelings generated by the prohibition fight. It was characteristic of Reynolds that he would not stay silent during the prohibition struggle even if it was apparent that his reelection chances would be damaged. By no means did this battle end his political career, however.[30]

Longshore won another term in 1910 with the same thin 51 percent of the vote that he received in 1904, but his majority went from sixty to a whopping sixty-one votes. It was his first victory on a Republican ticket and the first time since the late 1860s that a Republican had held the county's highest office; in addition, the county elected a GOP state legislator. After the election Longshore began to play an active role in Republican politics. Elections in which he was a candidate in Shelby County continued to be decided by thin margins until he retired from politics after 1922. Other general election races in the county from 1910 to 1922 were also hotly contested and usually decided by less than two hundred out of twenty-five hundred to three thousand votes.[31]

The same highly competitive two-party politics marked Chilton County's general election contests and those of some other hill counties. The narrow defeat of Reynolds in 1910 marked the first time a Democrat had won the office of probate judge in Chilton since 1886 and the first time a Populist or Republican ticket had not won all of the county offices since 1890. This fact did not mean that the anti-Democratic forces had lost their vitality; rather, the parties were evenly divided. In the same election in which Reynolds lost, a Republican candidate for circuit court clerk won by thirteen votes, and the Democratic candidate for sheriff defeated his GOP rival by only eight votes. One man claimed that Socialists, whose

A. P. Longshore *(top center, facing away)* with county officials and lawyers, Shelby County Courthouse, ca. 1920 (courtesy of Karl C. Harrison)

candidate for governor received sixty-eight votes in the county, took votes from the Populists.[32]

In Franklin County some Populists had returned to the Democratic party, but enough became Republicans to form a strong coalition with more traditional GOP members. Ex-Populist newspaper editor S. J. Petree was elected probate judge of Franklin County as a Republican in 1910 in an election that could not have been closer. Petree received 885 votes to his Democratic opponent's 884! Republican C. C. Scheuing was finally elected sheriff of Cullman County by sixteen votes in 1910 after a bitter dispute about the counting of the ballots.[33]

The situation of the Republican party in Marshall County was more desperate. The GOP was active and vital in Marshall, and in state and local elections between 1902 and 1910 it generally polled more than 40 percent of the vote, but in 1904 the Democratic party won control of the county government in elections that were not as close as in some other hill counties. Former Populist leader W. M. Coleman was elected to the legislature as a Democrat in 1906, and many ex-Populists reentered the Democratic party with him. This action did not signify that most of Marshall County's ex-Populists were Democrats again, but enough were, or a sufficient number had been disfranchised, to allow the Democratic party to gain control. Precincts that had given consistent majorities to the Populists in the nineties, however, either went into the Republican column in national and state elections between 1904 and 1920 or vacillated between Democrats and Republicans. The congressional election of 1910 and the presidential election of 1912 energized Marshall County's former Populists to fight the Democrats once again.[34]

Between 1904 and 1920, Marshall County's Oliver Street became a top figure in the state Republican party hierarchy. He never won an elective office, but he was an adept player in the Republican patronage game that obsessed state party leaders. His success at backstage political maneuvering eventually dulled his Populism. He brought other Populists into the GOP, but unlike Longshore and Reynolds, Street's reform instincts began to play a secondary role to his desire for power and place. By the 1920s few people in the state were more powerful. His influence was often critical in the appointment of federal judges, U.S. prosecuting attorneys, federal district court clerks, internal revenue collectors, customs collectors, postmasters, postal workers, and hundreds of other minor positions. Alabamians who wanted a federal position during the Harding, Coolidge, and Hoover administrations of the 1920s had to be cleared by Street. To rise to this position Street played a sometimes dangerous game in which he showed no compunctions about shedding one political faction to benefit from association with a more influential one.[35]

Street was a delegate to the state Republican convention in 1904, his first formal act as a Republican since appearing on the GOP ticket in 1902. He quickly aligned with the pro-Roosevelt, or J. O. Thompson, faction. Thompson was also appointed federal internal revenue collector for the state of Alabama by Roosevelt and placed close political friends into his office. Many Republicans believed that he should not hold such an important federal post and be chairman of the party at the same time. A resident of Tuskegee, Thompson was closely associated with Booker T. Washington and willingly acceded to the demands of President Roosevelt that some blacks be included in party affairs. Thompson was no advocate of civil rights, but he went along with these national directives so that he could maintain his close connection to Roosevelt. In 1903 he told Street that he did not believe that the politics of "color" would have a great impact on Republican politics, and he proved to be correct. Roosevelt soon backed away from any efforts to change the white power structure.[36]

In 1905 and 1906, opposition to the power of Thompson and his top associate, former Democrat Oscar Hundley, led to party divisions. Patronage disputes between pro- and anti-Thompson factions became so heated that at least one argument resulted in violence. Thompson was accused of circumventing local GOP organizations in the counties to put his own men in office. This accusation was probably true because some local GOP organizations were attached to the anti-Roosevelt Old Guard group in the state and national GOP.[37]

Not only did many Alabama Republicans dislike Roosevelt and the direction in which he was moving the Republican party, but also some were opposed to the rise of ex-Populists in the party. Walter Powell's nomination for Congress in 1904 marked the third successive time that Republicans had picked a Populist or ex-Populist for Congress from the Seventh District. Street had doubts about the loyalty of some of the GOP hierarchy to their cause. "Our chief obstacle in every campaign," he wrote Powell, "is the infidelity of the Republican office holders." In GOP campaigns in the Seventh District in which Street was conspicuously involved, he tried to include Populists. Thus, he played a major role in building the membership of the Upcountry Republican party with ex-Populists. When objections were made to J. O. Thompson about the influence of Powell and Street, he sided with the ex-Populists.[38]

In December 1905 criticism of Thompson became so strong that he considered resigning his post and offered to endorse Street for party chairman. Street agreed to seek the chairmanship and wrote Thompson that he would accept his support. Thompson reiterated his support of Street and then went off to Washington to discuss state party affairs with national leaders. In early January 1906 Thompson returned home and wrote Street that he had changed his mind about resigning. "We will have to suffer the ills we have rather than those we know not of," he said, and Street was relieved by Thompson's decision. Despite this outcome, the serious offer of the chairmanship to Street was evidence of the growing power of Hill Country ex-Populists in the party.[39]

In 1907 Street used his connections with state Republican leaders to win an appointment from President Roosevelt as United States district attorney for the Northern District of Alabama and began serving an interim term until the Senate confirmed him to a full term on January 12,

1908. One Democratic senator who voted to confirm this Republican nominee was an old friend of the Street family, Joseph Forney Johnston, who had come to the Senate in 1907. The shrewd Street had played the political game well both with Republicans and with Democrats, but he served at the pleasure of the president, and after the election of William Howard Taft in 1908 he was forced to choose between competing factions of the state Republican party to keep his job.[40]

Between 1906 and 1908 the Alabama state party was split into two patronage factions, one led by Thompson and the other headed by Birmingham attorney Julius Davidson. The Davidson faction claimed that Thompson had abandoned the chairmanship when the executive committee he chaired refused to nominate a statewide ticket in 1906. Davidson's group formed a competing executive committee and placed a ticket on the ballot. Each faction claimed to be the legitimate state party, and both sent delegates to the Republican national convention in 1908. Thompson's faction won recognition from the Republican national committee, but the other faction had powerful backers, including ex-congressman W. F. Aldrich, editor and publisher of the *Birmingham Times*. At the time of the split between the two party factions, neither could be characterized as clearly conservative or progressive, but differences between them over national politics became clearer during the first two months of 1908. The *Birmingham Times*, official organ of the Davidson faction, argued that the policies of Roosevelt resembled those of William Jennings Bryan, and it called for the nomination of a candidate on a truly "Republican platform."[41]

Aldrich and conservative Republicans had reason to be worried about the direction of Roosevelt. On January 31, 1908, the president sent a message to Congress that endorsed federal inheritance and income taxes, federal regulation of interstate corporations and stock market transactions, more extensive federal regulation of railroad rates, a postal savings bank, limitations on the power of federal courts to grant injunctions against the activities of organized labor, workers' compensation, an employers' liability law, and the extension of the eight-hour day. These far-reaching programs were only part of a message that included a sweeping attack on the influence of organized capital. Roosevelt referred to "lawbreaking corporations" and "lawbreaking men of wealth" who had debased politics. Later, in April 1908, when remnants of the national Populist party met and nominated Tom Watson for another futile try at the presidency, the group adopted a platform that endorsed practically every measure mentioned in Roosevelt's speech.[42]

It was apparent that the nominee of the national GOP in 1908 would be William Howard Taft. Roosevelt had declared that he would not run, and he endorsed Taft to be his replacement back in 1907. Taft seemed to be a Roosevelt progressive, and because he was Roosevelt's choice, some people who would be in his corner in 1912 were against him in 1908. Oliver Street and Joseph Oswalt Thompson were Taft men. Street went to the 1908 GOP national convention as attorney for the delegation chosen by the state's regular Republican party. The Davidson faction challenged the right of the regular delegation to be seated, and Street appeared on behalf of chairman Thompson before a committee called to rule on the challenge. Street's argument was successful, and Davidson's faction was sent packing while Thompson's was seated.[43]

Roosevelt was firmly in control of the 1908 convention and actively campaigned for Taft, but without the charismatic president at the head of the GOP ticket, voter turnout in the old Populist counties lagged. Taft did lead Democratic nominee William Jennings Bryan in six hill counties, including Chilton, Shelby, and Franklin, and lost St. Clair County by only thirty-eight votes. The election of Taft created a new dilemma for Oliver Street, who owed his job and influence in the party to J. O. Thompson's Roosevelt faction. Yet, Street could not continue as United States district attorney unless he demonstrated his loyalty to Taft, whose close advisors were increasingly suspicious of those who were loyal to the former president. Almost immediately, a dispute occurred that pulled Street into the middle of an intraparty patronage war and left him little alternative except to choose sides.[44]

Roosevelt's appointment of Birmingham attorney Oscar Hundley to a federal district judgeship in 1907 languished in the Senate as anti-Roosevelt Republicans and southern Democrats held up the confirmation. Hundley was Thompson's closest ally, and the state chairman's prestige was at stake. Bitter conflict over the appointment swept through the Alabama GOP when it became obvious that Taft's friends in Alabama were not necessarily friends of Thompson, Hundley, or other Roosevelt loyalists. Thompson continued to fight for the appointment in spite of overwhelming opposition, but other Republicans began to angle for the job. In February 1909 the Roosevelt administration's last month in office, Street still refused to recommend any job applicants who had opposed Hundley's appointment. Street soon found, however, that he would have to abandon Thompson to maintain his post as federal prosecutor, and he began private maneuvers unknown to the Roosevelt faction.[45]

On March 13, 1909, just nine days after Taft took office, the crafty Street wrote a shrewd letter about Hundley's appointment to Charles P. Taft, the president's brother and an able politician involved in handling Republican patronage for the administration. Street informed Taft that Hundley's interim appointment as judge continued but that the Senate had twice failed to confirm the appointee. Then, in guarded language, Street wrote that he was "a friend and supporter of Judge Hundley for this place and would not knowingly say one word or be guilty of any act whatever that would in the least injure his chances." After laying this important predicate, Street made his move. He wanted Hundley confirmed, "yet if this cannot be had, we do want some other Taft republican." They could not suggest another "Taft applicant," noted Street, until it was "definitely known to us" that Hundley would not be appointed. The president should dispose of Hundley one way or the other, and "then we want notice of that fact so that we can put forward another man." Without overtly opposing Hundley, Street had let Taft know that it was time for the administration to abandon Thompson's close friend publicly.[46]

Taft withdrew Hundley's nomination and, to the consternation of many Alabama Republicans, appointed a Democrat to the position. Putting a Democrat in the job could not have pleased Street, but he was able to use his letter as proof that he had helped ease Hundley out, and this action would prove his loyalty to the Taft men rather than to Thompson. Street was one of the few Alabama Roosevelt appointees in Alabama to be kept on by Taft.[47]

In 1910 Joseph O. Thompson, still unaware of the double-dealing on the Hundley nomination, asked Street to be chairman of the Seventh District congressional campaign. By the time Thompson made this request a strong movement had developed to give former Populist congressman Milford Howard the Republican nomination. Street should manage the campaign, said Thompson, because of his "congeniality with the man whom it seems now will undoubtedly be nominated by our people, Hon. M. W. Howard." Thompson also noted, with more irony than he knew, that Street had impressed national Republicans such as Charles Taft and that he might be able to get them to contribute funds to Howard's campaign. The eccentric Howard, who had combined support for free silver with support for high tariffs, had two major problems that hurt him with older Republicans. He had never participated in Republican politics and had campaigned against prohibition. Because Street had favored the prohibition amendment and made speeches on behalf of the anti-saloon league, he could deflect prohibitionist criticism of Howard, but he could not make Howard a conventional Republican.[48]

Walter Powell argued that Howard would be the strongest candidate "if he would make a declaration as a Republican." DeKalb County Republican R. J. Guest commented that voters in his county would be "tickled to death to get Howard" but that he must "formally declare himself a republican." Yet, if they nominated a candidate who could get the votes only of avowed Republicans, "it is the same old story of defeat." Republican congressional candidates received less than 45 percent of the vote in both 1906 and 1908, and the total vote for Republican candidates had fallen by one thousand from that obtained by Oliver Street in 1902. Guest understood that the congressional candidate had to stir the former Populists to action. Nevertheless, some Republicans were opposed to nominating a Populist. Etowah County's Gordon Ashley argued that Howard was still "too much of a Populist," but Street dismissed his comments as coming from one who had "always been unfriendly to that element of the party which came from the Populists."[49]

From the beginning, Howard was a difficult candidate. He won the GOP nomination but would not say he was running as a Republican. J. O. Thompson wanted "no pledges from me," said Howard, who said that the GOP chairman did not want Howard "embarrassed or handicapped in any way." Yet, some Republicans continued to complain that Howard was not a party man. Howard's speeches sometimes sounded Republican, said one party loyalist, but he did not "claim to belong to the party." Despite such complaints, Street understood the nature of the Seventh District electorate, and he supervised the compilation of a list of "republicans or populists" from each beat in the district.[50]

As in other Seventh District congressional campaigns, a lack of money hampered Howard, who often complained about it. He made two speeches a day in September and October, but sometimes he did not have enough money to mail campaign materials. Not only did the national Republican party fail to provide monetary support, but also his own state party acted in a miserly fashion. The chairman of the state Republican campaign wrote to say that he was sorry about the "self sacrifice" Street had to make on Howard's behalf but that it was probably "better for Howard's campaign to be like it is," for he was a "whole team within himself." Howard did, indeed, inspire Hill Country crowds. One Cherokee County man wrote that Howard had just finished speaking in his county and that the "woods are on fire." At a campaign stop in Cullman County, Howard reported speaking to two thousand people.[51]

The vigorous campaign almost paid dividends. Howard received 8,977 votes, or 48.6 percent of the total, to 9,496 for incumbent congressman John Burnett. Howard increased the Republican vote in the Seventh District 28 percent compared with that received by the 1908 GOP congressional candidate and doubled that received by the 1906 GOP nominee. He received the most votes won by an anti-Democratic congressional candidate in the Seventh District since he was elected to the Congress as a Populist in 1894. The excitement was palpable in Marshall County, where Howard trailed Burnett, but the county Republican congressional vote rose from 825 in 1908 to 1,321 in 1910, whereas Burnett gained only 49 votes. Howard lost St. Clair County by five votes, won Franklin by eight, and lost Cullman and DeKalb by only twenty-five and thirty-eight votes respectively.[52]

The Seventh District race, like those for local offices in Franklin, Chilton, and Shelby, indicated how close the entire Hill Country was to creating a two-party system. Republican J. B. Sloan was elected to the state senate from the district that included Blount, Cullman, and Winston Counties, and Winston County Republican J. J. Curtis became the first Republican elected to the post of state circuit court judge since Reconstruction. His district included Winston and Walker Counties.[53]

In the summer of 1911 Milford Howard exchanged letters with Oliver Street about the Republican party. Howard denounced "pie counter" Republicans, said he would join the party if GOP leaders stood for anything except patronage, and told Street that he would not get involved in the internal political fight between Joseph O. Thompson and Prelate D. Barker of Mobile, Taft's patronage referee in Alabama. Howard charged that Barker and other older Republican leaders had opposed him, and if it had not been for the "factional fight in the party and treachery and indifference I would have been elected to congress." The older party leaders did not want a "real party." Howard moved his law practice to Birmingham and entered into a partnership with the Roosevelt Republican Oscar R. Hundley.[54]

Roosevelt's progressive, even radical, rhetoric began to shock some Taft Republicans. Shortly after Taft's inauguration, Roosevelt went on a world tour and made few public statements about public policy for a year. He did not return to the United States until June 18, 1910, but he was privately informed by close advisors that Taft had moved the Republican party to the political right. The party's future was thrown into a state of uncertainty when Roosevelt embarked on a speaking tour for GOP congressional candidates in late summer. He did not criticize the president directly and acted as the loyal party man, but he took every opportunity to emphasize differences between himself and Taft. The speeches put him squarely in the camp of progressive Republican "insurgents," who were in open revolt against the president.[55]

Roosevelt's words sounded like good Populist doctrine. "The essence of any struggle for liberty," he said at Osawattomie, Kansas, "has always been, and must always be to take from one man or class of men the right to enjoy power, or wealth, or position, or immunity, which has not been earned by service to his or their fellows." Government had to "destroy privilege." Quoting Lincoln but sounding like an advocate of producerism, Roosevelt said that labor was "prior to," "independent of," and "superior to" capital. Capital was "only the fruit of labor." Judges should not be allowed to suppress labor activities with injunctions, and the president had a duty to protect people from the "legal cunning, hired by wealthy interests, to bring national activities to a deadlock." Speaking in the "tradition of the Jacksonians," Roosevelt wanted to stop the "corrosive influence" of big business on the country. Like Jackson, he said the nation's executive had to be the "steward of the public welfare." He recommended a complete reorganization of the nation's financial system, restrictions on child labor, and graduated income and inheritance taxes.[56]

The Osawattomie speech raised a firestorm of criticism within Republican circles. "Eastern conservatives," writes a Taft biographer, reacted as if Roosevelt had "become an anarchist and communist," and his attacks on property and the courts were tantamount to attacks on the "bulwarks of civilization." Taft informed close associates of his anger at the remarks of his old friend and benefactor and wrote his brother that Roosevelt had proposed "a program which it is absolutely impossible to carry out except by revision of the federal Constitution." The effort to protect the Republican party machinery from Roosevelt began in earnest. Months before any candidate had announced for president, a showdown occurred between the Thompson and Barker forces for control of the state Republican party. This showdown put the old Populists in a precarious situation. Even though many of them favored Roosevelt, the former president had not announced that he would run, and it was not apparent that he would.

Ex-Populists such as Longshore, who had just become Republicans and whose party loyalty was already suspect to men such as Barker, had little choice but to remain openly loyal to the incumbent Republican president.[57]

By the summer of 1911 it did become clear to Joseph O. Thompson that Oliver Street had betrayed him. Street went to a Birmingham meeting called by Barker's pro-Taft group, and with Street's backing, Barker pushed through a resolution that committed them to remove Thompson as state chairman and replace him with Walker County's Pope Long, son of the late Benjamin M. Long. Barker worried that ex-Populists Reynolds, Longshore, or Howard might, "in the interests of Thompson," attempt a takeover of the party. The outspoken Reynolds irritated Barker the most. "I am very much interested in Chilton," wrote Barker, "not only to keep that blatherskite Reynolds out of the state convention, but of the district convention, where he might do harm. . . . You know he is a regular firebrand."[58]

When the state convention met in August 1911, Reynolds, Longshore, and Howard did not cause any problems. The delegates removed Thompson, named Long chairman, and selected Barker as Alabama's new representative on the Republican national committee. Thompson left the room without a fight. The old Populists were in the minority, and although Reynolds had been loyal to Thompson for many years, he could not cut himself off from the party at this stage by opposing Taft. Barker had the power of the administration behind him, federal patronage under his control, and no Roosevelt candidacy in sight. Trouble for the Barker forces began only in the spring of 1912, after Roosevelt announced his candidacy for the GOP nomination and his forces began to organize.[59]

When the state Republican convention met in early March 1912, Roosevelt had been an announced candidate for less than a week, and the Taft forces, led by Prelate Barker and Oliver Street, were still in total control. They instructed Alabama's delegation to vote for Taft at the national convention; passed resolutions that condemned Roosevelt's candidacy; assailed Roosevelt's speeches as "anti-Republican," "radical," and even "revolutionary"; endorsed the stewardship of Pope Long as party chairman; and praised GOP national committeeman Prelate Barker. Events before and after the meeting made it clear that A. P. Longshore and Lewis Reynolds were for Roosevelt, but their only public objection to the convention's actions was to a resolution passed by the delegates that condemned the initiative, referendum, and recall. Longshore pointed out the advantages of the referendum, and Reynolds said that people ought to "have the right to recall the officials at all times who fail to do their duty." Their response to the rest of the resolutions passed by the convention was silence, but events soon moved them to action and proved that the majority of the rank-and-file Republican voters in Alabama were for Roosevelt.[60]

In May, Roosevelt supporters held meetings in many state counties to organize their campaign. At a Birmingham meeting, some Republicans formed a statewide pro-Roosevelt campaign team, and in May the two brothers of Lewis Reynolds created a local Roosevelt club in Chilton County. Reynolds, who opened a clothing store after his defeat in 1910, began to describe his business as the "home of the square deal," a direct reference to the name Roosevelt had given to the progressive policies of his administration. Both Lewis Reynolds and A. P. Longshore remained publicly silent until after the GOP national convention. Only after Taft was selected as the nominee did they openly break with the Republican president.[61]

Roosevelt delegates were selected to attend the Republican national convention and challenged the delegation of the regular Republican party. At the GOP national convention in Chicago, Oliver Street presented the case for Alabama's pro-Taft delegation. Three members of the regular delegation, two from the Wiregrass and one from the Upcountry's Seventh District, announced that they would vote for Roosevelt despite their instructions from the state Republican convention. They argued, with some justice, that they had been told to vote for Taft before the Roosevelt campaign actually began. Street appeared as counsel for the regular delegation before a national GOP committee assembled to decide on the credentials of the delegates, and Oscar Hundley accused him of misrepresenting the facts about the selection of the Ninth Congressional District delegates, but Street and Prelate Barker again triumphed, and the Roosevelt delegates were rejected.[62]

After Roosevelt announced his willingness to enter the campaign as a third-party candidate, the former Populists from Shelby County and Chilton County finally took action. Lewis Reynolds turned down the Republican nomination for Congress to become a Progressive. On July 24, 1912, A. P. Longshore was in Birmingham at the first meeting of Alabama's Progressive party. The attendees met to select delegates to the actual state Progressive party convention and selected a Progressive party state executive committee. Longshore was named a state-at-large member of the committee. J. O. Thompson and Oscar Hundley were the leading figures at the meeting, and older Republican officeholders who had not fared well under Taft, including former GOP chairman William Vaughn, also attended.[63]

The state Progressive party convention was certainly not dominated by ex-Populists, but they played a prominent role. Lewis Reynolds and Longshore spoke to the delegates, as did former Chilton County probate judge Samuel Adams, who had previously returned to the Democratic party. In a later convention, Adams was selected as a presidential elector but refused the honor because he would be out of the state during the fall campaign. He made it clear, however, that he favored the "platform and objects of the Progressive party." Longshore accepted the Progressive nomination for Congress from Alabama's Fourth District. Former Populist editor Frank Crichton of Chilton County, who had returned with Adams to the Democratic party in 1900, endorsed the Progressive party and supported it in editorials in September and October.[64]

The state Progressive convention and executive committee were all-white gatherings, and blacks were excluded from participation. This was no surprise, for the regular Republican organization was lily-white as well, and Progressives did not want to be tagged as the new "black and tan" party. The public exclusion of blacks by Progressives, and a widely publicized letter written by Roosevelt to Georgia newspaper editor Julian Harris in support of an all-white party, was followed by Booker T. Washington's endorsement of Taft. This act must have shocked Roosevelt, who had always treated Washington as the country's premier black leader.[65]

Some commentators argue that the Harris letter and Roosevelt's capitulation to racist forces led to increased support for Bull Moosers among white southern Republicans, but support for the Progressive party among ex-Populists in Alabama's Upcountry came before the Harris letter was revealed. There is no evidence from statements that Longshore and Reynolds made after the Progressive convention, or from editorials in the pro-Roosevelt newspapers in Chilton and Shelby Counties, that race played any role in the decision of ex-Populists to become Progressives. Little or no discussion of the Harris letter occurred in these counties. If race was the motivator, insurgents in these counties could just as easily have supported Taft, who adopted an all-white policy in dispensing patronage early in his administration that did not alter prior to the election. Because there was no evidence that blacks were a patronage threat and because they could not vote in Alabama, there was little reason to worry about the matter of race.[66]

In August, the Republican executive committees of both Chilton and Shelby Counties, with almost no dissent and some jubilation, voted to affiliate with the Progressive party. In a series of articles written in August, Frank Crichton endorsed the national Progressive party platform, which was closely patterned after the "new nationalism" Roosevelt had announced at Osawattomie two years earlier. The platform, wrote Crichton, was the "most progressive ever offered by any political party and proposes radical changes in the affairs of the country." The "progressive people of Chilton County" should join Roosevelt's new party. Crichton denounced the old parties for their refusal to take action to change the economic conditions of the country and called for the citizens of the county to attend a mass meeting on August 30 in Clanton at which Judge A. P. Longshore of Shelby County would explain the Progressive party platform.[67]

One of Crichton's readers expressed his delight that "not only Republicans and old time Populists" were for Roosevelt but also "a large number of Democrats." An index to the continued existence of a reform mentality in the old Populists can be discerned from comments by former Populist editors about the possibility that Socialists would take votes from the Progressive party. Progressives in Chilton were quick to invite Socialists into their ranks. In Shelby County in October, as the election neared, Frank Norris was far more worried about a Socialist ticket that was nominated there than about the Democrats. Democrats, he contended, had urged Socialists to enter the races in an effort to siphon votes from the Progressive ticket, which Norris persisted in describing as the "Populist and Republican" ticket.[68]

In his last issue of the *People's Advocate* before the election, Norris ran a front-page article with the headline "Stop, Look, and Listen, Socialists" and signed by "A Socialist," who argued that "every vote that went to a Socialist ticket would come out of the Populist and Republican party." The writer reminded those who might vote for the Socialists that "the Populists, Republicans and Socialists of Shelby County" were the "farmers and laborers," who were only "slightly in the majority" when combined, but "divide them and see where you stand."[69]

Norris and Crichton were rightly worried about the attraction of ex-Populists and Progressives to Socialism in 1912. The state Socialist party platform synthesized popular features of both Populism and the reforms advocated by Roosevelt. It endorsed a minimum wage; an end to child labor; abolition of the poll tax; free textbooks for public school students; "collective ownership of intrastate public utilities"; abolition of convict leasing; the initiative, referendum, and recall; women's suffrage, the eight-hour day; and the abolition of injunctions in labor disputes. For farmers, the Socialists proposed a plan very much like the subtreasury proposal of the Farmers' Alliance. The Socialist presence made it imperative for supporters of the Progressive ticket to emphasize the reform credentials and pro-labor attitudes of national, state, and local progressives and the continuity of the Bull Moose movement with Populism.[70]

A pro-Roosevelt editor in Chilton County wrote that the Progressive party was the "new people's party," and a former Populist in Chilton wrote to a local newspaper that "the people's cause has borne different names, yet it is the same people battling for the right." The Progressive party was against the dishonest political practices that Populism had opposed, he added, and the letter ended with a favorable comment on the memory of the late Populist leader Frank Baltzell. In a show of support for the Progressive party's endorsement of graduated income and inheritance taxes, the executive committee of Chilton County's Progressive party denounced taxes that had been piled on the "common people" while the "corporations horde their millions and practically pay no tax."[71]

The new party's purpose, wrote Crichton, was to "strike the shackles of slavery from the laboring people of the country" and to bring respect to those who work. If the Progressives were elected, the "man in his overalls and woman who does his cooking and washing will be equally respected with those who, living off their labor, have an easier time in life." White people would continue to rule under the Progressives, "but not the Black Belt aristocracy, who effect to despise the men and women who work." The *Clanton Union-Banner* endorsed women's suffrage and ran two front-page articles endorsing the efforts of the leaders of the suffrage movement in Alabama.[72]

The Bull Moose campaign in Alabama was aided by a personal appearance from Theodore Roosevelt. In late September, accompanied by Joseph O. Thompson and Oscar Hundley, he made a brief stop at Calera in Shelby County before his train went on its way to Montgomery. In Montgomery, Roosevelt argued that the South would not be seriously considered in national affairs until it abandoned its traditional allegiance to the Democratic party. He chastised southerners for living in the past and indelicately criticized the memory of Jefferson Davis, a mistake for which the Alabama press blasted the Bull Moose leader.[73]

Roosevelt failed to crack the "Solid South" and received only 20 percent of Alabama's vote, but in the hill counties that had been most loyal to

Populism he won remarkable support. In Marshall County, where Taft had managed only 923 votes in 1908, the combined Roosevelt-Taft vote was 1,612, or an increase of 73 percent compared with Taft's previous total. The Democratic presidential vote grew in Marshall by only 11 percent compared with that received by Bryan in 1908, and although Democratic nominee Woodrow Wilson won the county, he managed only a plurality. The excitement that drove additional Marshall County voters to the polls was clearly not about Wilson or Taft, but almost entirely about Theodore Roosevelt, who received more than 70 percent of the anti-Democratic vote. In the Seventh Congressional District Wilson did not get a majority, and the Progressive party won more than three-quarters of the opposition vote. Roosevelt defeated Wilson in Cullman and Winston Counties, and he lost Cherokee County by only fifteen votes. He won both Chilton and Shelby Counties, and he received more than 80 percent of the anti-Democratic vote in both.[74]

Precinct returns from Shelby, Chilton, and Marshall Counties demonstrate that Roosevelt consistently defeated Wilson and Taft in precincts that were loyal to Populists in the nineties. At Jemison, the Populist stronghold where Lewis Reynolds was born and where he operated the Farmers' Alliance store, Roosevelt received eighty-four votes to fifty-two for Wilson, twenty-five for Taft, and nineteen for Eugene Debs. In the twelve precincts in Marshall County that went to Populist candidates for governor in both 1896 and 1898, Roosevelt received 801 votes to 636 for Wilson and only 248 for Taft. At Rock Spring in Marshall County, where Reuben Kolb received 124 votes to his opponent's 11 in 1892, Roosevelt won 92 votes to 52 for Wilson and only 6 for Taft. In Franklin County, Roosevelt won both precincts that had given a majority to Populist gubernatorial candidate Grattan Crowe in 1900.[75] In several other north Alabama counties where Populism was strong but where precinct returns are unavailable, Roosevelt won more than 40 percent of the vote. In Shelby, Chilton, and Marshall Counties alone, more than thirty-five hundred voters cast ballots for the Bull Moose candidate.[76]

It would be absurd to contend that these thousands of rural voters, mostly small farmers, turned out in such large numbers to cast their ballots for the Progressive party because they were concerned about how federal patronage might be dispensed. The conclusion can more credibly be drawn that they voted for Roosevelt because they preferred that his policies, or certainly that his attitudes, predominate in the nation's capital. Such a finding is at odds with contentions that there was no continuity between Populism and progressivism in Alabama, that Populists were never reformers, or that Populists lost their reform impulse after 1896.

Longshore won only Chilton and Shelby Counties in his race for Congress, and in Shelby the outcome ran true to form, as he squeaked out a forty-five vote lead over the incumbent Democrat. Longshore and Lewis Reynolds remained in the Progressive party through 1916, and Longshore accepted the party's nomination for the United State Senate in 1914, but received only a handful of votes outside Shelby and Chilton Counties. He won only in Chilton and suffered his first defeat in Shelby since his congressional race as a Populist in 1892. His poor showing occurred, in part, because of the nature of his new party. Progressives were a "party" in name only, for their entire influence revolved around the figure of Theodore Roosevelt. Without him on the ballot in 1914, they had little chance of success. The uncertainty of whether Roosevelt would continue his quest for the White House in 1916 led many Shelby County Progressives to return to the regular Republicans. The GOP offered a statewide ticket and split the anti-Democratic vote. Progressives and Republicans constituted a majority of the county's voters, but like all anti-Democratic movements in Shelby, they could not win if they were divided. The Democrats also recaptured Shelby's seat in the state legislature in 1914.[77]

In the presidential campaign of 1916, many GOP leaders worried that Roosevelt would take a majority of the state's Republican electorate again. As the 1916 elections approached, Oliver Street wrote to Prelate Barker that Longshore and Reynolds were "unalterably committed to Roosevelt against the field." Another leading Republican wrote to party chairman Pope Long that J. O. Thompson still wanted control of the Republican party, but "his only asset in Alabama is the popularity of Col. Roosevelt." If Thompson were "stripped of the Roosevelt popularity" he would not be a problem. If Progressives returned to the regular Republican party, wrote another prominent Republican, they "would have an overwhelming majority" of the rank and file in their camp.[78]

Luckily for Republicans, Roosevelt did not run in 1916, but Lewis Reynolds ran impressively on his county Progressive party ticket. Reynolds won back the probate judgeship he had lost to a Democrat in 1910. Longshore was still judge, but he had been stripped of most of his power by Democratic legislators. The probate judge had traditionally been a voting member and chairman of the county board of revenue in Shelby County, but a legislative act had made the board chairmanship an elective office independent of the judgeship. Much to the Democrats' chagrin,

Longshore decided not to seek reelection as judge, but successfully ran for chairman of the board of revenue. His election to the legislature in 1918 as a Republican was his last victory in politics.[79]

Longshore and Reynolds had both returned to the regular Republican party by 1918, and they would stay in the GOP to the end of their political careers. Oliver Street never defected to the Progressives and became one of his party's most powerful members, but in a private letter to a national Republican leader he maintained that he was a "progressive" at heart because of his past association with the Populist party. His actions did not fit his words. He labored for the success of his party only, and he had no compunctions about serving its conservative wing. That was not true of Reynolds and Longshore, who acted and sounded like progressive reformers after 1916 despite the demise of Roosevelt's party.[80]

Lewis Reynolds won the GOP nomination for the U.S. Senate in 1920, and his acceptance speech could have been given by Robert La Follette or another nationally known progressive. It was at odds with the conservative mentality exhibited by a majority of the nation's Republicans in the 1920s. "I am for women's suffrage," he said, "and voted to give them the right to vote when I was in the constitutional convention of 1901." The "farmers and laboring people," said the former Populist, "should have the same protection and the same assistance from our government that other classes have." Reynolds concluded with a Jacksonian flourish. "I believe that one of the purposes of the organization of our government was to protect the weak against the strong and not to give the corporations the power to oppress other citizens." Reynolds also expressed opposition to the League of Nations proposed by Woodrow Wilson and stated that he favored prohibition, both of which stands aligned him with the Senate's prominent progressive Republicans. Reynolds won only 30 percent of the state's vote against incumbent Democratic senator Oscar Underwood, but he won eight counties in the Hill Country.[81]

A. P. Longshore demonstrated his consistent reform stance during the campaign for the 1920 GOP presidential nomination. He supported California senator Hiram Johnson, a progressive who had been Roosevelt's vice-presidential running mate in 1912. Prelate Barker wrote Oliver Street early in the year to complain that the more "crazy" members of the Roosevelt wing of the Alabama GOP favored Johnson or progressive senator William Borah of Idaho. Street wrote Barker that he could find only one Alabama delegate to the GOP national convention who supported the eventual winner, conservative Ohio senator Warren G. Harding. Longshore was a delegate, and his support for Johnson put him in the minority in Alabama's delegation, but they held out for the Californian through at least the first five ballots of the convention. Johnson gained support in Alabama's delegation before the delegates finally accepted Harding as a compromise nominee. Longshore also won the GOP nomination for Congress in 1920 and was defeated, but he polled in excess of 40 percent of the vote. In 1921 he lost a special election for Congress, and in 1922 his political career finally ended when he sought reelection to the legislature and was defeated in another close race.[82]

Post-1960s historians argue that Populism and progressivism were fundamentally different. Progressives were more concerned about protecting consumers than producers, had a more sanguine view of the marketplace, accepted the urban-industrial-corporate world, and had no desire to redistribute wealth. These historians say that Roosevelt was no radical, did not intend to decentralize big business, was a conservative kind of progressive who wanted to stave off radical upheavals by offering piecemeal changes to satisfy the masses, and sometimes capitulated to the demands of gigantic corporations. Therefore, support for Roosevelt did not necessarily mean support for true reform.[83]

These analyses of the subtle differences between Populism and progressivism, and of Roosevelt's essential conservatism, are tinctured with hindsight. They underrate the difficulties of achieving radical reforms in the context of the early twentieth century, and they do not accurately gauge how ex-Populists or other reform-minded people viewed progressives in that time, rather than how historians view them from the standpoint of the late twentieth century. Roosevelt's brand of reform, and that of other progressive leaders, did differ in many respects from Populism, but from 1900 to 1912 such differences were not always perceptible, and they were often masked by political rhetoric. Roosevelt did popularize anti-monopoly and pro-labor sentiment, and if ex-Populists in Alabama's Hill Country believed that he would stand up for the people against sinister corporate interests or that he derived his power from the masses rather than from elites or party bosses, such perceptions were not unreasonable.

Conclusion

In Alabama's Hill Country, thousand of ex-Populists entered the Republican party after 1900. Some did so immediately after the 1896 presidential election, but others were so dedicated to Populism or had such an inherited dislike of the state and national Republican party that they denominated themselves "Populists" through the first decade of the new century. The refusal of Populists to return to the Democratic party grew from a variety of factors, which included their anger over events surrounding the adoption of the 1901 constitution and their bitterness about elections stolen by Democrats. They were further encouraged to become Republicans because their home counties had a history of disloyalty to the Democrats that predated Populism. The Upcountry political culture that nourished the Populists had never engendered loyalty to a post–Civil War Democratic party that Upcountry farmers genuinely believed had betrayed its most important ideals.

The postwar Alabama Democratic party not only allowed former Whigs into its highest councils after the war but also changed its name to the Democratic and Conservative party to make the Whigs feel at home. Democratic party leaders began to adopt Whiggish policies. In the 1870s they seemed intent on pleasing Black Belt planters, railroad interests, and men who held bonds on the state. A Democratic gubernatorial candidate was defeated in 1872, in part, because he lost support from white Hill Country farmers who resented the growing influence of both the Black Belt and the rising industrial interests in the party. Before the war, the Upcountry had been devoted to a Jacksonian ideology that infused the Democratic party. Special privileges for wealthy elites such as planters, financiers, and industrialists violated prewar Jacksonian tenets that were political orthodoxy in the hills.

Democratic leaders sensed the necessity of returning Upcountry whites to the party, and in 1874 they abandoned the Whiggish policies of the immediate postwar era. During the 1874 election campaign the rhetoric of Democrats from all ranks and regions was once again filled with Jacksonian sentiments. Republicans were blamed not only for turning state government over to greedy bondholders and railroad men but also for giving power to blacks and their carpetbagger allies. Racial anxieties, combined with the renewed Democratic commitment to old principles, succeeded in unifying white voters and effectively removed the Republican threat for the remainder of the century. Hill counties played a role in redeeming the state, but rising economic distress in the Upcountry, the domination of the Democratic party by Black Belt interests, efforts to stifle dissent within and outside the party, and policies that favored wealthy elites drove many Tennessee Valley and Hill Country whites into new anti-Democratic movements. Most of the new dissenters had never been Reconstruction Republicans, but they believed that the Democratic party no longer represented the small farmers of the Upcountry.

Democratic party nominating processes were particularly obnoxious to Hill Country farmers, who had inherited a radically democratic ideology. So many whites of all political persuasions were gathered under the Democratic party roof that party leaders thought it was imperative to control who was nominated so that dissidents could be kept out of office. Black Belt leaders were particularly interested in such control because their chief aim was white supremacy. Black Belters believed they were under siege from blacks who might regain power. Therefore, they had to control elections in their region and gain power over who was nominated in the Upcountry. If the wrong people won office in the hills, Black Belt control would be threatened. State laws that controlled black sharecroppers and tenants in the old plantation area, but which also applied to small white farmers and farm laborers in the Upcountry, might be repealed if a lower-class coalition of lowcountry blacks and Hill Country whites could be assembled.

Black Belt planters formed beneficial coalitions with Upcountry white commercial-industrial elites. When the wrong kind of people seized control of Upcountry county Democratic parties, or when third-party candidates won office, Black Belt leaders in the legislature or on the state Democratic executive committee stepped in to quell the opposition. The power of this coalition of elite groups, the election laws they created, and the way in which they ran the Democratic party were resented in hill counties, where local revolts against county-level Democrats grew in the late 1870s and early 1880s. When state Democratic leaders stepped up their efforts to control the party by actually nullifying the elections of some Upcountry dissidents, the motivation for revolt expanded. Independent movements sprouted in most hill counties in elections throughout the 1880s. In counties with large aggregations of white Unionist-Republicans, GOP voters formed coalitions with those bolting the Democrats.

Anger at Democratic leaders grew in tandem with discontent over agricultural conditions. Upcountry Farmers had inherited the Jeffersonian-Jacksonian ideal of the independent farmer who owned his own land and owed no one. Freedom came only to people who were not dependent on others. As cotton prices fell, as tenancy and sharecropping spread in the Upcountry, and as farmers who had once been self-sufficient were threatened with the loss of their land, farmers began to look to the political process to bring back their independence. In the Tennessee Valley and a few hill counties this economic dimension led to the rise of the Greenback movements in the late 1870s, and as the marketplace took more and more farmers under its tentacles by the mid-eighties, the desire for currency and credit reform spread into other hill counties. The desire to restore grassroots democracy was then connected with the rising anger over the loss of economic autonomy.

Upcountry dissenters were also thoroughly disgusted with the policies of the national Democratic party, which was under the sway of its northeastern financial wing and was led by the reactionary Grover Cleveland. Such editors as Robert McKee took great delight in informing their readers that northern Democrats were the tools of Wall Street, and when some southern Democrats joined postwar efforts to use the national government to benefit corporate interests, the party of Jackson began to look like the party of railroad magnates and the "money power." Some southern Democrats chafed under the influence of the Clevelandites, but many of them succumbed to the temptation to support subsidies for railroads and other private interests. A perception grew that small farmers in Alabama had no party at any level that represented them.

When the Farmers' Alliance sought members in the Hill Country they found people already prepared for a political war on eastern interests, Black Belt planters, crooked merchants, and election thieves. Hill Country voters had no compunctions about leaving the party of their fathers because, in their view, it had abandoned its principles. Most Upcountry counties had already elected, or nearly elected, an independent, Greenbacker, or Republican to some office between 1876 and 1888. In south Alabama's Wiregrass the Alliance also found great strength, but Alliance lecturers there had to convert committed Alliancemen to the cause of opposition to the entrenched Democratic party, whereas in the Hill Country they were preaching to already confirmed anti-Democrats.

When Alliance membership spread quickly in the volatile Upcountry, local Democratic hierarchies reacted vigorously against the new organization. Upcountry elites, outnumbered by Alliance supporters, called on state Democratic officials to step in and stop the Alliance from dominating county parties. When state party officials interfered in county politics, anger spread, and the Alliance gained new adherents. In some counties, Alliancemen nominated by local Democratic conventions were nevertheless forced to run against anti-Alliance Democrats who had been recognized by the state Democratic executive committee as "regular" party nominees. Alliance candidates who were victorious at the local level then sought to take control of the state Democratic party. When the party hierarchy denied them nominations that they believed should have been theirs, they joined one of two new parties.

The most radical of the party bolters, or those most committed to the program of the Farmers' Alliance, joined the Populist party. More moderate elements and those merely ambitious for political office were more likely to become Jeffersonians. The two dissident parties cooperated in state elections, but those Jeffersonians who were attracted to Democratic moderates and free-silver men hoped to reunite with the Democrats. However, Democratic leaders controlled the election machinery, and they were in no mood for negotiations with bolters of any stripe. Because of their ability to manipulate the votes of lowcountry blacks, Democrats won all statewide elections in the nineties despite overwhelming support for third-party candidates in the Upcountry and Wiregrass.

Although they lost statewide contests, Populists won control of local governments in several hill counties, and their greatest strength was in Chilton, Marshall, St. Clair, and Shelby Counties, where they dominated politics through the nineties. In these counties an overwhelming majority of Populists had once been Democrats, independents, or Greenbackers, but not Republicans. In other counties such as Walker and Winston, Unionist-Republicans outnumbered the ex-Democrats who became Populists, but the two groups joined forces in some elections in the nineties. In a few counties competition between the third party and the Democrats was so close that a small number of GOP voters held the balance of power. In those counties third-party men could not win elections unless they cooperated with or fused their tickets with Republicans. Thus, a strained but necessary working relationship developed between Upcountry Populists and Republicans in counties such as Shelby and Franklin. The relationship between the two parties was a pragmatic one, but some

Upcountry Republican farmers had never had much in common with the pro-business wing of their party, and they found the Populist program attractive.

The various party coalitions that formed, and the relative strength of Populism as a movement, differed from county to county and was often dependent on the quality of Populist leadership in each place. In some counties, particularly in Chilton, Shelby, and Marshall, men of extraordinary ability led third parties to victory even though their emphasis on issues differed. Lewis Reynolds and A. P. Longshore were committed to the programs put forward by the Farmers' Alliance and the Populist party. Thomas Atkins Street and Oliver Day Street seemed less committed to the economic programs of the Alliance and more concerned with the maintenance of grassroots political democracy. Judge Street championed the cause of those small farmers who needed land and lashed out at the Black Belt elite who controlled the state Democratic party, but said nothing about the subtreasury.

Alabama's Populists and Jeffersonians, regardless of what they thought about various remedies put forward by the Alliance or the national Populist party, were strongly influenced by the Jacksonian ideology that had permeated the antebellum Upcountry Democracy. Jacksonians had been antigovernment, but Populists believed that it was necessary to use government to bring parity back to economic life. They did not think that this new attitude violated the Jacksonian faith, but continued to believe that they were the most loyal adherents to the old Democratic creed.

The impulse behind Jacksonianism was the same one that drove the Populists. Jacksonianism grew from the "strong and quite reasonable apprehension that new classes of monied men were rising to positions of exclusive power, with no public accountability whatsoever, to corrupt American independence and equality." Like Jacksonians, Populists wanted to "sustain and to enlarge democracy in the midst of manifest political inequalities between the monied few and the producing, dependent many." Hill Country independents, Alliancemen, and Populists believed in the myth that the party that existed in the time of Jackson stood for the common man. That was the party they hoped to resurrect in the Populist moment. The postwar Democratic party that "Redeemed" the state had proven to be a "Trojan horse" no longer impelled by the dynamics that had motivated it before the Civil War.[1]

The number and variety of party revolts that spread through the Hill Country before Populism, connections between those revolts and the larger movement of the nineties, and the continued success of Upcountry anti-Democratic politicians for at least another twenty years after 1900 demonstrated that voters in the region were part of an unusually independent political culture. They were not controlled by parties, "old captains," memories of the "lost cause" or appeals to white unity.

When the national Populist party went into decline between 1896 and 1900, some Populists wandered back and forth, in and out of the Democratic party, before becoming Republicans. The legend of Radical Republican venality and GOP racial liberalism that grew from Reconstruction was strong, and many Populists could not make the transition to the GOP easily. Some hoped for a progressive takeover of the state Democratic party, but events between 1898 and 1904 indicated that state and national Democrats were moving in a reactionary direction. Returning to the Democrats would have forced men such as Longshore to go "hat in hand" to those who had fought him with every weapon at their command since 1888. It became increasingly difficult for Populists, however, to sustain their local party in the absence of an influential national People's party organization.

A new progressive wing of the Republican party, represented by Theodore Roosevelt, made the GOP a palatable alternative. By 1910, even such militant Populists as Longshore had become Republicans. In many ways, the elitist Roosevelt was the antithesis of Upcountry Populism, but Reynolds and Longshore did not view him as a conservative in reform clothing. They believed that his progressive Republican movement, particularly the Bull Moose party of 1912, stood in direct line of descent from prior movements against elite privilege and power. When James B. Weaver, the former presidential candidate of both the Greenback and the Populist parties, died in 1912, Populist editor Frank Norris said that Weaver was the "first Republican reformer or progressive" and that he had been "a pioneer in that kind of politics."[2]

Academic historians have debated the question of whether continuity existed between Populism and progressivism or whether Populists remained reformers after 1900. Among the reforms that Lewis Reynolds, A. P. Longshore, and Frank Norris supported at various times between 1900 and 1912 were new taxes for schools and roads; government ownership and operation of public utilities; women's suffrage; the right of women to engage in professions usually restricted to men; the right of labor to bargain with employers; the eight-hour day; an end to convict leasing; severe restrictions on child labor; the right of labor to strike; the break-up of monopolies; and the initiative, referendum, and recall. They opposed all restrictions on the political power of the masses and fought Democratic antiboycott laws aimed at stifling labor unions. These varied reform attitudes constituted progressivism, as most historians have defined it. When joined with evidence of the support Theodore Roosevelt received in former Populist strongholds, the thesis of continuity between Populism and progressivism in Alabama's Hill Country is sustained. One may define the elusive concept of progressivism in such a way as to leave ex-Populists out, but one can hardly deny their post-1900 reform impulse.

In *Populism to Progressivism in Alabama,* Sheldon Hackney portrays Populists as retrograde agrarians longing for a Jeffersonian past that could never recur and describes Democratic governor Braxton Bragg Comer by contrast as the quintessential Alabama progressive. Progressives such as Comer believed in a "leadership elite" who were "realistically concerned with the problems of an urbanizing and industrializing society." Hackney admits that Comer "dragged his feet on certain progressive measures," but his support of higher taxes for increased government services was "the real test" that confirmed his progressivism.[3]

Comer's progressivism did not include concern for children tethered to textile machines, for miners working in dangerous conditions, or for the right of the masses to participate in politics. Comer was a product of the Black Belt, and as a grown man in his midtwenties he had taken up weapons to stop black people and white Republicans from voting in his native Barbour County in the 1874 general election. Later he became an influential textile magnate who had no compunctions about children working in his mills, and he did not oppose ratification of the 1901 constitution that enshrined into law what he had earlier tried to enforce with a gun. Comer's ethos was rooted in the elite paternalism of the planter class, and he transferred that ethos into the treatment of the cotton mill workers whose productive labor had made him rich. The whip and the gun always lurked just behind the noblesse oblige exterior that planters donned to pacify their slaves, and after he became governor B. B. Comer had no hesitation about breaking strikes with the state militia. He had also supported the use of such force by previous governors.[4]

The support by former Populists for labor and their opposition to voting restrictions differentiated their progressivism from the elitist variety championed by Comer. Like Jacksonians, Populists wanted "producers" and workers to control their own economic destiny. Comer, despite his self-serving attacks on railroad corporations that charged him high prices to ship his products, wanted a large supply of cheap labor tightly control-led for the benefit of his class. Between 1900 and 1904, he organized opposition to legislation that would have restricted child labor. If pro-gressivism was, as some historians think, motivated by a "deep outrage against the worst consequences of industrialism" or by "anti-business emotion," then Comer was no progressive.[5]

The exclusion of either Comer Democrats or ex-Populists from pro-gressive ranks depends on the definition of progressivism used by the his-torian doing the excluding. Sheldon Hackney's assumption that Populists should be left out because they did not share with Comer a sanguine faith in the modernizing impulse, in the ameliorative impact of bureaucratic agencies, and in the beneficent motives of those who were trying to raise their taxes is insufficient to deny them status as reformers. A liberal his-torian who inherited a strong commitment to the legacy of the New Deal and who wrote about Populists in the late 1960s—when liberals placed their faith in the success of Great Society programs to alleviate poverty and ensure racial equality—could be excused for concluding that Popu-lists were shortsighted and narrow-minded.

Populists distrusted economic modernization because they were more concerned and more realistic than Comer about the human costs of ur-ban-industrial development. They opposed taxes, particularly those on land, because of their concern for small farmers operating on the eco-nomic margins who comprised the vast majority of Alabama's work force. Populists were suspicious of the rise of a bureaucratic state because they feared that such a state might facilitate the growth of giant corporations and banks that would control the state and because they understood that a government agency was only as good as those who were placed in charge of it. Longshore and Reynolds were not naive enough to believe that regu-latory schemes proposed by a cotton mill boss such as Comer or a Bir-mingham banker such as Joe Johnston were simply offered to help "the people." The ex-Populists' commitment to progressive era reforms must be viewed in the context of those times, and their mentalities should not be measured against those of New Dealers, Great Society Democrats, or post–1954 civil rights activists.

Notes

Introduction

1. Letter of T. A. Street, *Montgomery Journal*, May 20, 1901, as cited in Wayne Flynt, *Poor But Proud: Alabama's Poor Whites* (Tuscaloosa: University of Alabama Press, 1990), 272–73.

2. V. O. Key, *Southern Politics in State and Nation* (New York: Alfred A. Knopf, 1949), 37; John Egerton, *Speak Now against the Day: The Generation before the Civil Rights Movement in the South* (New York: Alfred A. Knopf, 1994), 391 (for all quotes).

3. Key, *Southern Politics*, 36–57; see also William Warren Rogers, Robert David Ward, Leah Rawls Atkins, and Wayne Flynt, *Alabama: The History of a Deep South State* (Tuscaloosa: University of Alabama Press, 1994), 288–375, 411–42, 494–544, and J. Mills Thornton III, "Alabama Politics, J. Thomas Heflin, and the Expulsion Movement of 1929," *Alabama Review* 21 (April 1968):83–112.

4. Rogers, Ward, Atkins, and Flynt, *Alabama*, 343–54; Carl Grafton and Anne Permaloff, *Big Mules and Branchheads: James E. Folsom and Political Power in Alabama* (Athens: University of Georgia Press, 1985), 38–55; Flynt, *Poor But Proud*, 243–77.

5. Key, *Southern Politics*, 36–57; J. Mills Thornton III, *Politics and Power in a Slave Society: Alabama, 1800–1860* (Baton Rouge: Louisiana State University Press, 1978), 41–42, 240, 345–46; Flynt, *Poor But Proud*, 3–35, 367–79; Roger, Ward, Atkins, and Flynt, *Alabama*, 173–74; Dewey W. Grantham, *The Life and Death of the Solid South: A Political History* (Lexington: University Press of Kentucky, 1988), 33 (quote), 33–35.

6. Key, *Southern Politics*, 36–37, 42.

7. Dewey W. Grantham, *Southern Progressivism: The Reconciliation of Progress and Tradition* (Knoxville: University of Tennessee Press, 1983), 46–51, and *Life and Death of the Solid South*, 33–35, 93–94; Alexander Heard, *A Two-Party South?* (Chapel Hill: University of North Carolina Press, 1952), 37–52; Paul Casdorph, *Republicans, Negroes and Progressives in the South, 1912–1916* (University: University of Alabama Press, 1981).

8. Casdorph, *Republicans, Negroes and Progressives;* Dewey W. Grantham,

The Democratic South (Athens: University of Georgia Press, 1963), 42 (quote), 26, and Life and Death of the Solid South, 24.

9. Grantham, Southern Progressivism, 10, 35–36, and Life and Death of the Solid South, 8–11, 23–25 (quote on 24); J. Morgan Kousser, The Shaping of Southern Politics: Suffrage Restriction and the Establishment of the One-Party South, 1880–1910 (New Haven: Yale University Press, 1974), 11–44, 224–27.

10. Key, Southern Politics, 282–83 (all quotes).

11. Allen Johnston Going, Bourbon Democracy in Alabama, 1874–1890 (University: University of Alabama Press, 1951), 49–54, 213–31; Congressional Quarterly's Guide to U.S. Elections, 4th ed. (Washington D.C.: Congressional Quarterly, Inc., 1994); Louis Loveman, comp., "The Presidential Vote in Alabama," a county-by-county compilation of all of Alabama's presidential elections results in order by year but not by page number, Birmingham [Alabama] Public Library (n.p., 1983).

12. Loveman, "Presidential Vote in Alabama"; Guide to U.S. Elections; see Alabama Official and Statistical Register, 1903, 204–46 and the Official and Statistical Register, 1911, 264–301; see also the Montevallo Weekly Review, November 18, 1910, the Clanton Union and Banner, November 7, 1912, and the Cullman Tribune, November 4, 1920, for accounts of two-party competition; Grantham, Southern Progressivism, 119–20 (quote).

13. Official and Statistical Register, 1923, 344–56; Loveman, "Presidential Vote in Alabama."

14. Official and Statistical Register, 1923, 344–48.

15. Official and Statistical Register, 1931, 511–12, and see presidential elections results for 1924 and 1928 in Loveman, "Presidential Vote"; Oliver D. Street to Charles J. Scott, August 24, 1918, and to O. W. Tucker, September 2, 1918, O. D. Street Collection, Gorgas Library, University of Alabama; on the death of Burnett see the Boaz Leader, May 15, 1919; for election results in 1919 special election and 1920 general election in Marshall County see the Guntersville Democrat, October 8, 1919, and November 10, 1920.

16. See accounts of elections in Shelby and Chilton Counties and citations to sources of precinct returns in each county in Samuel L. Webb, "Two-Party Politics in the One-Party South: Alabama Hill Country, 1880–1920" (Ph.D. diss., University of Arkansas, 1991), 69–232, 307–76.

17. Going, Bourbon Democracy in Alabama, 214–31; Loveman, "Presidential Vote"; Official and Statistical Register, 1923, 364–65; Maurice McGee, "DeKalb Voters March to Different Drummer," Landmarks News 14 (summer-fall 1984):1, 3, 20–21.

18. See voting percentages for each congressional election in the *Guide to U.S. Elections;* for county totals in 1910 campaign see the *Official and Statistical Register, 1911,* 272; for 1919 and 1920 congressional races see the *Official and Statistical Register, 1923,* 345; *Guntersville Democrat,* October 8, 1919, and November 10, 1920; and *Centre Coosa River News,* October 3, 1919.

19. Gene Clanton, *Populism: The Humane Preference in America, 1890–1900* (Boston: Twayne Publishers, 1991), 3.

20. T. A. Street, *Montgomery Journal,* May 20, 1901, as cited in Flynt, *Poor But Proud,* 272–73; *Clanton Banner,* August 28, 1902 (second quote).

21. William F. Holmes, "Populism in Search of a Context," *Agricultural History* 64 (Fall 1990):57 (quote).

1. The Old Guard and the Populists

1. John M. Blum, *Liberty, Justice, Order: Essays on Past Politics* (New York: W. W. Norton, 1993), 34.

2. John Milton Cooper, Jr., *Pivotal Decades: The United States, 1900–1920* (New York: W. W. Norton, 1990), 169–75, 173 (quote).

3. Paul Casdorph, *Republicans, Negroes and Progressives,* 94–96; *Birmingham Times,* June 28, 1912; William Henry Harbaugh, *Power and Responsibility: The Life and Times of Theodore Roosevelt* (New York: Farrar, Straus and Cudahy, 1961), 432–36, 433 (quote).

4. *Columbiana People's Advocate,* June 27, 1912; Harbaugh, *Power and Responsibility,* 435.

5. *Talladega Daily Home,* July 25, 1912; *Birmingham News,* July 24 and 25, 1912; Paul Casdorph, *Republicans, Negroes and Progressives,* 125–27.

6. Robert Crunden, *Ministers of Reform: The Progressives' Achievement in American Civilization, 1889–1920* (New York: Basic Books, 1982), 200–224; Harbaugh, *Power and Responsibility,* 442–44, 443 (quote from Roosevelt), 450 (quote from socialist).

7. Crunden, *Ministers of Reform,* 210–19; Harbaugh, *Power and Responsibility,* 443–44.

8. Harbaugh, *Power and Responsibility,* 413–14 (quote), 423, 438–39.

9. Harbaugh, *Power and Responsibility,* 311 (quote); Lewis L. Gould, *Reform and Regulation: American Politics from Roosevelt to Wilson* (New York: Alfred A. Knopf, 1986), 121–59; John Milton Cooper, *The Warrior and the Priest: Woodrow Wilson and Theodore Roosevelt* (Cambridge, Mass.: Harvard University Press, Belknap Press, 1983), 143–63, and Cooper, *Pivotal Decades,* 147–48.

10. *Memorial Record of Alabama,* 2 vols. (1893; reprint, Spartanburg, S.C.: Reprint Co., 1976), 2:508; Thomas M. Owen, *History of Alabama and Dictionary of Alabama Biography,* 4 vols. (Chicago: S. J. Clarke, 1921), 3:99; Oliver D. Street to P. D. Barker and to William L. Chenault, February 2, 1916 (references to the "Major"), Street Collection.

11. *Memorial Record of Alabama,* 2:508; Owen, *History of Alabama and Dictionary,* 3:99; Casdorph, *Progressives, Negroes and Republicans,* 82–83, 94–96; for rise of Barker in party see the *Birmingham Times,* January 20, May 26, June 2, 16, 30, and September 1, 1911; Barker to Pope M. Long on September 19 and 24, 1912, Street Collection.

12. Barker to Oliver D. Street, March 20, July 23, August 21 and 25, 1911, Street Collection.

13. Milford Howard to Oliver D. Street, July 11 and August 1, 1911, Street Collection; Louis R. Harlan, *Booker T. Washington: The Wizard of Tuskegee, 1901–1915* (New York: Oxford University Press, 1983), 8, 24, 125; see also Sarah Woolfolk Wiggins, *The Scalawag in Alabama Politics, 1865–1881* (University: University of Alabama Press, 1977) and Casdorph, *Republicans, Negroes and Progressives,* for all sections relating to Alabama.

14. Owen, *History of Alabama and Dictionary,* 3:150, 248, 492, and 4:1761–62; see Wiggins, *Scalawag in Alabama Politics,* 94, 137–39, 142–46, 151–53 for mention of these men and their activities; Joel C. Dubose, *Notable Men of Alabama,* 2 vols. (Atlanta: Southern Historical Association), 1:25–28, 41–42, 149–50; *Memorial Record of Alabama,* 2:612–14; for further information on Bingham see the *Huntsville Republican,* June 28, August 9, and November 15, 1902.

15. Harlan, *Washington, Wizard,* 8–9, 24; *Huntsville Republican,* October 12, 1901, August 9, November 15, and December 6, 1902; *Birmingham Alabamian,* February 6 and June 13, 1903.

16. Lewis L. Gould, *The Presidency of Theodore Roosevelt* (Lawrence: University Press of Kansas, 1991), 22–23, 118–22.

17. Thomas R. Cripps, "The Lily White Republicans: The Negro, the Party and the South in the Progressive Era" (Ph.D diss., University of Maryland, 1967); Harlan, *Washington, Wizard,* 8, 24–25, 125; Gould, *Presidency of Theodore Roosevelt,* 118–22; Casdorph, *Republicans, Negroes and Progressives.*

18. Harlan, *Washington, Wizard,* 8, 24–25, 124; Gould, *Presidency of Theodore Roosevelt,* 22–24; see letters of Joseph Oswalt Thompson to Booker T. Washington, in Louis R. Harlan, ed., *Booker T. Washington Papers,* 13 vols. (Urbana: University of Illinois Press, 1972), 4:231, 7:277.

19. Harlan, *Washington Papers,* 4:231, 7: 277; Harlan, *Washington, Wizard,*

8–24, 25, 342; *Birmingham Times,* November 27, 1903; Dubose, *Notable Men of Alabama,* 2:397–98.

20. Gould, *Reform and Regulation,* 51–55, and *Presidency of Theodore Roosevelt,* 129–32, 133 (quote); *Birmingham Alabamian,* February 6, 1903; *Birmingham Times,* February 12, 1904; Harlan, *Washington, Wizard,* 8.

21. *Huntsville Republican,* November 15, 1902; *Birmingham Times,* May 13, 1904; *Birmingham Alabamian,* May 12, 1904; Owen, *History of Alabama and Dictionary,* 3:869–70.

22. Harlan, *Washington, Wizard,* 342; see all issues of *Birmingham Times* for January, February, March, and April of 1907, and January 1 and 8, March 19, and April 16, 1909; *Birmingham Republican,* January 2, 1909; Casdorph, *Republicans, Negroes and Progressives,* 50–52.

23. Oliver D. Street to Mary Emma Street, July 3, 1911, Street Collection; *Columbiana People's Advocate,* July 13, 1911; *Birmingham Times,* August 21, September 1, and September 22, 1911, and March 8, 1912; Cooper, *Warrior and the Priest,* 159.

24. Allen W. Trelease, "Who Were the Scalawags?" *Journal of Southern History* 29 (November 1963):445–68; Michael W. Fitzgerald, "Radical Republicanism and the White Yeomanry during Alabama Reconstruction, 1865–1868," *Journal of Southern History* 54 (November 1988):565–96; Wiggins, *Scalawag in Alabama Politics,* 109–27; William M. Cash, "Alabama Republicans during Reconstruction: Personal Characteristics, Motivations, and Political Activity of Party Activists, 1867–1880" (Ph.D diss., University of Alabama, 1973); Paul Haynes Horton, "Testing the Limits of Class Politics in Postbellum Alabama: Agrarian Radicalism in Lawrence County," *Journal of Southern History* 57 (February 1991):63–84.

25. See the *Official and Statistical Register, 1903,* and for all succeeding years through 1923, and Loveman, "Presidential Vote," for party voting statistics between 1900 through 1920.

26. Harlan, *Washington, Wizard,* 8–9; *Huntsville Republican,* August 12 and 16, 1902; Paul McWhorter Pruitt, "Joseph C. Manning, Alabama Populist: A Rebel Against the Solid South" (Ph.D. diss., The College of William and Mary, 1980).

27. Pruitt, "Joseph C. Manning," 1–4, 9–24, 32–57, 308–37, 348–86.

28. *Montgomery Evening Journal,* August 12, 13, 14, and 18, 1902; *Montgomery Advertiser,* August 15, 1902; *Huntsville Republican,* August 16, 1902; Harlan, *Washington, Wizard,* 8–9.

29. *Huntsville Republican,* August 16, 1902; *Montgomery Evening Journal,* August 14 and 18, 1902.

30. Owen, *History of Alabama and Dictionary,* 3:16–17.

31.   For fusion in Shelby County see the *Columbiana People's Advocate*, July and August 1896 and 1898 and October and November 1898; for examples of how fusion worked in a statewide election, see William Warren Rogers, *The One-Gallused Rebellion: Agrarianism in Alabama, 1865–1896* (Baton Rouge: Louisiana State University Press, 1970), 293–327, 308–11.

32.   Rogers, *One-Gallused Rebellion*, 296, 308–11, 326–27.

33.   Owen, *History of Alabama and Dictionary*, 3:16–17.

34.   Harlan, *Washington, Wizard*, 8, 8 n, 24–25; *Montgomery Evening Journal*, August 14 and 18, 1902 (Manning's remarks); for the rise of Thompson in the GOP, see the *Huntsville Republican*, November 2 and 23, 1901, November 15, 1902, April 4, 1903, and the *Birmingham Alabamian*, May 12, 1904.

35.   *Official and Statistical Register, 1903*, 237–38.

36.   *Official and Statistical Register, 1903*, 115, 117; *Official and Statistical Register,1907*, 155; and *Official and Statistical Register, 1911*, 201, 203.

37.   M. F. Parker to O. D. Street, June 14, 1911 (quotes), Street Collection; see all correspondence between Barker and Street during 1911 and early 1912 in the Street Collection.

38.   Sketches of both Oliver and Thomas Atkins Street in Owens, *History of Alabama and Dictionary*, 4:1632–33; *Birmingham Times*, April 11, 1909; Oliver D. Street to Charles W. Taft, March 13, 1909, Street Collection; Casdorph, *Republicans, Negroes and Progressives*, 94–95.

39.   David Alan Harris, "Campaigning in the Bloody Seventh: The Election of 1894 in the Seventh Congressional District," *Alabama Review* 27 (April 1974):127–38; Rogers, *One-Gallused Rebellion*, 327–28, 200, 223, 284, 315.

40.   Barker to O. D. Street, July 23, August 21 and 25, 1911, Street Collection.

41.   *Birmingham Times*, March 8, 1912; Gould, *Reform and Regulation*, 27; Cooper, *Pivotal Decades*, 161.

42.   *Birmingham Times*, March 8, 1912.

43.   O. D. Street to Lewis Reynolds, July 6, 1912, Street Collection; *Talladega Daily Home*, July 25, 1912; *Clanton Union and Banner*, August 8, 15, and 29, 1912; Loveman, "Presidential Vote."

44.   *Birmingham Age-Herald*, April 3 and July 24, 1912; *Birmingham Times*, June 2 and September 22, 1911; Casdorph, *Republicans, Negroes and Progressives*, 126.

45.   Albert Burton Moore, *History of Alabama*, 3 vols. (Chicago: American Historical Society, 1927), 3:470; *Guntersville Democrat*, November 6, 1902; see correspondence of Street and Kennamer in the file marked

"1906" in the Street Collection; J. O. Thompson to Oliver Street, May 3, 1910, Street Collection.

46. Barker to Pope M. Long, September 19 and September 24, 1912, Street Collection; *Clanton Union and Banner,* July 18, August 8, 16, and 29, 1912.

47. Loveman, "Presidential Vote"; see *Official and Statistical Register* for 1911 and 1913, returns in presidential elections located in both volumes at pages 264–65.

48. *Official and Statistical Register, 1911* and *Official and Statistical Register, 1913,* pp. 264–65 (both volumes).

49. See issues of the *Geneva Reaper* and the *Geneva Journal* for the early years of the twentieth century; Loveman, "Presidential Vote."

50. Loveman, "Presidential Vote"; Going, *Bourbon Democracy,* 215–31; for gubernatorial returns see the *Journal of the House of Representatives of the State of Alabama* for all years from 1872 to 1900; U.S. Bureau of the Census, *United States Census, 1910,* 2:776.

51. Numan V. Bartley, "In Search of the New South: Southern Politics after Reconstruction," in *The Promise of American History: Progress and Prospects,* ed. Stanley I. Kutler and Stanley N. Katz (Baltimore: Johns Hopkins University Press, 1982), 155; Sheldon Hackney, *Populism to Progressivism in Alabama* (Princeton, N.J.: Princeton University Press, 1969), 30–31, 77–88, 114–21, 326–31.

2. James Lawrence Sheffield and the Roots of Hill Country Independence

1. Eugene Genovese, "Yeoman Farmers in a Slaveholders Democracy," *Agricultural History* 49 (April 1975):334.

2. Owen, *History Of Alabama and Dictionary,* 4:1633; *Ashville Southern Aegis,* September 9 and 16, 1874.

3. Going, *Bourbon Democracy,* 1–26, 213–17; Rogers, Ward, Atkins, and Flynt, *Alabama,* 259–64; Michael Perman, *The Road to Redemption: Southern Politics, 1869–1879* (Chapel Hill: University of North Carolina Press, 1984), 156–58.

4. Fitzgerald, "Radical Republicanism and the White Yeomanry," 565–96; Trelease, "Who Were the Scalawags," 445–68; Rogers, Ward, Atkins, and Flynt, *Alabama,* 244–64; J. Mills Thornton III, "Fiscal Policy and the Failure of Radical Reconstruction in the Lower South," in *Region, Race and Reconstruction: Essays in Honor of C. Vann Woodward,* ed. J. Morgan Kousser and James M. McPherson (New York: Oxford University Press, 1982), 349–94.

5. *Ashville Southern Aegis,* September 9, 16 (first quote), and 30 (second quote), 1874.

6. Rogers, Ward, Atkins, and Flynt, *Alabama,* 259–65; Going, *Bourbon Democracy,* 30–31; *Selma Southern Argus,* June 20 and 27, July 4, and August 15, 1873.

7. *Selma Southern Argus,* June 20 (first and last quotes) and July 4, 1873 (second quote).

8. Rogers, Ward, Atkins, and Flynt, *Alabama,* 260; Perman, *Road to Redemption,* 234–35, 242–47; article from the *Opelika Times* reprinted in the *Huntsville Weekly Democrat,* June 4, 1874; *Columbiana Shelby Guide,* April 30, 1874.

9. *Selma Southern Argus,* February 13 and April 10, 1874, and in the July 30, 1875, *Argus* see the article titled "Morgan County Affairs"; *Huntsville Advocate,* June 25, 1872, as cited in Going, *Bourbon Democracy,* 6; Michael R. Hyman, *The Anti-Redeemers: Hill Country Political Dissenters in the Lower South from Redemption to Populism* (Baton Rouge, Louisiana State University Press, 1990), 23–25; W. David Lewis, *Sloss Furnaces and the Rise of the Birmingham District: An Industrial Epic* (Tuscaloosa: University of Alabama Press, 1991), 35–69; Wiggins, *Scalawag in Alabama Politics,* 79–84.

10. Owen, *Alabama History and Dictionary,* 4:1540; Katherine McKinstry Duncan and Larry Joe Smith, *The History of Marshall County, Alabama* (Albertville, Ala.: Thompson Printing Co., 1969), 50–51; Stewart Sifakis, *Who Was Who in the Civil War* (New York: Facts on File Publications, 1988), 585.

11. See file card on Nicholas Sheffield, Alabama Department of Archives and History, Montgomery, Alabama, and see U.S., Manuscript Census, 1830, for Madison County; Owen, *Alabama History and Dictionary,* 4:1540, 2:954–58; Albert Burton Moore, *History of Alabama* (Chicago: American Historical Association, 1927), 29–33; John M. Allman, "Yeoman Regions in the Antebellum Deep South: Settlement and Economy in Northern Alabama, 1815–1860" (Ph.D. diss. University of Maryland, 1979), 422–38; John Noel Story, "The History of Marshall County, Alabama, Prior to 1860" (master's thesis, University of Alabama, 1930), 11–54.

12. James L. Sheffield to O. D. Street, May 25, 1890, Street Collection; Lewy Dorman, *Party Politics in Alabama from 1850 through 1860* (Wetumpka, Ala.: n.p., 1935); Thornton, *Politics and Power,* xv–xxi, 3–58.

13. Thornton, *Politics and Power,* 19–54, 335–42, 442; Hyman, *Anti-Redeemers,* 29–35.

14. Eric Foner, *Reconstruction: America's Unfinished Revolution, 1863–1877* (New York: Harper and Row, 1988), 11–13; Thornton, *Politics and Power,*

288–89, 345–46; Steven Hahn, *The Roots of Southern Populism: Yeoman Farmers and the Transformation of the Georgia Upcountry, 1850–1890* (New York: Oxford University Press, 1983), 15–49.

15. Allman, "Yeomen Regions," 387–411; Grady McWhiney, "The Revolution in Nineteenth-Century Agriculture," *Alabama Review* 31 (October 1978):3–32; Hahn, *Roots of Southern Populism*, 58–61, 52 (quotes); J. Crawford King, "The Closing of the Southern Range: An Exploratory Study," *Journal of Southern History* 48 (February 1982):53–58.

16. Thornton, *Politics and Power*, xviii (quote), 26–47, and Thornton "The Ethic of Subsistence and the Origins of Southern Secession," *Tennessee Historical Quarterly* 48 (Summer 1989):67–85; Flynt, *Poor But Proud*, 4–10.

17. Thornton, *Politics and Power*, xviii, 5–8, 50–52, 323–42; Lawrence F. Kohl, *The Politics of Individualism: Parties and the American Character in the Jacksonian Era* (New York: Oxford University Press, 1989), 21–61; Harry L. Watson, *Liberty and Power: The Politics of Jacksonian America* (New York: Noonday Press, 1990), 61–65.

18. Thornton, *Politics and Power*, 323–42; Kohl, *Politics of Individualism*, 56–62, 96–99, 190–94; Watson, *Liberty and Power*, 62–64; Marvin Meyers, *The Jacksonian Persuasion: Politics and Belief* (1957; reprint, New York: Vintage, 1960), 11–12.

19. Robert C. McMath, *American Populism: A Social History* (New York: Hill and Wang, 1993), 52 (first quote); J. Mills Thornton, "Jacksonian Democracy," in *Encyclopedia of Southern Culture,* ed. Charles Reagan Wilson and William Ferris (Chapel Hill: University of North Carolina Press, 1989), 630 (second and fourth quotes), and Thornton, *Politics and Power*, 50 (third quotation), 74–76, 151–55.

20. Dorman, *Party Politics*, 222, 96–98; Thornton, "Fiscal Policy," 349–60.

21. Thornton, *Politics and Power*, 20–58; Flynt, *Poor But Proud*, 3–10; Watson, *Liberty and Power*, 146.

22. Leah R. Atkins, "Williamson R. W. Cobb and the Graduation Act of 1854," *Alabama Review* 38 (January 1975):20–21.

23. Owen, *Alabama History and Dictionary*, 4:1540; U.S., Manuscript Census, 1850, Marshall County; *Guntersville Democrat*, June 30, 1892.

24. W. J. Cash, *The Mind of the South* (New York: Alfred A. Knopf, 1941), 14; U.S., Manuscript Census, 1860, Marshall County; U.S., Bureau of the Census, *Agriculture, 1860*, 2:223.

25. U.S., Bureau of the Census, *Agriculture, 1860*, 2:193, 223.

26. Sean Wilentz, "The Original Outsider," *New Republic* (June 22, 1992), 34–38, 37 (quote); Thornton, "Ethic of Subsistence," 74–85; Lacy K.

Ford, *The Origins of Southern Radicalism: The South Carolina Upcountry, 1800–1860* (New York: Oxford University Press, 1988), 272–73, 335–37.

27.   Thornton, "Ethic of Subsistence," 74–85; Ford, *Origins of Southern Radicalism*, 335–37; Bradley G. Bond, *Political Culture in the Nineteenth Century South: Mississippi, 1830–1900* (Baton Rouge: Louisiana State University Press, 1995), 73–82.

28.   Owen, *History of Alabama and Dictionary*, 2:957–58, 4:1540.

29.   Rogers, Ward, Atkins, and Flynt, *Alabama*, 183–84; Thornton, *Politics and Power*, 344; James L. Sheffield Scrapbook, O. D. Street Papers, Department of Archives and History, Montgomery, Alabama; Owen, *History of Alabama and Dictionary*, 4:1540.

30.   Bessie Martin, *Desertion of Alabama Troops from the Confederate Army* (1932; reprint, New York: AME Press, 1966), 26–62, 234–55; Flynt, *Poor But Proud*, 36–46; Donald B. Dodd, "Unionism in Northwest Alabama" (master's thesis, Auburn University, 1966), 31–43, 57; William Stanley Hoole, *Alabama Tories: The First Alabama Cavalry, U.S A., 1862–1865* (Tuscaloosa: Confederate Publishing Co., Inc., 1960), 5–20.

31.   Foner, *Reconstruction*, 15–17, 16 (first quote); Flynt, *Poor But Proud*, 42–52, 43 (second quote).

32.   Sifakis, *Who Was Who in the Civil War*, 585; Owen, *History of Alabama and Dictionary*, 4:1633.

33.   Owen, *History of Alabama and Dictionary*, 4:1540.

34.   Ibid., 3:964; John R. Kennamer and Louis Garfield Kennamer, *The Kennamer Family* (Nashville: McQuiddy Printing Co., 1924), 322–23; Fitzgerald, "Radical Republicans and the White Yeomanry," 574.

35.   Owen, *History of Alabama and Dictionary*, 4:1633; see article from the *Huntsville Independent* by E. M. Ragland, editor, in the James L. Sheffield Scrapbook, Street Papers (quote); U.S., Manuscript Census, 1880, Marshall County.

36.   Ellis C. Moody, "The Origin, Rise and Organization of the Republican Party in Marshall County from 1860 to 1902" (twenty-page paper deposited in the Alabama Department of Archives and History, Montgomery, Alabama, 1939), 7–9; Owen, *History of Alabama and Dictionary*, 3:118, 4:1633; see also Sheffield Scrapbook, Street Papers, for information on Beard.

37.   Fitzgerald, "Radical Republicanism and the White Yeomanry"; Trelease, "Who Were the Scalawags."

38.   Fitzgerald, "Radical Republicanism and the White Yeomanry"; Going, *Bourbon Democracy*, 215–31; Loveman, "Presidential Vote."

39. See newspaper articles, with dates and names uncited, in the James L. Sheffield Scrapbook (no page numbers), Street Papers.

40. See the *Ashville Southern Aegis,* September and October, 1874; James L. Sheffield, "Circular to the People of the Fifth Congressional District of Alabama" (Huntsville: A. H. Brittain Mercantile Job Printers, 1874); *Huntsville Weekly Democrat,* August 27, 1874.

41. Sheffield, "Circular"; *Ashville Southern Aegis,* September 16, 1874; *Guide to U.S. Elections,* 1028, incorrectly lists Sheffield as a Republican.

42. *Ashville Southern Aegis,* September 9 and 16, 1874; Owen, *History of Alabama and Dictionary,* 3:189–90; Perman, *Road to Redemption,* 156–58; Going, *Bourbon Democracy,* 69.

43. Thornton, "Fiscal Policy," 349 (quote) and *Politics and Power,* 442; Perman, *Road to Redemption,* 157, 213–15, 220.

44. C. Vann Woodward, *Origins of the New South, 1877–1913* (Baton Rouge: Louisiana State University Press, 1951), 47–50, 75–77, and *Reunion and Reaction: The Compromise of 1877 and the End of Reconstruction* (Boston: Little, Brown and Co., 1951), 22–50, 112–49; Thornton, *Politics and Power,* 442; Hyman, *Anti-Redeemers,* 29–33.

45. Woodward, *Origins,* 27–28; Dan T. Carter, *When the War Was Over: The Failure of Self-Reconstruction in the South, 1865–1867* (Baton Rouge: Louisiana State University Press, 1985), 45–47; Perman, *Road to Redemption,* 16, 58–59, 101–102, 157–58; Going, *Bourbon Democracy,* 28, 43; Cash, "Alabama Republicans during Reconstruction," 151 (quote).

46. Going, *Bourbon Democracy,* 61–78; Mark W. Summers, *Railroads, Reconstruction, and the Gospel of Prosperity: Aid under the Radical Republicans, 1865–1877* (Princeton: Princeton University Press, 1984), chap. 5, 250–57; Thornton, *Politics and Power,* 321–42, 327–28; Rogers, Ward, Atkins, and Flynt, *Alabama,* 165–66.

47. Carter, *When the War Was Over,* 45–47; Horace Mann Bond, "Social and Economic Forces in Alabama Reconstruction," *Journal of Negro History,* 23 (July 1938): 290–348; Summers, *Railroads,* chap. 13.

48. Thornton, *Politics and Power,* 321–42, 326 (map); Dorman, *Party Politics,* 203; *Journal of the Convention of the People of the State of Alabama Held at the City of Montgomery Commencing on the 7th Day of January, 1861* (Montgomery: Shorter and Reid, 1861), 5, 49, 100–101.

49. Carter, *When the War Was Over,* 45–47.

50. Bond, "Social and Economic Forces"; Lewis, *Sloss Furnaces,* 47–53; Woodward, *Origins,* 8–10, 126–27; Rogers, Ward, Atkins, and Flynt, *Alabama,* 278–83.

51. Lewis, *Sloss Furnaces,* 47–55; Summers, *Railroads,* chap. 13; Bond, "Social and Economic Forces."

52. Summers, chap. 5, chap. 13, 250–57.

53. Summers, *Railroads,* 221–33; *Journal of the House of Representatives, 1870–71,* 348–52.

54. Going, *Bourbon Democracy,* 61–69, 120; see editorials of McKee in the *Selma Southern Argus* for February, March, April, and May 1871; for activities of Boyd in the 1870–1871 legislative session see the *Journal of the House of Representatives, 1870–71,* 60–61, 132–33, 230–31, 437–38, 465–67; Hackney, *Populism to Progressivism,* 125–26.

55. Owen, *History of Alabama and Dictionary,* 3:189, 4:1120; Perman, *Road to Redemption,* 156–58.

56. *Columbiana Shelby Guide,* February 15 and August 30, 1870, April 20, September 7, October 5, and November 30, 1871, January 18, February 8 and 15, 1872, and February 20, 1873; Perman, *Road to Redemption,* 157; *Journal of the House of Representatives, 1870–71,* 230–31, 437–38, 460, 465–67.

57. Samuel L. Webb, "A Jacksonian Democrat in Postbellum Alabama: The Ideology and Influence of Journalist Robert McKee," *Journal of Southern History* 62 (May 1996):254–58.

58. *Selma Southern Argus,* February 24 (quote in first three sentences), March 3, 1871 (quote in fourth and fifth sentences), and June 2, 1871 (quote in last two sentences).

59. Winston to Robert McKee, February 21, 1871, Robert McKee Papers, Alabama Department of Archives and History, Montgomery, Alabama, as cited in Going, *Bourbon Democracy,* 67; Wiggins, *Scalawag in Alabama Politics,* 79–83, maps on pages 70 and 84; Perman, *Road to Redemption,* 174–82; Joseph Andrew Fry, *John Tyler Morgan and the Search for Southern Autonomy* (Knoxville: University of Tennessee Press, 1992), 25–33; Going, *Bourbon Democracy,* 9–26.

60. Wiggins, *Scalawag in Alabama Politics,* 86–99; see editorials on the economic dimension of the election in the *Selma Southern Argus,* November 21, 1873, January 9, 1874, and May 15, 1874; Foner, *Reconstruction,* 394, 408–9, 512–16.

61. *Selma Southern Argus,* May 15, 1874 (first quote), November 21, 1873 (second quote).

62. Thornton, "Fiscal Policy"; Rogers, Ward, Atkins, and Flynt, *Alabama,* 260; *Centre Cherokee Advertiser* quoted in the *Selma Southern Argus,* July 3, 1874; Perman, *Road to Redemption,* 174–77.

63. *Columbiana Shelby Guide,* October 22, 1874; Ralph B. Draughon, Jr.,

"George Smith Houston and Southern Unity, 1846–49," *Alabama Review* 19 (July 1966):186–207; Horace Mann Bond, *Negro Education in Alabama: A Study in Cotton and Steel* (1939; reprint, Tuscaloosa: University of Alabama Press, 1994), 38–42; Rogers, Ward, Atkins, and Flynt, *Alabama,* 158–59, 262–68.

64. Perman, *Road to Redemption,* 157, 174–76; letter (name of writer illegible) to E. H. Moren, April 6, 1874, E. H. Moren Papers, Alabama Department of Archives and History, Montgomery, Alabama.

65. Perman, *Road to Redemption,* 157 (quote in first sentence), 174 (quote in second sentence); *Centre Cherokee Advertiser* editor quoted in the *Selma Southern Argus,* July 3, 1874; *Selma Southern Argus,* May 8, 1874 (last quote from McKee).

66. Fry, *John Tyler Morgan,* 25–33; Perman, *Road to Redemption,* 174–77; Rufus K. Boyd to Robert McKee, May 17, 1874, McKee Papers, as cited in Going, *Bourbon Democracy,* 69 (quote).

67. Wiggins, *Scalawag in Alabama Politics,* 97–98; Rogers, Ward, Atkins, and Flynt, *Alabama,* 259–64; Perman, *Road to Redemption,* 156–58, 174–77.

68. *Guide to U.S. Elections,* 1024 and 1028; *Columbiana Shelby Guide,* November 19, 1874; see the *Montgomery Daily State Journal,* October 25, 1876, for comparison of county-by-county gubernatorial returns for 1872, 1874, and 1876.

69. *Guide to U.S. Elections,* 1024 and 1028; *Ashville Southern Aegis,* November 4, 1874.

70. Kousser, *Shaping of Southern Politics,* 51–52.

71. Going, *Bourbon Democracy,* 20–26; Perman, *Road to Redemption,* 188–91, 199–203, 228–36.

72. Perman, *Road to Redemption,* 208, 213, 235–36, 242–47; *Selma Southern Argus,* August 27, 1875; Rogers, Ward, Atkins, and Flynt, *Alabama,* 266; Malcolm Cook McMillan, *Constitutional Development in Alabama, 1798–1901: A Study in Politics, the Negro, and Sectionalism* (Chapel Hill: University of North Carolina Press, 1955), 189–210, 211–16; Hyman, *Anti-Redeemers,* 1–9, 75–166, 192–203; Thornton, *Politics and Power,* 442.

73. Hyman, *Anti-Redeemers,* 102–3; Going, *Bourbon Democracy,* 99; *Selma Southern Argus,* May 5, 1876; see remarks of Joseph H. Sloss in the *Tuscumbia North Alabamian,* March 23, 1877; *Columbiana Shelby Guide,* January 28, 1875.

74. Going, *Bourbon Democracy,* 97–98; Rogers, *One-Gallused Rebellion,* 14–19; Hyman, *Anti-Redeemers,* 36–37.

75. Webb, "Jacksonian Democrat," 264–65.

76. *Selma Southern Argus,* February 25 (quotes from McKee), March 24 (quote from *Advertiser*), and April 14, 1876; Going, *Bourbon Democracy,* 75; *Troy Enquirer,* April 29, 1876.

77. Charles W. Raisler to Robert McKee, March 21, 1876, McKee Papers, as cited in Going, *Bourbon Democracy,* 74.

78. Terry L. Seip, *The South Returns to Congress: Men, Economic Measures, and Intersectional Relationships, 1868–1879* (Baton Rouge: Louisiana State University Press, 1983), 253–54; *Selma Southern Argus,* May 7, 1875, March 15 and July 13, 1877; Woodward, *Reunion and Reaction,* 38, 101–21; *Tuscumbia North Alabamian,* March 15 and July 13 (quotes), 1877.

79. Seip, *South Returns to Congress,* 253–54; *Selma Southern Argus,* May 7, 1875 (quote).

80. Going, *Bourbon Democracy,* 50–51; Wiggins, *Scalawag in Alabama Politics,* 114–15.

81. Hyman, *Anti-Redeemers,* 182; Going, *Bourbon Democracy,* 33–35; *Guide to U.S. Elections,* 1032, 1036, 1040, 1048; Kousser, *Shaping of Southern Politics,* 11–29.

82. Going, *Bourbon Democracy,* 29–30.

3. The Growth of Dissent: Anti-Democrats, 1876–1887

1. *Huntsville Advocate,* November 5, 1879, as cited in Hyman, *Anti-Redeemers,* 29.

2. Hyman, *Anti-Redeemers,* 12–16; Lawrence W. Goodwyn, *Democratic Promise: The Populist Moment in America* (New York: Oxford University Press, 1976), 11–33; Hahn, *Roots of Southern Populism,* 137–69; Richard Franklin Bensel, *Yankee Leviathan: The Origins of Central State Authority in America, 1859–1877* (Cambridge: Cambridge University Press, 1990), 416–19.

3. E. G. Walker to the *Columbiana Shelby Sentinel,* September 23 and 30, 1875; Hyman, *Anti-Redeemers,* 12–16; U.S., Bureau of the Census, *Agriculture, 1880,* 3:30–31, *Agriculture, 1890,* 5:120–21, *Agriculture, 1900,* 5:58–59.

4. Goodwyn, *Democratic Promise,* 11–21; Bensel, *Yankee Leviathan,* 416–36; Woodward, *Origins of the New South,* 107–41.

5. Goodwyn, *Democratic Promise,* 26–31; Rogers, *One-Gallused Rebellion,* 12–30; Edward L. Ayers, *The Promise of the New South: Life after Reconstruction* (New York: Oxford University Press, 1992), 92–94; Flynt, *Poor But Proud,* 59–91, 367–77.

6. *Selma Southern Argus,* May 8, 1874, November 30, 1877, and June 21,

1878; Hyman, *Anti-Redeemers*, 27–53, 194–95; letters of E. G. Walker to the *Columbiana Shelby Sentinel*, September 23 (quote) and 30, 1875; see editorials of *Columbiana Shelby Guide* against aid to railroads, January 18, February 15, and February 29, 1872.

7. U.S., Bureau of the Census, *Agriculture, 1880,* 3:30–31 and *Population, 1880,* 1:49, 93–98, 380; Hyman, *Anti-Redeemers,* 22.

8. Going, *Bourbon Democracy,* 57–59; *Columbiana Shelby Sentinel,* June 20, 1878; Hyman, *Anti-Redeemers,* 18–23, 41–42; Goodwyn, *Democratic Promise,* 11–21.

9. Jerry W. DeVine, "Free Silver and Alabama Politics, 1890–96," (Ph.D. diss., Auburn University, 1980), 13; *Selma Southern Argus,* May 17, 1878.

10. Frances Roberts, "William Manning Lowe and the Greenback Party in Alabama," *Alabama Review* 5 (April 1952):100–121; Owen, *History of Alabama and Dictionary,* 4:1075; on Madison County see Bureau of the Census, *Agriculture, 1860,* 2, 3, 4, 193, and 223, and *Population, 1880,* 1:380.

11. Roberts, "William Manning Lowe," 100–105; Rogers, *One-Gallused Rebellion,* 199 (map).

12. Roberts, "William Manning Lowe," 102–3.

13. Ibid., 107–8.

14. *Guide to U.S. Elections,* 1036; U.S., Bureau of the Census, *Population, 1880,* 1:49, 380; Roberts, "William Manning Lowe," 108, 108 n.

15. *Columbiana Shelby Sentinel,* August 22, 1878.

16. Roberts, "William Manning Lowe," 113–18; *Guide to U.S. Elections,* 1040.

17. Going, *Bourbon Democracy,* 58; Rogers, *One-Gallused Rebellion,* 53; DeVine, "Free Silver," 1–17.

18. *Gadsden Times* (undated), as reprinted in the *Columbiana Shelby Sentinel,* July 20, 1882 (quote in second sentence); *Selma Morning-Times,* July 8, 1882; *Guntersville Democrat,* July 15, 22, and 29, 1882.

19. *Journal of the House of Representatives, 1882,* 60–63; comparisons between Sheffield's vote and that received by other gubernatorial candidates between 1874 and 1882 may be made by looking for the official state voting returns in the *Journal* of the lower house for each election year.

20. *Guntersville Democrat,* August 12, October 5, and October 19, 1882; for comparison of the continuation of anti-Democratic dissent in Marshall County, see precinct election returns in the *Democrat* for August 5, 1882, August 4, 1892, August 6, 1896, August 11, 1898, and November 17, 1910, and in the *Albertville Banner,* November 14, 1912; Loveman,

"Presidential Vote"; *Guide to U.S. Elections,* 1044; Sheffield Scrapbook, Street Papers; *Huntsville Advocate,* October 31, 1884.

21.   U.S., Manuscript Census, 1880, for Chilton County; U.S., Bureau of the Census, *Population, 1880,* 1:49, 380, and *Agriculture, 1880,* 3:30–31; *Clanton Banner,* January 19, 1893 (quote) and August 11, 1898; T. E. Wyatt, *Chilton County and Her People: History of Chilton County, Alabama* (Montevallo, Ala.: Times Printing Company, 1976), 127; Owen, *History of Alabama and Dictionary,* 1:250–51; see letter to "Southern Lumberman," reprinted in the *Clanton Chilton View,* March 10, 1887.

22.   Samuel L. Webb, "From Independents to Populists to Progressive Republicans: The Case of Chilton County, Alabama, 1880–1920," *Journal of Southern History* 59 (November 1993):714–17; Loveman, "Presidential Vote"; see *Journal of the House of Representatives* for 1876, 1878, 1880, 1882, 1884, and 1886, for official returns in state elections.

23.   Going, *Bourbon Democracy,* 225; *Clanton Chilton County Courier,* March 23, April 13, and May 11, 1877; *Clanton Chilton View,* August 12, 1880, June 29, August 3, 10, and 17, October 2, 1882, March 6, 1884 (first quote), and letter from "Julius," June 19, 1884 (second quote); *Calera Shelby Sentinel,* August 4, 1884.

24.   *Calera Shelby Sentinel,* March 27, July 3 and 31, and August 6, 1884, January 15 and August 6, 1885; July 15, 1886, and September 22, 1887.

25.   Ibid., May 27, June 24, July 15 (quotation), and August 5, 1886.

26.   Ibid., August 5, 12, and 19, 1886.

27.   Ibid., November 4, 1886.

28.   Owen, *History of Alabama and Dictionary,* 3:1066–67; James C. Bonner, *Georgia's Last Frontier: The Development of Carroll County* (Athens: University of Georgia Press, 1971), 90, as cited in Hahn, *Roots of Southern Populism,* 216; see also Joe Cobb, *Carroll County and Her People* (n.p., n.d.), available at the Birmingham, Alabama, public library.

29.   Dodd, "Unionism in Northwest Alabama," 93–96; U.S., Bureau of the Census, *Population, 1880,* 1:49, 380, and *Agriculture, 1880,* 3:30–31; Loveman, "Presidential Vote"; Saffold Berney, *Handbook of Alabama,* Tutwiler Collection of Southern History, Birmingham Public Library, (Birmingham: Roberts & Son, 1892), 47–74, 334; see Long's comment on tariffs and wages in the *Jasper True Citizen,* October 29, 1886; Foner, *Reconstruction,* 478–82.

30.   Owen, *History of Alabama and Dictionary,* 3:1066–67; Hahn, *Roots of Southern Populism,* 216; for activities of Long see Rogers, *One-Gallused Rebellion,* 184, *Jasper True Citizen,* August 12 and October 29, 1886, *Jasper Protectionist,* April 10, 1888, *Jasper Mountain Eagle,* May 6, 1890 and

May 6, 1896, and the *Oakman Mountain News,* August 9 and October 4, 1894.

31. Owen, *History of Alabama and Dictionary,* 4:1549; see Long's views in the *Jasper Protectionist,* February through November 1888, particularly February 21 and April 10, 1888; *Columbiana Shelby Sentinel,* September 5, 1878; Herbert G. Gutman, "Black Coal Miners and the Greenback-Labor Party in Redeemer Alabama, 1878–1879," *Labor History* 10 (summer 1969):506–35.

32. Chester McArthur Destler, *American Radicalism, 1865–1901* (Chicago: Quadrangle Books, 1966), 32–77; Owen, *History of Alabama and Dictionary,* 4:1549; Woodward, *Origins of the New South,* 81 (quote); Going, *Bourbon Democracy,* 58; see comment on Long and miners in the *Jasper True Citizen,* October 15, 1886.

33. *Journal of the House of Representatives, 1878–79,* 11, 80–81, 89.

34. Going, *Bourbon Democracy,* 35–36 (quote); Hyman, *Anti-Redeemers,* 182.

35. Owen, *History of Alabama and Dictionary,* 4:1064–67.

36. Wilbur R. Miller, "The Revenue: Federal Law Enforcement in the Mountain South, 1870–1900," *Journal of Southern History* 65 (May 1989):204–10; *Jasper True Citizen,* October 29, 1886; *Tuscumbia North Alabamian,* February 15, 1878; Loveman, "Presidential Vote."

37. Going, *Bourbon Democracy,* 227, 229, 231; Owen, *History of Alabama and Dictionary,* 4:1549; *Jasper True Citizen,* August 12, 1886.

38. *Jasper True Citizen,* October 15 and 29, 1886; see quote from the *Birmingham Labor Union* in the *Jasper True Citizen,* October 15, 1886.

39. *Jasper True Citizen,* October 15 and 29, 1886; *Guide to U.S. Elections,* 1052; *Vernon Courier,* November 26, 1886.

40. *Jasper Protectionist,* February 21 (first quote), March 6 (other quotes from newspaper), and April 10, 1888.

41. *Guntersville Democrat,* August 12, 1882, July 24, and August 14, 1884, April 1, 15, 22, and May 20, 1886; see also the article from the *Fort Payne Journal* in the *Democrat* dated October 14, 1886, attacking Sheffield's party loyalty.

42. U.S., Bureau of the Census, *Population, 1880,* 1:49, 380, and *Agriculture, 1880,* 3:30–31; Berney, *Handbook of Alabama,* 327–29, 456–70, 470–74.

43. Karl N. Rodabaugh, "Agrarian Ideology and the Farmer's Revolt in Alabama," *Alabama Review* 36 (July 1983):195–217, and see the description of the "clique" in Shelby County at 209–11; for views of Lewis and Roberts see the *Columbiana Shelby Guide,* October 15 and November 30, 1871, January 18, February 8, 15, 29, April 2, and June 11, 1872, and February 20, 1873, and Seip, *South Returns to Congress,* 253–54.

44. *Columbiana Shelby Guide,* June 18, 1874; Owen, *History of Alabama and Dictionary,* 2:1246, 3:16–17; Robert H. McKenzie, "Reconstruction Historiography: The View from Shelby," *Historian* 36 (February 1974):218–19, and "Reconstruction of the Alabama Iron Industry, 1865–1880," *Alabama Review* 25 (July 1972):178–91; Berney, *Handbook of Alabama,* 327–29, 456–70; Woodward, *Origins of the New South,* 10–11; Lewis, *Sloss Furnaces,* 42, 63, 66.

45. U.S., Bureau of the Census, *Population, 1880,* 1:95–97; *Official and Statistical Register, 1903,* 148, 170–72; Martha Mitchell Bigelow, "Birmingham's Carnival of Crime, 1871–1910," *Alabama Review* 3 (1950):123–33; *Columbiana Shelby Guide,* June 12, 1873; Lewis, *Sloss Furnaces,* 247.

46. *Official and Statistical Register, 1903,* 150, 183; Going, *Bourbon Democracy,* 128; Rogers, *One-Gallused Rebellion,* 25, 25 n; U.S., Manuscript Census, 1880, Shelby County; U.S., Bureau of the Census, *Mining, 180,* 15:40, 643.

47. Lewis, *Sloss Furnaces,* 151–54; Going, *Bourbon Democracy,* 181–90; Flynt, *Poor But Proud,* 138–39, 250; *Clanton Chilton View,* August 8, 1885; McKenzie, "Reconstruction of the Alabama Iron Industry"; Rodabaugh, "Agrarian Ideology," 209–17 (quote).

48. *Columbiana Shelby Guide,* May 25, 1876 (first quote); Rodabaugh, "Agrarian Ideology," 209–17; Moore, *History of Alabama,* 3:477; *Memorial Record of Alabama,* 2:907–8; T. A. Deland and A. David Smith, eds., *Northern Alabama* (1888; reprint, Spartanburg, S.C.: Reprint Co., 1976), 162; see accounts of Shelby's Democratic conventions and executive committee meetings in the *Columbiana Shelby Sentinel,* May 23, 1878, May 20, 1880, July 6, 1882, the *Calera Shelby Sentinel,* May 1, 1884, and the letter of E. G. Walker in the *Calera Shelby Sentinel,* April 29, 1886.

49. Woodward, *Origins of the New South,* 10–11; Deland and Smith, *Northern Alabama,* 166; Lewis, *Sloss Furnaces,* 56–59; Perman, *Road to Redemption,* 201–2; Rodabaugh, "Agrarian Ideology," 209–11.

50. *Columbiana Shelby Sentinel,* March 14, 1878.

51. Rodabaugh, "Agrarian Ideology," 209–11; see *Columbiana Shelby Sentinel,* the article titled "Calera!" dated December 11, 1879, and the *Sentinel,* August 10, 1882; *Calera Shelby Sentinel,* August 27, 1885; U.S., Bureau of the Census, *Population, 1880,* 1:380; on Mardis see Owen, *History of Alabama and Dictionary,* 4:1158, and the *Columbiana Shelby Guide,* June 24 and December 14, 1869.

52. Fitzgerald, "Radical Republicanism and the White Yeomanry," 585 n, 592–93; Loveman, "Presidential Vote"; Rodabaugh, "Agrarian Ideology," 210–11.

53. *Columbiana Shelby Sentinel,* December 11, 1879, August 17, 1882; *Calera*

Shelby Sentinel, August 23, 1883, March 27 and May 22, 1884, August 27, 1885, June 10, 1886; Berney, *Handbook of Alabama,* 491–92.

54. *Columbiana Shelby Sentinel,* July 20, 1882; *Calera Shelby Sentinel,* May 29, 1884; see address of Hardy in the *Calera Shelby Sentinel,* October 7, 1886.

55. *Columbiana Shelby Sentinel,* July 26, August 2, and August 9, 1877, June 20 (first quote) and September 5, 1878 (second quote).

56. Ayers, *Promise of the New South,* 35; *Columbiana Shelby Sentinel,* July 26 and August 2, 1877.

57. *Columbiana Shelby Sentinel,* May 9, 23, and September 5, 1878, May 20 and August 12, 1880; on the Harrisons see sketch of Dr. Henry W. Harrison in Dubose, *Notable Men of Alabama,* 1:456, the activities of William E. Harrison in the *Columbiana People's Advocate,* March 31 and November 10, 1904, November 7, 1916, and November 11, 1920, and a sketch of Karl Cecil Harrison in the *Official and Statistical Register, 1955,* 319–20.

58. *Columbiana Shelby Sentinel,* May 20, 1880.

59. *Columbiana Shelby Sentinel,* August 12, 1880; for information on Bear Creek see William L. Barney, *The Secessionist Impulse: Alabama and Mississippi in 1860* (Princeton: Princeton University Press, 1974), 298, and the *Columbiana Shelby Guide,* November 14, 1872.

60. *Columbiana Shelby Sentinel,* August 12, 1880.

61. Ibid., July 20 and 27, August 3, and December 28, 1882.

62. Ibid., August 17, 1882; *Selma Morning-Times,* August 17, 1882.

63. *Selma Morning-Times,* August 17, 1882; *Columbiana Shelby Sentinel,* August 17, 1882.

64. *Calera Shelby Sentinel,* April 17, 1884 ("Q.R.X." letter) and April 10, 1884 (letter of "Progress").

65. Ibid., May 1, 8, 15, and 29, 1884; for previous activities of Walker see *Columbiana Shelby Sentinel,* July 6 and 27, 1882, and September 23 and 30, 1875.

66. *Calera Shelby Sentinel,* May 15 and June 5, 1884.

67. Ibid., May 29, July 10, August 14, 1884; *Columbiana Shelby Chronicle,* July 3 and 10, 1884.

68. *Calera Shelby Sentinel,* May 15 and 29 and July 3 ("Englishman" quote), 10, and 31, and August 14, 1884.

69. Ibid., August 14, 1884; *Columbiana Shelby Chronicle,* November 13, 1884; for behavior of county precincts compare precinct returns as reported in the *Columbiana Shelby Sentinel,* August 12, 1880, November 11, 1880,

and August 17, 1882, the *Calera Shelby Sentinel,* August 14, 1884, and the *Columbiana Shelby Chronicle,* November 13, 1884.

70.   *Calera Shelby Sentinel,* November 13, 1884 and reprint of article from the *Selma Times* in the *Calera Shelby Sentinel,* August 7, 1884.

71.   *Calera Shelby Sentinel,* November 13 and 20, 1884; Hyman, *Anti-Redeemers,* 156–57.

72.   *Calera Shelby Sentinel,* December 11, 1884; *Journal of the House of Representatives, 1884–85,* 461–62.

73.   *Ashville Southern Aegis,* August 11, 1886 (statewide county results); *Jasper Mountain Eagle,* August 11, 1886 (see statewide county results); see statement in the *Vernon Courier,* June 29, 1888 about 1886 elections in Franklin County; *Jasper True Citizen,* August 12, 1886; *Tuscumbia North Alabamian,* August 13, 1886; see also Horton, "Testing the Limits of Class Politics," 63–84.

74.   *Journal of the House of Representatives, 1886–87,* 148, 263–64, 758, 761–62, 683–86.

75.   *Journal of the Senate, 1886–87,* 263.

76.   Going, *Bourbon Democracy,* 223–31.

4. Alliancemen, Populists, and Republicans, 1888–1892

1.   Thornton, *Politics and Power,* 442

2.   Goodwyn, *Democratic Promise,* xvii (quotes in second sentence), 11–21; Bensel, *Yankee Leviathan,* 416–36; McMath, *American Populism,* 83–107; Woodward, *Origins of the New South,* 107–41, 185–204, 291–92.

3.   McMath, *Southern Populism,* 66–107.

4.   Goodwyn, *Democratic Promise,* 166–68.

5.   Rogers, *One-Gallused Rebellion,* 56–79, 121–46; Ayers, *Promise of the New South,* 218–22.

6.   Ayers, *Promise of the New South,* 217–56; see the role of the Alliance in politics discussed in the *Columbiana Shelby Chronicle,* July 5, 1888.

7.   Rogers, *One-Gallused Rebellion,* 121–31, 137–38; Horton, "Testing the Limits, 64–79.

8.   Ayers, *Promise of the New South,* 230–34; Rogers, *One-Gallused Rebellion,* 141–46.

9.   *Clanton Chilton View,* June 30, July 17, August 4 and 11, 1887, and March 29, 1888; for comparison of precinct elections returns for independents Alliance Democrats see the *View,* August 4, 1884, August 5 and 12, 1886, and August 9 and 16, 1888.

10.   Ibid., June 30 (quote), July 7 and 14, 1887, March 29, April 12, and October 18, 1888, and October 24, 1889.

11.   Rogers, *One-Gallused Rebellion*, 165–66; *Clanton Chilton View*, March 29, April 5, 12 (first quote), 19 (second quote), and May 3, 1888.

12.   *Clanton Chilton View*, May 10, June 4, August 9 and 16, and October 18 (quote), 1888.

13.   Ibid., August 9 and 16, 1888.

14.   Ibid., January 2 (last quote) and 16 (first three quotes), 1890.

15.   *Calera Shelby Sentinel*, July 28 and August 11, 1888; letter from "Semi-Occasional" in *Sentinel*, July 14, 1888; letters from John W. Pitts in the *Sentinel*, July 21 and September 1, 1888; letter from Walthall in the *Sentinel*, August 25, 1888.

16.   Owen, *History of Alabama and Dictionary*, 4:1368, and Dubose, *Notable Men of Alabama*, 1:413; *Journal of the House of Representatives, 1878–79*, 443, 461–62, 671, 697; *Columbiana Shelby Sentinel*, March 20, 1880; *Calera Shelby Sentinel*, May 1, 1884.

17.   *Calera Shelby Sentinel*, February 23, March 15, and April 12, 1888, and October 24, 1889.

18.   Ibid., September 22, 1887, February 23, March 1, and April 12, 1888; Rogers, *One-Gallused Rebellion*, 165–74; Hackney, *Populism to Progressivism*, 10.

19.   For biographical sketches of Longshore see Moore, *History of Alabama*, 3:202–3, *Memorial Record of Alabama*, 908–9, and Dubose, *Notable Men of Alabama*, 2:404.

20.   Dubose, *Notable Men of Alabama*, 2:404; Moore, *History of Alabama*, 3:202–3; *Dadeville Lone Star*, July 4, 11, 18, 25, August 22, and September 26, 1884; also see letter from T. H. Bulgar to the *Calera Shelby Sentinel*, July 26, 1888, explaining Longshore's financial support of his family; *Calera Shelby Sentinel*, June 3, 1886.

21.   *Calera Shelby Sentinel*, May 13, 1886; *Columbiana Banner of Liberty*, January 14, 1886; *Columbiana Shelby Chronicle*, July 8 and August 5, 1886, March 24, 31, August 18, September 1, and December 8, 1887.

22.   *Calera Shelby Sentinel*, June 17, August 12, October 28, and November 12, 1886.

23.   *Calera Shelby Sentinel*, May 10, 1888; see letters on the convention dispute in the *Columbiana Shelby Chronicle*, May 31, June 7, 14, 21, 28, 1888.

24.   *Columbiana Shelby Chronicle*, June 28, 1888; see letters of Pitts in the *Chronicle*, May 31 and July 5, 1888, and the reply July 12, 1888.

25.   *Calera Shelby Sentinel*, June 21, July 19 and 26, 1888, and see the *Sentinel*, May 15 and August 14, 1884.

26. *Columbiana Shelby Chronicle,* July 26 and August 30, 1888 (quotes).

27. *Calera Shelby Sentinel,* August 16 and 23, 1888; see the letter of J. L. Vandiver in the *Columbiana Shelby Guide,* September 17, 1874.

28. *Columbiana Shelby Chronicle,* August 16, 23 and 30, 1888; *Calera Shelby Sentinel,* October 24, 1889 (quote).

29. *Calera Shelby Sentinel,* October 24, 1889.

30. Hackney, *Populism to Progressivism,* 71–76, 212–13, 328; *Calera Shelby Sentinel,* January 10 and February 14, 1889; see letter attacking Longshore in *Columbiana Shelby Chronicle,* August 1, 1889, and a defense of him in the *Chronicle,* August 29, 1889.

31. *Guntersville Democrat,* April 1, 15, 22, and May 20 1886; see article from the *Fort Payne Journal* in the *Guntersville Democrat,* October 14, 1886.

32. Thomas Kermit Hearn, "The Populist Movement in Marshall County," (master's thesis, University of Alabama, 1935), 49–50; *Guntersville Democrat,* February 18, April 8, and May 6, 1882.

33. Hearn, "Populist Movement in Marshall County," 49–50.

34. Rogers, *One-Gallused Rebellion,* 165–87; *Clanton Chilton View,* May 8, 15, and 22, June 5, July 3 and 24, 1890; *Columbiana Shelby Chronicle,* March 19, April 9 and 30, May 7 and 28, June 4 and 25, 1890.

35. *Clanton Chilton View,* May 8 (all quotes), 15, and 22, 1890.

36. J. L. Sheffield to Oliver D. Street, Street Collection, May 25, 1890; Hearn, "Populist Movement in Marshall County," 25–33.

37. Rogers, *One-Gallused Rebellion,* 180–87.

38. Sheffield to Oliver D. Street, May 25, 1890, Street Collection; Rogers, *One-Gallused Rebellion,* 184.

39. Rogers, *One-Gallused Rebellion,* 184; Going, *Bourbon Democracy,* 53–54.

40. *Jasper Headlight,* August 5, 1890; *Oakman Mountain News,* June 7, 1894; *Jasper Mountain Eagle,* May 6 and August 5, 1896.

41. *Columbiana Shelby Chronicle,* March 9, April 9 and 30, May 5 and 28, 1890.

42. Ibid., June 4 and 25, and July 9, 1890; *Calera Shelby County News,* July 24 and 31, 1890.

43. *Calera Shelby County News,* August 14, 1890; *Columbiana Shelby Chronicle,* June 4, 1890.

44. *Calera Shelby County News,* July 31, 1890.

45. McMath, *American Populism,* 7, 110, 51–53; Bruce Palmer, *"Man Over Money": The Southern Populist Critique of American Capitalism* (Chapel Hill: University of North Carolina Press, 1980), 12–13, 114; Goodwyn, *Democratic Promise,* 379 (quote in second sentence).

46. *Columbiana Shelby Chronicle*, July 30, 1890.

47. *Calera Shelby County News*, August 14, 1890; see the "Harpersville Locals" in the *Columbiana Shelby Chronicle*, September 10, 1891.

48. *Clanton Chilton View*, May 22, June 5, July 3 and 24, 1890, and January 1, 1891.

49. Hearn, "Populist Movement in Marshall County," 32–33; *Guntersville Democrat*, November 6, 1890; *Albertville Alliance News*, September 12, 1891.

50. *Guntersville Democrat*, June 26, 1890 and November 20, 1890; see also the James L. Sheffield Scrapbook, Street Papers.

51. See election returns for secessionist delegates compiled by O. D. Street in the James L. Sheffield Scrapbook, Street Papers; James L. Sheffield to O. D. Street, May 25, 1890, Street Collection; on Denson and Taliferro see Rogers, *One-Gallused Rebellion*, 181, 184–85, 207–14.

52. John S. Hughes, *The Letters of a Victorian Madwoman* (Columbia: University of South Carolina Press, 1993), 1–45; *Guntersville Democrat*, November 20, 1890; see accounts of the trial and Sheffield's subsequent activities in the James L. Sheffield Scrapbook, Street Papers.

53. *Guntersville Democrat*, March 17 and 24, 1892; Hearn, "Populist Movement in Marshall County," 45–51.

54. Hearn, "Populist Movement in Marshall County," 45–51.

55. Rogers, *One-Gallused Rebellion*, 193–216; Pruitt, "Joseph C. Manning," 37–46.

56. Rogers, *One-Gallused Rebellion*, 211–16; *Columbiana People's Advocate*, June 9, 1892.

57. *Columbiana People's Advocate*, June 9, 1892; Pruitt, "Joseph Manning," 44–57; Rogers, *One-Gallused Rebellion*, 211–12.

58. *Columbiana People's Advocate*, June 2, 1892.

59. *Calera Shelby County News*, April 27, May 12, and June 9, 1892 (first quote); *Calera Journal*, May 13, 1892 and July 2, 1892 (last quote); see Goodwyn, *Democratic Promise*, 432–36, for explanation of "mid-roaders."

60. Pruitt, "Joseph Manning," 69–71.

61. Ibid., 71–72.

62. *Calera Journal*, June 25, 1892; Wyatt, *Chilton County and Her People*, 130–32; *Columbiana Shelby Chronicle*, February 25, 1892; *Clanton Chilton View*, September 10, 1891, April 7, 14 and 21, and July 14, 1892.

63. *Clanton Chilton View*, April 21, June 30, July 14, and August 4, 1892.

64. Ibid., April 14, 1892.

65. Ibid., April 14, 1892.

66. Ibid.; Palmer, *"Man Over Money,"* 39–48, 114; Worth Robert Miller, "The Republican Tradition," in *American Populism,* ed. William F. Holmes (Lexington, Mass.: D. C. Heath and Co., 1994); McMath, *American Populism,* 51–53; M. J. Heale, *The Making of American Politics* (London: Longman Group Ltd., 1977), 170, 177; Chester McArthur Destler, *American Radicalism,* 5–6, 16–17; on Longshore and Ocala see the *Columbiana Shelby Chronicle,* March 16, 1892.

67. Hearn, "Populist Movement in Marshall County," 51–52, 64–70; *Guntersville Democrat,* June 30, 1892.

68. *Guntersville Democrat,* May 5, June 2, and August 4, 1892; Hearn, "Populist Movement in Marshall County," 69–70.

69. *Guntersville Democrat,* June 30, 1892, and November 10, 1893 (quote); Moody, "Origin, Rise and Organization," 15.

70. Hearn, "Populist Movement in Marshall County," 63–64, citing the *Albertville Alliance News,* July 13, 1892; Owen, *History of Alabama and Dictionary,* 4:1540.

71. Rogers, *One-Gallused Rebellion,* 221–22; Hackney, *Populism to Progressivism,* 22; letter of Robert McKee to Frank Baltzell, August 7, 1892, McKee Papers; McKee to James E. Cobb, March 26, 1893, McKee Papers.

72. Editorial in the *Birmingham Age-Herald* printed in the *Columbiana People's Advocate,* August 11, 1892.

73. Rogers, *One-Gallused Rebellion,* 223; *Clanton Chilton View,* August 4, 1892; *Calera Shelby County News,* August 18, 1892; *Guntersville Democrat,* August 4, 1892.

74. Owen, *History of Alabama and Dictionary,* 3:412–13; *Columbiana People's Advocate,* November 3, 1892; *Calera Journal,* November 10, 1892.

75. Berney, *Handbook of Alabama,* 539.

76. *Columbiana Shelby Chronicle,* March 16, 1892.

77. Berney, *Handbook of Alabama,* 539; on Wood see the *Huntsville Advocate,* October 31, 1884, and the *Birmingham People's Weekly Tribune,* May 14, 1896.

78. Rogers, *One-Gallused Rebellion,* 228–33; Loveman, "Presidential Vote."

79. Loveman, "Presidential Vote"; E. C. Sternes, "Letter from Isney," *Butler Choctaw Alliance,* November 2, 1892.

80. *Columbiana People's Advocate,* November 10, 1892; *Clanton Banner,* December 23, 1893; Cash, *Mind of the South,* x, 30–60, 161–75; Norman Pollack, *The Just Polity: Populism, Law, and Human Welfare* (Urbana: University of Illinois Press, 1987), 100–102.

81. Pollack, *Just Polity,* quotes at 10, 100, and 102; Norman Pollack, *The Hu-*

mane Economy: Populism, Capitalism, and Democracy (New Brunswick, N.J.: Rutgers University Press, 1990), 35–37, 78–83.

82. Pollack, *Humane Economy*, 83; see Cash, *Mind of the South*, 161–75, 51–54 (on blacks); see a favorable review of Pollack's work in Worth Robert Miller, "A Centennial Historiography of American Populism," *Kansas History* 16 (Spring 1993):59–60, 63, 65.

5. Who Were the Populists, and What Did They Believe?

1. McMath, *American Populism*, 17, 50.

2. Miller, "Centennial Historiography," 54–69.

3. Hackney, *Populism to Progressivism*, 30–31.

4. Ibid., 27–29.

5. Flynt, *Poor But Proud*, 253–55, 367–68, 378.

6. Hackney, *Populism to Progressivism*, 27–30, 77–80, 85–88, 326–28.

7. See biographical sketches of Populist leaders and officials in the *Clanton Banner*, January 19 (on Honeycutt) and 26, February 2, 9, 16, and 23, March 2 (teacher), 9, 16, and 23, and April 6, 1893.

8. *Ashville Southern Alliance*, May 12, 1893; Owen, *History of Alabama and Dictionary*, 3:595.

9. Owen, *History of Alabama and Dictionary*, 3:379.

10. Dubose, *Notable Men of Alabama*, 2:273; Owen, *History of Alabama and Dictionary*, 3:125–26; *Memorial Record of Alabama*, 1:1013.

11. Owen, *History of Alabama and Dictionary*, 3:830, 875–76; Dubose, *Notable Men of Alabama*, 1:456; *Memorial Record of Alabama*, 1:646.

12. Owen, *History of Alabama and Dictionary*, 3:13, 96; *Clanton Banner*, January 19, 1893.

13. Dubose, *Notable Men of Alabama*, 1:364–65; *Memorial Record of Alabama*, 1:736–37; Owen, *History of Alabama and Dictionary*, 4:1368.

14. Owen, *History of Alabama and Dictionary*, 4:1069; catalogue, class roll records, and grades for the 1872–73 school year kept at the main library, Washington and Lee University.

15. U.S., Manuscript Censuses, 1880 and 1900, for Chilton, Marshall, and Shelby Counties. These conclusions were reached by compiling lists of male (potential voters) heads of households from 1880 and 1900, in alphabetical order, and comparing the lists.

16. McMath, *American Populism*, 123–27; Flynt, *Poor But Proud*, 250–51.

17. Rodabaugh, "Agrarian Ideology"; Hahn, *Roots of Southern Populism*, 15–49, 170–203; U.S., Bureau of the Census, *Agriculture, 1880*, 3:30–31.

18. U.S., Bureau of the Census, *Agriculture, 1880*, 3:30–31, *Agriculture, 1890*, 5:120–21, and *Agriculture, 1900*, 5:58–59.

19. U.S., Bureau of the Census, *Agriculture, 1880*, 3:30–31, *Agriculture, 1890*, 5:120–21, and *Agriculture, 1900*, 5:58–59.

20. U.S., Bureau of the Census, *Agriculture, 1880*, 3:30–31, *Agriculture, 1890*, 5:120–21, and *Agriculture, 1900*, 5:58–59.

21. Rogers, *One-Gallused Rebellion*, 331.

22. See the reprint of the article from the *Birmingham Age-Herald* in the *Columbiana People's Advocate*, August 11, 1892.

23. *Clanton Banner*, October 15, 1896.

24. Hackney, *Populism to Progressivism*, 85; Goodwyn, *Democratic Promise*, x-xi; McMath, *American Populism*, 17–53.

25. Owen, *History of Alabama and Dictionary*, 4:992–95 (Kolb); Fry, *John Tyler Morgan*, 1–3 (Philander Morgan); see sketches of other men cited above in this chapter; Jean Baker, *Affairs of Party: The Political Culture of Northern Democrats in the Mid-Nineteenth Century* (Ithaca: Cornell University Press, 1983), 27–45, 46–49.

26. Baker, *Affairs of Party*, 27–45, 46–49; Bond, *Political Culture in the Nineteenth Century South*; Cash, *Mind of the South*, 100–102; Hackney, *Populism to Progressivism*, 27–47, 85–88, 326–27.

27. Arthur S. Link and Richard L. McCormick, *Progressivism* (Arlington Heights, Ill.: Harlan-Davidson, Inc., 1983), 33; Hackney, *Populism to Progressivism*, 71–75, 326–28, 213.

28. John F. Hughes, "The Jacksonians, the Populists and the Governmental Habit," *Mid-America: An Historical Review* 76 (Winter 1994):5–25; Hyman, *Anti-Redeemers*, 29–33; Bruce Palmer, "The Roots of Reform: Southern Populists and Their Southern History," *Red River Valley Historical Review* 4 (Summer 1979):34–35, 41–42, 50–51, 54–55, 58; *Birmingham People's Weekly Tribune*, April 23, 1896; Thornton, *Politics and Power*, 442; Webb, "Jacksonian Democrat."

29. Hughes, "The Jacksonians, the Populists"; see the *Columbiana People's Advocate*, December 15, 1892, for letter signed by Longshore and other leading Populists and Jeffersonians, and on December 20, 1894, for editorial on "banks of issue"; Thornton, "Jacksonian Democracy," 629–31.

30. *Columbiana People's Advocate*, August 2, 9, and 16, 1893.

31. Ibid.

32. *Ashville Southern Alliance*, January 20, 1893; see Miller, "Republican Tradition," 211–12.

33.	Article from the *Piedmont Enquirer* in the *Columbiana People's Advocate,* June 2, 1892; Palmer, *"Man Over Money,"* 42; McMath, *American Populism,* 51–53; Miller, "Republican Tradition," 212.

34.	*Columbiana People's Advocate,* October 6, 1892 (quote) and September 8, 1892; Lewis Reynolds to the *Clanton Chilton View,* April 14, 1892; Samuel M. Adams in the *Columbiana People's Advocate,* August 25, 1892.

35.	*Columbiana People's Advocate,* July 14, 1892 (first quote) and June 9, 1892 (platform); Goodwyn, *Democratic Promise* (for phrase "Populist moment"); *Guntersville Democrat,* June 30, 1892 (quote from Street).

36.	McMath, *American Populism,* 175 (first quote); *Columbiana People's Advocate,* August 25, 1892 (second quote); *Ashville Southern Alliance,* February 10 and October 26, 1893 (other quotes).

37.	*Clanton Banner,* December 30, 1893; *Columbiana People's Advocate,* June 2, 1892 (Longshore quotes); Kohl, *Politics of Individualism,* 26, 46, 191, 197; Meyers, *Jacksonian Persuasion,* 10–11.

38.	J. Mills Thornton, "Hugo Black and the Golden Age," *Alabama Law Review* 36 (Spring 1985):899–913, 912; Palmer, *"Man Over Money,"* 14, 39–49; Lewis Reynolds to the *Clanton Banner,* April 14, 1892.

39.	*Clanton Banner,* July 2, 1896.

40.	Pruitt, "Joseph C. Manning," 71–72, 348–86, 400–8; *Columbiana People's Advocate,* February 14 and 21, 1894.

41.	*Columbiana People's Advocate,* May 2, 1894, and August 23, 1893 (quote on "loafers").

42.	*Columbiana People's Advocate,* October 27, 1892, and March 7, 1895.

43.	Webb, "Jacksonian Democrat," 272; letter of John Tyler Morgan to Robert McKee, February 4, 1892, McKee Papers.

44.	Webb, "Jacksonian Democrat," 239–74; letter of McKee to James E. Cobb, September 3, 1893, McKee Papers.

45.	Street to McKee, September 10, 1891, McKee Papers; *Columbiana People's Advocate,* June 2, 1892, October 11, 1894.

46.	Denson to McKee, July 9, 1893, McKee Papers.

47.	Hackney, *Populism to Progressivism,* 53–54; Webb, "Jacksonian Democrat," 245–46, 268–69, 271–72; Clanton, *Populism,* xiii–xvi, citing Worth Robert Miller, *Oklahoma Populism: A History of the People's Party in the Oklahoma Territory* (Norman: University of Oklahoma Press, 1987), 265; Rogers, *One-Gallused Rebellion,* 246.

48.	McMath, *American Populism,* 50–53, 110 (first quote); Palmer, "Roots of Reform," 34 (other quote).

6. Triumph, Tragedy, and Disillusionment, 1893–1898

1. Goodwyn, *Democratic Promise,* 502.

2. Ibid., 404–7; Rogers, *One-Gallused Rebellion,* 236–48, 271–317; Palmer, *"Man Over Money,"* 157–68.

3. Goodwyn, *Democratic Promise,* 404–7; Rogers, *One-Gallused Rebellion,* 298–304.

4. Rogers, *One-Gallused Rebellion,* 246, 276–77, 294–311; oral interview by Wayne Flynt with Mrs. L. A. House, Sylacauga, Alabama, July 10, 1974, Oral History Collection, Harwell G. Davis Library, Samford University, Birmingham, Alabama.

5. Rogers, *One-Gallused Rebellion,* 237–41; Pruitt, "Joseph Manning," 112–15.

6. Kousser, *Shaping of Southern Politics,* 134–37; editorial from the *Montgomery Alliance Herald,* reprinted in the *Columbiana People's Advocate,* February 2, 1893.

7. *Columbiana People's Advocate,* June 21, 1893; *Ashville Southern Alliance,* June 30, 1894; *Boaz Sand Mountain Signal,* November 17 and December 15, 1893.

8. *Ashville Southern Alliance,* May 12, 19, and 26, and September 14, 1893.

9. Ibid., September 14, 1893; *Columbiana People's Advocate,* September 13, 1893, and February 14, 1894; *Clanton Banner,* August 31 and September 14, 1893; Rogers, *One-Gallused Rebellion,* 241–43, 247–48; Pruitt, "Joseph Manning," 131–40.

10. *Ashville Southern Alliance,* February 15, 1894.

11. *Columbiana People's Advocate,* July 26, August 2, and August 9, 1894; *Columbiana Shelby Chronicle,* August 6, 1894.

12. *Columbiana Shelby Chronicle,* August 6, 1894; *Columbiana People's Advocate,* April 11 and June 20, 1894; *Vernon Courier,* August 2, 1894 (quotes).

13. Robert David Ward and William Warren Rogers, *Labor Revolt in Alabama: The Great Strike of 1894* (University: University of Alabama Press, 1965); Hackney, *Populism to Progressivism,* 59–62; Flynt, *Poor But Proud,* 252–53.

14. Hearn, "Populist Movement in Marshall County," 82, 77 (quote from *Advertiser*), and 92, citing the *Boaz Sand Mountain Signal,* July 21, 1893, and June 22, 1894.

15. *Clanton Banner,* May 5 and 19 and August 11 and 18, 1894.

16. Official returns for 1892 in Berney, *Handbook of Alabama,* 538–39, and for 1894 in the *Journal of the House of Representatives, 1894–95,* 98–101;

Rogers, *One-Gallused Rebellion*, 273, 280; Kousser, *Shaping of Southern Politics*, 131–38; *Birmingham Times*, August 29, 1894.

17. Pruitt, "Joseph Manning," 211–13.

18. David Alan Harris, "The Political Career of Milford W. Howard, Populist Congressman from Alabama" (master's thesis, Auburn University, 1957), 11–27, and Harris, "Campaigning in the Bloody Seventh," 127–38, 129, 130; Hackney, *Populism to Progressivism*, 78–80.

19. Milford W. Howard, *If Christ Came to Congress* (Washington D.C.: Howard Publishing Co., 1894); Hackney, *Populism to Progressivism*, 80–87.

20. Harris, "Campaigning in the Bloody Seventh," 130–31.

21. Ibid., 128–35; Harris, "Political Career," 46–48.

22. Rogers, *One-Gallused Rebellion*, 287–88; *Calera Shelby Sentinel*, October 18 (first quote) and November 8, 1894 (second quote).

23. *Calera Shelby Sentinel*, November 8, 1894; *Columbiana Shelby Chronicle*, November 15, 1894; *Columbiana People's Advocate*, November 25, 1894.

24. *Columbiana People's Advocate*, November 25, 1894; *Columbiana Shelby Chronicle*, November 15, 1894.

25. *Columbiana Shelby Chronicle*, November 8, 1894; *Clanton Banner*, November 8 and 15, 1894.

26. Rogers, *One-Gallused Rebellion*, 288–89.

27. Hackney, *Populism to Progressivism*, 70–76, 343 (map).

28. Ibid., 74; *Journal of the House of Representatives, 1894–95*, 944–45, 976–77, 1098–1102.

29. *Journal of the House of Representatives, 1894–95*, 976–77, 1102.

30. Hackney, *Populism to Progressivism*, 74–75; *Journal of the House of Representatives, 1894–95*, 276.

31. Hackney, *Populism to Progressivism*, 73; Pruitt, "Joseph Manning," 228–31.

32. Pruitt, "Joseph Manning," 226; Hackney, *Populism to Progressivism*, 72–73.

33. Pruitt, "Joseph Manning," 232–33.

34. Karl Rodabaugh, "Fusion, Confusion, Defeat and Disfranchisement: The Fadeout of Populism in Alabama," *Alabama Historical Quarterly* 34 (Summer 1972):131–54.

35. *Columbiana People's Advocate*, September 5, 1895; Hackney, *Populism to Progressivism*, 91–92.

36. *Ashville Southern Aegis*, October 3, 1900 (on Spears); Frank Lathrop to J. O. Thompson, September 13, 1904, Street Collection (on Powell); on Walker County see the *Oakman Mountain News*, October 4 and 25,

1894, and the *Birmingham Times,* April 1, 1896; see the letter of Charles Kennamer in the *Birmingham Times,* January 15, 1896; see domination of GOP candidates on Winston County fusion ticket in the *Double Springs Winston Herald,* August 11, 1892.

37. Hackney, *Populism to Progressivism,* 92–93; Rogers, *One-Gallused Rebellion,* 308–10; Pruitt, "Joseph Manning," 285–88, 293–94.

38. Hackney, *Populism to Progressivism,* 13–14; Rogers, *One-Gallused Rebellion,* 177; Kousser, *Shaping of Southern Politics,* 132.

39. Johnston to Robert McKee, January 19, 1894, McKee Papers; Hackney, *Populism to Progressivism,* 94–95, 118–20, 127; R. W. Cobb to Robert McKee, July 20, 1898, Frank O'Brien to Robert McKee, May 17, 1899, and Chappell Cory to Robert McKee, January 5, 1897, McKee Papers.

40. Fry, *John Tyler Morgan,* 123–25; Rogers, *One-Gallused Rebellion,* 277; Pruitt, "Joseph Manning," 327; Hackney, *Populism to Progressivism,* 127; Karl Louis Rodabaugh, "Fusion, Confusion," 131–34.

41. Rogers, Ward, Atkins, and Flynt, *Alabama,* 316; *Columbiana People's Advocate,* January 30, 1896; Hackney, *Populism to Progressivism,* 95.

42. Hackney, *Populism to Progressivism,* 94–95.

43. Rogers, *One-Gallused Rebellion,* 303, 307, 318–19.

44. *Greenville Living Truth,* June 11, 1896; *Columbiana Shelby Chronicle,* July 16, 1896; J. E. Brown to O. D. Street, n.d., 1896, Street Collection.

45. *Columbiana People's Advocate,* July 23 and 30, 1896; Rogers, *One-Gallused Rebellion,* 319–23; Pruitt, "Joseph Manning," 329–30, 345 n. 62; Rodabaugh, "Fusion, Confusion," 141–42.

46. Goodwyn, *Democratic Promise,* 484–88, 491–502; DeVine, "Free Silver and Alabama Politics," 200–201.

47. Rodabaugh, "Fusion, Confusion," 141; DeVine, "Free Silver in Alabama Politics," 207–9; Pruitt, "Joseph Manning," 332–35.

48. Pruitt, "Joseph Manning," 327–28; DeVine, "Free Silver and Alabama Politics," 202–5.

49. J. E. Brown to O. D. Street, December 14, 1896, Street Collection.

50. *Columbiana People's Advocate,* May 14 and 28, August 13 and 20, 1896; Rogers, *One-Gallused Rebellion,* 327.

51. *Columbiana People's Advocate,* January 31 (postal quote), March 14, 1895 (second quote), and July 2 (on Graham) and 30, 1896 (on Bryan); *Anniston Alabama Leader,* October 3, 1895, as cited in Palmer, "Roots of Reform," 57 n (cited incorrectly as written in 1892 [newspaper cited existed in 1895 only]); Palmer, *"Man Over Money,"* 274 n. 177 (third quote).

52. *Calera Shelby Sentinel,* June 18 and July 30, 1896.

53. Rogers, *One-Gallused Rebellion*, 314–16.

54. *Jasper Mountain Eagle,* May 6 and August 5, 1896; *Double Springs Winston Herald,* August 14, 1896.

55. *Jasper Mountain Eagle,* August 5, 1898; *Oakman Mountain News,* August 3, 1898; see also the *Official and Statistical Register, 1903,* 204–5, 218–19, 237, 246, 84–85; *Guntersville Democrat,* November 12, 1896.

56. *Columbiana People's Advocate,* August 13 and 20, 1896.

57. Ibid.

58. *Columbiana People's Advocate,* October 15, 1896; *Columbiana Shelby Chronicle,* October 15 and 22, 1896.

59. *Columbiana People's Advocate,* October 15, 1896, and the *Columbiana Shelby Chronicle,* October 15 and 22 (quotes), 1896.

60. *Clanton Banner,* August 6, September 24, and October 29, 1896.

61. Ibid., October 15, 1896.

62. Hearn, "Populist Movement in Marshall County," 98–110; *Boaz Sand Mountain Signal,* January 24, 1896; *Guntersville Democrat,* March 26, 1896; *Albertville Marshall County News,* February 6, 1896.

63. *Guntersville Democrat,* March 26, (first quote) and August 6, 1896; *Boaz Sand Mountain Signal,* February 14, 1896 (second quote).

64. *Guntersville Democrat,* August 6, 1896.

65. Harris, "Political Career of Milford W. Howard," 99–110; sketch of Curtis in *Official and Statistical Register, 1913,* 64.

66. *Montgomery Advertiser,* October 15, 1896; Harris, "Political Career of Milford W. Howard," 106; *Clanton Banner,* October 29, 1896.

67. Harris, "Political Career of Milford W. Howard," 111, citing the *Montgomery Advertiser,* November 20, 1896; Loveman, "Presidential Vote."

68. Loveman, "Presidential Vote."

69. Rogers, Ward, Atkins, and Flynt, *Alabama,* 320–23; see treatment of Johnston in David Alan Harris, "Racists and Reformers: A Study of Progressivism in Alabama, 1896–1911" (Ph.D. diss., University of North Carolina at Chapel Hill, 1967).

70. Hackney, *Populism to Progressivism,* 122–46.

71. *Journal of the House of Representatives, 1896–97,* 8–9, 248–49; *Calera Shelby Sentinel,* February 4, 1897; *Clanton Banner,* November 26, 1896.

72. Hackney, *Populism to Progressivism,* 135–37.

73. Ibid., 136; see the *Columbiana Shelby Chronicle,* February 18, 1897, for the appointment of W. J. Wood, formerly of the L & N, to Johnston's new tax commission; Hackney, *Populism to Progressivism,* 251–56.

74. Rogers, *One-Gallused Rebellion,* 328–29; Alfred Lee to O. D. Street, August 20, 1898, Street Collection; N. B. Spears to O. D. Street, August 25, 1898, Street Collection.

7. What Happened to the Upcountry Populists? 1898–1904

1. Napoleon B. Spears to W. T. Coggin, October 18, 1902, Street Collection.

2. *Columbiana People's Advocate,* November 14, 1897, and see two versions of the paper beginning April 14, 1898, and continuing through the August elections; *Columbiana People's Advocate,* August 11, 1898, for control by Frank Norris and Longshore.

3. *Columbiana People's Advocate* (Pitts version), April 14 and 21; *Columbiana Shelby Chronicle,* August 11, 1898.

4. *Columbiana People's Advocate* (Norris version), August 4, 1898.

5. *Columbiana People's Advocate* (Norris version), July 28, 1898; King, "Closing of the Southern Range," 53–70.

6. Hahn, *Roots of Southern Populism,* 239–68; Hyman, *Anti-Redeemers,* 180; McMath, *American Populism,* 55; Letter from "J. S. F." in the *Calera Shelby Sentinel,* November 26, 1885.

7. Webb, "From Independents to Populists," 722–23; *Columbiana People's Advocate,* March 15 and July 5, 1900.

8. See editorial in the *Columbiana Shelby Chronicle* reprinted in the *Columbiana People's Advocate,* December 1, 1898.

9. *Clanton Banner,* June 30, 1898.

10. Ibid., March 31, 1898.

11. Ibid., May 5, June 6, June 23, and August 11, 1898.

12. *Guntersville Democrat,* August 11, 1898

13. L. W. Watson to T. W. Powell, August 5, 1897, Street Collection; Hackney, *Populism to Progressivism,* 78–81; Rogers, *One-Gallused Rebellion,* 307–8; Hearn, "Populist Movement in Marshall County," 139–40, citing the *Boaz Sand Mountain Signal,* August 11, 1898; Harris, "Political Career of Milford W. Howard," 99–138.

14. Harris, "Political Career of Milford W. Howard," 126–35.

15. Letters to O. D. Street from Alfred Lee, August 20, 1898, T. W. Powell, August 22, 1898, and Napoleon Spears, August 25, 1898, Street Collection.

16. T. W. Powell to O. D. Street, August 22, 1898, Street Collection; John J. Durham to T. W. Powell, October 12, 1898, Street Collection.

17. Pruitt, "Joseph Manning," 365–68; Harlan, *Washington, Wizard,* 8; Rogers, *One-Gallused Rebellion,* 308–9; T. W. Powell to O. D. Street, Au-

gust 22 and October 13, 1898, Street Collection; R. H. Lackey to T. W. Powell, Street Collection.

18. Alfred Lee to O. D. Street, August 20, 1898, N. B. Spears to O. D. Street, August 25, 1898, and W. T. Gast to O. D. Street, August 31, 1898, Street Collection; Hearn, "Populist Movement in Marshall County," 140.

19. T. W. Powell to Thomas E. Watson, October 14, 1898, and to O. D. Street, September 20, 1898, Street Collection; on Populist national nominees see John W. Hicks, *The Populist Revolt: A History of the Farmers' Alliance and the People's Party* (1931; reprint, Lincoln: University of Nebraska Press, 1961), 384–87.

20. O. D. Street to J. L. Brasher, September 10, 1898, Street Collection; Harris, "Political Career of Milford W. Howard," 138, citing the *Gadsden Times-News*, November 22, 1898.

21. Brock to Street, November 11 and September 30, 1898, Street Collection; Jesse Stallings to Thomas A. Street, December 4, 1899, and February 7, 1900, Street Collection; Hearn, "Populist Movement in Marshall County," 145, citing correspondence of Joseph F. Johnston to T. A. Street in November 1899 and February 1900.

22. Hackney, *Populism to Progressivism*, 158–70.

23. *Calera Shelby Sentinel*, April 13, 1899; *Columbiana People's Advocate*, May 11, 1899; *Clanton Banner*, July 13, 1899; Johnston to O. D. Street, January 22, 1900, Street Collection; Hackney, *Populism to Progressivism*, 116, 127, 171, 173, 227–28.

24. *Clanton Banner*, April 20, August 17, and November 23, 1899.

25. Ibid., November 23 and 30, 1899; *Columbiana People's Advocate*, December 14, 1899.

26. Joseph A. Fry, *John Tyler Morgan*, 133; *Clanton Banner*, May 3 and 17, 1900; Hearn, "Populist Movement in Marshall County," citing letter of I. L. Brock to O. D. Street, March 2, 1900.

27. Fry, *John Tyler Morgan*, 143; Hackney, *Populism to Progressivism*, 172–73.

28. *Clanton Banner*, May 3, 1900; Hicks, *Populist Revolt*, 399–400 (quote).

29. *Clanton Banner*, May 31, June 7, and July 5 and 12, 1900.

30. Ibid., July 12, 1900; *Official and Statistical Register, 1903*, 204–5.

31. *Columbiana People's Advocate*, September 30, October 4 (quotes), 11, 25, and November 1, 1900.

32. Ibid., November 1, 1900.

33. *Official and Statistical Register, 1903*, 242; *Clanton Banner*, September 6 and 20 and October 4, 1900.

34. Letter of Spears Campaign Committee with Lathrop as chairman, October 18, 1900, Street Collection.

35. *Ashville Southern Aegis,* October 3, 1900; Owen, *History of Alabama and Dictionary,* 4:1605.

36. *Russellville Franklin Times,* September 28, 1900; Noah Hood to O. D. Street, October 6, 1900, Street Collection.

37. See letter of Spears attached to letter of H. A. Fitzpatrick to O. D. Street, September 4, 1900, Street Collection; Frank Lathrop to J. H. Bingham, October 18, 1900, Street Collection.

38. *Guide to U.S. Elections,* 1085; Loveman, "Presidential Vote."

39. *Russellville Franklin Times,* November 23, 1900.

40. Reprint of article from *Anniston Hot Blast* in the *Montevallo Shelby Sentinel,* November 15, 1900.

41. *Clanton Banner,* November 8, 1900; *Columbiana People's Advocate,* November 15, 1900.

42. Woodward, *Origins of the New South,* 457–59, 458 (quote).

43. Kousser, *Shaping of Southern Politics,* 165–71, 264–65; *Columbiana People's Advocate,* December 6, 1900.

44. Flynt, *Poor But Proud,* 272–73, citing the *Montgomery Journal,* May 20, 1901.

45. Hearn, "Populist Movement in Marshall County," quoting letter of Oliver Street to Hearn, August 23, 1935.

46. *Official and Statistical Register, 1903,* 141–42; Hackney, *Populism to Progressivism,* 209–14, 351–61.

47. Webb, "Independents to Populists," 722–23.

48. *Columbiana Shelby Chronicle,* June 14 and 21, 1900; *Columbiana People's Advocate,* June 21, July 3, and October 4, 1900; *Clanton Banner,* February 21, 1901.

49. Webb, "Independents to Populists," 724–25.

50. Ibid.

51. Ibid.

52. Kousser, *Shaping of Southern Politics,* 169–70; Grafton and Permaloff, *Big Mules and Branchheads,* 95–97.

53. *Columbiana People's Advocate,* September 5 (quotes in first two sentences), October 31 and November 7 (last quote), 1901.

54. Kousser, *Shaping of Southern Politics,* 166–67; *Official and Statistical Register, 1903,* 141–42.

55. *Official and Statistical Register, 1903,* 141–42; *Columbiana People's Advo-*

cate, November 14, 1901 (quote from Norris), August 13, 1896, August 4, 1898, and August 16, 1900.

56. *Montgomery Advertiser,* April 8, 1902; *Clanton Banner,* January 2, 1902.

57. Webb, "Independents to Populists," 726–27.

58. Hackney, *Populism to Progressivism,* 233–36; N. P. Renfro to O. D. Street, August 13, 1902, Street Collection; Joseph F. Johnston to Thomas A. Street, August 30, 1902, Street Collection.

59. Webb, "Independents to Populists," 727, citing the *Clanton Banner,* July 31, 1902.

60. Webb, "Independents to Populists," 727; *Clanton Banner,* August 21 (quotes from Reynolds and Crichton), August 28, and September 4, 1902; *Birmingham Alabamian,* June 13, 1903 (quotes from critic).

61. Webb, "Independents to Populists," 727–28, citing the *Clanton Banner,* August 14 (quotes in third sentence) and 28, September 4 and 25, October 9 (quote from Adams), 1902.

62. *Clanton Banner,* September 4 and November 13, 1902.

63. Ibid., August 16, 1900, and November 13, 1902; *Official and Statistical Register, 1903,* 204–5, 218–19; *Guide to U.S. Elections,* 1085, 1090; U.S., Bureau of the Census, *Agriculture, 1910,* 2:776.

64. Webb, "Independents to Populists," 728, citing the *Clanton Banner,* November 27 (first two quotes) and December 11, 1902 (last quote).

65. Hackney, *Populism to Progressivism,* 234, 241–42; Kousser, *Shaping of Southern Politics,* 239–42; Johnston to Street, August 30, 1902, Street Collection.

66. W. F. Standifer to O. D Street, September 2, 1902, J. J. Curtis to Street, September 10, 1902, and N. B. Spears to Street, September 10, 1902, Street Collection.

67. Noah Hood to O. D. Street, September 10, 1902, and I. L. Brock to O. D. Street, September, 13, 1902, Street Collection.

68. William Vaughn to O. D. Street, September 24, 1902, and J. M. Babcock to O. D. Street, October 3, 1902, Street Collection.

69. Johnston to Street, September 30, 1902, Street Collection; J. J. Curtis to Walter Powell, October 27, 1902, Street Collection.

70. J. M. Babcock to O. D. Street September 30 and October 3, 1902, Street Collection.

71. N. B. Spears to O. D. Street, October 1, and Spears to W. T. Coggin, October 18, 1902 (quotes), Street Collection; J. J. Curtis to Walter Powell, October 27 and November 2 (quote), 1902, Street Collection.

72. S. J. Petree to Street, October 13, 1902, Street Collection; *Official and*

Statistical Register, 1903, 240; Guntersville Democrat, November 6, 1902; Oliver D. Street to Theodore Roosevelt, November 17, 1902, Street Collection.

73. E. C. Street to O. D. Street, November 8, 1902, Street Collection.

74. Webb, "Independents to Populists," 728–29, citing the *Clanton Union*, September 24 and October 22, 1903; Hackney, *Populism to Progressivism*, 246–48.

75. *Montgomery Journal*, February 19, 1903; Harlan, *Washington, Wizard*, 8–9.

76. *Clanton Union*, January 6, 1904; *Birmingham Times*, February 12, 1904.

77. *Clanton Union*, March 3, 10 (Reynolds quotes) and 17, 1904; *Clanton Banner*, March 17 (Thompson quote), 1904; Harlan, *Washington, Wizard*, 8–9, 24, 125.

78. *Birmingham Times*, March 18, 1904; *Clanton Banner*, November 17, 1904; *Clanton Union*, August 24, October 19 and 26, 1905.

79. *Columbiana People's Advocate*, October 22, 1903, July 14, October 13, 1904, and November 10, 1904.

80. *Columbiana People's Advocate*, February 27 and August 7, 1902, January 8, 15, and 22, February 19 and 26, October 22, 1903, and July 14, 1904.

81. Ibid., February 27 and April 17, 1902, November 26, 1903.

82. Ibid., July 7 and 28, August 4, September 15 and 29, October 13 and 27, and November 3, 1904.

83. Ibid., July 28, August 25, September 25, October 6, and November 10, 1904.

84. Ibid., November 10, 1904, and August 16, 1900.

85. Loveman, "Presidential Vote."

86. *Columbiana People's Advocate*, November 17, 1904 (all quotes from Longshore); *Montevallo Shelby Sentinel*, November 24, 1904.

87. *Columbiana People's Advocate*, December 8, 1904.

88. *Clanton Banner*, March 31, 1904.

8. From Populists to Progressive Republicans, 1904–1912

1. *Columbiana People's Advocate*, July 2, 1908.

2. Harlan, *Washington, Wizard*, 8–9.

3. *Birmingham Times*, May 22, 1895 (quote from Franklin editor).

4. Key, *Southern Politics*, 284 (first quote); *Double Springs Observer*, January 17, 1895; *Birmingham Times*, March 20, 1895 (quote from Cherokee editor I. L. Brock).

5. Link and McCormick, *Progressivism,* 31–39; Gould, *Reform and Regulation,* 31–57, 76–95.

6. Gould, *Reform and Regulation,* 50–57, 79, 85, 98–100, 121–47; Link and McCormick, *Progressivism,* 41.

7. Link and McCormick, *Progressivism,* 21–58.

8. *Columbiana People's Advocate,* March 16, April 13, and July 27, 1905, August 2 and 23, 1906, and July 2, 1908.

9. Link and McCormick, *Progressivism,* 47–53; Harbaugh, *Power and Responsibility,* 235; Gould, *Reform and Regulation,* 36–38, 73–74.

10. Link and McCormick, *Progressivism,* 33; *Columbiana People's Advocate,* September 27, 1906, and July 2, 1908; *Clanton Union,* August 23, 1906.

11. James L. Sundquist, *The Dynamics of the Party System* (Washington, D.C.: Brookings Institution, 1983), 178–79 (first two quotes); Gould, *Reform and Regulation,* 66–77; *Columbiana People's Advocate,* December 1, 1904.

12. *Columbiana People's Advocate,* January 19, 1905, September 27, 1906 (Republican committee quote); *Clanton Union,* August 23, 1906.

13. Webb, "Independents to Populists," 729–31; *Clanton Banner,* August 24, September 21, October 19 and 26, 1905.

14. *Columbiana People's Advocate,* July 27, 1905, August 23, 1906 (quote), and July 2, 1908.

15. See reprint of Street's 1905 letter to Watson in the *Birmingham Times,* April 11, 1909.

16. Letter of H. W. Caffey to the *Clanton Banner,* November 8, 1906.

17. *Columbiana Shelby Sentinel,* September 5, 1907 (quote from Crichton).

18. L. B. Pounds to the *Clanton Banner,* August 3, 1903; Thomas N. Freeman of the Socialist Party of Alabama to O. D. Street, November 1, 1903, Street Collection.

19. *Columbiana People's Advocate,* August 6, 13, and 27, and September 10, 1908, and March 25, 1909 (quote).

20. Hackney, *Populism to Progressivism,* 255–323, 316–23; Rogers, Ward, Atkins, and Flynt, *Alabama,* 369–70; Kousser, *Shaping of Southern Politics,* 231 (first quote); *Columbiana People's Advocate,* August 20 (third quote) and September 10 (second quote), 1908.

21. *Columbiana People's Advocate,* May 6 and July 22, 1909, and February 3 and 10 (quotes), 1910.

22. *Columbiana People's Advocate,* August 2, 1906.

23. Ibid.

24. Ibid., July 2 (quote) and July 30, 1908.

25. Ibid., May 25, June 1, and November 22, 1905; *Columbiana Shelby Sentinel,* October 25, 1906.

26. See reprint of editorial from the *Columbiana Shelby Sentinel* in the *Columbiana People's Advocate,* September 23, 1909.

27. *Columbiana People's Advocate,* July 22, August 26, September 2 and 23, 1909, and February 24, 1910.

28. Ibid., March 3, May 5, and June 30, 1910.

29. Hackney, *Populism to Progressivism,* 302–5, 316; *Columbiana People's Advocate,* October 7, 1909; Brooks Lawrence of the Anti-Saloon League to O. D. Street, November 13, 1909, and G. W. Palmer to O. D. Street, May 13, 1910, Street Collection; Wyatt, *Chilton County,* 130–32; *Clanton Record,* November 11, 1909.

30. *Clanton Record,* November 11, 1909; *Clanton Banner,* November 17, 1910; Wyatt, *Chilton County,* 130–32.

31. *Montevallo Weekly Review,* November 18, 1910; see also the *Columbiana People's Advocate,* November 14, 1912, November 14, 1918, November 14, 1920, and November 16, 1922.

32. C. L. Langston to the *Clanton Banner,* October 13, 1910; *Clanton Banner,* November 17, 1910.

33. *Russellville Franklin Times,* November 17, 1910; *Columbiana People's Advocate,* October 26, 1911.

34. See the Marshall County precinct returns in the *Guntersville Democrat,* November 13 and 20, 1904, and November 15, 1906, the *Albertville Sand Mountain Record,* November 17, 1910, and compare with the returns in the *Guntersville Democrat* for August 6, 1896, and November 6, 1902; see also Loveman, "Presidential Vote," for results in Marshall County.

35. See the hundreds of letters dealing with patronage in the files from 1909 through 1932 in the Street Collection, and see particularly J. O. Thompson to Street, May 21, 1914; *Birmingham Age-Herald,* June 6, 1920.

36. O. D. Street to J. O. Thompson, September 12, 1905, Street Collection; *Birmingham Times,* May 13, 1904; *Birmingham News,* May 6–11, 1904; Thompson to O. D. Street, March 24, 1903, Street Collection.

37. *Birmingham Times,* March 3, 10, and 24, 1905; see letter from Chambers County Republican complaining about Thompson in the *Birmingham Times,* August 25, 1905; John Tyler Morgan to the *Birmingham Times,* December 1, 1905; J. O. Thompson to the *Birmingham News,* March 25 and March 31, 1905.

38. T. W. Powell to Street, March 24, June 27, July 18, and August 6, 1904, and O. D. Street to Powell, August 28, 1905, Street Collection.

39. Street to Thompson, December 15 and December 29, 1905, and Thompson to Street, January 1 and 10, 1906, Street Collection.

40. See interim appointment letter to Street July 31, 1907, and John H. Bankhead to Street, January 13, 1908, Street Collection.

41. *Birmingham Times,* September 14, 21, and 28, October 12, 19, and 26, 1906, and January 24, 1908.

42. Gould, *Presidency of Theodore Roosevelt,* 275–76; C. Vann Woodward, *Tom Watson: Agrarian Rebel* (1938; reprint, New York: Oxford University Press, 1963), 398–400; Arthur M. Schlesinger, Jr., and Fred L. Israel, eds., *History of American Presidential Elections, 1789–1968* (New York: McGraw-Hill, 1971), 2110–12.

43. Gould, *Reform and Regulation,* 106–8; *Birmingham Republican,* May 30, June 6, and June 30, 1908; J. O. Thompson to Street, May 3, 1910, Street Collection.

44. Loveman, "Presidential Vote."

45. W. H. Standifer to O. D. Street and Street to Standifer, February 16 and 17, 1909, Street Collection.

46. Street to Charles P. Taft March 13, 1909, Street Collection.

47. Harlan, *Washington, Wizard,* 342; *Birmingham Times,* January 8, March 19, and April 16, 1909.

48. Thompson to Street, May 3, 1910, Street Collection.

49. Powell to Street, March 22, 1910, Guest to Street, March 26, 1910, Street to W. A. Stinson, May 13, 1910 (on Ashley), Street Collection; *Guide to U.S. Elections,* 1090, 1095, 1100, 1105.

50. Howard to Street, March 30, 1910, R. J. Guest to Street, March 26, 1910, Street to Howard, May 20, 1910 (on lists of Populists), and letters of complaint about Howard, May 3 and October 13, 1910, Street Collection.

51. Howard to Street, August 1, 1910 (on Cullman speech), October 2, 1910, and Frank Lathrop (campaign chairman) to Street, October 4, 1910, and J. F. Slone (Cherokee County) to O. D. Street, September 17, Street Collection.

52. *Official and Statistical Register, 1911,* 269, 272; *Guide to U.S. Elections,* 1100, 1105, 1110.

53. *Official and Statistical Register, 1911,* 61, 74, 298, 299.

54. Howard to Street, July 11 and August 1, 1911, Street Collection.

55. Gould, *Reform and Regulation,* 138–39; Harbaugh, *Power and Responsibility,* 390–91.

56. Harbaugh, *Power and Responsibility,* 391–92.

57. Ibid., 392–93; Paolo E. Coletta, *The Presidency of William Howard Taft* (Lawrence: The University Press of Kansas, 1973), 110–11.

58. Barker to Street, July 23, August 21 (on Reynolds), and 25, 1911.

59. *Birmingham Times,* August 25, September 1 and 8, 1911.

60. *Birmingham Times,* March 8, 1912.

61. Ibid., May 17, 1912; *Clanton Union and Banner,* May 2, 9, 16, and 23.

62. Casdorph, *Republicans, Negroes and Progressives,* 94–95; *Official Report of the Proceedings of the Fifteenth Republican National Convention, Chicago Illinois, June 18, 19, 20, 21, 22* (Washington, D.C.: Republican National Committee, 1912), 169–89.

63. *Talladega Daily Home,* July 25, 1912; *Clanton Union-Banner,* July 18 and 25 (on Reynolds); see a description of the proceedings of the state Progressive party convention by A. A. Jackson in the *Clanton Union-Banner,* September 12, 1912; *Birmingham News,* July 24 and 25, 1912.

64. *Clanton Union-Banner,* August 29, 1912; A. A. Jackson to the *Clanton Union-Banner,* September 12, 1912; see Crichton editorials in the *Union-Banner.*

65. *Birmingham News,* July 24 and 25, 1912; Harbaugh, *Power and Responsibility,* 444–45; Arthur S. Link, "Theodore Roosevelt and the South in 1912," *North Carolina Historical Review* 23 (July 1946):313–24.

66. Coletta, *Presidency of William Howard Taft,* 30.

67. *Clanton Union-Banner,* August 8 (quote on platform), 15 (other quotes), 22 and 29, 1912.

68. *Clanton Union-Banner,* September 5, 1912 (Socialists), and letter of A. A. Jackson to the *Union-Banner* September 12, 1912; *Columbiana People's Advocate,* October 24 and 31, 1912.

69. *Columbiana People's Advocate,* October 31, 1912.

70. *Official and Statistical Register,* 1913, 294–96.

71. Webb, "Independents to Populists," 734; *Clanton Union-Banner,* September 5 (quote from resolution), October 10 (second quote) and 24 (first quote), 1912.

72. *Clanton Union-Banner,* October 17 and 31, 1912.

73. Howard Smith, "The Progressive Party and the Election of 1912 in Alabama," *Alabama Review* 9 (January 1956):14–16; Casdorph, *Republicans, Negroes and Progressives,* 123, 127–28.

74. *Official and Statistical Register,* 1913, 264–65; Loveman, "Presidential Vote."

75. *Clanton Union-Banner,* November 7, 1912; *Guntersville Democrat,* August 6, 1896, August 11, 1898, and the *Albertville Banner,* November 14,

1912; *Columbiana People's Advocate,* November 14, 1912; *Russellville Franklin Times,* August 5, 1900, and November 14, 1912.

76. Loveman, "Presidential Vote."

77. *Official and Statistical Register, 1913,* 267; *Official and Statistical Register, 1915,* 366–67, 394, 134–35.

78. Webb, "Independents to Populists," 734; O. D. Street to Prelate Barker, February 15, 1916 (first quote), C. B. Kennamer to Pope Long, March 8, 1916 (second quote), and Julian Bingham to Pope Long, February 10, 1916 (third quote), Street Collection.

79. *Columbiana People's Advocate,* November 9 and 16, 1916, and November 14, 1918.

80. Street to Frank H. Hitchcock, February 15, 1916, Street Collection.

81. Webb, "Independents to Populists," 734–35; *Birmingham Age-Herald,* August 26, 1920.

82. *Birmingham Age-Herald,* June 6, 7, 8, 9, and 12, 1920; *Birmingham News,* June 12 and 13; Pope Long to Longshore, April 10, 1920, Street Collection; Street to Barker, May 28, 1920, Street Collection; *Official and Statistical Register, 1923,* 345; *Columbiana People's Advocate,* November 11, 1920, June 16 and 23, July 7, 1921, and November 16, 1922.

83. Robert W. Cherny, *Populism, Progressivism, and The Transformation of Nebraska Politics, 1885–1915* (Lincoln: University of Nebraska Press, 1981), 151–52, 154, 157–66, as cited in Holmes, *American Populism,* 197, and also see articles cited by Holmes at 222; Cooper, *The Warrior and the Priest,* 40–43, 76–86, 109–17; see also Gabriel Kolko, *The Triumph of Conservatism: A Reinterpretation of American History, 1900–1916* (New York: Free Press, 1963), which is critical of Roosevelt's reform efforts.

Conclusion

1. Wilentz, "The Original Outsider," 37–38.

2. *Columbiana People's Advocate,* February 22, 1912.

3. Hackney, *Populism to Progressivism,* 330–31 (first two quotes) and 311–12 (last two quotes).

4. Dan T. Carter, *The Politics of Rage: George Wallace, the Origins of the New Conservatism, and the Transformation of American Politics* (New York: Simon and Schuster, 1995), 36–37; Hackney, *Populism to Progressivism,* 128–39, 59–62, 316–23.

5. Link and McCormick, *Progressivism,* 21.

Bibliography

Archival Materials

McKee, Robert. Papers. Department of Archives and History, State of Alabama, Montgomery, Alabama.

Moren, E. H. Papers. Department of Archives and History, State of Alabama, Montgomery, Alabama.

Street, O. D. Collection. Amelia Gayle Gorgas Library, Department of Special Collections, University of Alabama, Tuscaloosa, Alabama.

Street, O. D. Papers. Department of Archives and History, State of Alabama, Montgomery, Alabama.

Government Documents

Alabama. *Alabama Official and Statistical Register,* 1903, 1907, 1911, 1913, 1915, 1919, 1923, 1931, 1955. Montgomery, Alabama.

Alabama. *Journal of the Convention of the People of the State of Alabama Held at the City of Montgomery Commencing on the 7th Day of January, 1861.* Montgomery: Shorter and Reid, 1861.

Alabama. *Journal of the House of Representatives of the State of Alabama,* 1870–71, 1876–77, 1878–79, 1880–81, 1882–83, 1884–85, 1886–87, 1892–93, 1894–95, 1896–97, 1903. Montgomery, Alabama.

Alabama. *Journal of the Senate of the State of Alabama,* 1886–87, 1894–95. Montgomery, Alabama.

U.S. Bureau of the Census. *Agriculture, 1860, 1880, 1890, 1900, 1910.* Washington, D.C.: U.S. Government Printing Office.

———. *Mining, 1880.* Washington, D.C.: U.S. Government Printing Office.

———. *Population, 1880.* Washington, D.C.: U.S. Government Printing Office.

U.S. Manuscript Census, 1830, Madison County.

U.S. Manuscript Census, 1850, Marshall County.

U.S. Manuscript Census, 1860, Marshall County.

U.S. Manuscript Census, 1880, Chilton, Marshall, and Shelby Counties.

U.S. Manuscript Census, 1900, Chilton, Marshall, and Shelby Counties.

Newspapers

Albertville Alliance News, 1891
Albertville Banner, 1912
Albertville Marshall County News, 1894–96

Albertville Sand Mountain Record
Anniston Alabama Leader, 1895
Anniston Hot Blast, 1900
Ashville Southern Aegis, 1886–1912
Ashville Southern Alliance, 1892–99
Birmingham Age-Herald, 1890–1934
Birmingham Alabamian, 1903–4
Birmingham Labor Union, 1886
Birmingham News, 1892–1934
Birmingham People's Weekly Tribune, 1896
Birmingham Republican, 1907–9
Birmingham Times, 1894–1912
Boaz Leader, 1919
Boaz Sand Mountain Signal, 1894–96
Butler Choctaw Alliance, 1892
Calera Journal, 1890–93
Calera Shelby County News, 1890–92
Calera Shelby Sentinel, 1883–90
Centre Cherokee Advertiser, 1874–78
Centre Coosa River News, 1896–1920
Clanton Banner, 1893–1912
Clanton Chilton County Courier, 1877–78
Clanton Chilton View, 1880–93
Clanton People's Party Banner, 1892–93
Clanton Record, 1909
Clanton Union, 1904–12
Clanton Union and Banner, 1912–14
Clanton Union-Banner, 1914
Columbiana Banner of Liberty, 1886
Columbiana People's Advocate, 1892–1924
Columbiana Shelby Chronicle, 1884–1904
Columbiana Shelby County Reporter, 1924–30
Columbiana Shelby Guide, 1866–77
Columbiana Shelby Sentinel, 1877–83, 1893–1903, 1904–9
Cullman Tribune, 1920
Dadeville Lone Star, 1884–85
Double Springs Observer, 1895
Double Springs Winston Herald, 1886–1904
Fort Payne Journal, 1886–1912
Gadsden Times-News, 1904
Geneva Journal
Geneva Reaper
Greenville Living Truth, 1896
Guntersville Democrat, 1881–1934
Huntsville Advocate, 1872–86

Huntsville Independent, 1872
Huntsville Republican, 1899–1904
Huntsville Tribune, 1904
Huntsville Weekly Democrat, 1874
Jasper Headlight, 1888–90
Jasper Mountain Eagle, 1886–1934
Jasper Protectionist, 1887–88
Jasper True Citizen, 1886–88
Jasper Walker County News, 1912
Mobile Daily Register, 1870–80
Montevallo Shelby Sentinel, 1900–1904
Montevallo Star, 1866
Montevallo Weekly Review, 1910
Montgomery Advertiser, 1874–1934
Montgomery Alliance Herald, 1893
Montgomery Daily State Journal, 1876
Montgomery Evening Journal, 1902
Montgomery Journal, 1901–2
Montgomery Weekly-Advertiser, 1882–85
Oakman Mountain News, 1896
Piedmont Enquirer, 1891–92
Russellville Franklin Times, 1899–1912
Selma Morning-Times, 1882–86
Selma Southern Argus, 1869–81
Talladega Daily Home, 1912
Troy Enquirer
Tuscumbia North Alabamian, 1876–78
Vernon Courier, 1894

Books, Articles, and Other Publications

Alexander, Thomas B., Peggy Duckworth Elmore, Frank M. Lowery, and Mary
    Jane Pickens Skinner. "Persistent Whiggery in Alabama and the Lower
    South, 1860–67." *Alabama Review* 12 (January 1959): 35–52.
———. "Persistent Whiggery in the Confederate South, 1860–1877." *Journal of
    Southern History* 27 (August 1961): 305–29.
———. "The Basis of Alabama's Antebellum Two-Party System." *Alabama Re-
    view* 19 (October 1966): 243–76.
Allman, John M. "Yeoman Regions in the Antebellum Deep South: Settlement
    and Economy in Northern Alabama, 1815–1860." Ph.D. diss., University
    of Maryland, 1979.
Atkins, Leah. "Williamson R. W. Cobb and the Graduation Act of 1854." *Ala-
    bama Review* 38 (January 1975): 16–31.
Ayers, Edward L. *The Promise of the New South: Life After Reconstruction.* New
    York: Oxford University Press, 1992.

Baker, Jean. *Affairs of Party: The Political Culture of Northern Democrats in the Mid-Nineteenth Century.* Ithaca: Cornell University Press, 1983.

Barnard, William D. *Dixiecrats and Democrats: Alabama Politics, 1942–1950.* Tuscaloosa: University of Alabama Press, 1974.

Barney, William L. *The Secessionist Impulse: Alabama and Mississippi in 1860.* Princeton: Princeton University Press, 1974.

Bartley, Numan V. "In Search of the New South: Southern Politics after Reconstruction." In *The Promise of American History: Progress and Prospects,* edited by Stanley I. Kutler and Stanley N. Katz. Baltimore: Johns Hopkins University Press, 1982.

Bensel, Richard Franklin. *Yankee Leviathan: The Origins of Central State Authority in America, 1859–1877.* Cambridge: Cambridge University Press, 1990.

Berney, Saffold. *Handbook of Alabama.* Tutwiler Collection of Southern History, Birmingham [Alabama] Public Library. Birmingham: Roberts & son, 1892.

Bigelow, Martha Mitchell. "Birmingham's Carnival of Crime, 1871–1910." *Alabama Review* 3 (1950): 123–33.

Blum, John M. *Liberty, Justice, Order: Writings on Past Politics.* New York: W. W. Norton & Company, 1993.

Boles, John B., and Evelyn Thomas Nolen, eds. *Interpreting Southern History: Historiographical Essays in Honor of Sanford W. Higginbotham.* Baton Rouge: Louisiana State University Press, 1987.

Bond, Bradley. *Political Culture in the Nineteenth-Century South: Mississippi, 1830–1900.* Baton Rouge: Louisiana State University Press, 1995.

Bond, Horace Mann. "Social and Economic Forces in Alabama during Reconstruction." *Journal of Negro History* 23 (July 1938): 290–348.

——. *Negro Education in Alabama: A Study in Cotton and Steel.* 1939. Reprint, Tuscaloosa: University of Alabama Press, 1994.

Bonner, James C. *Georgia's Last Frontier: The Development of Carroll County.* Athens: University of Georgia Press, 1971.

Brewer, Willis. *Alabama, Her History and Resources, War Record and Public Men.* Montgomery: N.p., 1872.

Carter, Dan T. *When the War Was Over: The Failure of Self-Reconstruction, 1865–1867.* Baton Rouge: Louisiana State University Press, 1985.

——. *The Politics of Rage: George Wallace, the Origins of the New Conservatism, and the Transformation of American Politics.* New York: Simon and Schuster, 1995.

Casdorph, Paul. *Republicans, Negroes and Progressives in the South, 1912–1916.* University: University of Alabama Press, 1981.

Cash, W. J. *The Mind of the South.* New York: Alfred A. Knopf, 1941.

Cash, William M. "Alabama Republicans during Reconstruction: Personal Characteristics, Motivations, and Political Activity of Party Activists, 1867–1880." Ph.D. diss., University of Alabama, 1973.

Cherny, Robert W. *Populism, Progressivism, and the Transformation of Nebraska Politics, 1885–1915.* Lincoln: University of Nebraska Press, 1981.

Clanton, Gene. *Populism: The Humane Preference in America,* 1890–1900. Boston: Twayne Publishers, 1991.

Cobb, Joe Pvt. *Carrol County and Her People.* Birmingham [Alabama] Public Library. N.p., n.d.

Coletta, Paolo E. *The Presidency of William Howard Taft.* Lawrence: University of Kansas Press, 1973.

Congressional Quarterly's Guide to Congressional Elections. Washington, D.C.: Congressional Quarterly Inc., 1994.

Cooper, John Milton, Jr. *The Warrior and the Priest: Woodrow Wilson and Theodore Roosevelt.* Cambridge: Harvard University Press, Belknap Press, 1983.

———. *Pivotal Decades: The United States, 1900–1920.* New York: W. W. Norton & Company, 1990.

Cresswell, Stephen Edward. *Multiparty Politics in Mississippi, 1877–1902.* Jackson: University Press of Mississippi, 1995.

Cripps, Thomas R. "The Lily White Republicans: The Negro, the Party and the South in the Progressive Era." Ph.D. diss., University of Maryland, 1967.

Crow, Jeffrey, Paul D. Escott, and Charles L. Flynn, eds. *Race, Class and Politics in Southern History: Essays in Honor of Robert F. Durden.* Baton Rouge: Louisiana State University Press, 1989.

Crunden, Robert. *Ministers of Reform: The Progressives' Achievement in American Civilization, 1889–1920.* New York: Basic Books, Inc., 1982.

Degler, Carl N. *The Other South: Southern Dissenters in the Nineteenth Century.* New York: Harper & Row, 1974.

Deland, T. A., and A. David Smith. *Northern Alabama: Historical and Biographical.* 1888. Reprint, Spartanburg, S.C.: Reprint Co., 1976.

Destler, Chester McArthur. *American Radicalism, 1865–1901.* 1946. Reprint, Chicago: Quadrangle Books, 1966.

DeVine, Jerry W. "Free Silver and Alabama Politics, 1890–96," Ph.D. diss., Auburn University, 1980.

Dodd, Donald. "Unionism in Northwest Alabama." Master's thesis, Auburn University, 1966.

Dorman, Lewy. *Party Politics in Alabama from 1800 to 1860.* Wetumpka, Ala.:N.p., 1935.

Draughon, Ralph B., Jr. "George Smith Houston and Southern Unity, 1846–49." *Alabama Review* 19 (July 1966): 186–207.

Dubose, Joel C. *Notable Public Men of Alabama.* 2 vols. Atlanta: Southern Historical Association, 1904.

Duncan, Katherine McKinstry, and Larry Joe Smith. *The History of Marshall County, Alabama.* Albertville, Ala.: Thompson Printing Company, 1969.

Egerton, John. *Speak Now Against the Day: The Generation Before the Civil Rights Movement in the South.* New York: Alfred A. Knopf, 1994.

Fitzgerald, Michael R. *The Union League Movement in the Deep South.* Baton Rouge: Louisiana State University Press, 1989.

Fitzgerald, Michael W. "Radical Republicanism and the White Yeomanry During Alabama Reconstruction, 1865–1868." *Journal of Southern History* 54 (November 1988): 565–96.

Flynt, Wayne. *Poor But Proud: Alabama's Poor Whites.* Tuscaloosa: University of Alabama Press, 1990.

Foner, Eric. *Reconstruction: America's Unfinished Revolution, 1863–1877.* New York: Harper & Row, 1988.

Ford, Lacy K. *The Origins of Southern Radicalism: The South Carolina Upcountry, 1800–1860.* New York: Oxford University Press, 1988.

Fry, Joseph A. *John Tyler Morgan and the Search for Southern Autonomy.* Knoxville: University of Tennessee Press, 1992.

Genovese, Eugene. "Yeoman Farmers in a Slaveholders Democracy." *Agricultural History* 49 (April 1975): 331–42.

Going, Allen Johnston. *Bourbon Democracy in Alabama, 1874–1890.* University: University of Alabama Press, 1951.

Goodwyn, Lawrence W. *Democratic Promise: The Populist Moment in America.* New York: Oxford University Press, 1976.

Gould, Lewis L. *Reform and Regulation: American Politics from Roosevelt to Wilson.* New York: Alfred A. Knopf, 1986.

———. *The Presidency of Theodore Roosevelt.* Lawrence: University of Kansas Press, 1991.

———, ed. *The Progressive Era.* Syracuse: Syracuse University Press, 1974.

Grafton, Carl, and Anne Permaloff. *Big Mules and Branchheads: James E. Folsom and Political Power in Alabama.* Athens: University of Georgia Press, 1985.

Grantham, Dewey W. *The Democratic South.* Athens: University of Georgia Press, 1963.

———. *Southern Progressivism: The Reconciliation of Progress and Tradition.* Knoxville: University of Tennessee Press, 1983.

———. *The Life and Death of the Solid South: A Political History.* Lexington: University of Kentucky Press, 1988.

Gutman, Herbert. "Black Coal Miners and the Greenback-Labor Party in Redeemer Alabama, 1878–1879." *Labor History* 10 (Summer 1969): 506–35.

Hackney, Sheldon. *Populism to Progressivism in Alabama.* Princeton: Princeton University Press, 1969.

Hahn, Steven. *The Roots of Southern Populism: Yeoman Farmers and the Transformation of the Georgia Upcountry, 1850–1890.* New York: Oxford University Press, 1983.

Harbaugh, William Henry. *Power and Responsibility: The Life and Times of Theodore Roosevelt.* New York: Farrar, Straus and Cudahy, 1961.

Harlan, Louis, ed. *Booker T. Washington Papers.* 13 vols. Urbana: University of Illinois Press, 1972.

Harlan, Louis R. *Booker T. Washington: The Wizard of Tuskegee, 1901–1915.* New York: Oxford University Press, 1983.

Harris, David Alan. "The Political Career of Milford W. Howard, Populist Congressman From Alabama." Master's thesis, Auburn University, 1957.

———. "Racists and Reformers: A Study of Progressivism in Alabama, 1896–1911." Ph.D. diss., University of North Carolina, 1967.

———. "Campaigning in the Bloody Seventh: The Election of 1894 in the Seventh Congressional District." *Alabama Review* 27 (April 1974): 127–38.

Heale, M. J. *The Making of American Politics.* London: Longman Group Ltd., 1977.

Heard, Alexander. *A Two-Party South?* Chapel Hill: University of North Carolina Press, 1952.

Hearn, Thomas Kermit. "The Populist Movement in Marshall County." Master's thesis, University of Alabama, 1935.

Hicks, John W. *The Populist Revolt: A History of the Farmers' Alliance and the People's Party.* 1931. Reprint, Lincoln: University of Nebraska Press, 1961.

Hofstadter, Richard. *The Age of Reform: From Bryan to FDR.* New York: Alfred A. Knopf, 1955.

Holmes, William F. "Populism in Search of a Context." *Agricultural History* 64 (Fall 1990).

———, ed. *American Populism.* Lexington, Mass.: D. C. Heath & Co., 1994.

Hoole, William Stanley. *Alabama Tories: The First Alabama Cavalry, U.S.A., 1862–65.* Tuscaloosa: Confederate Publishing Co., 1960.

Horton, Paul Haynes. "Lawrence County, Alabama, in the Nineteenth Century: A Study in the Other South." Master's thesis, University of Texas, 1985.

———. "Testing the Limits of Class Politics in Postbellum Alabama: Agrarian Radicalism in Lawrence County." *Journal of Southern History* 57 (February 1991): 63–84.

Howard, Milford W. *If Christ Came to Congress.* Washington, D.C.: Howard Publishing Co., 1894.

Hughes, John F. "The Jacksonians, the Populists and the Governmental Habit." *Mid-America: An Historical Review* 76 (Winter 1994): 5–25.

Hughes, John S., ed. *The Letters of a Victorian Madwoman.* Columbia: University of South Carolina Press, 1993.

Hyman, Michael R. *The Anti-Redeemers: Hill-Country Political Dissenters in the Lower South From Redemption to Populism.* Baton Rouge: Louisiana State University Press, 1990.

Kennamer, John R. *The Kennamer Family.* Nashville: McQuiddy Printing Co., 1924.

Key, V. O. *Southern Politics in State and Nation.* New York: Alfred A. Knopf, 1949.

King, J. Crawford. "The Closing of the Southern Range: An Exploratory Study." *Journal of Southern History* 48 (February 1982): 53–70.

Kirby, Jack Temple. *Darkness at the Dawning: Race and Reform in the Progressive South.* Philadelphia: J. B. Lippincott, 1972.

Kohl, Lawrence F. *The Politics of Individualism: Parties and the American Character in the Jacksonian Era.* New York: Oxford University Press, 1989.

Kolko, Gabriel. *The Triumph of Conservatism: A Reinterpretation of American History, 1900–1916.* New York: Free Press, 1963.

Kousser, J. Morgan. *The Shaping of Southern Politics: Suffrage Restriction and the Establishment of the One-Party South, 1880–1910.* New Haven: Yale University Press, 1974.

Kousser, J. Morgan, and James M. McPherson. *Region, Race and Reconstruction: Essays in Honor of C. Vann Woodward.* New York: Oxford University Press, 1982.

Kutler, Stanley I., and Stanley N. Katz, eds. *The Promise of American History: Progress and Prospects.* Baltimore: Johns Hopkins University Press, 1982.

Lewis, W. David. *Sloss Furnaces and the Rise of the Birmingham District: An Industrial Epic.* Tuscaloosa: University of Alabama Press, 1994.

Link, Arthur S. "Theodore Roosevelt and the South in 1912." *North Carolina Historical Review* 23 (July 1946): 313–24.

Link, Arthur, and Richard L. McCormick. *Progressivism.* Arlington Heights, Ill.: Harlan-Davidson, 1983.

Loveman, Louis, comp. "The Presidential Vote in Alabama." Birmingham [Alabama] Public Library. N.p.: 1983.

Martin, Bessie. *Desertion of Alabama Troops from the Confederate Army.* 1932. Reprint, New York: AME Press, 1966.

McGee, Maurice. "DeKalb Voters March to Different Drummer." *Landmark News* 14 (Summer-Fall 1984): 1, 3, 20–21.

McKenzie, Robert H. "Reconstruction of the Alabama Iron Industry, 1865–1880." *Alabama Review* 25 (July 1972): 178–91.

———. "Reconstruction Historiography: The View from Shelby." *The Historian* 36 (February 1974): 213–19.

McKinney, Gordon B. *Southern Mountain Republicans, 1865–1900.* Chapel Hill: University of North Carolina Press, 1978.

McMath, Robert C., Jr. *American Populism: A Social History, 1877–1898.* New York: Hill and Wang, 1993.

McMillan, Malcolm Cook. *Constitutional Development in Alabama, 1798–1901: A Study in Politics, the Negro, and Sectionalism.* Chapel Hill: University of North Carolina Press, 1955.

McWhiney, Grady. "The Revolution in Nineteenth-Century Agriculture." *Alabama Review* 31 (October 1978): 3–32

Memorial Record of Alabama. 2 vols. 1893. Reprint, Spartanburg, S.C.: Reprint Co., 1976.

Meyers, Marvin. *The Jacksonian Persuasion: Politics and Belief.* 1957. Reprint, New York: Vintage, 1960.

Miller, Wilbur. "The Revenue: Federal Law Enforcement in the Mountain South, 1870–1900." *Journal of Southern History* 65 (May 1989): 195–216.

Miller, Worth Robert. *Oklahoma Populism: A History of the People's Party in the Oklahoma Territory.* Norman: University of Oklahoma Press, 1987.

———. "A Centennial Historiography of American Populism." *Kansas History* 16 (Spring 1993): 54–69.

———. "The Republican Tradition." In *American Populism,* edited by William F. Holmes. Lexington, Mass.: D. C. Heath and Co., 1994.

Moody, Ellis C. "The Origin, Rise and Organization of the Republican Party in Marshall County from 1860–1902." Paper deposited in the Alabama Department of Archives and History.

Moore, Albert Burton. *History of Alabama.* 3 vols. Chicago: American Historical Association, 1927.

Official Report of the Proceedings of the Fifteenth Republican National Convention, Chicago, Illinois, June 18, 19, 20, 21, 22. Washington, D.C.: Republican National Committee, 1912.

Owen, Thomas M. *History of Alabama and Dictionary of Alabama Biography.* 4 vols. Chicago: S. J. Clarke, 1921.

Palmer, Bruce. "The Roots of Reform: Southern Populists and Their Southern History." *Red River Valley Historical Review.* 4 (Spring 1979): 34–58.

———. *"Man Over Money": The Southern Populist Critique of American Capitalism.* Chapel Hill: University of North Carolina Press, 1980.

Perman, Michael. *The Road to Redemption: Southern Politics, 1869–1879.* Chapel Hill: University of North Carolina Press, 1984.

Pollack, Norman. *The Populist Response to Industrial America.* Cambridge: Harvard University Press, 1962.

———. *The Just Polity: Populism, Law and Human Welfare.* Urbana: University of Illinois Press, 1987.

———. *The Humane Economy: Populism, Capitalism, and Democracy.* New Brunswick: Rutgers University Press, 1990.

Pruitt, Paul McWhorter. "Joseph C. Manning, Alabama Populist: A Rebel Against the Solid South." Ph.D. diss., The College of William and Mary, 1980.

Rabinowitz, Howard N. *The First New South, 1865–1920.* Arlington Heights, Ill.: Harlan-Davidson, 1992.

Roberts, Frances. "William Manning Lowe and the Greenback Party in Alabama." *Alabama Review* 5 (April 1952): 100–21.

Rodabaugh, Karl N. "Fusion, Confusion, Defeat and Disfranchisement: The Fadeout of Populism in Alabama." *Alabama Historical Quarterly* 34 (Summer 1972): 131–54.

———. "Agrarian Ideology and the Farmer's Revolt in Alabama." *Alabama Review* 36 (July 1983): 195–217.

Rogers, William Warren. *The One-Gallused Rebellion: Agrarianism in Alabama, 1865–1896.* Baton Rouge: Louisiana State University Press, 1970.

Rogers, William Warren, Robert David Ward, Leah Rawls Atkins, and Wayne

Flynt. *Alabama: The History of a Deep South State.* Tuscaloosa: University of Alabama Press, 1994.

Roller, David C., and Robert W. Twyman, eds. *The Encyclopedia of Southern History.* Baton Rouge: Louisiana State University Press, 1979.

Schlesinger, Arthur M., Jr., and Fred L. Israel, eds. *History of American Presidential Elections, 1789–1968.* New York: McGraw-Hill, 1971.

Seip, Terry L. *The South Returns to Congress: Men, Economic Measures, and Intersectional Relationships, 1868–1879.* Baton Rouge: Louisiana State University Press, 1983.

Sheffield, James L. "Circular to the People of the Fifth Congressional District of Alabama." Huntsville, Ala.: A. H. Brittain Mercantile Job Printers, 1874.

Sifakis, Stewart. *Who Was Who in the Civil War.* New York: Facts on File Publications, 1988.

Smith, Howard. "The Progressive Party and the Election of 1912 in Alabama." *Alabama Review* 9 (January 1956): 5–19.

Story, John Noel. "The History of Marshall County, Alabama, Prior to 1860." Master's thesis, University of Alabama, 1930.

Summers, Mark W. *Railroads, Reconstruction, and the Gospel of Prosperity: Aid Under the Radical Republicans, 1865–1877.* Princeton: Princeton University Press, 1984.

Sundquist, James L. *The Dynamics of the Party System.* Washington D.C.: The Brookings Institution, 1983.

Thompson, J. A. *General History of Marshall County, Alabama.* Albertville, Ala.: Creative Printers, 1989.

Thompson, Wesley S. *The Free State of Winston: A History of Winston County, Alabama.* Winfield, Ala.: Pareil Press, 1968.

Thornton, J. Mills III. "Alabama Politics, J. Thomas Heflin, and the Expulsion Movement of 1929." *Alabama Review* 21 (April 1968): 83–112.

———. *Politics and Power in a Slave Society: Alabama, 1800–1860.* Baton Rouge: Louisiana State University Press, 1978.

———. "Fiscal Policy and the Failure of Radical Reconstruction in the Lower South." In *Region, Race and Reconstruction: Essays in Honor of C. Vann Woodward,* edited by J. Morgan Kousser and James M. McPherson. New York: Oxford University Press, 1982.

———. "Hugo Black and the Golden Age." *Alabama Law Review* 36 (Spring 1985): 899–913.

———. "The Ethic of Subsistence and the Origins of Southern Secession." *Tennessee Historical Quarterly* 48 (Summer 1989): 67–85.

———. "Jacksonian Democracy." In *Encyclopedia of Southern Culture,* edited by Charles Reagan Wilson and William Ferris. Chapel Hill: University of North Carolina Press, 1989.

Trelease, Allen W. "Who Were the Scalawags?" *Journal of Southern History* 29 (November 1963): 445–68.

Ward, Robert David, and William Warren Rogers. *Labor Revolt in Alabama: The Great Strike of 1894.* University: University of Alabama Press, 1965.

———. *Convicts, Coal and the Banner Mine Tragedy.* Tuscaloosa: University of Alabama Press, 1987.

Watson, Harry L. *Liberty and Power: The Politics of Jacksonian America.* New York: Noonday Press, 1990.

Webb, Samuel L. "Two-Party Politics in the One-Party South: Alabama Hill Country, 1880–1920." Ph.D. diss., University of Arkansas, 1991.

———. "From Independents to Populist to Progressive Republicans: The Case of Chilton County, Alabama, 1880–1920." *Journal of Southern History* 59 (November 1993): 707–36.

———. "A Jacksonian Democrat in Postbellum Alabama: The Ideology and Influence of Journalist Robert McKee, 1869–1896." *Journal of Southern History* 62 (May 1996): 239–74.

Weiner, Jonathan M. *Social Origins of the New South: Alabama, 1860–1885.* Baton Rouge: Louisiana State University Press, 1978.

Wiggins, Sarah Woolfolk. *The Scalawag in Alabama Politics, 1865–1881.* University: University of Alabama Press, 1977.

Wilentz, Sean. "The Original Outsider." *New Republic,* June 1992, 34–38.

Wilson, Charles Reagan, and William Ferris, eds. *Encyclopedia of Southern Culture.* Chapel Hill: University of North Carolina Press, 1989.

Woodward, C. Vann. *Tom Watson: Agrarian Rebel.* 1938. Reprint, New York: Oxford University Press, 1963.

———. *Origins of the New South, 1877–1913.* Baton Rouge: Louisiana State University Press, 1951.

———. *Reunion and Reaction: The Compromise of 1877 and the End of Reconstruction.* Boston: Little, Brown and Company, 1951.

Wyatt, T. E. *Chilton County and Her People: History of Chilton County, Alabama.* Montevallo, Ala.: Times Printing Co., 1976.

Index

18; Reconstruction in, 31–33, 42; society in, 119–20; state legislators from, 83–85, 139–42, 153–54; stock laws in, 156–57, 170; two-party system in, 202, 217–18. *See also* Chilton County; Democratic party; Marshall County; Populism; Progressive (Bull Moose) party; Republican party; Secession; Seventh Congressional District; Shelby County; St. Clair County; Walker County

Hollis, Dr. Jonathan S., 117

Honeycutt, Riley Monroe, 106–7, 116, 117, 118–19, 122, 123, 149–50; breaks with Populists, 157–59; independent leader, 66–67, 89–90; free silver and, 149–50

Hood, Noah B., 166

Houston, George Smith, 50–52, 54, 55, 57, 64, 76

Howard, Milford W., 6, 131, 152, 160, 164, 204; author, 136; ideology, 200–201; Populist congressional candidate, 136–37, 139, 151, 161; denounces Republican leaders, 202; embarrassing behavior, 159; opposes fusion with Republicans, 141–42; opposes nomination of W. J. Bryan, 144–45; opposes prohibition, 194, 201; supports Populist remedies, 137; Republican congressional candidate, 200–202; supports Tom Watson, 145; Dingley tariff and, 159; supports Oliver Street, 178. *See also* Seventh Congressional District

Hundley, Oscar R., 12, 17, 18, 20, 197, 202; ally of J. O. Thompson, 17–18, 199, 205; appointment as federal judge, 18, 199–200; Progressive (Bull Moose) party leader, 12, 205–6, 208

Huntsville, Alabama, 34, 63

Huntsville Advocate, 59, 63

Hurst, Dr. James Alpheus, 117

If Christ Came to Congress, 136. *See also* Howard, Milford W.

Independents and Independent movements, 28, 29, 31–32, 44, 52–53, 55–57, 59, 64, 66–85, 96, 102, 111, 156, 214–16; motives behind, 61–62, 67–68, 188, 214–15; variety of, 61–62, 67–85, 89–97, 100, 101,

102, 156; legislators, 83–85. *See also* Chilton County; Marshall County; Shelby County; Walker County

Indian tribes, 34, 37

Internal improvements: antebellum, 36, 37; postbellum, 45–52, 56, 125

Internal Revenue: untaxed liquor and, 72–73

Jackson, Andrew, 34, 37, 56, 59, 104, 107, 123, 126–27, 181, 185, 192, 215

Jackson County, 31, 37, 61, 63, 66

Jacksonianism, 11; as antebellum ethos, 34–38, 101, 104, 213, 215; in post–Civil War period, 45–46, 48–52, 54, 56, 59, 64, 65, 86, 90, 100–101, 103, 146, 172, 211, 213, 217; dualistic view of politics, 127; Jacksonians on Thomas Jefferson, 127, 130; Populism and, 86, 101, 104, 107, 108–9, 123–30, 185, 188, 217; Theodore Roosevelt and, 11, 188, 203

Jasper, Alabama, 73

Jasper Protectionist, 73

Jefferson, Thomas, 104, 107, 127, 130, 181; Jeffersonian ideology, 127, 130, 215

Jefferson County, 46, 66, 75, 104, 134, 139

Jeffersonian Democratic party, 103–6, 108–11, 124, 129–30, 131, 138, 141, 143–45, 216–17; 1894 election and, 133–35; differences with Populists, 133, 216; dominated by Reuben Kolb, 133; party platform, 133; state legislators, 139. *See also* Kolb, Reuben F.; Street, Thomas Atkins

Jeffersonian Republicans, 107

Jelks, William Dorsey, 174, 176

Jemison, Alabama, 106, 118–19, 209

John, Sam Will: Democratic leader in state legislature, 139–40

Johns Hopkins University, 117

Johnson, Andrew, 42

Johnson, Hiram W., 12, 25, 186; A. P. Longshore and, 211–12

Johnston, Joseph Forney, 177, 220; background, 142–44; appeal to Populists 155, 162, 174; campaign for U.S. Senate, 162; election of 1896 and, 147–50; election of 1898, 154; election of 1902 and, 176; reform or "silver" Democrats and, 142–

About the Author

Samuel L. Webb is associate professor of history at the University of Alabama at Birmingham. He received his doctorate from the University of Arkansas.